SICILY BEFORE HISTORY

SICILY BEFORE HISTORY

an archaeological survey
from the Palaeolithic
to the Iron Age

Robert Leighton

Duckworth

First published in 1999 by
Gerald Duckworth & Co. Ltd.
61 Frith Street, London W1V 5TA
Tel: 0171 434 4242
Fax: 0171 434 4420
Email: duckworth-publishers.co.uk

A catalogue record for this book is available
from the British Library

ISBN 0 7156 2764 3 (hbk)
ISBN 0 7156 2770 8 (pbk)

Typeset by Ray Davies
Printed in Great Britain by
Redwood Books Ltd, Trowbridge

Contents

Acknowledgements

I am particularly grateful to Enrico Procelli and Rosa Maria Albanese Procelli for their generous assistance during the preparation of the text and comments on certain chapters. Claire Lyons, Ruth Whitehouse and Roger Wilson also read sections of the manuscript and made helpful suggestions. My thanks go to them, to the reader for Cornell University Press and to Deborah Blake at Duckworth for her patience and advice.

Several individuals kindly provided me with information concerning points of detail or gave permission to use photographs and illustrations. In this connection, I thank John E. Dixon, John D. Evans, R. Ross Holloway, Irene Lemos, Brian McConnell, Anna Revedin, Francesca Spatafora, Louise Steel, Antonio Tagliacozzo, Steve Thompson, David Trump, Sebastiano Tusa and Stefano Vassallo. Special thanks go to Gioacchino Falsone and Giovanni Mannino for photographs and offprints. Most of the illustrations are the result of my own labours, adapted from sources which are acknowledged individually. Without advice from Gordon Thomas they would have been less successful.

On a personal note, it is a pleasure and a privilege to recall the friendships and exchanges of ideas which I have enjoyed over many years with archaeologists in Sicily. I also feel indebted to those with whom I have worked on excavations and surveys in Calabria, the Belice valley, at Motya and Morgantina, and to Lydia, my Italian mother, for teaching me her native language. My father, Kenneth, first encouraged my interest in archaeology and it is to his memory that this work is affectionately dedicated.

Abbreviations and conventions

The following abbreviations for chronological periods are used as adjectives:
EN = Early Neolithic
MN = Middle Neolithic
LN = Late Neolithic
CA = Copper Age
ECA = Early Copper Age
LCA = Late Copper Age
EBA = Early Bronze Age (BA1 = phase 1; BA2 = phase 2)
MBA = Middle Bronze Age
LBA = Late Bronze Age (encompassing the Recent and Final Bronze Ages in Italian terminology)
EIA = Early Iron Age

Radiocarbon dates in the text are given as a calibrated 1σ (one standard deviation) range (see also table 4).

Measurements are given as follows:
cm = centimetres
km = kilometres
m = metres
m asl = metres above sea level
H = height
L = length
W = width
Ø = diameter

Introduction: past research
and recurrent themes

Archaeological research in Sicily has a long history. Speculation about the remote past can be traced back to the Presocratic philosopher, Xenophanes, who noted the presence of fish and seaweed fossils in the quarries of Syracuse, and to the philosophical discourses of the Sicilian Greek, Empedocles.[1] The island's rich fossil record also attracted the attention of Boccaccio, Kircher and Sicilian writers of the 16th-18th centuries, such as Fazello, Valguarnera and Mongitore, whose works reflect gradual changes in ideas about antiquity and an early interest in antiquarian pursuits. Some of them explored burials and caves and regarded the bones of prehistoric animals as the remains of giants, doubtless encouraged by the Church to reconcile Biblical accounts of human origins with those of ancient writers, such as Thucydides, for whom Sicily was originally the home of Laestrygones and Cyclopes.

From the middle of the 18th century, the island became a popular destination for foreign visitors and often marked the climax of an extended Grand Tour. Educated gentlemen and aristocrats came to see Mount Etna and the picturesque ancient sites, such as Taormina, Syracuse and Agrigento, and some of them, including William Hamilton and Goethe, also took an interest in remoter antiquity and the natural sciences, as reflected in early cabinets of curiosities and antiquarian collections. At the same time, the varied and often dramatic Sicilian landscape attracted the attention of several prominent naturalists and geologists: Dolomieu visited the island in 1781, examined prehistoric rock-cut tombs and scorned theories about giants and troglodytes, while Charles Lyell's ideas about the extended time-scale of earth history were profoundly influenced by his visit to Etna in 1828.

The official excavation of 1830 in the San Ciro cave by Scinà confirmed the identification of extinct animals, extracted from a mass of bone concretions, and stimulated an interest in palaeontology. Of historical significance too are the excavations of Hugh Falconer in the Maccagnone cave and the work of Anca and Gemmellaro in the 1860s, when many caves were being plundered for bones and stalactites. These pioneers were primarily interested in the evolution of mammalian fauna, but were also finding prehistoric artefacts and coming to the conclusion that human

1

settlement in the island extended back to a very remote period. Closely linked with advances in the natural sciences, the earliest prehistoric periods were the subject of study from the mid-19th century, even though local historiography was dominated by classical antiquities and the accounts of ancient writers.

The work of Paolo Orsi (1859-1935) marks a decisive break with the dilettantism of local antiquarian traditions.[2] Orsi was the great pioneer of archaeological exploration in Sicily and a major figure in the history of Italian archaeology. Working from his base at the Syracuse museum, his tireless research is emblematic of new attitudes that were evolving rapidly in the late 19th century, when the first professionals, inspired by a more scientific outlook and using more rigorous techniques, were engaged in systematic fieldwork, the organisation of state museums and the definition of archaeological cultures in space and time. Although some of his interpretations have been superseded, Orsi's fieldwork is of an unusually high standard for his day and well documented in a vast array of published articles and monographs, spanning a long career, which concentrated on Sicilian prehistory but also encompassed classical and early Christian archaeology.

Space prevents mention of several others associated with archaeological research in Sicily. If Orsi's work characterizes an early pioneering phase, much progress in the second half of the 20th century can be associated with the extensive and influential research of Luigi Bernabò Brea, author of the first comprehensive synthesis of Sicilian prehistory.[3] His continuing work, in collaboration with Madeleine Cavalier, has revealed numerous sites and a long sequence of human occupation in the Aeolian archipelago. The prehistory of this island group is unusually well documented in several monographic publications, which serve as an important point of reference for Sicily and southern Italy.

Despite changes in methodology since Orsi's day, certain themes obviously recur in Sicilian archaeology, which are partly dictated by the nature of the evidence, the potential of the landscape and the position of the island in relation to larger landmasses. Despite being surrounded by sea, Sicily has often seemed to archaeologists and historians to be the least island-like of all the Mediterranean islands, being at once too big, too close to the centre of the Mediterranean and to the Italian mainland to have experienced isolation for prolonged periods.[4] While providing a good context for the study of local cultural developments, the island is also a barometer of wider processes of interaction and may be described as a meeting-place of cultures or a crucible of interaction. By comparison with some smaller or more remote islands, such as Malta or Sardinia, the prehistory of Sicily was more in step with developments in South Italy.

From a geographical perspective, despite the physical separation created by the narrow Straits of Messina, Sicily can be regarded in part at least as a southern extension of the peninsula, albeit its most distinctive

2

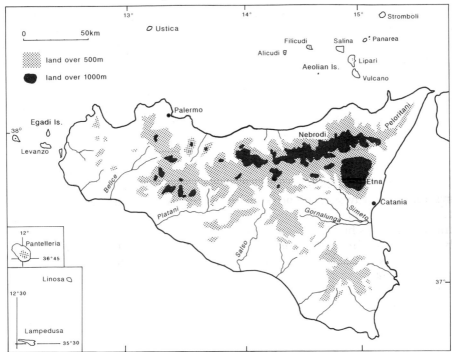

Fig. 1. Sicily

region, which contrasts with adjacent areas (fig. 1).[5] Backed by rugged terrain, much of Calabria's coastline is comparatively unwelcoming, whereas Apulia has wide expanses of flat land. Cultural adaptations in each of these southern regions were bound to differ. Moreover, the southern and western coasts of Sicily face a different stretch of water from the rest of Italy. Without modern communications, the distance from the peninsula must have seemed all the greater. In fact, the inhabitants of these parts are as far from central Italy as their counterparts in southern Sardinia. In addition, although the northeastern mountains are related geologically to the Calabrian Apennines, their steep slopes look more like a barrier than a gateway to the Italian mainland. From a psychological point of view, therefore, it might be argued that Sicily is very much an island and that its population has always had a detached 'island mentality', however hard to define.

Plainly, correlations can be made between physical and cultural units (in the more limited archaeological sense of a recurrent assemblage, or *facies* in Italian terminology), while patterns are visible in relationships with surrounding territories and islands. Northeastern Sicily and southern Calabria shared many cultural traits in prehistory. The Apennine-Peloritani-Nebrodi chain delimited a sphere of coastal and

3

maritime interaction in this corner of the Tyrrhenian basin in which the narrow seaboard and the Aeolian islands played an important role: the latter, in particular, as the source of obsidian and a nodal point in a wider trading network during the Neolithic, and as a convenient port of call for boats entering the western Mediterranean during the Bronze Age. Set beside this northeastern province is the great mass of Etna, Europe's largest volcano, characterized by an extraordinary ecosystem. Here one may detect human adaptations peculiar to the environment of its lower slopes: well-watered, fertile, with a rich and varied fauna and flora, and numerous caves. If it were better documented, the archaeology of Etna would constitute a remarkable case study in European prehistory.

By contrast, the rolling hills and plains of central, southern and western Sicily, with the exception of the more imposing northwestern mountains, represent a gentler and less sharply differentiated landscape. This includes the central grain-growing heartland, which was more wooded before Greek and Roman times, extending across and beyond the provinces of Enna and Caltanissetta. This is sometimes regarded as a sub-region, for which the Salso river serves as a boundary between eastern and western zones. More readily distinguished are the Hyblaean tablelands in the southeastern corner, which, despite erosion, form a naturally favoured unit with localized volcanic formations, picturesque limestone canyons, springs, caves, terraced hillsides and a coastal plain with several good harbours on its eastern side. This area witnessed a succession of distinctive prehistoric cultures with a tradition of burial in rock-cut tombs, sometimes clustered into vast burial grounds.

The sandstones, conglomerates, clays and marly limestones of western Sicily have more in common with the opposite shore of Africa. However, there is little evidence for cultural ties with the Maghreb before the foundation of Carthage. During the Late Palaeolithic and Mesolithic periods, the open waters of the Sicilian channel were no doubt an obstacle to contact. On the other hand, the intervening islands of Lampedusa and Pantelleria had Neolithic and Bronze Age settlements, while Pantelleria obsidian as well as a few sites with impressed pottery are known in Tunisia. Much of North Africa still presents a glaring lacuna in Mediterranean prehistory, but new research may well discover greater evidence of contact with Sicily.

Within Sicily, cultural provinces are easier to identify in certain periods than others. While the late Neolithic was characterized by a certain uniformity over much of southern Italy, the Copper Age was a time of greater regionalism in which northern and southern zones are more clearly distinguishable. During the Middle and Late Bronze Ages, there were more noticeable differences between communities inhabiting coastal, inland or small island sites. In the early historical period, different ethnic groups (Phoenician, Greek and indigenous) can be associated with specific territories, as a result of colonisation. In all periods, however, size and diversity were key factors, permitting the island, which is well endowed with fertile soils and other essential resources, to support substantial populations in different areas.

Despite its proximity to Italy, Sicily has always had considerable potential for local autonomy. It also provides a good example of F. Braudel's concept of a 'continent in miniature'.[6] The trajectory of its cultural evolution differed, therefore, from that of its nearby satellite islands. Smaller, closer to the larger landmass and with more limited resources and fragile ecosystems, the latter were more exposed to disruption by outsiders. It was more difficult for them to develop autonomously for long, especially in the case of the Aeolian archipelago but also, to a lesser degree, in the case of Ustica and Pantelleria. The exception is Malta, which is larger, further away and evidently enjoyed a period of relatively undisturbed development that allowed the remarkable and unique architectural and cult traditions of the temples to flourish, between about 3500 and 2500 BC. By the Early Bronze Age, however, even Malta was tied into more widespread patterns of cultural evolution.

The prehistory and history of Sicily cannot be understood in isolation from that of Italy or the central Mediterranean in general. In fact, links with western and eastern Mediterranean areas have generally underlain assumptions about the causes of cultural change in the island in prehistoric as well as later periods. Considerable weight has usually been given to exogenous factors, whether in the form of external stimuli and influences deriving from trade or migrations. This is not surprising: Palaeolithic hunter-gatherers, like certain species of contemporary fauna, are thought to have entered the island from Italy; farming was introduced from southern Italy, but ultimately from the eastern Mediterranean; beakers had a western origin, while other items in the 3rd millennium BC point eastward and foreshadow the internationalism of the 2nd millennium BC, when relations with the Mycenaean world became close, followed by a return to a western sphere of interaction prior to Greek and Phoenician colonisation in the 8th century BC.

These external connections, traditionally highlighted by prehistorians, are the result of changing alignments and wider processes of interaction in Mediterranean prehistory. It could be argued that they also anticipate the shifting relationships of the island in historical times, with the obvious proviso that the later political domination of Sicily by external forces (Phoenician, Greek, Roman, Byzantine, Arab, Norman, Spanish, Austrian) was a result of competition between states with nationalistic or imperialistic ambitions and international strategic interests. The latter have no real parallel in prehistory. It is perhaps only with the Middle-Late Bronze Ages that the future potential of the island as a major power base becomes apparent. Exposure to influences or incursions from eastern or western areas, albeit a recipe for political instability in historical times, was also a cause of dynamic cultural interaction and change, as reflected in the Phoenician-Greek or Arab-Norman polarities.

The attention given to international developments and external forces, as opposed to local and sometimes more mundane realities, is also a reflection of historiographic traditions. For the majority of historians since the 16th century, the history of Sicily was one of successive invasions and therefore of radical shifts, discontinuities and impositions by outsiders. Social historians have even concluded that this has obscured Sicilian identities or made them unusually complex or ambiguous.[7] On the other hand, different attitudes to Sicilian history and culture have emerged in the 20th century, which may emphasize its indigenous roots and local characteristics, its relationship with the wider Mediterranean world, or more specifically with Italy.

Island traditions and external influences, local responses to outside stimuli, and conservatism versus innovation represent dialectical forces in Sicilian prehistory, as in later times, which archaeologists are better able to examine as they acquire a broadening range of evidence. However, there is much room for debate about the manner in which exogenous factors led to changes in this specific island setting and about how much importance should be attributed to them. The way in which archaeological cultures, whether as a result of migrations, forms of trade, interaction or endemic processes, adapted or moved towards a new identity is a subject of recurrent interest. If the work of L. Bernabò Brea, in the tradition of V. Gordon Childe, has stressed the importance of diffusionist processes, ample possibilities remain for different or complementary prehistories of Sicily, or changes of emphasis, in which more prominence is given to local developments and identities, multiple causes of change, broader economic relationships and convergences that are not simply due to movements of people.

In the Neolithic, for example, although I see no real basis for challenging a traditional paradigm which envisages an arrival of settlers who imported the raw materials and techniques of farming, it is the nature of the new regime in its local context that governs the dynamics of change. At the same time, there may be a danger of reducing a major development in human history to a series of subsistence transitions. Important though these are, a welcome broadening of horizons in recent years has lead to renewed interests in trade or exchange, for example, which is a key element in Italian Neolithic economies and one which may account for many of the alignments, affinities and changes noted over wide areas of the western Mediterranean between 6000 and 3000 BC. More recently, the attempt to understand Neolithic ideologies, with reference to burials or other manifestations of cult activity, presents an exciting opportunity for new debate.

There was probably no period in prehistory during which the island was out of touch with surrounding regions and when at least small groups of people did not arrive from contiguous areas and sometimes from more distant parts. Most of them will have left no archaeological traces and probably had little, if any, effect on local developments. During the 3rd millennium BC, which partly coincides with the Copper Age, there are

6

signs of periodic small-scale infiltrations and what might be called diffuse network contacts, which probably reflect movements of individuals as well as trade goods. Mostly we are able to detect no more than certain affinities with other regions, suggested by pottery styles for example, but sometimes complemented by more specific analogies between individual items, such as the Camaro figurines, the Monte Venere spearhead and the famous bossed bone plaques of the Early Bronze Age. In the case of the 'beaker connection' there is a more substantial body of evidence to suggest that an external relationship was on a scale likely to have been significant for local cultural developments. However, even in this case it has been shown that beaker elements were quickly absorbed within the local cultural environment. This is a reminder that models of change or tacit assumptions based on a knowledge of recent history, which credit outside forces as 'prime movers', are not always appropriate in prehistory. In fact, this largest of Mediterranean islands has a correspondingly greater capacity to absorb and then transform immigrants. The visitors are more likely to start imitating the residents than vice versa.

From the end of the 3rd millennium BC, however, we can trace the growth of a steadier relationship between Sicily, Greece and the eastern Mediterranean which, by the middle of the 2nd millennium BC, was exerting a profound effect on the island's cultural development. It contributed to the emergence of 'proto-urban' centres, which had an important role in international trade and encouraged the formation of more articulated social structures. Sicily had a special if not privileged status in relations with the Mycenaean world. Several reasons, partly geographical and partly cultural, can be suggested for this. Although the impetus for the connection probably came mainly from an opportunistic and dynamic element in Mycenaean societies, the relationship can only be properly understood as a bilateral one. The island was a key player in the wider spectrum of Bronze Age interaction and yet remains one of the most neglected in recent research and one of the least understood. Once again, it is the ability of the local cultures to absorb, adopt and transform external elements, which is striking at this time. A better understanding of this period demands that more attention be paid to the local cultural context as well as to the study of imported artefacts.

In the history of Sicily's external relations, the end of the Bronze Age and the Iron Age represent a change in emphasis and a return of the island to an essentially western Mediterranean sphere of interaction, in which relations with the Italian peninsula are most significant. This period also coincided with marked social and ideological changes and the emergence of new centres of power. There is little archaeological evidence from the island for continuity of relations with Greece or the eastern Mediterranean after the demise of the Mycenaean palaces and before the arrival of Greek and Phoenician colonists in the 8th century BC, although it would not be surprising to find that intermittent contacts occurred.

The colonizing movements of the 8th century BC represent the beginning of a new chapter in Sicilian history, which gradually led to a complete transformation of the indigenous culture. However, in recent years there has been a growing interest in this process and in the 'indigenous world', which is not entirely separable from that of the first Greek and Phoenician settlers, but needs to be evaluated on its own terms if the historical situation is to be properly understood. It is striking that local traditions survived well into the Archaic period (6th century BC) in many parts of Sicily. Neglected by Greek writers, this is an area of research which should hardly differ in approach and methodology from that of prehistoric archaeology, and in which both prehistoric and classical archaeologists have much to learn from each other.

Throughout this volume, I have used the traditional period names of European prehistory, which reflect 19th-century concerns with technological developments and which suffer from obvious conceptual limitations. This is of course an old problem and attempts have been made for over a century to focus attention on social evolution as a way of classifying prehistoric societies. In recent years, the terms bands, tribes (or segmentary societies) and chiefdoms (sometimes classed as 'simple' or 'complex', or called middle-range societies) have been applied to European prehistoric groups thought to reflect different degrees of complexity in their socio-political structure. Sicilian prehistory presents the full range of these 'types'. I have made passing reference to these terms, while aware that they have been used rather loosely by archaeologists and anthropologists and that they therefore need to be accompanied by explicit statements about the kind of social formations which are being inferred and so labelled.

Space prevents further discussion of method and theory, although the interpretations which have been promoted in Sicilian archaeology are obviously influenced by the methodological and theoretical approaches of the archaeologists involved. It is undeniable that the bulk of attention in Sicily is directed at sites of the historical periods, which are often the ones which make the most visibly pressing demands on the resources of the island's archaeological Superintendency. With some important exceptions, such as the Uzzo cave and a growing number of new excavations being conducted with up-to-date techniques, there have been rather few large-scale research excavations of prehistoric sites run by universities using the full range of modern interdisciplinary techniques, nor has Sicily benefited from a long history of international research, which has characterized archaeological activity in some other Mediterranean islands, such as Crete and Cyprus.[8]

Much of the emphasis in past research has been placed on conventional artefact studies, concerned with chronology and external connections, but without the great benefit of scientific and interdisciplinary applications, whether directed at a better understanding of these same artefacts, chronology (by techniques such as radiocarbon dating) or the environment. There is a laudable concern with enlarging and improving the empirical database by new excavations, although few complete site reports have yet appeared, and the older publications are often inadequate from the point of view of modern research interests. Cultural adaptations and transformations as a result of social, economic and environmental factors within the island have therefore received limited consideration to date. Nor has much discussion yet taken place within the framework of explicit theory, with reference to debates stimulated by different approaches (by positivists, Marxists, processualists or post-structuralists to name but a few) in the historical and social sciences. As the limitations of viewing cultural change in prehistory based on a narrow selection of historical models are visible, a wider range of possibilities needs to be explored. This should promote a better understanding of external relations without losing sight of the importance of endemic traditions and local originality, most obviously reflected, for example, in crafts, cult activities, burial practices and cultural adaptations unique to Sicily, many of which endured for a remarkably long time.

The present volume cannot deal with all these matters in depth. My aim is essentially to provide a new synthesis of the prehistoric periods, accompanied by a selection of illustrations and bibliography, while highlighting local developments with reference to wider processes in Mediterranean archaeology.[9] A concise introductory survey was therefore envisaged for the benefit of those with no specialist knowledge in which several basic themes would be brought to attention: dating, settlement patterns and structures, funerary practices, subsistence, economic and social organisation. The selection of topics partly reflects personal choices and priorities within the conventional framework of a regional study in chronological outline, although I have abandoned the straitjacket of chapter divisions by conventional period names in favour of a more thematic approach. Certain periods, such as the Late Copper and Early Bronze Ages, and the Middle Bronze Age and beginning of the Late Bronze Age, have been kept within the same chapter, albeit subdivided, in order not to lose sight of underlying themes. The shortcomings of the archaeological record are familiarly frustrating ones of incomplete, uneven and biased evidence. However, correlations need to be made visible before causation can be discussed with any conviction. In considering long periods of time in chronological succession, I hope that the reader will gain a sense of continuities as well as discontinuities and be stimulated to think about causes and effects. Essentially, I hope to have provided a useful guide to the current state of research and an indication of the potential for new work and for new approaches in the future.

1

Early Faunal and Human Populations

Headlines in hunter-gatherer studies

The earliest and longest periods of human prehistory, from the Lower to the Upper Palaeolithic (or Pleistocene), are not usually represented in the archaeological record of Mediterranean islands. This is probably because smaller and more remote islands, deficient in large game, held few attractions for hunter-gatherers. Apart from Sicily, only Sardinia can currently claim to have been inhabited during the Upper Palaeolithic and possibly also during the Lower Palaeolithic, although the evidence for the latter has only begun to emerge recently and has been challenged.[1] Likewise, the presence of human residents in Sicily during the Lower Palaeolithic is not easy to prove, since it rests on little more than collections of stone tools from secondary contexts, lacking secure associations with extinct fauna and geometric dating. However, new discoveries may yet vindicate the theory of a very early human presence in the island, contemporary with a few sites in peninsular Italy and North Africa.

Throughout these periods, Sicily was represented by a series of evolving land formations that were significantly different from the island of today. This chapter begins, therefore, with a survey of geological, palaeogeographic and ecological factors, which provide a regional framework for a study of the first human cultures. At least four Pleistocene faunal associations have been recognised in recent years, although detailed vegetational sequences have yet to be elaborated and the task of associating insular ecological and climatic changes with broader continental patterns is only just beginning.

The widespread and rich assemblages of the late Upper Palaeolithic (or Epigravettian) and Mesolithic (table 1) have much in common with those of southern Italy, which is partly to be explained as a result of contact between these regions. An ultimately Italian provenance for the faunal and human populations of the Upper Palaeolithic, facilitated by crossings of the Straits of Messina, is the favoured hypothesis. However, the gentler relief and slightly milder climate of southern Sicily must have rendered it more hospitable and perhaps more populous than much of Apennine Italy, especially during the coldest glacial phases. Caves are recurrent on ancient limestone cliff-lines and have traditionally been the main focus of

11

archaeological research, while the number of outdoor sites known from surface surveys is now growing rapidly.

The elaboration of stone tool typologies has attracted much attention in the past, although certain ambiguities remain in these studies, based partly on materials from old excavations without radiocarbon dates. In particular, the distinction between late Palaeolithic and Mesolithic assemblages remains blurred, arguing in favour of cultural continuity between these periods. New evidence from Mesolithic sites also gives the impression that, at least in terms of their tool-kits, Sicilian Mesolithic groups had much in common with their peninsular neighbours. At the same time, variations existed in subsistence strategies, geared to the exploitation of a wide range of natural resources, which result from marked contrasts in terrain and relief within the island. The stratified faunal samples from the Uzzo cave show an increase in the exploitation of marine resources in the late Mesolithic and a more diversified subsistence base, although red deer still predominate. There is no evidence of independent domestication of plants or animals.

The archaeological record of the late Palaeolithic and Mesolithic in Sicily is also enriched by two kinds of more unusual findings, which attest a broadening of the cognitive faculties associated with *Homo sapiens*: cave burials, which have provided new information about the lifestyle and ceremonial behaviour of early populations; and a remarkable concentration and repertoire of cave art, which consists of incised animals and humans, including the numerous naturalistic figures in the Addaura and Levanzo caves, as well as more enigmatic linear motifs. Some of these images have been discussed at length, while others are less well known. Despite a long history of research, many problems of dating and interpretation remain, which typify the study of Palaeolithic art in general. Nevertheless, several different approaches (structuralist, post-structuralist or simply intuitive) have contributed to a better understanding of this repertoire and serve at least to impart a sense of its multifunctional potential.

Landscape evolution

From a structural point of view, Sicily consists essentially of three units, which eventually came to resemble the island of today as a result of tectonic movements at the boundary of the European and African plates, during the Miocene and Early Pliocene, between 25 million and 4 million years ago (fig. 2).[2] One major unit is the Hyblaean limestone plateau in the southeast; a second consists of the predominantly terrigenous or land-derived sediments of the central-western region; and a third is represented by the more variable associations and lithologies of the northern zone, mainly limestone in the northwest (the mountains of Palermo), and metamorphic or terrigenous sediments in the northeast (the Nebrodi and Peloritani mountains).

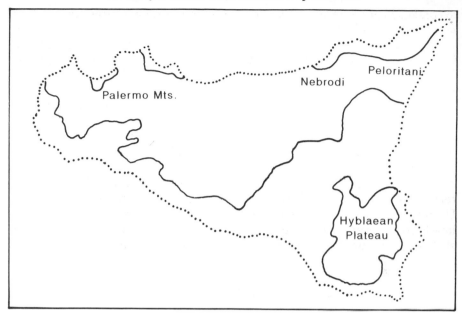

Fig. 2. Lower Pleistocene land forms (continuous line)

Tectonic activity and regional geological evolution during the Pliocene generated a series of deep marine basins, which surrounded the main structural units until the end of the Lower Pleistocene (about 700,000 years ago). During the Middle Pleistocene, after an increase in elevation of the three units, their borders subsided and a combination of tectonic movement (uplift) and sea-level changes, caused by glaciation cycles, led to the formation of marine terraces and coastal plains, as well as numerous caves aligned on ancient limestone cliffs.

The Hyblaean plateau continued to resemble an island surrounded by warm seas until well into the Middle Pleistocene, when the earliest Etnean volcanic activity occurred underwater (approximately 700,000 years ago). Stratigraphic sequences suggest that the southeastern plateau and the western part of the island were joined towards the end of the Lower Pleistocene. At an early stage of the Pliocene, the Straits of Messina resembled a deep marine basin separating the crystalline massifs of the Peloritani mountains from Aspromonte (Calabria). As a result of local tectonic activity, these mountains have undergone steady uplift since the Pliocene. During the Middle Pleistocene, the intervening area of the Straits was probably occupied by a land-bridge, consisting of a series of gravels on a south-facing bay backed by an isthmus, known as the Messina Formation. This feature, which is thought to have formed as a result of tectonic movements rather than sea-level changes, must have facilitated the spread of fauna between the island and southern Italy.

13

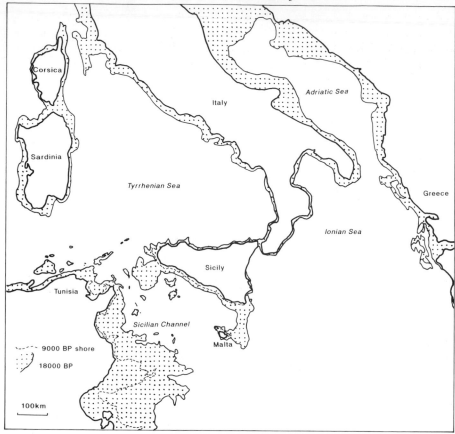

Fig. 3. Extended coastlines of the late glacial periods

During the last glacial periods of the Upper Pleistocene (from about 70,000 years BP) sea-level is estimated to have fallen by up to 120m, causing some dramatic changes to the Italian coastline, especially in the northern Adriatic, where steppe-like plains stretched southward for an additional 300km or so. The southern and western shores of Sicily also expanded considerably and the Maltese islands were joined, intermittently at least, to the Hyblaean plateau, until the intervening plate was finally submerged around 12,000 years BP (fig. 3). The possible existence of an isthmus at the western end of the island, which could have important implications for links with African faunal or human populations, was discussed by several scholars in the 19th century, although later authors have tended to dismiss the idea of a direct link with Tunisia.[3]

Nevertheless, this question merits further research as new information about sedimentation and tectonic movements becomes available. A glance at the bathymetry of the Sicilian channel shows that there are extensive stretches of relatively shallow water covering the Pelagian shelf, despite

14

a deeper trough, known as the Pantelleria Rift. The crossing to Africa must have narrowed from the 150km of today to about 40km, and was probably dotted with islets inbetween. The deeper section consists of a complex sequence of deposits (known as a 'horst and graben' system) on the edge of the African plate in a region that was prone to faulting, stretching, upwarping and subsidence. Volcanism resulted in the emergence of the small islands, Pantelleria and Linosa, but temporary formations are also known to have existed: 'Ferdinand's isle' appeared in 1831 only to disappear after a few years as a result of sea erosion or subsidence. The complex interplay of these palaeogeographical variables presents a major challenge for future research. It still remains to be established to what extent Italy was a geographical cul-de-sac for early mammals, which could only be entered from the north.

Climate and environment

Only general observations about climate and flora can be made, derived partly from research in Italy and the study of ocean cores, with the proviso that Sicily's more southerly latitude would have made it a rather more comfortable environment than central or northern Italy during the coldest phases of glaciation.[4] An early population of small mammalian fauna (fig. 5), possibly Villafranchian in date, may belong to a generally warmer pre-glacial phase of the Lower Pleistocene. Pollen diagrams from Calabria for the Lower Pleistocene show different phases with forests rich in *Taxodiaceae* (cypress family), woodlands with *cathaya* (an *Abietacea*, now extinct in Europe), open parklands, deciduous woodland, or conifer woods including cedars at higher altitudes.

The second and third Sicilian faunal associations, described below, belong approximately within the Middle Pleistocene, when interglacial periods were milder but not as warm as once thought. Deer were predominant on higher plateaus inland, which were probably well wooded, while hippo frequented broad coastal plains with lakes, as attested by the upper deposits of the new excavations at Fusco (Syracuse), where there is evidence for a range of Middle Pleistocene flora: holm-oak (*Quercus ilex*), flowering ash (*Fraxinus ornus*), pine (*Pinus* sp.), hornbeam (*Ostryga carpinifolia*), members of the Cypress family (*Cupressaceae*), as well as typical Mediterranean coastal shrubs (*Phillyrea*) and grasses (*Urticaceae* and *Laminaceae*).[5] During the Eemian interglacial phase of the Upper Pleistocene (about 120,000-80,000 BP), which was probably slightly warmer (by 1.5-3°C) and damper than today, an expansion of deciduous habitats occurred throughout Italy, with mixed oak and elm also spreading in the South. During the long cold periods of the Upper Pleistocene, particularly from about 70,000 BP (traditionally known as the Würm phase), clusters of small glaciers extended over the highest slopes of the Apennine chain down to Calabria. In central and northern Italy, there is ample evidence for loess (wind-blown silt) formation, associated with cold steppe-like conditions even on the Tyrrhenian side.

The situation may not be matched exactly in Sicily, where more endemic (unique local) species were able to survive. Plant cover naturally varies considerably with altitude. However, late glacial pollen sequences from the Madonie mountains suggest alternating cold phases, characterized by above-average rainfall (pluvial periods), with cooler steppe-like interstadials, favouring the spread of beech woods and the persistence of evergreen forests with laurel and holly.[6] From Upper Palaeolithic levels in the San Teodoro cave, carbonised remains of several broadleaf species attest the presence locally of mixed woodland including oaks, maples, wild plums and pears, suggesting damp and cool conditions (fig. 4). This fits broadly with the evidence of Upper Palaeolithic faunas, which are similar to their continental counterparts and associated with the colder conditions of the last glacial periods.

From about 10,000 BC, through the Pre-Boreal and Boreal phases (about 8000-6000 BC), climate and environment altered rapidly concurrently with a rise in average temperature of 8-10°C, until the Atlantic phase (5500-2500 BC). Apennine glaciers disappeared and rising sea-level (the Versilian transgression) led to the submersion of broad coastal plains (especially in the Adriatic), the separation of Malta from Sicily, Sardinia from Corsica, Elba from Italy, and a probable extension of the gap across the Straits of Messina. Over much of Italy, this period also saw the gradual restriction of pines to higher altitudes and the spread of mixed oak woodland, with evergreen oaks, hazel, beech, pine, elm and lime creeping upward into the Apennine foothills, accompanied by typical Mediterra-

LAYER	A(I)	B(II)	C(III)	D(IV)	D-E(IV-VI)
Pedunculate/English oak (*Quercus robur*)	4	1	10	5	4
Cf. Turkey oak (*Quercus cerris*)			1		
Oak family (sp. undetermined)			2		
Sycamore (*Acer Pseudo-platanus*)	1	2			2
Field maple (*Acer campestre*)	3	3	4	3?	3
Italian maple (*Acer opalus*)		3		3?	
Montpellier maple (*Acer monspessulanum*)			1		
Maple (sp. undetermined)	2	2	3	5	16
Pear (*Pyrus malus/communis*)	1	2	3	1	3
Plum (*Prunus domestica*)		1	3		1
Hawthorn (*Crataegus sp.*)			1		1
Blackthorn (*Prunus spinosa*)				1	
Cf. Chestnut (*Castanea* sp.)	1				
Buckthorn (*Rhamnus saxatilis*)	1				
Cf. Willow (*Salix* sp.)					1

Fig. 4. Wood charcoal from Grotta di San Teodoro, Upper Palaleolithic levels A-E (I-VI)

nean species, such as pistachio, arbutus, olive, cistus and boxwood. Similar developments probably occurred in Sicily, although beech seems to predominate in postglacial pollens from the Madonie mountains in competition with mixed oak (especially *Quercus robur*), by contrast with today's rather scruffy garrigue of broom and holm oak. However, more detailed associations and evidence of the temporary return to cooler drier conditions, widely associated with the Younger Dryas (about 11,000-10,000 BP), are lacking. Wood charcoal from early Holocene levels in the Uzzo cave point to a shift from a cooler and damper environment to a warmer and drier phase, dominated by an evergreen triad of holm oak (*Quercus ilex*), wild olive (*Olea* sp.) and *Phillyrea*, which are still typical of today's Mediterranean *macchia*, accompanied by wild strawberry (*Arbutus unedo*), wild grape (*Vitis sylvestris*) and some wild vetchlings or peas (*Lathyrus/pisum*).[7] Subsequent trends were of course increasingly affected by human action.

Pleistocene fauna

More evidence exists for Pleistocene fauna than vegetation as new research has begun to reassess the island's abundant palaeontological remains. As a preliminary working hypothesis, four main associations have been postulated, although their dating and the process of their evolution are not yet fully understood (fig. 5). A characteristic signature of the second and third groupings is the presence of species with markedly endemic characteristics.[8] In the case of large mammals, such as elephant or hippo, this is most apparent in their reduced size, although other minor traits also distinguish certain island species from their mainland counterparts. Paradoxically, in the case of some small vertebrates, such as mice, unusually large species are represented. For example, the smallest dwarf elephant in Sicily (*Elephas falconeri*) was the size of a large dog (about 1m in height), while certain 'giant' dormice (*Leithia melitensis*) were more like small rabbits. Giant swans and vultures are also known. This phenomenon, which recurs in several Mediterranean islands, is usually explained in terms of local adaptation to an insular environment, following a period of colonisation by mainland species.

In the early days of research, dwarf species were thought to be a result of degeneration caused by inbreeding. Today, it is more widely believed that changes in size were adaptive and in many ways advantageous. Small hippos and elephants not only require lesser quantities of food, but would have been more mobile, able to tackle rougher terrain and less dependent on water for keeping cool, while capable of a high reproductive rate. The absence of large predators may also have diminished the need for large size. By contrast, oversized rodents may have evolved as a means of protection or as a result of less competition for food. Insularity may also have had disadvantages. In the absence of predators, certain herbivores

17

Stage 1: (the 'Monte Pellegrino' stage):
    Weasel (*Mustelercta arzilla* De Gregorio)
    Hares (*Pellegrinia panormensis* De Gregorio; *Hypolagus* sp.)
    Fieldmouse (*Apodemus maximus* Thaler)
    Dormouse (*Leithia* sp.)

Stage 2: (the 'Spinagallo' stage):
    Dwarf elephant (*Elephas falconeri* Busk)
    Toads (*Discoglossus* cf. *pictus* Otth; *Bufo* cf. *viridis* Laurenti)
    Tree frog (*Hyla* sp.)
    Turtle (*Geochelone* sp.)
    Tortoises (*Testudo hermanni* Gmelin; *Emys orbicularis* Linnaeus)
    Lizards (*Lacerta viridis* Laurenti; *Lacerta siculimelitensis* Böhme & Maempel)
    Snakes (*Coluber* cf. *viridiflavus* Lacépède; *Natrix* sp.)
    Various bats (*Chiroptera*)
    Large dormouse (*Leithia melitensis* Adams)
    Dormouse (*Leithia cartei* Adams)
    Shrew (*Crocidura esuae* Kotsakis)
    Otter (*Lutra trinacriae*)
    Fox (*Vulpes* sp.)

Stage 3: (the 'Maccagnone' stage):
    Hippo (*Hippopotamus pentlandi* Meyer)
    Elephant (*Elephas mnaidriensis* Adams)
    Tortoise (*Testudo* sp.)
    Deer (*Cervus siciliae* Pohlig)
    Elk-like deer (*Megaloceros messinae* Pohlig; *Megaloceros carburangelensis* De Gregorio)
    Wild cattle (*Bos primigenius* Bojanus; *Bos primigenius siciliae* Pohlig)
    Bison (*Bison priscus* Bojanus)
    Boar (*Sus scrofa* Linnaeus)
    Bear (*Ursus* cf. *Arctos* Linnaeus)
    Wolf (*Canis lupus* Linnaeus)
    Cave hyena (*Crocuta spelea* Goldfuss)
    Cave lion (*Felis leo spelea* Goldfuss)

Stage 4: (the 'Castello' stage):
    Hedgehog (*Erinaceus europaeus* Linnaeus)
    Fox (*Vulpes vulpes* Linnaeus)
    Wild equids (*Equus caballus* Linnaeus; *Equus hydruntinus* Regalia)
    Boar (*Sus scrofa* Linnaeus)
    Wild cattle (*Bos primigenius* Bojanus)
    Red deer (*Cervus elaphus* Linnaeus; *Cervus siciliae*?)
    Bear (*Ursus* sp., uncommon)
    Wolf (*Canis* cf. *Lupus*, uncommon)
    Marten (*Martes*, uncommon)
    Hare (*Lepus europaeus* Pallas)
    Common toad (*Bufo bufo*)

Fig. 5. Pleistocene faunal associations

have a propensity to overbreed and periodically fall victim to mass starvations, perhaps caused by overgrazing.

In Sicily and many other islands, the presence or absence of endemic species raises questions about palaeogeography, the degree of insularity and the likelihood of replenishment with new arrivals from the mainland. It seems logical to correlate periods of markedly endemic fauna with periods of greater isolation, caused by sea-level or land-level changes, which determined distances across the Straits of Messina or the Sicilian-Tunisian channel. By this reasoning, the more balanced nature of later Pleistocene faunal associations can be correlated with periods of lesser insularity, when contacts with continental land masses were easier. To some extent, the factors conditioning processes of biological evolution have a parallel in later periods, when the subject of discussion is human cultural evolution; the latter was also influenced by insularity, or the presence and absence of external contacts. The spread of mammalian faunas into the island is also relevant to the study of early human residents, since it is quite likely that the latter arrived by similar routes.

A very early faunal association, known only from Monte Pellegrino (Palermo) in western Sicily, consists of small vertebrates, such as weasels, fieldmice, dormice and hare, possibly reflecting links with Africa.[9] This association is not easy to date on present evidence, although it may go back to a Villafranchian stage. The second association, recorded in the Hyblaean plateau and the Palermo mountains, comprises species with markedly endemic characteristics, notably the dwarf elephant (*Elephas falconeri*), as well as several kinds of reptiles, amphibians, rodents and small mammals. Geochemical dating (amino-acid racemization) of *Elephas falconeri* remains from the Spinagallo cave has provided an approximation of 550,000 years BP, while stratigraphic data suggest an earlier date at the beginning of the Middle Pleistocene for similar fossil remains from lake deposits.[10]

The origins of this faunal group are not obvious. Equivalent species have not yet been found in either northeastern Sicily or Calabria and a crossing of the Straits of Messina may have been impeded by a larger and deeper stretch of water at this time. The markedly endemic features of certain species in this group, such as *Elephas falconeri*, which is also recorded in Malta, have suggested a slow movement over an extensive area, possibly an archipelago, along which certain gradual modifications in characteristics occurred. A North African link with some elements in this Middle Pleistocene faunal group is only a faint possibility and cannot be proven.

The third faunal association is spread throughout Sicily and has less markedly endemic traits. It is characterized by the presence of a hippo (*H. pentlandi*) and an elephant (*E. mnaidrensis*), which is notably larger than the earlier dwarf species. A significant context for the study of this association are the layers just outside the San Teodoro cave at Acquedolci, where huge quantities of fossilized hippo bone accumulated gradually in an ancient lake bed as their carcasses sank to the bottom.[11] Geochemical dating of a hippo tooth provided an approximation of 190,000 ± 50,000 years BP. The more broadly balanced characteristics of this grouping, the presence of carnivores and the fact that several species also occur in southern Italy during the Middle Pleistocene, argues for a closer relationship with Italy as a result of an easier passage across the Straits of Messina. However, much new evidence for this stage is coming to light from the Fusco deposits, where younger dates around 146,000 BP (± 19,500) have been obtained.[12] The lower level indicates that the small elephant (*E. mnaidriensis*; H about 2m), was partly contemporary with a larger species (*Elephas* sp., possibly *antiquus*; H up to 4m) and a wide range of other vertebrates which survive into later layers, by which time the elephants had been largely substituted by hippo.

How long did these species last? While some of their descendants are present in the succeeding association, contemporary with humans, it seems that the hippo and elephant died out before or soon after the onset of the last glacial period in peninsular Italy and were replaced by woolly rhino and mammoth. They were never seen, therefore, by Late Palaeolithic peoples. In Cyprus, however, contrary to expectations, recent excavations have suggested that pygmy hippos and elephants were still current around 10,000 BC and that they were hunted by early settlers. There is nothing to prove that the same is true for Sicily, although little is known about the survival potential of these species into colder phases.[13]

The last faunal grouping (stage 4) is recorded mainly in caves, where it is often associated with Upper Palaeolithic stone industries and partly reflects the diet of local hunter-gatherers (fig. 9). A much lesser degree of bone fossilisation usually characterizes these remains as well as the presence of non-endemic mammals, which resemble their counterparts in Italy: deer are most common, mainly smallish red deer (*Cervus elaphus*), although a small local variety (*Cervus siciliae*) may still be current. Some doubts surround the presence of fallow deer (*Dama dama*); the few recorded bones of the preceding stage may have been confused with megacerines. One typical species of this period is the wild ass-like equid (*Equus hydruntinus*), present from the early Upper Pleistocene and characteristic of open park-land. Its remains have been found in several Sicilian caves, especially in the Palermo region. An early study of Sicilian wild cattle suggested the presence of two rather small subspecies, resembling *Bison priscus* and *Bos primigenius*, more typical of stage 3, although new studies are now required. In fact, the bones of *Bos primigenius* from the Upper Palaeolithic rock-shelter at Pedagaggi are consistent with the large continental species. Other mammals attested at this time include wild boar and possibly lynx.[14] This group, and doubtless the associated humans, must derive from Italy and denotes colder conditions than before.

Some of these species lasted into later periods and their subsequent history is clearly bound up with that of human exploitation and animal domestication. In the more wooded and hilly country of central and northeastern Sicily and in the forests of Etna, red deer and wild boar survived until historical times. By contrast, wild equids probably died out early in the Holocene as the coastal plains became much narrower, while the last wild cattle could have been cross-bred with domesticates during the early Neolithic.

The first stone tools?

Bedevilled by false expectations and uncertain contexts, the controversy surrounding the dating of many stone tools originated in the 19th century, when a few axes were assumed to be Lower Palaeolithic.[15] An assessment of the age of simpler stone tools on the basis of typology alone can be a risky exercise, even for experienced practitioners (fig. 6). Ideally, recourse should be made to geostratigraphic observations, scientific dating, or other associations. In the absence of the latter, it is not surprising that divergent opinions have been expressed periodically about certain stone implements in Sicily.[16] Some claims have been shown to be flawed and others remain inconclusive.

Significant quantities of material come from two provinces (fig. 7). The first is the Catania plain, where surface surveys have recovered numerous scrapers, points, denticulates and choppers, mainly of quartzite, but occasionally of flint and other rock. These are generally large in size and with simple retouched edges, and have often been dated to the Lower Palaeolithic. If proven, this would imply an unusually dense concentration of sites in this area. Likewise, in the province of Agrigento, denticulates,

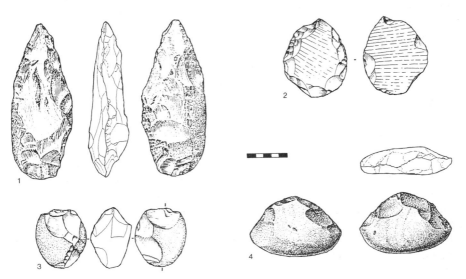

Fig. 6. Bifacial, discoidal and pebble chopping tools: (1) Rocca Vruaro; (2-3) sporadic; (4) Faro Rossello

scrapers and large quartzitic bifacials have been found at several locations. In 1968, P. Graziosi noted an undeniable similarity between some bifacials from earlier collections and the classic European and North African Palaeolithic hand-axes of Acheulean type, reviving the notion of a Lower Palaeolithic date. During the 1970s, numerous implements resembling even more archaic pebble tools (of Clactonian and earlier types) were collected at various locations on the southwestern coast by G. Bianchini and in recent years quartzitic choppers of archaic appearance have been found in the Belice region.[17]

However, despite the initial enthusiasm for an early date, an alternative hypothesis has steadily gained ground in recent years. New research into Holocene stone industries of Campignian type has shown that the late Neolithic, Copper and Early Bronze Ages saw a profusion of large roughly worked axe-like tools (tranchets, bifacials and many others), evidently used by agriculturalists (chapter 2), some of which closely resemble Palaeolithic forms. Pebble choppers are also known from Neolithic and later sites.[18] As a result, the identification of Lower Palaeolithic implements on purely morphological grounds has been thrown into question and many specialists have now adopted a more cautious position.

On the other hand, the discovery of an indisputable Lower or Middle Palaeolithic site in the island would not generate much surprise. There is good evidence for early humans in Italy, for example at Isernia (La Pineta) in the Molise before 730,000 BP. Archaic chopping tools have been found in Middle Pleistocene deposits in Calabria (Casella di Maida, Rosaneto), while pre-neanderthal fossils are documented elsewhere in southern Italy.[19] At Notarchirico (Basilicata), bifacials are associated with elephant bones and choppers around 360,000 BP. After France, Italy has more direct fossil evidence for *Homo sapiens neanderthalensis* than any other European country: well represented by the Circeo skulls (Lazio), and also at sites in Calabria (Iannì di S. Calogero, Archi). In North Africa, archaic pebble tools are common in Algeria. It seems unlikely, therefore, that Sicily should have remained deserted even in these very early periods; but this theory needs to be vindicated by new research.

The Upper Palaeolithic

The Italian Epigravettian or late Upper Palaeolithic, datable from about 18,000 BC and roughly contemporary with the Solutrean and Magdalenian periods in France, is divided into three main phases: early, evolved and final (table 1). The final phase has the most numerous sites and shows increasing evidence for regional variation in hunting and gathering strategies as a result of local adaptations to contrasting habitats. A striking characteristic of the period is the evidence for a broadening of the cognitive faculties of contemporary humans, reflected, in particular, by cave art, decorated artefacts and burials.

By the later stages of the Upper Palaeolithic, Sicily was widely inhab-

1. Early Faunal and Human Populations

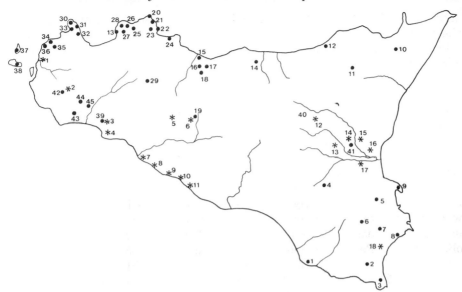

Fig. 7. *Bifacial and pebble tools* (*): 1 Guarrato, Granatello, Marausa; 2 Fiume Grande-Bovara; 3 Menfi; 4 Bertolino di Mare; 5 S. Stefano di Quisquina; 6 Rocca del Vruaro; 7 Eraclea Minoa; 8 Faro Rossello; 9 Realmonte; 10 Maddaluso; 11 Mandrascava; 12 Agira; 13 Ramacca; 14 Muglia Nord; 15 Fontanazza, Poggio Monaco; 16 Gerbini; 17 Piano Meta; 18 Noto. *Upper Palaeolithic/Mesolithic sites* (•): 1 Fontana Nuova; 2 Riparo Stafenna; 3 G. Corruggi; 4 Palike; 5 Pedagaggi; 6 Riparo San Corrado; 7 Canicattini Bagni; 8 G. Giovanna; 9 G. Acquasanta; 10 Riparo di San Basilio; 11 Riparo San Marco; 12 G. San Teodoro; 13 San Cataldo; 14 Piano di S. Foca; 15 Riparo del Castello; 16 G. Geraci, Natale, Puleri; 17 G. di Nuovo; 18 Contrada Franco; 19 G. di Acqua Fitusa; 20 G. Perciata; 21 G. Addaura; 22 Riparo Primo Pizzo; 23 G. Niscemi; 24 G. San Ciro; 25 G. di S. Rosalia; 26 G. Carburanceli; 27 G. Maccagnone; 28 G. dei Puntali, Za' Minica; 29 Contrada Drago; 30 G. di Cala Mancina; 31 G. Capreria; 32 G. dell'Uzzo; 33 G. Racchio, Isolidda; 34 G. Mangiapane; 35 G. Miceli; 36 G. Emiliana, Martogna; 37 G. dei Genovesi and other Levanzo caves; 38 Favignana caves; 39 Contrada Tardara; 40 Riparo Longo; 41 Perriere Sottano; 42 Roccazzo; 43 Parche di Bilello; 44 Cisternazza-Vallesecco; 45 Pizzo Don Pietro

ited, as indicated by numerous sites with characteristic assemblages known from excavations mainly in caves located near the sea and from a growing number of surface collections inland (fig. 7). The majority are assigned on stylistic grounds to the later phase of the Epigravettian and some ^{14}C dates, ranging from about 15,000 to 10,000 cal.BC, support this conclusion (table 4). Sites with radiocarbon dates and trustworthy stratigraphies obviously provide the ideal basis for interpretation. However, the current framework has gaps and uncertainties despite diligent classifications of stone tools, which attempt to trace sequences of development using the method devised by G. Laplace.[20] In fact, most sites lack radiocarbon dates, many are known only from old excavations and others are merely surface scatters of stone tools. Dating the latter can be very difficult, especially when atypical forms occur or when the more common types appear to be absent.

23

One site that may be much older than the rest is Fontana Nuova (Ragusa), a small rock-shelter (8m wide, 2m deep and 3m high) located at 145m asl near the top of a rocky ridge about 3km from the modern shore. It is known from a small collection of tools and bones extracted early this century and a later test excavation of residual deposits, which provided a rough stratigraphic outline. The absence of microliths and the predominance of a laminar blade industry with some typical Aurignacian forms (especially endscrapers, a few notched and denticulated tools) has led several authors to regard it as the most southerly Aurignacian site in Europe (fig. 8:A).[21] In Italy this period is dated from about 33,000-30,000 BP by conventional ^{14}C dates and up to 40,000 BP by accelerator dates. The site resembles a temporary shelter, whose occupants relied heavily on deer (over 90% of bones), represented by individuals of mixed ages and a high proportion of limb bones with frequent signs of burning, which were probably butchered nearby. There is no evidence of *Equus hydruntinus* which is recurrent in later Epigravettian sites. Two varieties of flint were used for making tools, one local and the other from a source at Monte Iudica, about 100km away, as well as occasional jasper and limestone implements, including an incised cylinder. Five human bones may belong to a single adult and include two teeth, one of which has an artifical 'toothpick' groove, a feature which recurs on certain Neanderthal as well as Upper Palaeolithic Italian specimens. Although they cannot be taken as evidence for Neanderthals, the large dimensions of the teeth place them near the upper limit of the size range for the Upper Palaeolithic.

In the rest of Italy, this early phase of the Upper Palaeolithic, associated with anatomically modern humans, is represented by few sites. It is followed by the Gravettian (from French terminology, about 28,000-20,000 BP), for which there is no evidence for human occupation in Sicily. If this lacuna is taken at face-value, it would appear that the island was only resettled in a later Epigravettian phase. However, new discoveries may eventually fill this gap.

The dating of Sicilian Epigravettian sites rested initially on the typological studies of Laplace, who assigned two assemblages (Canicattini Bagni and Grotta Niscemi) to an early Epigravettian typified by denticulates, notched, truncated and backed blades, and two others (San Corrado and Grotta Mangiapane) to the second or evolved phase. A recent study of material from old excavations at the Riparo Castello (Termini Imerese) has also raised the possibility of an early Epigravettian or even late Gravettian date for certain microgravettes, although the assemblages from all these sites were probably from mixed levels and cannot be dated before the Final Epigravettian with much confidence.

There are also risks in assuming that stone tools followed a straightforward evolution. Lithic assemblages are clearly influenced by the nature of local activities and subsistence. Different activities undertaken at the same site, for example on a seasonal basis, can also lead to significant

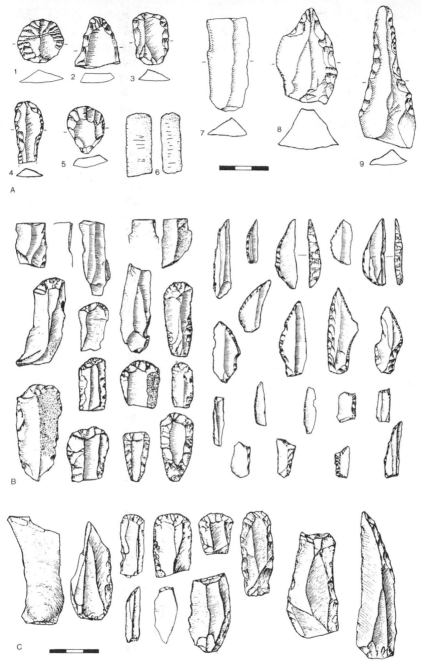

Fig. 8. (A) Fontana Nuova lithic implements: (1-5,8) endscapers; (6) incised limestone cylinder; (7) angled burin; (9) blade; (B) Acqua Fitusa, Final Epigravettian types, first geometric phase; (C) Final Epigravettian types, San Teodoro upper layers, second non-geometric phase

25

intra-site variability. Contemporary sites in different environments, therefore, can have considerable variation in their tool kits, and partially excavated sites may present a distorted view. Because of the marked changes in environment and relief encountered within Italy, even over relatively short distances, the degree of variation in cultural assemblages may well be greater than that found in the larger expanses of more uniform landscape in northern Europe.

It is only with the better-known and more numerous sites of the Final Epigravettian that approximate dates can be assigned with confidence. Even so, there may be considerable spatial variation in these assemblages and the presence or absence of microliths, for example, may not be a reliable indication of date. Moreover, a date from Acqua Fitusa (14,959-14,109 cal.BC) seems early for a site where the assemblage has much more in common with Final Epigravettian forms. However, this is often regarded as one of the earlier sites of the Sicilian Final Epigravettian, along with Grotta Giovanna (13,436-13,003 cal.BC) and San Teodoro (lower layers D-C), to which the more recently discovered sites of Cisternazza, Roccazzo, Pedagaggi and Passo Falcone may be added.[22] Vigliardi describes this early phase as one characterized by the development of truncated backed forms and especially geometrics: triangular, lunate, trapezoidal and rhomboidal forms, as well as elongated retouched scrapers (fig. 8:B). The faunal samples associated with this material are dominated by deer, followed by wild boar; those from Grotta Giovanna also include wild cattle, equids, wolf, cave hyena, marine molluscs and occasional land snails (fig. 9).

Probably slightly later within the Final Epigravettian are the upper layers (B-A) at San Teodoro, layer 3 in the Grotta dei Genovesi on Levanzo (11,764-11,094, and 11,034-10,737 cal.BC), and the bottom layers of some trenches in the Grotta dell'Uzzo. In these contexts, geometric and microlithic forms are absent, whereas truncated backed forms, points, denticulates and scrapers predominate (fig. 8:C). In northwestern Sicily, therefore, this second phase is often distinguished as one in which geometrics are absent, although there is some suggestion of a subsequent cycle with geometrics marking the beginning of the Mesolithic in about the 9th millennium BC (below).

At Levanzo, where the faunal remains show signs of burning and breakage typical of culinary debris, deer bones are by far the most frequent, followed by much smaller quantities of wild cattle, equids, boar, fox, small mammals and many species of birds (figs. 9-10). Marine molluscs were also collected, although there is no evidence for fishing in this earlier layer. Deer also predominate at other sites and may include a small local variety as well as *Cervus elaphus*. In eastern Sicily, similar species are recorded from a rock-shelter at Pedagaggi as well as a possible lynx and various birds. Careful sifting of deposits in the Uzzo cave has allowed a wide range of avifauna to be identified, although it is not certain whether the bones in the lowest layers were introduced by humans or by natural

1. Early Faunal and Human Populations

	Deer	Boar	Cattle	Fox	Equid	Roe	Other
PALAEOLITHIC							
Fontana Nuova	92.6	2.8	3.7	0.1			0.5
San Teodoro A-B	64	27	9				
San Teodoro C-D	61	24.5	14	0.5			
Grotta Genovesi 3	69	2	17	3	9		
Pedagaggi	22	24	14		30		10
PALAEO-MESOLITHIC							
Grotta Genovesi 2/4	55	31	8		6		
Uzzo F/48-33	92.5	1.6	2.6	1.6			1.7
Sperlinga S. Basilio	65	17.4		4.7	1.5	11.1	
Grotta Corruggi	44	3	4	23	15		11
MESOLITHIC							
Uzzo F/32-23	86.1	5	0.4	7.3			1.3
Uzzo F/22-15	69.8	25.6	2.2	2.1			0.4
Uzzo F/14-11	66.5	26.1		5			2.4

Fig. 9. Palaeolithic-Mesolithic fauna (*Cervus elaphus, Sus scrofa ferus, Bos primigenius, Vulpes vulpes, Equus hydruntinus, Capreolus capreolus*), % of bone nos

	PALAEOLITHIC		MESOLITHIC			
	Uzzo	Genovesi	Genovesi	Uzzo	Uzzo	Uzzo
	F48-33	St3/5	St2/4	F32-23	F22-15	F14-11
Grebes	1			1		
Ducks			1	3		
Rails, gallinules, coots	4		1		2	2
Shearwaters		1	10		2	2
Falcons	4	1		7		
Hawks			5	1		
Buzzard				1	3	1
Hen harrier			1			
Quails and partridges	49	2	1	59	28	26
Woodcock				6	1	
Herons and bitterns			1			1
Crane			3			
Great bustard		1	2			
Geese			2			1
Pigeons and doves	21	1	2	168	50	52
Owls	2		1	16	8	4
Swift	1				4	3
Jays and crows	29		1	156	32	2
Roller		1				

Fig. 10. Palaeolithic-Mesolithic avifauna; number of remains

processes (fig.10). Some species, such as rock partridges and doves, still thrive in the neighbouring mountainous areas and rocky coastline. On the other hand, the presence of choughs suggests some markedly cold phases.

The overall impression is that Sicily was essentially an extension of southern Italy in a cultural sense during the later Palaeolithic. Links with Africa are much harder to discern and the contemporary Iberomaurusian of northern Tunisia, with its specialized tool-kits and different burial and artistic manifestations, need owe nothing to the Epigravettian or vice versa.[23] This does not rule out the possibility of occasional crossings of the Sicilian channel. However, since Levanzo and Favignana (Egadi islands) were still joined to Sicily and the small islands seem to have been uninhabited, there is no sign of a willingness on the part of early residents to cross ample stretches of sea, perhaps due more to a lack of motivation than ability. Little off-shore islands, such as the Aeolian group, deficient in large game, would not have had much to offer hunter-gatherers. The first evidence of visits to Lipari dates to the Mesolithic.

However, while the Sicilian late Epigravettian has many features in common with that of southern Italy, the island's slightly milder climate and less rugged terrain must have rendered it more hospitable than much of Apennine Italy, especially during the coldest phases of the last glaciation. It was probably more populated too, especially around the coasts, which were of greater breadth prior to the last marine transgression.

Caves and rock-shelters were plainly both dwellings and places of ritual importance (for burial and art), but outdoor camps must have been common too, especially inland, as recent evidence from surface surveys suggests. Some sites are known at considerable altitudes: a surface scatter, usually regarded as Final Epigravettian, from Rocca San Marco at 1225m asl in the Nebrodi mountains must surely represent a summer hunting camp.[24] Deer hunting was prevalent and ubiquitous, but marine and land molluscs were also collected. Large numbers of *Patella* were found earlier this century in the Riparo Castello and in other caves on the northern shore as well as several marine and land species (*Monodonta*, *Conus Mediterraneus*, *Columbella* and *Helix*), which could well belong to the late Palaeolithic, despite the uncertainties of the stratigraphy. Red deer was most abundant at this site, followed by equids, boar, wild cattle, roe deer, fox, hare and birds, but modern investigations of subsistence behaviour with reference to microfauna and plant foods are lacking. There was probably little difference in lifestyle between the inhabitants of the northern coast and their neighbours in southern Tyrrhenian Italy. At Grotta della Cala in Campania and Grotta della Madonna in Calabria a rather mixed subsistence strategy is encountered, in which red deer predominate, although roe, ibex, chamois, large quantities of bird bones and molluscs are also attested. By comparison with their Magdalenian contemporaries in northern Europe, who were more reliant on single large species, such as reindeer, these southern Mediterranean Epigravettian communities seem rather less specialised. From the point of view of

1. Early Faunal and Human Populations

CONTEXT	MESOLITHIC				NEOLITHIC	
	Genovesi St2/4	Uzzo F32-23	Uzzo F22-15	Uzzo F14-11	Uzzo F10-6	Uzzo F5-1
MARINE SHELLS						
Patella ferruginea		23	54	24	13	6
Patella caerulea		11	236	4199	4236	699
Patella rustica		2	38	1123	1388	299
Patella sp.	✓		176	745	607	187
Gibbula sp.			11	113	291	47
Monodonta turbinata		15	795	1492	1169	227
Monodonta articulata			18	52	60	13
Mitra sp.				2	20	7
Cerithium sp.				4	18	9
Columbella rustica			29	119	526	127
Conus mediterraneus			1	5	12	6
Hexaplex sp.			1	9	15	7
Pisania striata			1	7	17	7
Trochus	✓					
Triton	✓					
LAND SHELLS						
Helix	✓	270	137+	20	8	
FISH						
Grouper (Epinephelus sp.)	117	1	35	422	386	144
Dentex (Dentex sp.)	4			12	13	
Sea-bream (Sparus sp.)	9			4	8	1
Grey mullet (Mugil cephalus)		1	3	5	5	
Moray eel (Muraena helena)			1	12	29	2
Sea-bream (Pagellus sp.)				1	4	
Striped bream (Lithognatus mormyrus)			1		2	
White bream (Diplodus sargus)			1	14	10	
Sarpa (Sarpa salpa)				4	2	
Black bream (Spondyliosoma cantharus)				2		2
Umbrina (Sciaena umbra)				1	6	2
Amberjack (Seriola dumerili)				1		
Wrasse (Labrus merula)			3	13	13	1
Scorpion fish (Scorpaena scrofa)					1	
Angler fish (Lophius piscatorius)					1	
MARINE MAMMALS						
Loggerhead turtle (Caretta caretta)	2	1			1	
Monk seal (Monachus monachus)	1		3		2	
Pilot whale (Globicephala melaena)			7	21		
Large whale (Balaeonoptera/Physeter)				14		
Risso's dolphin (Gramphus griseus)				3		
Common dolphin (Delphinus delphis)				2		

Fig. 11. Mesolithic-Neolithic molluscs (minimum number of individuals), fish and marine species (number of remains)

subsistence, therefore, it is not surprising that many of their traditions persisted into the Mesolithic.

The Mesolithic

The term Mesolithic is more problematic in the Italian context than in northern Europe. Many characteristics of the period originated in the course of the Final Epigravettian so that the distinction between the two phases is not clearly demarcated. The term Epipalaeolithic is occasionally used to stress this. Some authors play down the significance of the transition, which is seen in little more than chronological terms: a label applied to the last practitioners of a hunting and gathering lifestyle who lived at a time of climatic and environmental change following the Pleistocene-Holocene transition, from roughly 9000 BC. Others prefer a definition based on cultural rather than environmental or chronological principles. Traditionally, new developments in technology and the increase in microlithic tools, connected with the use of the bow and arrow, have been taken as a hallmark of the Mesolithic. Changes in subsistence strategies are now increasingly the subject of research, while sedentism is also regarded as a significant factor.

In Italy, the picture is a complex one and the standard view may be less applicable further south and in Sicily.[25] Changes in technology or a simple progression towards microlithic industries are not clearly demonstrable in a uniform pattern. Variations existed between regions and sites and even within the same site as a result of spatial or temporal factors. There are also problems of dating. Geometric microliths are not always predominant in Mesolithic sites and can occur in Final Epigravettian contexts too. For example, the Grotta Corruggi and the Sperlinga di San Basilio are somewhat ambiguous: both have an abundance of microlithic implements. Circular scrapers, trapezoidal and triangular geometrics predominate at Corruggi, a cave in southeast Sicily, while triangular geometrics and curved forms are common at San Basilio (layer III), a rock-shelter high above sea level (600m) in the Peloritani mountains. It seems most likely

Fig. 12. Shells of *Columbella rustica* with incised lines, sometimes filled with ochre: *left* Uzzo cave; *right* Perriere Sottano

that they represent Mesolithic occupation, although some would not exclude the possibility of an earlier Epigravettian phase with geometrics.

Two radiocarbon-dated sites (Uzzo and Perriere Sottano) provide ample evidence for the Mesolithic. Early Mesolithic layers at Uzzo contain only a few microlithic implements (not all geometric in form), followed by more mixed types in later layers with simple or denticulated retouch, accompanied by bone points, spatulas and shell beads or pendants, sometimes incised and filled with ochre (fig. 12). At Perriere Sottano, a rock-shelter in eastern Sicily of about 8000-7500 cal.BC, the tool-kit shows the persistence of Final Epigravettian forms and the appearance of non-geometric microliths, comparable with Sauveterrian types, widely associated with the Pre-Boreal and Boreal phases (ca. 8000-6000 BC), suggesting a pattern of development like that of peninsular Italy (fig.13:1-8). The second layer (st. 2/4) of the Genovesi cave on Levanzo probably also belongs to the Mesolithic, or to the very end of the Epigravettian, on account of its stratigraphic position and similarities between its faunal remains and those of Uzzo.

Many other caves have probably lost their Mesolithic deposits as a result of human disturbance. It is also difficult to identify changing settlement patterns on the basis of cave sites alone. As regards subsistence, the Mesolithic seems to reflect gradual change and flexibility, as may be expected of foragers living at a time of climatic and environmental change. It may well have been more common now to follow wild fauna (especially deer) and flora (summer fruits and berries) into higher terrain away from the coast, as part of a seasonal cycle. At coastal sites, the diet embraced a widening range of natural resources, with a new emphasis on fishing and shellfish.

These developments are best documented at the Uzzo cave, where deep soundings span the transition to the Neolithic, from about 9000 to 5500 cal.BC (figs. 9-11). The bones of wild mammals (36.1%), small mammals (32.1%) and birds (30.6%) predominate in the earlier Mesolithic layers (tr.F 32-23). From a nutritional point of view, red deer is the most important species, followed by wild boar, fox and wild cattle. The variety of bird bones (notably partridges, doves and jackdaws) is striking. The later Mesolithic layers (22-15), which probably cover much of the 8th millennium BC, also contain a high percentage of red deer (70%), mainly adult examples, which provide a good return in terms of meat, skins and antler. Wild boar (25%) was more common, wild cattle (2.2%) infrequent and birds (5%) less common than before. By contrast, there is more evidence for fishing (up to 7.7%) and for the collection of marine molluscs, accompanied by occasional bones of the monk seal and pilot dolphin.

Fishing (25.8%) grew steadily in importance through the latest Mesolithic levels (14-11), which are dated in part to the early 7th millennium BC. Groupers were most common (86%), followed by Moray eel, white bream, wrasse and various species, which still occur in local waters. Likewise, a large quantity of sea shells (mainly *Patella* and *Monodonta*)

31

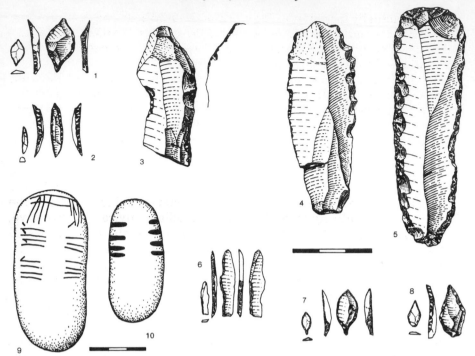

Fig. 13. (1-8) Perriere Sottano, Mesolithic flint tools; (9-10) Grotta Genovesi painted pebbles

bear witness to the exploitation of marine resources. More unusual are the finds of vertebra from several species of dolphin and a sperm whale, one of the largest cetaceans known to visit the Mediterranean, probably reflecting beach strandings. Red deer still predominate among the mammals (66%) and are well represented by young adults between 3 and 5 years of age that might well have come from bachelor herds and could, therefore, suggest a considered form of exploitation or herd management. Slightly smaller than their continental counterparts, these deer may be an island variant of the species. By contrast, wild boar (26%) were mostly killed at a very young age. Fox (5%), the occasional wild cat (2.3%) and possibly wolf or dog are recorded too. A plant-food economy at Uzzo can be traced from early Mesolithic layers, represented by the strawberry (*Arbutus unedo*), certain wild legumes, a vetchling or pea (*Lathyrus* or *Pisum*), and subsequently by oak acorns, wild grape (*Vitis sylvestris*) and wild olive (*Olea* sp.).[26]

Aside from several burials at Uzzo (below), structural remains include a late Mesolithic floor surface (Q) traced over 5m² and associated with a hearth and an unusual installation, consisting of a fire-hardened clay platform, about 50cm long and 2-3cm thick, set into the floor, reminiscent of the clay cooking bases found in later prehistoric contexts (fig. 14).[27] Evidently this late Mesolithic group was already making some use of clay, albeit not actually for pottery. The study of the wild boar and deer remains from the floor indicates that several individuals were killed in the late summer or early autumn; one of several seasonal episodes in the long occupational history of this cave.

Overall, the sequences at the Uzzo and Genovesi caves show changing emphases in the use of local resources, the most obvious of which is the growing exploitation of marine life. Herein lies the potential for a more stable pattern of residence at coastal sites, which is to some extent confirmed by a study of the fish bones, indicating catches at different times of year. The presence of various birds, including winter migrants, reinforces the idea of multi-seasonal if not year-round occupation, following a pattern of radiating mobility: stable occupation of a base from which forays were made for specific tasks. The presence of marsh and lake birds in the faunal sample, unlikely to be from the immediate environs of the cave, indicates a hunting territory encompassing flatter shorelands several miles away. Plainly, a more diversified subsistence strategy was advantageous as an adaption to a changing postglacial environment in which herds of large game (notably *Bos* and *Equus*) were becoming scarcer. One constant feature, however, is the persistence of deer, evidently the favoured quarry of both Palaeolithic and Mesolithic hunters in many parts of the island.

As in the previous period, the assemblage from north Sicilian coastal caves is most closely matched in southern Tyrrhenian Italy. Mesolithic levels (7532-7258 cal.BC) in the Grotta della Madonna (Calabria) also show an increase in marine molluscs and wild boar.[28] Further afield, the subsistence pattern at Uzzo has certain similarities with that of the Franchthi cave in Greece. To some extent it was probably typical of southern Mediterranean coastal sites. In different environments, however, a different regime prevailed. At Perriere Sottano in the Catania plain, bones of wild cattle and smallish red deer were found in roughly equal quantity, as well as a few of wild boar and just three marine molluscs, one of which was an ornament. This was evidently a locally wooded habitat with ample open areas frequented by wild cattle. Sites at high altitudes, such as the San Basilio rock-shelter, are more likely to represent seasonal camps visited in the summer months, when the emphasis was on hunting red and roe deer, species which are inclined to follow annual altitudinal movements.

The overall impression during the Mesolithic is of local diversity, which to some extent reflects the variations in subsistence activities and habitats documented throughout peninsular Italy. As before, there is no compelling evidence for influential contacts with the Maghreb, where the early Holocene Capsian hunter-gatherers are associated with *escargotières* (in Tunisia) and hunting of large bubal antelope.[29] Nevertheless, the Mesolithic provides the first evidence of island visits, as attested by the presence of Lipari obsidian at Perriere Sottano. This is also witnessed elsewhere in the Mediterranean: for example, obsidian from Melos occurs at the Franchthi cave and some large islands, such as Corsica, were probably settled at this time.

The transition from hunting and gathering to farming, one of the most significant developments in prehistory, naturally focuses attention on early plant cultivation and animal domestication. However, there is nothing very convincing at Uzzo to suggest a precocious or autonomous move towards the domestication of wild animal species or plant cultivation in late Mesolithic layers. In fact, occasional claims for independent developments of this kind in the western Mediterranean have often evaporated on closer inspection.[30] At Uzzo, the nature of the stratigraphy changes from layer 10 upward, which correlates with a radiocarbon date of 5711-5558 cal.BC and a pattern of subsistence behaviour which can confidently be described as fully 'Neolithic'. A cautious view, therefore, would be that the first cereal grains need not have arrived before about 6000 cal.BC at this site, probably from an external source such as a nearby farming village.

It could be argued that some late Mesolithic groups developed behavioural patterns that would have pre-disposed them to adopt farming practices, although there are several hypothetical elements in the arguments. The exploitation of certain wild species (boar at Uzzo, cattle at Perriere Sottano) which were subsequently domesticated is noteworthy, although the emphasis on red meat and sea-food might have militated against food-storage. Fishing may have permitted a greater degree of sedentism accompanied by new skills and technological innovations, an increasing competence in sea travel and an extended range of social contacts. This also led to the discovery and acquisition of obsidian from the island of Lipari, an unusual raw material that was central to the subsequent development of the Neolithic economy in this region. The discussion must therefore be resumed in the next chapter.

Burials and bones

Evidence of human burial exists for the Middle Palaeolithic, but it was only during the Upper Palaeolithic that the practice became widespread in Europe. Italy has more examples than usual for this period: about 60 cases have been recorded so far, covering a time-span of about 15,000 years, although the majority (about 40 individuals) date to the Final Epigravettian.[31] Burials from Italian Mesolithic sites, including Corsica, comprise less than 40 individuals and nearly half of them are from Sicily. One must be wary of generalizations or attempts to characterize hunter-gatherer populations on the basis of such a small sample, and yet the evidence merits special attention. Where preservation is good, excavation conducted rigorously and analysis undertaken with scientifically credible methods, it can illuminate a new dimension of life in the past.

Cave burials throughout Italy have certain recurrent features: the deceased were usually placed singly but occasionally in pairs, in pits or

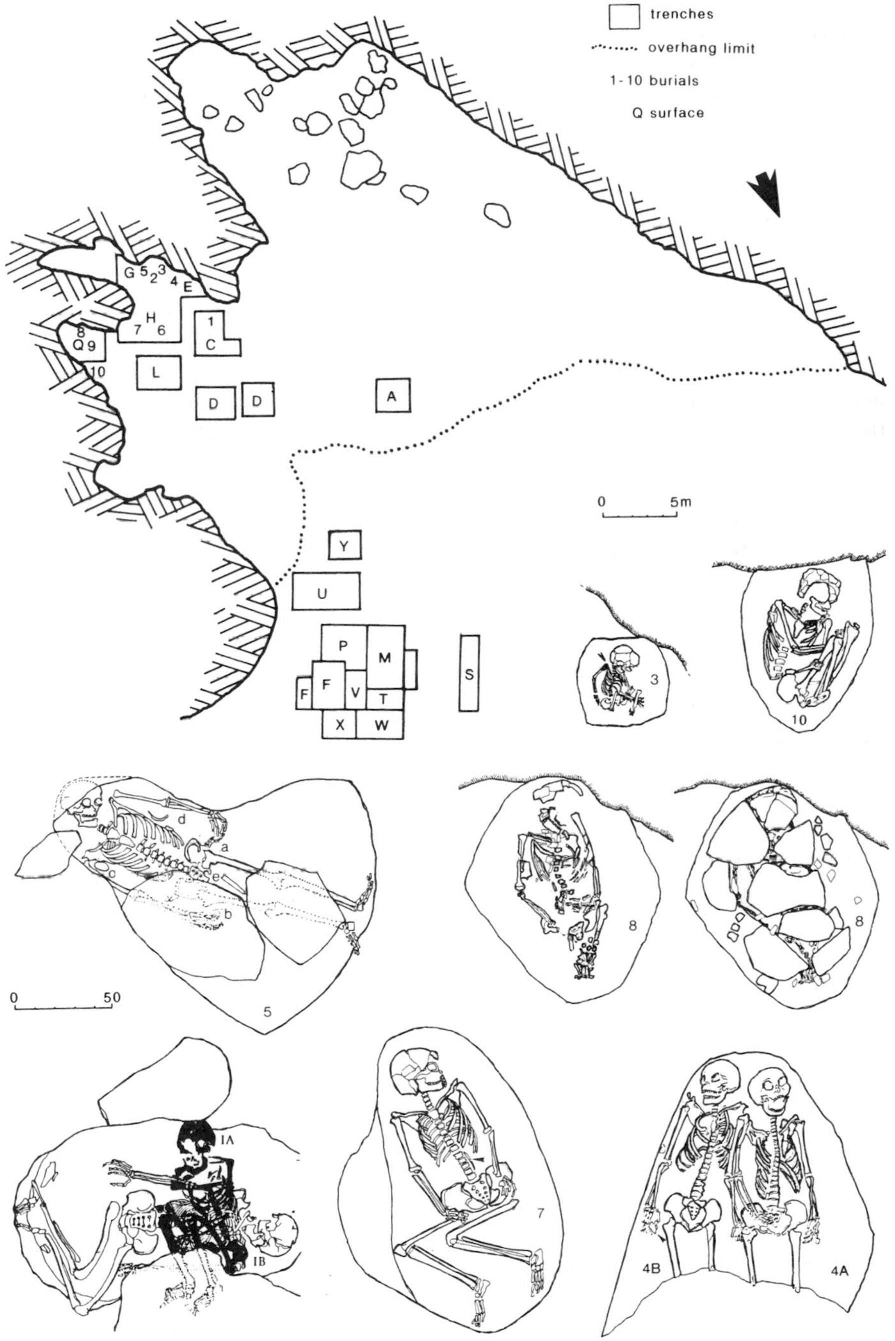

1. Early Faunal and Human Populations

Fig. 14. Uzzo cave plan and Mesolithic burials: (3) infant, chipped pebble; (10) female adult; (5) male adult, deer bones (a,b,d) shell (c) and cattle rib (e); (8) female? adult; (1A-B) male + female adult; (7) male adult, bone pin; (4A-B) male + female adult, flint blade and shell

trenches, sometimes covered with stones or red ochre, without grave goods or with just a few items of materials such as flint, shell and bone. Pendants, necklaces or attachments to clothing are known as well as antler, organic materials and occasionally inscribed stone plaquettes. Both sexes and a wide range of ages, from infants to adults over 50, are represented by Final Epigravettian skeletons. A fairly marked degree of sexual dimorphism (gender-specific contrast) has been noted: medium-tall males (166-174cm) of fairly robust stature and well-developed musculature contrast with medium-short females (150-154cm) of slighter build, both with good dentition, which is typical of hunter-gatherers, and little evidence for any infectious diseases which leave traces in bones.

Remains of seven human skeletons were found between 1937 and 1942 in the San Teodoro cave in Sicily: one (ST1) was well preserved and others damaged by treasure hunters or incomplete.[32] Four (ST1-4) were buried at the base of several strata (layer E) and are therefore thought to represent the earliest human occupants of the cave. They were placed separately, a metre or so apart, probably in shallow pits, on their backs or on one side in an extended position, with different alignments. Various items, perhaps a mixture of offerings and personal possessions, were found, mostly with ST4: antler and deer bones, smooth pebbles, possibly a hyena skull (with ST4), and a necklace of perforated deer teeth (probably with ST1). Once covered with earth, much of the cave floor over these burials was sprinkled with a thin layer of red ochre, a substance that was also used in the funerary ceremonies of later periods (chapter 3). A cranium and a few bones of another individual (ST5) were found at a higher level (layer B), near a hearth, mixed with animal bones and lithic material; this one was either never formally buried or had been disturbed.

The excavators regarded six skeletons as mature males, of between 25 and 50 years of age, but new analyses have overturned some of these findings and it now transpires that ST1, ST4 and probably ST6, were adult females (tables 2-3).[33] Their height has been estimated at around 164cm (ST1 & 4), which is rather tall by comparison with Upper Palaeolithic females and above the average for females from burials of all subsequent periods in Sicily. It is also noteworthy that ST1 and ST4 were associated with grave goods. In other words, it can no longer be claimed that these burials represent a purposeful selection of adult males. In fact, the new findings are more consistent with those elsewhere. The nearest neighbours of San Teodoro in the Grotta del Romito in Calabria, of similar date (11,710-11,250 cal.BC), were found in single and double burials containing males and females. The rather stereotypical notion that mature males, hunters par excellence, enjoyed the highest status in these societies is not, therefore, consistent with the latest research.

In Sicily, there are comparable burials in the Molara and Uzzo caves, although probably later in date (8th-7th millennium BC).[34] Three graves in the Grotta della Molara contained at least three adults in a crouched position, while eight single and two double graves (U1-10) from Uzzo held twelve individuals: probably five mature males, four mature females, one child and two infants. This is one of the largest groups of Mesolithic burials in the Mediterranean region and might suggest a cross-section of a Mesolithic band, although we do not know why certain individuals were selected for burial in this period. They were found in shallow pits dug into occupation or earlier sterile layers, placed mostly on their backs with legs bent, or in a crouched position and covered with soil or stones (fig. 14). Two double burials (U1 and U4) each contained an adult male and probably an adult female. Three small clusters might suggest areas for consanguine groups, although many features of the graves vary, such as their alignment, the position, age and sex of the deceased. The presence of ashy deposits just above the fill covering several burials could suggest a lighting of fires as part of a funerary ceremony.

Grave goods were either absent or modest, with little sign that they denoted prestige or gender, although U5 (an adult male) had five items, including a bone dress pin, which is more than the others. In one double burial, U4B (probably adult female) held a flint blade in one hand, while the accompanying male had nothing. Certain objects, such as a perforated shell and the odd flint blade suggest practical or ornamental items. More enigmatic and perhaps symbolic was a broken pebble, next to the shoulder of an infant (4-6 months old, U3) and the rib cut lengthwise of wild cattle (a rare species in the faunal sample), placed between the legs of U5, perhaps a genital covering. Noteworthy too is the occasional presence of deer bones (a very common species in the faunal sample): part of a forehead with U2, and a fragment of jaw and an indeterminate bone held in each hand by U5. Perhaps these were food offerings or items of symbolic or magical significance.

The skeletal report for Uzzo suggests that the degree of sexual dimorphism was less than that of present-day Europeans, with an average height difference of less than 10cm. Italian Mesolithic groups are generally reckoned to have been slightly shorter and less robust than their Palaeolithic predecessors, although one of the Molara males (M2, at least 50 years old) was unusually robust and tall (H 170.7cm). Both sexes had probably become shorter (males averaging 166cm and females 154cm), although it is not certain whether the changes (with the exception of facial and upper limb measurements) were a result of strictly environmental, biological or cultural factors, or perhaps all three. The teeth and bones show wear patterns and trace elements consistent with a varied diet in which marine products figured prominently; a finding which agrees well with the evidence for subsistence represented by the mollusc, fish and faunal remains from the site. The frequency of dental caries and wear (9.5% of 263 teeth) might also be correlated with increasing consumption of natural sugars or of food containing abrasive contaminants and a non-alimentary use of the teeth. Skeletal pathology revealed odd instances of muscle, back and joint strains, presumably due to various physical activities, which may have included habitual lifting and carrying, as well as sitting in a crouched position. Less marked right-handedness and slight changes in arm musculature might also be correlated with changes in hunting techniques and the development of fishing.

Art

Over 20 sites with cave (or parietal) art are recorded in Sicily. Most of these have linear incisions, several have only one or two intelligible figures, while three caves (Addaura, Genovesi and Niscemi) stand out for the exceptional quantity and quality of figurative subjects. Their concentration in the northwest of the island is perhaps partly due to the existence of suitable limestone formations and a long history of cave exploration in this area, but it may well also reflect a strong local tradition.[35] Eastern Sicily has little to compare with it, except for a few schematic incisions in the San Corrado rock-shelter and the portable (or mobiliary) art from the Grotta Giovanna. It is not known if rock-faces in the open were also decorated. Much has undoubtedly been lost, but new discoveries are still occasionally made and more examples of portable art can be expected from future excavations.

Nearly all the images were engraved and are usually assigned, principally on grounds of style and content, to the late Upper Palaeolithic (Final Epigravettian). However, the tradition may well have persisted into the Mesolithic and it is hard to be sure when it began. Final Epigravettian stone industries are most frequently associated with Sicilian caves, some images have been found beneath Mesolithic layers and two detached blocks of stone incised with bovids are datable stratigraphically to the Final Epigravettian: the less naturalistic one from a test trench near the entrance to the Grotta dei Genovesi (11,034-10,737 cal.BC) is perhaps later than that from Grotta Giovanna, where 71 loose stones had non-figurative and occasional zoomorphic engravings (fig. 15:B-D). A minority opinion holds that the Addaura and Levanzo engravings belong mainly to the earlier 'evolved' phase of the Epigravettian, rather than to the final phase, although stylistic comparisons with earlier Gravettian cave art in Italy are inconclusive. In fact, it would be easier to argue from a purely stylistic point of view that the emphasis on human figures in the Addaura group points to a relatively late date: while the Niscemi and Genovesi animals are broadly consistent with the subject matter of Late Palaeolithic imagery elsewhere, the Addaura scene could be contemporary with the postglacial or Mesolithic art of the Spanish Levant in which slender human figures are more common, albeit painted rather than incised.[36] By contrast, the majority of painted images in Sicilian caves appear to be a later creation of agricultural societies of the Neolithic or Copper Age (chapter 2).

Certain features of the style and subject matter of Sicilian cave art recur in a broader province that includes southern Italy, an indication of shared traditions or contacts between widely scattered groups. Affinities can also be noted with the art of southern France and Spain, which probably stem

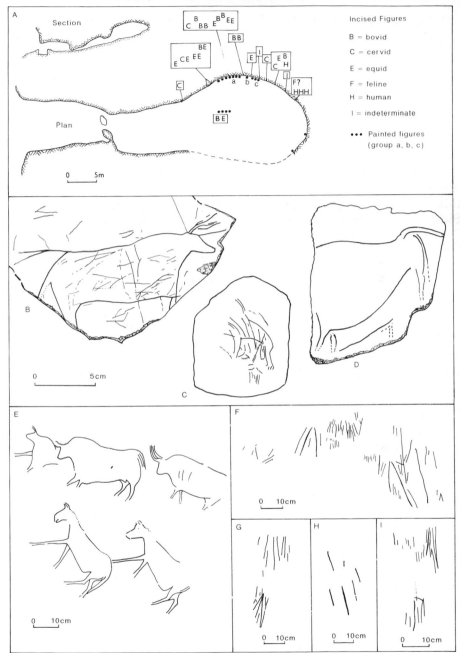

Fig. 15. (A) Grotta dei Genovesi plan and section. Incised stones: (B) Grotta dei Genovesi; (C-D) Grotta Giovanna. Incised parietal figures and lines: (E) Grotta Niscemi; (F-I) S. Rosalia caves

from parallel cultural patterns, although the larger scale and use of paint which characterizes some of the Franco-Cantabrian repertoire are missing. Moreover, the human figures in the Addaura cave are without parallel, while certain animals depicted in peninsular Italy, such as bison and ibex, are not found in Sicily, no doubt because they were rare or absent here. The inspiration, therefore, seems to come essentially from the local physical and cultural environment. Lively realism is another striking feature of many Sicilian engravings and has encouraged various authors to speak of a 'naturalistic Mediterranean style'. However, the degree of naturalism varies and much more has been written about the main or more realistic figurative motifs than the more schematic or linear signs. Overall, Sicilian cave art is sufficiently variable in content and style to defy a single definition and, like cave art elsewhere, it could have had several functions.

The Grotta dei Genovesi contains the greatest variety and number of images: 33 figures are distributed over an area of about 30m on the eastern wall of the large, dark internal chamber, entered by crawling through a narrow passage from the entrance hall, which is illuminated by daylight (fig. 15:A). That this location could have been a sanctuary for special ceremonial activities, such as initiation rites, comes readily to mind. It evokes a strong sense of privacy or secrecy, which is a recurrent theme in Palaeolithic art elsewhere and of the so-called cult caves used in the Italian Neolithic (chapter 2). The figures are outlined with a thin but deep single line in profile, except for three full-frontal humans and one bovid head (fig. 16). Only rarely are minor anatomical features indicated, such as eyes. Some figures are incomplete, while the scale is approximately consistent insofar as cattle are generally larger than cervids or equids, adults are larger than juveniles and males seem to be larger than females: they range from 15-50cm in length, while the largest human is 31cm in height. In this sense the animals could be said to respect each other, perhaps because they were executed over a limited period of time and represent a unitary conception. Quite accurate in their proportions, they display an easy naturalism in a variety of poses.

Equids and bovids occur in almost equal number (fig. 17). The large head and short ears of the former resemble the extinct ass-like species, *Equus hydruntinus*. Genitals are rarely shown, but there seem to be a mixture of ages and sexes: one bull seems to be a prime male, one deer sports large antlers, while others resemble juveniles (fig. 16:e,g). An incomplete quadruped might be a rare example of a feline, perhaps a species of wild cat occasionally attested in faunal samples (fig. 16:h). Limited superimposition occurs, while several animals are paired: certain bovids and equids walk in tandem, an alert deer is looking back and another has its head turned in a compellingly life-like gesture (fig. 16:d,f,b,a). Others may be running, walking or grazing and could pass as life studies from a naturalist's sketchbook.

By comparison, the place of humans is marginal. One almost insignifi-

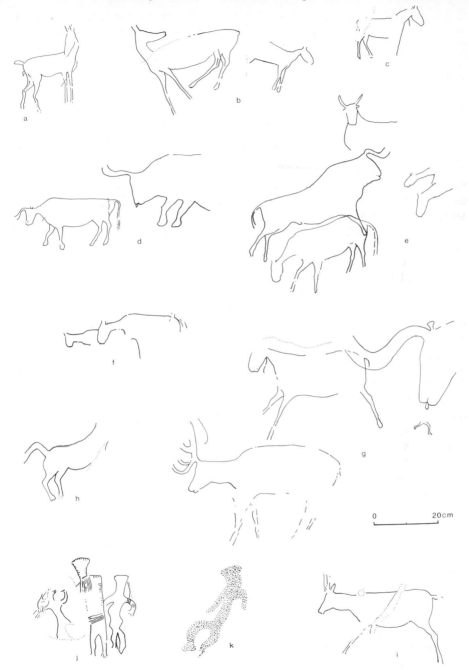

Fig. 16. Grotta dei Genovesi incised groups (a-j) and painted figure (k)

SITE	SPECIES/TYPE							
	E	B	D	H	F	I	P	L
G. Giovanna		1						✓
G. San Giovanni							1	
G. Addaura 2	12	2	4	17				✓
G. Addaura 1		2						
G. Niscemi	2	3	1					✓
G. Genovesi	11	10	6	4	1	1		
G. Uzzo								✓
G. Puntali	1	1	1					
G. Isolidde								✓
G. Luisa	1			?				
G. Maria								✓
G. Mastricchia								✓
G. Miceli								✓
G. Montagnola		1						✓
G. Racchio			2					✓
G. Rocca Giglio								✓
G. Rumena								✓
G. Vaccari								✓
G. Armetta 2 & 3								✓
G. Fico								✓
G. Vitelli								✓
G. Za' Minica 1			1					✓
G. San Basilio								✓
TOTAL	27	20	15	21	1	1	1	

Fig. 17. Incised images in caves: E=equid; B=bovid; D=deer; H=human; F=feline; I=indeterminate; P=pig; L=linear motif

cant pair of running legs, lacking a torso, is dwarfed by the looming head of a bull (fig. 16:g). By contrast with the naked realism of animals, three humans set low down are strange images, poised and gesticulating, perhaps dancing in cloaks and masks (fig. 16:j). The central figure could be a bearded male, flanked by a smaller form with a beaked head and a more sinuous female wearing arm-bands. They are all engraved, but there is also a human figure some distance away, painted in red ochre, which they closely resemble (fig. 16:k). The latter may also be attributed to the Palaeolithic and thereby separated from the great majority of other painted figures in the cave, which are black, different in style and obviously later in date (chapter 2).

What meanings or messages can be grasped? Leroi-Gourhan regarded the association or juxtaposition of such animals in terms of male and female symbols, represented in particular by equids and bovids, although the validity of this paradigm is not entirely convincing. From a subjective

Fig. 18. Grotta Addaura plan and incised figures

standpoint, there are perhaps too many blank spaces between figures to imply any photographic sense of place and yet the overall effect is not unlike a landscape in which animals roam in an unbounded manner which is characteristic of Palaeolithic art. In fact, herds of wild cattle, equids and deer were undoubtedly part of the local habitat, typical of the broad (now submerged) coastal shelf around Levanzo. These three species figure prominently in the faunal remains from the cave, and although deer predominated in the diet, whereas equids and bovids predominate as images, a correlation with large food mammals is unmistakable (figs. 9 and 17). Small animals, birds, fish, vegetation and inanimate objects are absent. Of course, in addition to culinary or hunting concerns, the species depicted could have been important in their own right or for other symbolic or cosmological reasons.

Two caves on Monte Pellegrino deserve special mention. The Grotta Niscemi, a narrow gallery with several niches, has a small number of incised figures in a naturalistic style: three stocky bovids (the largest 36cm long) appear in procession above a pair of equids just inside the entrance, with a young running deer and linear graffiti close by (fig. 15:E). Once again, the faunal remains from a test excavation comprised cervids, equids and bovids. However, the most famous mural engravings in Italy are those of the Grotta Addaura (recess 2), which is little more than a rock-shelter with a broad entrance, about 9m in depth and 3m in height, located beside two others, all easily accessible (figs. 18-20). Discovered in 1953, the engravings are in deep shadow but clearly visible on the rear wall, clustering in three groups with one or two separate figures nearby. The main frieze spreads diagonally for about 2.5m over a smooth tract of wall 2-3m above the current floor-level. It includes 16 humans (L 13-23cm) and about 10 animals (deer, cattle and equids, L 12-27cm). Four stages of execution have been postulated on the basis of superpositions and style, although some motifs are difficult to place in the scheme and the time intervals between stages are uncertain.[37] The materials from a small test trench nearby have suggested a broadly late Epigravettian date, although the cave was probably still used in the Mesolithic, and stylistic considerations may lead to divergent estimates, as noted above.

The first stage is represented by scattered shallow lines with no recognisable pattern. A second stage has a sequence of lightly engraved figures of humans and animals in naturalistic style. Two other areas of the rear wall also have lightly engraved and worn, incomplete animals as well as a striding human (no. 16), probably holding a spear over one shoulder. The famous group of human figures (nos. 1-10), which are more deeply engraved and appear in a roughly circular arrangement, is often assigned to a third stage, while one or two schematic bovids are sometimes regarded as later in date (stage 4). In addition, two bovids are represented in the neighbouring Addaura 1 shelter.

The contrast with Levanzo is mainly one of content and conception,

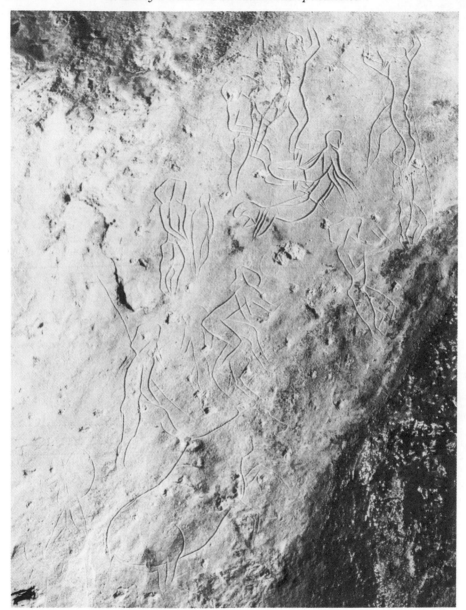

Fig. 19. Grotta Addaura figures

especially as regards the place of humans, who are now prominent and fairly naturalistic. One probable female (no. 13) with breasts and a slight paunch, carrying a large bundle or sack on her back, is perhaps following a taller male figure (no. 15) holding something (sticks, spears?) on his shoulders. Together with no. 16, they are striding away from and may well be unconnnected with the main group above.

The latter is one of the most striking representations of cave art, full of movement and unusually accomplished in its proportions and use of perspective (fig. 19). Observed from a raised viewpoint, the figures are poised in a kind of axonometric projection and are generally regarded as a unified composition or group scene, involving eight or more individuals arranged around the two placed horizontally.[38] With three possible exceptions (nos. 8, 10, 11), all are males, deftly outlined in vigorous poses, with slim but muscular figures. Apart from waist-bands and genitals, few details are shown and the heads are essentially blank, although apparently endowed with a great mass of hair, except for no.5. It is often said that several faces (notably nos.1-2) are covered by bird-masks and that this reveals a concern with ambiguous theriomorphic men. However, there could be some confusion here with what was simply a stylistic convention for beards.

Central to the upper part of the composition and to much past debate are two horizontal figures shown above one another, but perhaps to be understood as side by side, floating or flying through the air. Both have their legs bent back to their buttocks, possibly tied by a cord to the back of the neck, a prominent penis or covering sheath, with arms either stretched out or folded behind the neck. According to one interpretation, they are being tossed into the air (by nos. 1 and 2) and caught (by no. 10) in a kind of acrobatic performance. A more brutal action has also been suggested. If the horizontal figures are bound, they could represent captives being tortured or strangled, while experiencing erotic stimulation. The uniqueness of the scene inhibits judgement, although dance is such a recurrent activity in ethnographically documented cultures that one might favour this interpretation, in agreement with J. Bovio Marconi, rather than that of strangulation, suggested by A.C. Blanc and G. Chiappella. Plainly, this is an unusual example of cave art, quite different from depictions of nature or hunting, in which humans tend to appear in a secondary role. The concern with ceremony and ritual also anticipates the more prominent subject matter of cave art in subsequent periods.

Dozens of caves are dotted along the hills which crown the fertile amphitheatre of the Conca d'Oro (Palermo), spreading westward to Castellamare and Trapani. Some were explored by 19th-century pioneers of archaeological and palaeontological research, but most are still little known archaeologically. Only recently has it become clear that some contain linear markings and occasional figures, such as the two cervids in the Grotta Racchio.[39] In fact, linear signs, which are recurrent in Palaeolithic art elsewhere, are more common than figurative images in Sicily, although they are not so well documented and it is harder to make sense of them (fig. 15:F-I). That they should also be regarded as the work of hunter-gatherers is suggested in part by associations with figurative motifs. For example, a deer in the Za' Minica rock-shelter was bisected by

Fig. 20. Grotta Addaura human, no. 16, H 14.5cm

Fig. 21. Grotta Za' Minica cervid

deep vertical scores (fig. 21). In the San Basilio cave, scorings found beneath Neolithic layers could be associated with the Mesolithic layers below, while certain caves used mainly during the Mesolithic, like Uzzo, also have linear incisions. However, a move from figurative to more abstract forms of expression remains hypothetical, since it is certain that some figurative and abstract work co-existed in the Late Palaeolithic. The latter often predominates in portable art: the Grotta Giovanna has only a few plaquettes inscribed with recognisable figures, such as a bovid and possible bear or carnivore (fig. 15:C-D), but dozens of others bearing linear or unintelligible markings.

Groups of vertical or diagonal lines are often found by the entrances of caves, usually two or more metres above the floor. One of the Santa Rosalia caves had 120 lines divided into seven unequal groups, ranging from 5-30cm in length, from shallow scratches to thick grooves, either straight or sinuous. These have baffled scholars for years, although few would now dismiss them as by-products of stick-sharpening or casual doodling. On

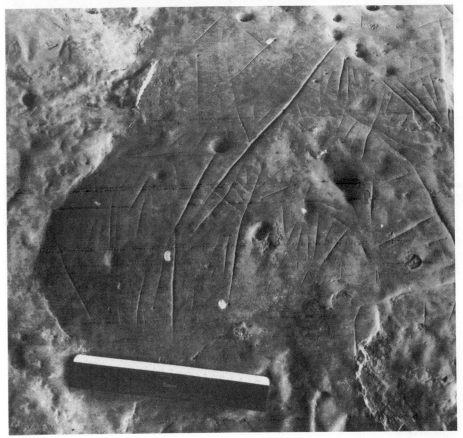

Fig. 22. Cup and line marks in the Riparo Armetta, 20cm scale

the other hand, it is impossible to prove a notational or counting system, however tempting this idea seems. It may be preferable to admit more than one meaning. In fact, those in the Armetta rock-shelter, juxtaposed in diagonal patterns or radiating from cup-marks, are clearly more complex (fig. 22). Elsewhere in southern Italy, there are schematized representations of a kind often said to symbolize females or males, the former associated with fusiform and possibly vulvar signs, which are basically triangular lines. Some of the Sicilian examples could be interpreted in like manner.

A magical or religious meaning is also possible. G. Mannino has noted that, by contrast with the more secret and hidden contexts of figurative imagery, these lines often occur in full daylight at the entrances of caves. One might think in terms of a kind of runecraft or notation for writing spells, or a magical protective device. In such a case, the precise form of the lines may not have mattered so much as the act of scoring the cave mouth. The bisected deer in the Za' Minica cave also suggests a magical or destructive purpose: perhaps an attempt to kill or to exert power over the animal. It is noteworthy too that burials have been found in certain caves with linear markings (Uzzo and San Teodoro), which might have heightened the spiritual significance of such places.

No less ambiguous is the significance of three pebbles painted with red ochre (fig. 13:9-10). Unfortunately from disturbed contexts, both examples from the Grotta dei Genovesi and that from Uzzo are of uncertain date: they could well be Mesolithic, although the habit of painting pebbles continued in the Italian Neolithic and R. Whitehouse regards this as an indication of continuity in cult practice, particularly at cave sites.[40] However, such items are more common in Azilian contexts in France and several similar Italian examples, from Grotta della Madonna in Calabria and Arene Candide in Liguria, are also Mesolithic. The lines on the Levanzo pebbles, which are symmetrically arranged in groups, could suggest a notational system, although the use of red ochre, which recurs in art and burial ritual, might have had a magical function. One ethnographic analogy for them, albeit purely formal, is that of Aboriginal 'churingas': ritual stones imbued with the spirit of an individual and stored after death in special places associated with ancestors.

2

The First Farming Societies

Neolithic genesis

An account of the origins and growth of farming societies in Sicily demands reference to changes over a wider geographical area and an assessment of relative chronologies, settlement patterns, subsistence and broader economic and social questions. A diffusionist theory for the spread of agriculture westward from an ultimate place of origin in the eastern Mediterranean was delineated in many of the influential works on European prehistory by V.G. Childe: the spread of farming through central Europe was seen in terms of movements of people identified with the Danubian or Bandkeramik cultures, and through the western Mediterranean by the expansion of impressed ware groups.

A more recent model of the process was formulated by A.J. Ammerman and L. Cavalli-Sforza, who used radiocarbon dates to measure the rate at which farming spread and to postulate a steady but not particularly rapid advance that might be understood as a gradual expansion of small farming groups into suitable adjacent territories, lured by the prospect of uncultivated land and encouraged by population growth being generated by a different lifestyle associated with food production.[1] However, views differ about the details and mechanisms involved. If migrating farmers advancing over virgin landscapes seemed to be the main agents of change to Childe, today one is more inclined to consider gradual and differentiated processes: regional adaptations, including a selective adoption of certain aspects of food production, the acculturation of indigenous hunter-gatherers, local continuity, and to speak in terms of a transition rather than a revolution.

As regards the origins of domesticated animals and cultigens, the lack of evidence for native ancestors of sheep and goat in Sicily, Italy and the western Mediterranean in general, suggests that these animals, which have remained at the heart of the subsistence economy until recently, were introduced from contiguous areas, and ultimately from a western Asiatic source. Likewise, it seems that the main cereal crops of the Neolithic economy must have been imported. The earliest sheep and goats, einkorn, emmer and barley in Italy come from Neolithic contexts possibly no earlier than about 6000 cal.BC. In the case of cattle and pig, the potential for local domestication existed insofar as wild varieties (*Bos primigenius*, *Sus scrofa ferus*) are well represented in Mesolithic faunal samples, but there

51

is no evidence of their autonomous domestication prior to the introduction of domesticates, pottery and other aspects of the assemblage generally subsumed by the term Neolithic. Local domestication of cattle in Apulia probably took place in a secondary stage by cross-breeding imported species with native wild cattle.[2] This may also have occurred in eastern Sicily and local wild pigs were perhaps domesticated in western Sicily at the beginning of the Neolithic in a similar manner.

The conclusion seems unavoidable, therefore, that the initial spread of farming to Italy and the western Mediterranean islands involved a form of diffusion and was not an autonomous development. Nor can the process have been simply the result of shifting cultivation or of the gradual and selective adoption of ideas by adjacent populations. There were occasions when more rapid movements and changes must have occurred, when routines were broken and natural barriers overcome. This is partly a matter of geography. One such moment can be inferred from the crossing of the southern Adriatic, probably at a narrow point of the Otranto channel between Apulia and Albania (70km today), or possibly between Dalmatia and the Gargano, where the gap is greater but has the benefit of the little Pelagosa islands in between. At this point, domestic animals, grain, personal possessions and family members had to be transported across stretches of open water. The numbers involved need not have been large and the feasibility of such crossings may well have been explored during the Mesolithic when sea-levels were lower and the distances shorter, but this must have been a deliberate migration.

Several factors conditioned the development of farming in southern Italy, Sicily and the smaller islands. Unlike the great plains of central Europe, these western Mediterranean landscapes change markedly over short distances: fertile soils are not so evenly distributed; coastal plateaus expand, contract and then vanish in front of hills and mountain ranges; seasonal rivulets are commoner than large fluvial basins and communications are often easier by sea than by land. In general, this varied landscape, with recurrent stretches of light cultivable soils, extensive woodlands, *macchia* and an increasingly warm climate, offered an ideal location for the establishment of a mixed farming regime, which had originated at a similar latitude, albeit at the eastern end of the Mediterranean. On the other hand, settlement, subsistence and population density were unlikely to be uniform in this setting.

One obstacle to a more detailed reconstruction is the limited number of radiocarbon dates (table 4). Within the logic of a diffusionist framework, the spread of farming to Sicily should have come about as an extension of developments in southern Italy. As the nearest landfall across the southern Adriatic, the first region to initiate farming would have been Apulia, where early farming sites on the Tavoliere plain possessing the 'full Neolithic package' of domestic animals, crops and pottery can be dated from about 6000 cal.BC, although the first settlers may have arrived a little earlier than the first radiocarbon dates currently indicate.[3] Several gen-

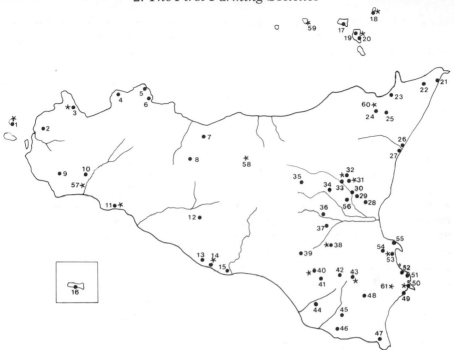

Fig. 23. *Early-Middle (•) and Late (*) Neolithic sites*: 1 G. Genovesi; 2 G. Maiorana; 3 G. Uzzo; 4 G. Puntali; 5 G. Regina; 6 M. Pellegrino; 7 G. Geraci; 8 Le Rocche; 9 Castelluccio; 10 Stretto; 11 Kronio; 12 Serra del Palco; 13 Piano Vento; 14 G. Zubbia/Infame Diavolo; 15 Casalicchio; 16 Cala Pisana; 17 Rinella; 18 Milazzese; 19 Lipari sites: Castellaro etc; 20 Lipari acropolis; 21 Boccetta; 22 Rometta; 23 Pietro Pallio; 24 M. Alfone; 25 Riparo di San Basilio; 26 Cutrufelli; 27 Naxos; 28 Valcorrente; 29 Fontana di Pepe; 30 Trefontane; 31 Biancavilla; 32 Adrano; 33 Fontanazza; 34 Muglia bassa; 35 Agira; 36 M. Alfone; 37 Torricella; 38 Palike; 39 Caltagirone; 40 Poggio Biddini; 41 Pirrone; 42 Calaforno; 43 G. Masella; 44 Paolina; 45 Bruca; 46 Scicli; 47 G. Corruggi; 48 M. Gisira; 49 Ognina; 50 Matrensa; 51 Capo Panagia; 52 Stentinello; 53 Megara; 54 Petraro; 55 Gisira; 56 Perriere Sottano; 57 Castello della Pietra; 58 G. Vecchiuzzo; 59 Filicudi: Capo Graziano; 60 Basicò; 61 G. Conzo, Chiusazza, Palombara

erations must have passed before agriculture became widely established on the Tavoliere. Nonetheless, the evidence is broadly consistent with an introduction of farming by immigrants replete with equipment and know-how, leading to a fairly rapid change in the human landscape, represented by a proliferation of EN sites, suggesting a marked increase in population.

From southern Apulia, farming must have followed two routes: up the Adriatic to northern Italy, where Neolithic settlements appear from about 5500 cal.BC, and along the Ionian coast to Calabria and Sicily. Movement in this direction was probably rapid. The earliest impressed ware settlements on the Tyrrhenian side of Calabria are dated in the first half of the 6th millennium BC.[4] In theory, a steadily advancing frontier could be enivsaged, although the process may have been less uniform if some seafaring groups ventured ahead and settled in favourable enclaves early on. Unfortunately, the impressed ware sites of eastern Sicily are undated by radiocarbon, but one would expect this to have been a primary region for the development of agriculture (or 'Neolithisation') in the island, which spread to western Sicily soon after 6000 BC, as indicated by radiocarbon dates from the Uzzo cave (5711-5558 cal.BC). The rapid spread could also suggest primary movements of people rather than a gradual process of cultural diffusion (the adoption of farming by local foragers). By the second half of the 6th millennium BC, impressed ware villages were widespread in coastal regions of southern Italy and Sicily, as also suggested by a date (5226-4941 cal.BC) from Piano Vento. By about this time too, Malta and some of the small surrounding islands had been settled.

A contrast has often been noted between the eastern and western Mediterranean basins in the adoption of farming. In the eastern zone (Greece, Crete, the southern Balkans), cultigens, domesticates, pottery and agricultural equipment seem to have appeared abruptly (about 7000-6500 BC), with little evidence of continuity from the Mesolithic. By contrast, the western zone (central and northern Italy, Sardinia and Corsica, Mediterranean France and Spain) has some evidence for Neolithisation, especially from caprines and pottery, between about 6000 and 5500 cal.BC, but less evidence for open-air settlements with substantial architectural developments or village life. This has encouraged the view that traditional hunting and gathering lifestyles further west were not so rapidly displaced and that only certain aspects of farming and material equipment were initially adopted by local peoples: specifically those elements (such as domestic animals), which could complement traditional foraging activities, while the transition to village life and cereal cultivation occurred later.[5]

Sicily and southern Italy occupy the border between the eastern and western basins. Insofar as they saw a rapid development of mixed farming and village life, albeit starting later than in Greece, they resemble the eastern zone. On the other hand, the contribution of native hunter-gatherers is hard to gauge. Were relations friendly and conducive to rapid assimilation, or hostile, leading to evictions or eradication, or merely indifferent, resulting in the persistence of traditional foraging communities in substantially separate territories? The situation probably varied from place to place, so that marked variations can be found between sites in different ecological zones. However, the areas where farming soon predominated (the Apulian Tavoliere, the Acconia coastal dunes in Calabria, eastern Sicily) and which are fairly well surveyed archaeologically, have no evidence for pre-existing Mesolithic occupation of any density. The prevailing impression in these areas, therefore, is of a rather dispersed antecedent population of hunter-gatherers; present no doubt, but perhaps only *'inutilement présent'*.[6]

Against this, it can be argued that coastal sites were submerged by the early Holocene rise in sea-level and that the limited visibility in the archaeological record of Mesolithic groups and their typically lightweight

Fig. 24. Uzzo cave

material culture hinders an objective assessment of their numbers. At least the potential for interaction with local foragers, through exchanges of goods for example, must have existed. The presence of microlithic implements at certain EN sites and the persistence of some traditional activities is a possible sign of continuity. For example, small flint and obsidian armatures are associated with Stentinello pottery at Petraro and the gathering of shellfish and fishing were recurrent in some coastal settlements of Apulia and Sicily. However, this was probably only a supplementary subsistence activity, and such evidence could reflect adaptive behaviour by incoming farmers or indigenous foragers.[7]

In the last chapter, more diversified food procurement, increased maritime activity and the possibility of a more sedentary lifestyle in the late Mesolithic were noted, which might have predisposed local foragers to adopt a food-producing economy. The nature and speed of the transition probably depended partly on the potential for a successful continuation of traditional foraging in appropriate ecological zones. There is no suggestion of hard-pressed foragers eager to take up farming in order to survive. At sites with prior Mesolithic occupation, such as the Uzzo cave, the 6th millennium BC witnessed only the gradual alteration of a traditional hunting and gathering way of life. Once again, this site merits a closer look.

There are many other contingent questions. Although contacts persisted across the Adriatic, the idea of endless waves of settlers crossing into Italy throughout the Neolithic, determining subsequent developments, is

A: Uzzo Tr.F layers:	10	9	8	7	6	NR TOT %	MNI TOT %
	Neolithic phase 1						
Cattle	2	23	13	3	6	47 = 3.5%	4 = 6%
Sheep/goat	11	36	27	38	50	162 = 12%	17 = 25%
Pig	89	135	48	30	51	353 = 26%	17 = 25%
Dog					5	5 = <1%	1 = 1.5%
Deer	221	126	81	43	69	540 = 40%	16 = 24%
Fox	37	52	18	15	23	145 = 11%	6 = 9%
Wild cat	13	32	22	9	13	89 = 7%	4 = 6%
Otter			1			1 = <1%	1 = 1.5%
Monk seal			1	1		2 = <1%	1 = 1.5%
TOTAL						1344	67

B: Uzzo Tr.F layers:	5	4	3	2	1	NR TOT %	MNI TOT %
	Neolithic phase 2						
Cattle	5	3	7	6	10	31 = 4%	4 = 6%
Sheep/goat	45	61	56	92	130	384 = 54%	31 = 46%
Pig	28	35	24	23	16	126 = 18%	12 = 18%
Dog		1		1	3	5 = <1%	3 = 4.5%
Deer	38	33	12	17	9	109 = 15%	9 = 13.5%
Fox	13	5	5	6	3	32 = 4.5%	4 = 6%
Wild cat	9	4	5	2	3	23 = 3%	3 = 4.5%
Hare				1		1 = <1%	1 = 1.5%
TOTAL						711	67

C

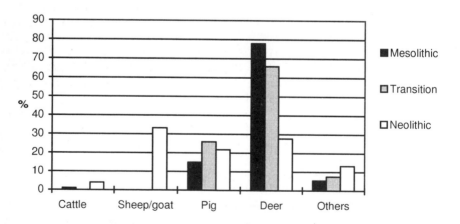

Fig. 25. Uzzo cave: (A-B) mammal bone numbers (NR) and minimum number of individuals (MNI) in Neolithic layers 1-10, Trench F; (C) Principal species proportions in different phases

hardly convincing. Affinities in pottery styles, for example between Italian painted wares and those of the Sesklo, Dimini and Danilo styles in Greece and southeastern Europe, need not imply more than intermittent or low levels of contact. Once introduced, it was the expansion and development of the new locally adapted regime of mixed and mobile farming that largely governed the dynamics of change. However, the new way of life did not lead to the rapid establishment of urban hierarchies with marked social inequalities. The visible features of Neolithic sites, perhaps represented initially by scattered homesteads and subsequently by larger agglomerations, suggest a collective or group-oriented culture of 'tribal' entities without emphatic internal differences in wealth. Nevertheless, these societies were capable of creating substantial earthworks, timber, daub and masonry structures as well as manufactured products of high quality, while maintaining extensive exchange networks that included a wide range of goods.

Subsistence transitions

A succession of levels attests continued occupation of the Uzzo cave after the Mesolithic (chapter 1).[8] The first Neolithic phase (tr.F, levels 10-6) has a ^{14}C date of 5711-5558 cal.BC (levels 7-9), although level 10 should be somewhat earlier, while the upper levels (5-1) are associated with Stentinello pottery and a curved stone wall delimiting the cave mouth. The faunal remains reflect both continuity and change insofar as hunting, gathering and fishing were still practised, while domesticates now had a significant role too (figs. 25-6). Botanical remains (trench W/15-14) include einkorn and emmer wheat (*Triticum monococcum* and *dicoccum*), vetchlings (*Lathyrus* sp.), domestic lentil (*Lens culinaris*) and fig (*Ficus carica*), with barley (*Hordeum* sp., *Hordeum vulgare*) present in subsequent levels.[9] Cultigens in trench F (levels 7-9) include bread and club wheat (*Triticum aestivum* and *compactum*), horse bean (*Vicia fava*), bitter vetch (*Vicia ervilia*), pea (*Pisum*), with more evidence for figs, almond (*Prunus amygdalus*) and wild olive. These species and the pattern of their adoption, which suggests that naked hexaploid wheats were subsequently more common, is similar to that observed in southern Italy.

Fish were still a primary source of food, represented by those species first seen in Mesolithic layers, including many large grouper, probably caught using both nets and lines, as suggested by hooks made from bone and boar's tusk (fig. 27:4,5,7). Likewise, the wide range and numbers of marine molluscs, especially *Patella*, remained constant, whereas land snails were rarer (fig. 11). Among the wild mammals, deer were still the main quarry, though declining steadily, while the persistence of hunting is confirmed by the recurrence of fox and wild cat, perhaps valued for their pelts and killed for the threat posed to lambs (fig. 25). Wild and domestic pig bones were not always separable, but pork was still a valued source of protein. By contrast, the number of bird bones, mainly partridges and

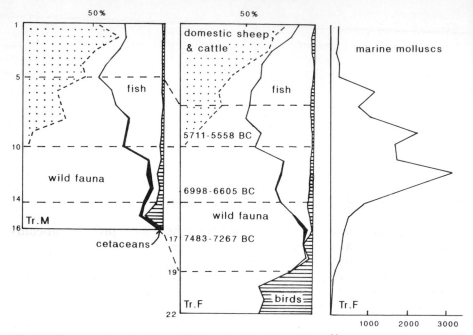

Fig. 26. Uzzo cave trenches F and M, faunal and mollusc ratios; ^{14}C dates at 1σ cal.BC

doves, diminished further. This varied diet is consistent with the continuing use of microlithic armatures for arrows alongside an expanding laminar stone industry.

An important development was the appearance of domestic sheep and goat (often inseparable from bones and hence termed caprines), cattle, pig and dog. Caprines increased steadily to become the dominant species by the upper levels. All parts of the skeleton were found, mainly from young animals reared for meat. By comparison with Italian counterparts, the sheep were of average size (66cm at the withers) and the goats fairly large. Despite the occasional presence of wild cattle (*Bos primigenius*) in Mesolithic layers there is no evidence of local domestication, from hybrids for example, and the bones from Neolithic levels are attributable to the smaller *Bos taurus*, presumably introduced already domesticated, although not in great numbers. The locally rough terrain is not well suited to rearing cattle, a species which has never been numerous around Uzzo. In rugged habitats, sheep and goat were doubtless always more common, as also seen on Lipari, where a small faunal sample exists for Neolithic layers. By contrast, pigs were abundant in both domesticated and wild form, mostly butchered while young, as before. The domesticated examples appear to be slightly smaller, although there is no real evidence for an autonomous local domestication of wild boar, or dogs.

The Uzzo data reflect a local habitat and cannot therefore be taken as a universal model of Neolithisation in Sicily and southern Italy. The

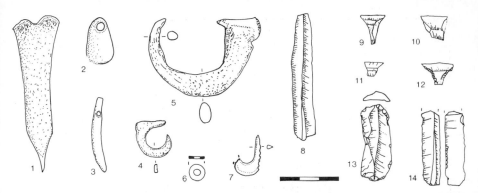

Fig. 27. Uzzo cave, Early Neolithic flint and bone implements

continuing importance of hunting and fishing here were probably encouraged by the local ecology and rough terrain. The situation was undoubtedly different in regions with more extensive light fertile soils, such as the coastal plains of eastern and southern Sicily, which were better suited to cereal cultivation and cattle, and presumably more attractive to farmers. As regards cultural evolution and interaction, it might be envisaged that the inhabitants associated with the first Neolithic levels at Uzzo were the descendants of local hunter-gatherers, who maintained many of their skills and traditions, while gradually adopting innovations from a community of agriculturalists, perhaps located not too far away. Alternatively, the changes in subsistence may have resulted from an influx of settlers to the general area, who were already acquainted with farming techniques and mixed with local foragers. Either way, some aspects of a long-established way of life evidently lasted longer in this region. By the Middle Neolithic, however, the cave was probably used mainly as a shelter for shepherds and their flocks.

Elsewhere, the transformation was perhaps more sudden, but is harder to follow. The old faunal samples from Orsi's excavations at ditched settlements on the eastern coastal plain are biased in favour of large bones (fig. 28), although cattle are well represented and two varieties of differing size are recorded at Stentinello (probably *Bos brachyceros* and *Bos taurus*), the larger of which could reflect a local domestication of the indigenous wild form (*Bos primigenius*).[10] This was a good environment for rearing cattle, many of which were butchered as mature adults. Sheep, goat and pig are present as well as dogs of a medium-small species, possibly resembling a spitz, and more likely to have been introduced with other domesticates than bred from local wolves. Orsi also kept a few samples of what were obviously abundant marine and land molluscs from these coastal sites, as well as the odd fish and turtle bone; fish may well have been a significant component of the diet. By contrast, evidence for hunting is limited to very few bones of deer, fox and wild cat, a situation reminiscent of the Tavoliere, where the main concern was also with mixed farming and non-specialised stock-rearing.

	Sheep/goat	Cattle	Pig	Boar	Equid	Dog	Deer	Fox
EARLY NEOLITHIC	NR/MNI							
Stentinello	225/29 38/33%	170/13 29/15%	139/24 23/27%			44/16 7/18%	11/3 2/3%	3/2 <1/2%
Megara	222/27 38/32%	203/21 34/25%	146/26 25/31%		1/1 <1/1%	8/7 1/8%	11/3 2/3%	
Matrensa	195/28 26/33%	373/34 50/40%	156/17 20/19%		4/2 <1/2%	12/4 2/5%	3/1 <1/1%	
MIDDLE NEOLITHIC	NR							
Lipari Trichrome	168	39	2					
Lipari Serra d'Alto	9	13						
LATE NEOLITHIC								
Grotta Genovesi 2/3	35	1	17	8			14	
San Basilio II	15	4		73		43	1	1
Lipari Diana	1	2						

Fig. 28. Neolithic faunal samples: bone numbers/minimum number of individuals

Environmental circumstances go some way towards explaining the diversity of EN subsistence strategies. The San Basilio cave, used as a hunting camp during the Mesolithic, was also frequented during the Neolithic and Copper Ages, perhaps on a seasonal basis. At this time, the lithic assemblage still included forms typical of hunting activity, such as geometric microliths (mainly trapezoidal and semi-lunate forms) of flint and obsidian (fig. 48:1-2) and a faunal sample still dominated by deer and wild boar. Game was evidently plentiful in the region, which was not much suited to agriculture. Rather than claim this as evidence for the survival of foraging groups from an earlier age, it may be taken as an indication of diverse lifestyles of Neolithic communities in different areas, not all of whom were committed farmers.

Pottery and chronology

The evolution of Neolithic pottery styles in Sicily and southern Italy has been understood in outline for decades, although uncertainty persists about absolute dates and the extent to which different styles overlapped (table 1).[11] The stratigraphy of the Lipari acropolis provides one useful guide for the Middle and Later Neolithic, while the evidence for the Early Neolithic has to be extrapolated from several sites, only some of which have informative stratigraphies. However, more radiocarbon dates are

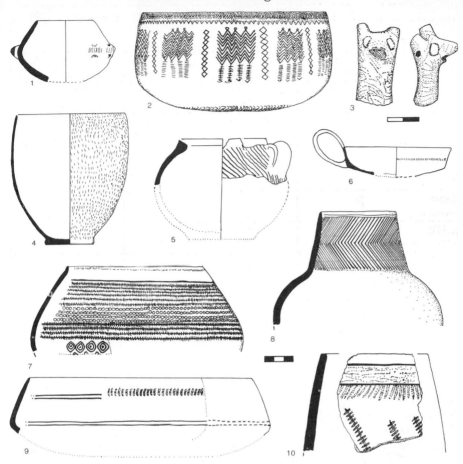

Fig. 29. Incised and impressed ware: (1,4-6) Antro Fazello; (2) Naxos; (3,7-10) Stentinello

needed, while much could still be learnt from new studies of pottery in existing collections.

Throughout the western Mediterranean, EN communities are associated with pottery decorated with stamped and incised motifs, known as 'impressed wares', although various regional styles can be discerned within their wide area of distribution (figs. 29, 30).[12] Those of southeast Italy bear a generic resemblance to those of western Greece and the Balkans, where such pottery is not so common, while various styles are identified in Malta, the small islands, Calabria and Sicily, usually called 'Stentinello ware' after the site near Syracuse where Orsi first found it in large quantity. Five Stentinello provinces have been tentatively distinguished: 1) western Calabria (including the Acconia and Nicotera sites); 2) southern Ionian Calabria (around Crotone); 3) Etna (including the sites of Trefontane, Poggio Rosso, Fontana di Pepe, and those near Adrano); 4) the southeastern coast (Stentinello, Megara, Matrensa, Ognina); 5) Malta (Ghar Dalam, Skorba, Ghajn Abdul). To these may be added a sixth province comprising western Sicily, named after the Monte Kronio sites.

This is currently no more than a working hypothesis and the challenge remains to distinguish temporal from spatial variations. The Calabrian material has been more closely studied in recent years than that from Sicily, where the full range of forms and decoration is not yet known. Comparisons are therefore difficult to make at present. The impressed ware tradition was of considerable duration, perhaps as long as 2000 years: radiocarbon dates in Calabria range from early in the 6th to late in the 5th millennium cal.BC. For example, in addition to plain and heavier coarse wares (some decorated with so-called cardial and rocker motifs, using the edge of a shell), Stentinello pottery from an early context (5950-5724 cal.BC) at Acconia in Calabria already comprises vessels elaborately decorated with zig-zags, diamonds, cord impressions, lines and occasional eye-motifs arranged in dense horizontal and vertical bands. By contrast, Stentinello contexts at Capo Alfiere are dated mainly in the 5th millennium cal.BC and can be more easily described as Middle Neolithic.[13]

The more complex designs of Stentinello pottery in eastern Sicily are on the fine wares: well-fired, thin-walled, smooth and burnished medium-sized vessels of dark grey, brown and black.[14] Typical forms include open bowls, jars with cylindrical necks, baggy bodies and curved bases. The finesse and regularity of the decoration is striking, and the potter's steady hand was clearly assisted by an assortment of stamps, combs, points and spatulas. White lime, gypsum or red ochre was used to fill the grooves after firing, graphically emphasizing the geometrical patterns. These fine wares and smaller vessels (cups and shallow bowls) are also contemporary with thicker-walled vessels (large jars), some plain or decorated with simpler incisions, finger-pinched or incised freehand.

There has been a growing tendency to assume that the more elaborately decorated pottery dates to the later 6th and 5th millennia BC and that the ditched Stentinello sites of eastern Sicily belong to a MN stage.[15] Evidence from Apulia suggests a progression from simpler ceramic forms with all-over decoration to more carefully structured and complex motifs on vessels with finer pastes (the Guadone phase).[16] In western Sicily, Antro Fazello at Monte Kronio has a stratigraphic sequence in which the earliest levels (15-17) contain coarser wares with 'coffee-grain' decoration and a smaller quantity of finer wares with triangular motifs, while later levels (8-14) are characterized by a richer repertoire of geometric designs on bowls and jars: the so-called Kronio style, which is more akin to that of Stentinello proper. At a later stage (levels 4-7), incised ware is associated with painted pottery of Capri and Serra d'Alto type, generally regarded as Middle Neolithic. The Uzzo cave also suggests that western Sicilian impressed wares were initially simpler in design, although the samples are small and it is conceivable that those from the early levels are mainly

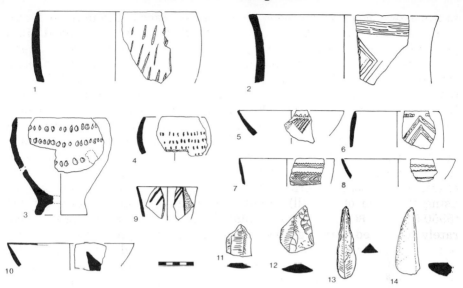

Fig. 30. Castellaro Vecchio, Lipari: (1-8) incised ware; (9-10) painted ware; (11-14) stone tools

coarse wares.[17] Moreover, the presence of ditched villages in eastern Sicily from an early stage in the Neolithic would not be surprising, since such sites typify EN Apulia.

When did painted wares start? This is an old problem in Italian Neolithic studies. Several Sicilian sites have red and black painted ware ('bichrome' and 'trichrome') associated with Stentinello pottery: for example, Serra del Palco (about 10% painted), the earlier contexts at Stretto, Piano Vento and Castellaro Vecchio on Lipari (about 10% painted), show that both styles were at least partly contemporary (fig. 30), although painted ware is rare or absent in the ditched sites of southeast Sicily. Some have argued that it was made from the very beginning of the Neolithic, albeit in small quantities.[18] However, limited stratigraphic evidence (from Monte Kronio, for example) and radiocarbon dates suggest that it began slightly later, perhaps by the middle of the 6th millennium BC, as a result of contacts with southeast Italy, where a wider variety of painted styles are documented at a fairly early stage. The more developed forms may date from the early 5th millennium BC, although there is a later date for trichrome levels on Lipari (4211-3977 cal.BC). Thermoluminescence dates from Serra del Palco for this material range mainly between 5800 and 4400 BC.[19]

Painted ware fabrics are often beige or brown, with little temper and a polished surface, decorated with zigzags, curvilinear motifs or red bands and rays bordered in black. Capacious multi-handled jars, small bowls and shallow dishes are typical (fig. 31). Similar forms occur on the Tyrrhenian coast of Italy, where they are often called Capri wares, representing a regional variety of central and southeastern Italian painted wares in the

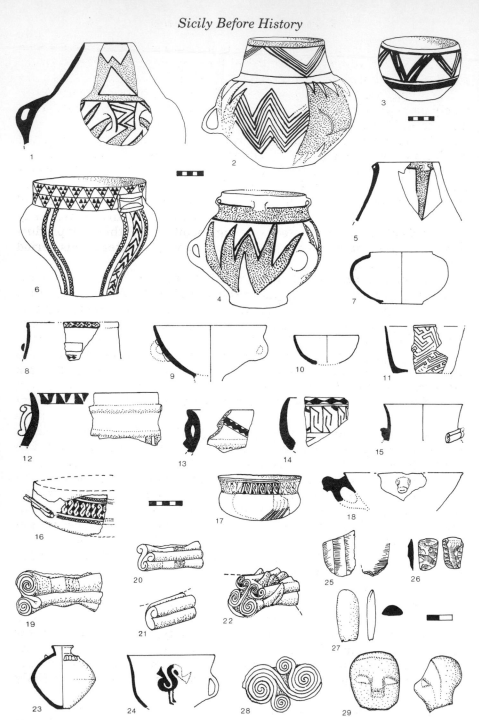

Fig. 31. Trichrome ware (1-5); Serra d'Alto pottery (6-24), stone tools (25-27), figurine (29), pintadera (28). From Lipari, except for 23 (Adrano), 24 (Stretto), 28 (Dessueri)

Ripoli style. On Lipari, trichrome pottery is associated with darker brown plain or burnished wares, decorated with fine incisions or painted motifs, some of which anticipate spiral-meander styles (fig. 31:11).[20]

There may well be an overlap between the later trichrome and elaborately painted spiral-meander pottery of Serra d'Alto style. Radiocarbon dates from Stretto (and Apulia) suggest that the latter was current by the early 5th millennium cal.BC. In fact, Serra d'Alto pottery is widespread in southern Italy and has much in common with the Balkan Danilo style. It is generally assigned to a MN stage, with the bulk of radiocarbon dates falling in the 5th millennium cal.BC. Serra d'Alto layers on Lipari are sandwiched between those with trichrome and Diana pottery and should logically belong in the later 5th millennium BC. This elegant style of finely decorated pottery, which represents a high point of Neolithic craft production, may have lasted for about 1000 years. As yet, few sites of this period are known in Sicily.

Disassembled, the decoration of Serra d'Alto pottery commonly consists of simple geometric motifs: small triangles and hooks, often dark brown on a beige background, combined in vertical and horizontal patterns to create a striking, almost *trompe l'oeil*, effect, possibly shared with decorations on textiles or skins. Stylized figures of birds are also known (fig. 31:24). Cups, bowls and jars provided with intricately scrolled and folded lug handles are common, while small unpainted jars (fig. 31:23) are sometimes associated with funerary contexts, heralding a move away from painted decoration in the succeeding period, named after the Diana site on Lipari.

In stratigraphic terms, the Diana phase concludes the pottery sequence just described and is traditionally regarded as Late Neolithic. Two radiocarbon dates from Lipari (4000-3544 and 3775-3638 cal.BC) and others from Calabria, Apulia and Malta (Red Skorba layers: 4221-3797 cal.BC) place it in the late 5th and first half of the 4th millennium cal.BC. However, there are a significant and growing number of ^{14}C dates for Diana sites in southern Italy that span the 5th millennium cal.BC, and some widely divergent dates from Grotta Cavallo in Sicily (5238-4720 cal.BC). It may be, therefore, that this style of pottery was already current for much of the 5th millennium cal.BC. Nevertheless, the wide discrepancy between dates is not easily resolved.

The pottery is characterized by fine red burnished surfaces, although coarser and duller forms are also known in Sicily and Calabria (often called Diana-Bellavista in southern Italy). The typical forms are shallow bowls and jars, many of which have tubular or trumpet-like handles near the rim (fig. 32). A late development of the style on Lipari, known as the Spatarella phase, has more in common with the Early Copper Age in Sicily (chapter 3).[21]

Sicily was clearly part of a broader cultural province during the Neolithic; ceramic sequences are in line with those of southern Italy and even find an echo in the Balkans and territories further west. The wide diffu-

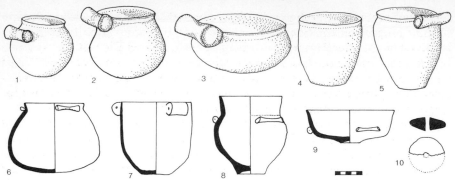

Fig. 32. Diana ware: (1-5) Lipari tomb; (6-7) Marmo; (8-9) Biancavilla; (10) Lipari acropolis, spindle-whorl

sion of impressed ware no doubt reflects the common background of early farming communities, while the development of various style provinces may suggest the emergence of more distinctive groupings as regional exchange networks grew. Preliminary studies suggest that style zones can also be discerned for painted wares, and that features of one style are often anticipated or elaborated in another. Changes probably occurred as a result of both local and regional processes. While not excluding stimuli from further afield or from more dynamic areas, such as coastal villages, there was probably no single centre of innovation. Nor are movements of people the only or even the most likely cause of change, since exchanges of goods and raw materials were a central feature of local economic systems, providing a means of communicating ideas and innovations. Pottery can be seen as an element in this broader network (below).[22] While the Middle Neolithic may have been a time of growing regional diversification, the Late Neolithic signals a return to a more homogeneous tradition, as reflected by the widespread occurrence of Diana ware. This coincides with evidence for more intensive exchange activities, documented most clearly by the distribution of Lipari obsidian.

Ditches and dwellings

The combined evidence for Sicily and southern Italy shows considerable diversity in the density, form and layout of Neolithic sites in different areas. Regional patterns emerge in the Early Neolithic when numerous ditched sites appear on the Apulian Tavoliere: the most common are small compounds (up to 7 hectares in area), probably holding individual or little groups of homesteads, followed by medium-sized sites (7-16 hectares), comprising various C-shaped compounds surrounded by one or more ditches.[23] A few very large sites with concentric ditches enclosing numerous C-shaped structures are probably Middle Neolithic in date and suggest a move towards larger aggregations in a secondary phase (about 5500-4200 BC). Up to about 1000 of these sites are estimated to have existed on the Tavoliere, covering the period from about 6000-4200 BC, although only a small proportion can have been contemporary. If the agricultural regime involved shifting cultivation, as many believe, the smaller sites may have had a short life-span. A different settlement pattern has been identified on the coastal dunes of western Calabria, comprising numerous single-roomed dwellings built with quantities of daub, often less than a kilometre apart, which may represent scattered homesteads.[24]

Sicily has many EN-MN sites that cannot yet be fitted into a regional pattern: some occupy a hillock near the coast (Piano Vento) or a hill-top further inland (Serra del Palco); several are known only from surface surveys along major river valleys, such as the Simeto, Gornalunga and Dirillo, or beside the smaller torrents of the northern coast; others occur around the foothills of Etna (fig. 23). Various caves (such as Monte Kronio, Uzzo and Corruggi) previously occupied by hunter-gatherers also have EN deposits, although these were probably not permanent habitation sites. Sites in favourable locations with a reliable source of water often have several occupation phases (EN-LN), such as Pirrone, which occupies a terraced promontory in the Dirillo valley.[25] Farming had spread to the hilly country of central Sicily by the end of the Stentinello or early trichrome phases, possibly before 5000 BC. A notable quantity of trichrome wares has come to light in the heart of western Sicily at Roccapalumba.

The density of sites was probably higher along the coastal plains, where open-air settlements with timber-framed structures and ditched compounds occur, not unlike those of Apulia and the Materano region. Three of these sites (Stentinello, Matrensa and Megara Hyblaea) on the coastal plain near Syracuse were first investigated by Orsi, who was struck by the quality and wide repertoire of the pottery and by the size of the ditches that delimited substantial settlement areas, representing feats of labour and construction without precedent locally.

At Stentinello, 8km north of Syracuse on a rocky shelf by the sea, which has eroded a corner of the site, large sections of the rock-cut ditch were excavated (fig. 33:A).[26] From 1.90-3.10m deep and 1.5-3.6m wide, it had some narrower points to facilitate crossing, traces of stone walling along the inner edge, and provided a roughly elliptical border to the settlement, which had a maximum diameter of about 250m. Further research in the 1950s revealed traces of postholes within the rather eroded compound. The ditch was rich in artefactual material: flints (mainly blades, one or two with sickle gloss); obsidian in slightly lesser quantity (mainly short blades and a few cores); basaltic ground axes; lava millstones; an abundance of coarse and finer pottery with a great variety of incised and impressed decoration ('Stentinello' ware); fragments of clay figurines including animal and human heads (fig. 29:3); land and marine shells, faunal remains and six fragments of human bone.

A few miles north of Stentinello, the Greeks who settled at Megara Hyblaea in the 8th century BC had laid the foundations of a temple above the ditch of a similar site.[27] This ditch had a slightly sinuous course, traced

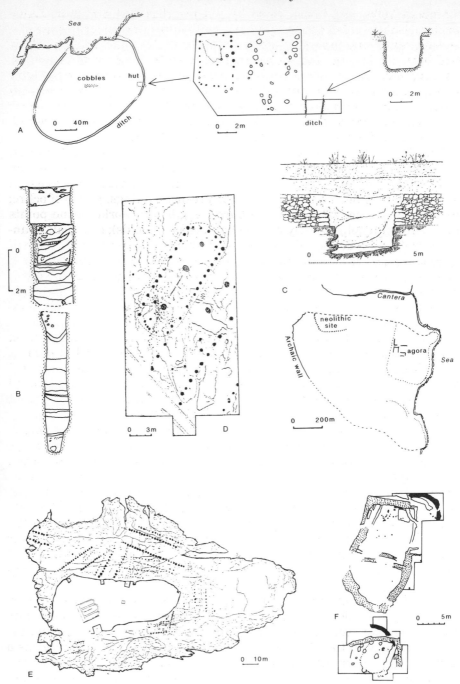

Fig. 33. Site plans and ditch profiles: (A) Stentinello, (B) Stretto, (C) Megara, (D) Gisira, (E) Ognina, (F) Serra del Palco

for about 100m and investigated by ten trenches laid across it. Later explorations revealed a roughly semicircular outline against the edge of a stream valley, encompassing a plateau of about 200 x 135m (fig. 33:C). It had been cut into the limestone crust for a depth of between 1 and 2m, varying from 1.70-4m across, although the upper edges were crowned with a stone wall so that the total depth was almost 4m in places. The wall (about 1.75m wide) was quite neatly constructed along the northern inner face, while traces of another wall on the opposite side were also noted. Post-holes and a burial (below) are recorded in the vicinity.

The fill contained a range of artefacts: flints (mainly short blades, scrapers and a core); obsidian in similar quantity (blades, flakes and cores); lava millstones and numerous handstones; basaltic ground axes; an axe-amulet and pebble-pendant; broken greenstone rings; pieces of ochre; animal bones, including split and burnt long bones, worked bone points and spatulae; shells (mostly marine but also land snails); charcoal; abundant plain and decorated potsherds of Stentinello type; and a small number of almost intact painted vessels found in the middle-upper fill of one trench. At the bottom of the ditch, a thin layer of sand contained fewer artefacts and some human bones (including a jaw, cranium, and limb bones), although others were probably mixed elsewhere in the fill. Two dozen fragments from adult skeletons are extant.

Much less is known about Matrensa, where great quantities of Stentinello pottery, as well as animal bones and three human bones came from ditches (3m wide by 4m deep) cut into bedrock and possibly divided into separate sections, 12-30m in length.[28] Near Ognina, another ditched settlement associated with Stentinello pottery has been largely destroyed by sea erosion.[29]

The function of such ditches, especially those in Apulia, has been much discussed and various suggestions have been made: defence, drainage, barriers for livestock, water sources and supplies of stone, all of which have some merit and are not necessarily mutually exclusive. Defence seems plausible in the case of Stentinello and Megara, given the addition of a wall. One recurrent feature of Neolithic ditched sites is the relatively high proportion of cattle in their faunal samples, perhaps increasing the need for water and security. The fills may have accumulated at a later time, when the original purpose had changed and they were perhaps used as rubbish tips. Lack of clear stratigraphic divisions at Stentinello suggested a single fill.

In the absence of evidence for social hierarchies, the ditches are generally thought to reflect communal labour projects and a desire to demarcate the domestic environment by separating it from the surrounding territory. This may suggest that duality or opposition, postulated by I. Hodder as a psychological metaphor common to much of Neolithic Europe, between the domesticated home environment of early farmers and the untamed landscape of hunter-gatherers.[30] However, for EN farmers, the digging of a ditch may have reinforced the definition of their homestead and the staking of a claim, as suggested by S. Tinè, reminiscent of the ceremonial ploughing of the *pomerium* when ancient towns were founded. The larger ditches, which are often later in Apulia, are as likely to reflect growing territorialism, competition and materialism generated by an increasing population concerned with land, property ownership and trade.

Stretches of most unusual ditches have survived modern quarrying operations at Stretto in western Sicily (fig. 33:B).[31] They are represented by several narrow fissures or trenches up to 120m long and about 13m deep in places, but only a few metres wide at the top and tapering to less than a metre at the bottom. The fill of ditch 1 consisted of alternating sandy layers and lenses with ashy and organic material, as well as artefacts: Serra d'Alto pottery, trichrome and some incised ware, predominantly at the bottom of the deposit; flint and obsidian; animal bones (mainly domestic sheep/goat, cattle and pig, but also deer, birds and occasional remains of other wild species); and fragments, including skulls, from at least seven disarticulated human skeletons.

A geomorphological study has suggested that the fill accumulated as a result of infiltration, presumably from the settlement above, and from water-deposited silt. The upper part of the trench may well have been enlarged by hand, but it was essentially a natural feature, created by a combination of erosion and fault-lines in the local calcarenite. A defensive function seems unlikely. Instead, the purpose may have been to drain the surrounding settlement, of which little survives, an idea supported by the evidence for water-borne material and erosion within the deposits, which may have formed after the site was abandoned. They could even be part of an irrigation system designed to channel water from a local stream to another adjacent area. The surrounding area has extensive rock-cuttings, including channels and an artificial gallery with steps leading down to a pool, perhaps created for practical or cult reasons. Another ditch has also come to light, 2.5m deep and 1.5m wide, with a flat bottom and vertical sides, which is more like the Stentinello ditches.

Information about residential structures is scarce. About 500m from the remains of a ditch at Ognina, on what is now a little offshore island but was probably once a coastal promontory, a thin deposit was excavated with Stentinello pottery, including many fragments of large jars, partially overlying a network of holes cut into the rock.[32] Although post-hole structures are known at other sites, those of Ognina are puzzling. Arranged in parallel alignments, 5.5 to 9.5m apart, sometimes flanked by a third row, they superficially resemble the ground plans of Neolithic longhouses in central Europe (fig. 33:E). However, the longest rows extend for over 40m, while the individual holes are large (Ø 0.80-1.30m) and closely spaced. They are more likely to be pits or silos. By contrast, the shorter alignments of smaller holes (complexes 7, 8 and 11) could be the foundations of once substantial timber-framed dwellings, of about 20 x 6.75m, 12 x 5m, and 13 x 7m respectively.

Similar alignments of post-holes are known from various locations at Gisira (Brucoli): on the upper slopes of the hill at least one LN or ECA structure has been discovered, 13 x 5m long, with three large central posts (fig. 33:D), although several additional parallel alignments are not easily reconstructed as dwellings.[33] A smaller rectangular post-hole structure (5.10 x 3.10m) was found a few metres behind the ditch at Stentinello, near other less regular alignments. By contrast, the central area of the site had tracts of a cobbled pavement, perhaps free of buildings.

At Piano Vento, 15km east of Agrigento, a Stentinello site has been uncovered on a gently sloping hillock (192m asl) near the shore.[34] Structural features in the earlier levels are associated with incised and impressed wares (5226-4941 cal.BC), but painted trichrome and Serra d'Alto pottery follows, suggesting continuity of occupation into the Middle Neolithic. The earliest structures, disturbed by the imposition of CA tombs (chapter 3), consisted of fire-hardened plastered and pebbled floors of half a dozen or so small circular or subcircular huts (Ø 2.50-3m), closely spaced, and built partly of daub with stones in the packing. One later, possibly MN, hut (no. 8) had five little clay-lined pits set into the floor, bordered by stones, with traces of burning. A figurine was found nearby, but is hardly sufficient to designate a cult building. In addition, a larger structure with an L-shaped stone wall was found, while some dwellings were delimited by a retaining wall or compound. Tracts of a rough stone perimeter wall, about 2.5m wide, preserved around the naturally weaker southern side of the hill-top are thought to represent a Neolithic defensive work.

Further inland, near Milena, new evidence for Neolithic settlement, associated with Stentinello and trichrome pottery, has come to light at Mandria on the hill-top promontory of Serra del Palco.[35] A precinct or compound (20 x 12m), built of stone, set on a flat shelf cut into the gently sloping ground, probably had multiple functions. Domestic installations (hearths, alcoves, possibly plastered floors) at one end were separated by a wall from the other apse-shaped end, perhaps for storage or sheltering animals (fig. 33:F). Parts of a second and possibly third compound lay a few metres away. The settlement perhaps consisted of several, each serving a family group. Middle and Late Neolithic settlement patterns and structures are even harder to assess. Sites with Serra d'Alto wares are scattered throughout the island, but none have been fully investigated. Finds of Diana pottery are more widespread, suggesting a period of expanding settlement, particularly inland, a pattern also encountered on Lipari (below). Field surveys in western Sicily have recorded Neolithic sites mainly on hill-tops, but also on terraces and along valleys.[36] There is also more evidence for the use of caves in the later Neolithic (below).

Overall, Neolithic settlement structures were surprisingly varied: compounds with masonry foundations; substantial free-standing rectangular timber-framed structures, reminiscent of central Europe; small circular and perhaps quadrangular dwellings with clay-packed walls, with affinities in the eastern Mediterranean and southeastern Europe; large ditched sites like those of Apulia. Many of these basic elements and techniques were elaborated or re-combined over succeeding millennia to produce a rich and varied spectrum of architectural traditions.

Small island colonisations

Lipari obsidian began to reach Sicily during the late Mesolithic, although no settlers are documented on this largest of the Aeolian islands before the Early Neolithic. They arrived in what was probably an uninhabited but familiar island, clearly visible from Sicily, and occupied various sites on the northwestern upland slopes, perhaps lured here by the presence of fertile soil, enriched by wind-blown volcanic granules, resembling a 'tuff-loess', and the proximity of fresh water. The best known site at Castellaro Vecchio is not much more than a scatter of sherds and lithics, associated with a hearth, a pit and a few flag-stones.[37] Local obsidian was used in abundance, but some of the flint blades were probably imported from Sicily. The pottery was mainly of Stentinello type, except for a few painted sherds (fig. 30). Although undated by radiocarbon and sometimes described as Middle Neolithic, the site could easily be earlier (6th millennium BC). Another small Stentinello site is known at Rinella on the nearby island of Salina, consisting of an oval hut (Ø 3.5 x 2.5m) with its floor cut into the volcanic tuff. Scattered homesteads seem typical of this period.

Aeolian settlements increased and expanded during the Middle and Late Neolithic. The volcanic bastion of the Lipari acropolis, or *castello*, offers a natural vantage over a bay on the eastern side of the island and was first occupied at a time when trichrome wares predominated. The same site was then inhabited recurrently in subsequent millennia and into historical times, as shown by the remarkable depth of the deposits (over 9m in places) and superposition of prehistoric buildings. Deep soundings reached Neolithic levels at several points, encountering plentiful pottery but scanty architectural remains. Above the lowest levels, Serra d'Alto pottery was found in various locations, suggesting an ample settlement area, followed by LN deposits. A sprawling settlement now developed on the adjacent coastal plain at contrada Diana, after which the LN assemblage of southern Italy and Sicily is named. Deposits with hearths, pottery, obsidian and millstones extend over 10 hectares, but the architectural remains were evanescent; a mixture of activity areas outdoors and structures made of perishable materials are implied. An expanding population on Lipari is also attested by the LN sites at Portinenti, Piano Conte, Spatarella and elsewhere on higher ground inland. The earliest material from the smaller islands of Filicudi and Panarea belongs to the Diana phase, also associated with the expansion and intensification of exchange networks in which local obsidian featured prominently.

2. The First Farming Societies

The Aeolian archipelago constitutes a special case in terms of its cultural development. There does not seem to have been an Aeolian culture *per se*, but rather an assemblage with a somewhat polymorphic character, much of which is almost indistinguishable from that of neighbouring regions. This is almost certainly because Lipari was too small and too close to Sicily and Calabria to have developed autonomously and was of special significance because of its obsidian. In the Neolithic and Bronze Ages, the island was enriched and informed by regular maritime contacts. The large numbers and diverse categories of imported goods indicate that exchange activities were an integral part of the way of life for these satellites, which maintained a close relationship with Sicily and the mainland.

The same cannot be said of the Maltese islands, further away and usually out of sight across a stretch of open sea that was undoubtedly less frequented. However, Malta was also settled before the end of the 6th millennium cal.BC, almost certainly from Sicily, as attested by the presence of Neolithic pottery of the Ghar Dalam phase at Skorba. The earliest ^{14}C date (5266-4846 cal.BC) represents a *terminus ante quem*, rather than the arrival date of the first settlers.[38] The Ghar Dalam pottery, with its mainly simple range of motifs, could easily date from an early stage in the development of impressed ware. The Grey Skorba and Red Skorba phases seem to be contemporary with Serra d'Alto and Diana respectively.

Malta is another special case with regard to its later cultural evolution, especially during the temple period, which constitutes a striking example of independent development after about 3500 BC. However, despite local traits in pottery styles and cult activities, there is little sign of this future divergence during the Neolithic, when building techniques were still similar to those in Sicily: the long stone wall at Skorba, perhaps enclosing small daub huts with pebble and clay floors and paved areas, are paralleled at Piano Vento for example. The domestic fauna and flora (sheep, goat, cattle, pig, dog, barley, emmer wheat and lentils) must also have been introduced from Sicily. Continuing exchanges with Sicily are reflected by the presence of obsidian, increasingly from Lipari rather than Pantelleria, and by small stone axes and other items made from non-local rocks.

Floating elusively between Sicily and Tunisia, although slightly closer to the latter (80km west of Cape Bon), Pantelleria was at least visited and perhaps settled during the Early Neolithic, since its obsidian occurs in Sicily, Malta and North Africa. More surprising is the evidence for Neolithic settlement, probably quite early in date, on the more remote and smaller island of Lampedusa, 210km from southern Sicily and 130km from Tunisia, attested by finds of incised pottery, resembling Stentinello ware.[39] Intrepid settlers no doubt came here from Malta or Pantelleria, the source of their obsidian blades, bringing caprines, pigs and cereals, as suggested by a few retouched flints with sickle gloss. Life on Lampedusa, and probably on all these small islands, also involved fishing, gathering shellfish and catching birds, which sometimes visit them during migration. Some of these settlers probably reached Tunisia, where finds of Stentinello pottery have been reported. Likewise, the little island of Ustica, visible from the shore about 50km north of Palermo, could easily have been settled in the Neolithic, even though the earliest evidence yet recovered is more likely to be Copper Age.[40]

Clearly, aside from important changes in subsistence, the Neolithic was a time of exploration, seafaring and island colonisation, which must have generated new designs of boats or rafts, perhaps already equipped with a basic sail. The cognitive horizons of Neolithic peoples extended well beyond their farmsteads, compounds and concerns with subsistence, as emphasized by new research into the wider spheres of economic and ritual activity.

Networks of exchange

Sicily and its neighbouring territories provide a rich context for the study of exchange (the trade of earlier prehistory). This is partly due to the stimulus provided by contrasting environments in which different resources are localized and to a maritime environment that facilitated the development of networks in which various items could move in several directions (fig. 34). The economic and social prominence of exchange may also account for many of the cultural similarities between Sicily, surrounding islands and parts of southern Italy in the Neolithic.

Of the various materials in circulation, obsidian has received most attention thanks to its high visibility, wide distribution and the relative ease with which it can be sourced.[41] It is a hard and glassy volcanic rock, which can be chipped in any direction, and is therefore an ideal utilitarian material for making sharp cutting and piercing implements. In the western Mediterranean, it occurs on four islands: Pantelleria, Lipari, Palmarola and Sardinia. Characterisation of these sources by such techniques as neutron activation analysis has been a notable success story of materials science research in archaeology. Neolithic communities in Sicily and most of southern Italy made considerable use of the grey-bluish calcalkaline obsidian from Lipari, which also travelled to northern Italy and beyond, where Sardinian obsidian was initially prevalent. The greenish peralkaline variety from the island of Pantelleria was also used in Malta, Sicily and North Africa, but in lesser amounts.

Although known to late Mesolithic hunter-gatherers, the first widespread use of Lipari obsidian coincided with the Early Neolithic, intensified during the later phases, and declined subsequently, occurring only sporadically after about 2500 BC. Hunter-gatherers looking across the water to Lipari during the 9th millennium BC might well have witnessed the volcanic eruptions which led to the formation of the Lami-Pomiciazzo obsidian flow, exploited during the Neolithic. It is still partly visible, but was mostly buried by a later flow in about the 8th century AD.[42] The raw

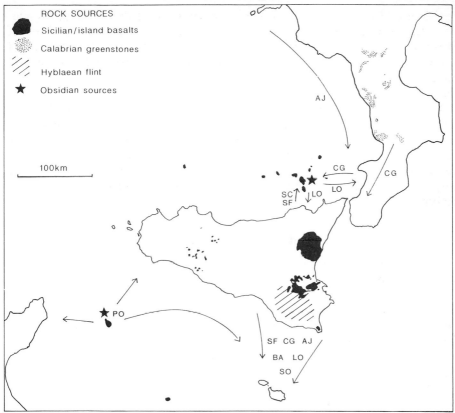

Fig. 34. Neolithic exchange networks, with arrows suggesting flow from sources only: AJ = Alpine jadeite; BA = Basaltic axes; CG = Calabrian greenstone; LO = Lipari obsidian; PO = Pantelleria obsidian; SC = Sicilian clay/ceramics; SF = Sicilian flint; SO = Sicilian ochre

material would have been easily collected at the source, in effect a vast natural quarry, either in the form of black nodules, conveniently prominent in deposits of white pumice, or by breaking chunks off swirling laminated bands, several metres across. Some initial reduction into more manageable blocks or pre-cores occurred here, as glimpsed by the presence of shatter fragments in places where the earlier flow is exposed.

Large quantities of obsidian were found during excavation of Aeolian Neolithic settlements, especially at the Diana site, where reduction activity is attested by waste products, collected in several hundredweights. Recurrent forms consist principally of cone-shaped cores, parallel-sided blades and occasional points. There was plainly no need to economize with a material that was so easily obtained locally, nor to restrict its use or retouch blades. However, the scale and nature of exploitation are not easy to gauge, and it may be misleading to speak in terms of industrial or intensified forms of production at specialised sites, such as workshops, with their modern connotations. In effect, one person reducing quarried blocks can generate large quantities of indestructible debris in just a few hours.

More has been learned from distribution patterns in western Calabria, where obsidian commonly accounts for 90% of the chipped stone tools at Neolithic sites. The material was probably moved directly to both Sicily and Calabria in lots that, at least in terms of volume and weight, consisted mainly of cores or 'pre-cores': roughly-shaped chunks requiring some further trimming before finished blades can be struck from them. The coastal communities opposite Lipari were perhaps most directly involved in obtaining the raw material and working it locally; they have been identified in the Acconia dunes of Calabria by sites with a high proportion of cores and evidence for reduction, and are probably present in northern Sicily too.[43] The sites where finished blades are more common could represent neighbours who subsequently obtained the material in finished form. Nevertheless, cores were also traded over long distances.

In central and western Sicily, Pantelleria obsidian is recorded at a few sites including the Uzzo cave.[44] In Neolithic contexts at Serra del Palco, obsidian accounted for between 20% and 40% of the lithic material and was still present in the Copper Age, but it is the material from Lipari which steadily predominated at the expense of that from Pantelleria, a pattern also noted on Malta. There is little evidence for cores and much of the material was perhaps exchanged as finished tools. It was used not only for blades, but for small armatures resembling Mesolithic hunting tools.

The dynamics of exchange systems are not easy to unravel from static patterns of archaeological data, but it is noteworthy that obsidian cores in Calabria tended to be smaller and more standardized in the later Neolithic, while blades tended to be thinner and narrower. Concurrently in northern Italy, Lipari obsidian became more popular, despite the greater distance it had to travel, but was obtained now mainly in the form of finished blades, not cores. One implication is that more efficient use was being made of the material in the course of the Neolithic and that there may have been a greater appreciation of the material as a prestige item, especially in places far from the source. This anticipates a feature of long-range exchanges between Sicily and the western Mediterranean during the Copper Age.

Unlike Calabria and the small islands, southern and central Sicily is endowed with numerous deposits of high-quality flint. One typical item in the Neolithic tool-kit, the sickle-blade, was often made of flint, retouched along the edges. The Hyblaean region in particular has abundant sources of coarse-grained Cretaceous flint and shiny fine-grained Miocene flint. Scattered cores and debris are known from open working areas, sometimes spread over several kilometres, for example along the Irminio and Dirillo valleys, where at least preliminary shaping took place. Although difficult to date, such contexts may be Neolithic in part. The galleries from which flint was mined in this region are usually assigned to the Early Bronze

Age, since they were used for mass burials at that date (chapter 3). However, the burials provide only a *terminus ante quem*, by which time extraction had ceased. Some earlier mining activity during the Neolithic cannot be excluded, and has recently been proven in the Gargano region of Apulia. The so-called Campignian tradition of flint-working in Sicily, while still current in the 4th and 3rd millennia BC, undoubtedly originated at least in the Middle Neolithic, when the first *petits-tranchets* blades are documented. Hyblaean flint was already being widely distributed in the Stentinello phase to sites in eastern Sicily, Malta, and perhaps to Lipari and further afield.

Equally prominent items of exchange were ground stone axes, common in Neolithic and later sites.[45] They reflect a knowledge of the properties of many different rocks, some common, some rare, and the exploitation of convenient sources, such as river-beds, where material could be found in pebble form. The fine-grained basalts from Etna and the Hyblaean hills were favoured for heavy work-axes, the more vesicular basalts for mill-stones. Smaller and frequently ornamental greenstone axes (serpentine and nephrite principally) probably originated in northern Calabria, although occasional jade or eclogite axes from western Alpine sources also reached southern Italy and Malta, at least towards the end of the Neolithic, perhaps in exchange for obsidian or other goods.

Lipari is a nodal point in the network, endowed with obsidian, but lacking several other raw materials (non-volcanic rocks, including flint, and good quality clay). It illustrates the reciprocal and complementary nature of Neolithic exchange transactions. Small stone axes and a few pebbles of various greenstones and another rare rock, known as fibrolite, occur with a certain regularity, especially in LN layers, and suggest a Calabrian or Sicilian provenance. The flint is most likely Sicilian in origin, represented mainly by finished implements. Clay analysis indicates that some of the pottery (group B pastes), especially the finer decorated wares of trichrome and Serra d'Alto styles, was imported either as finished vases or as unworked clay to be manufactured locally, most probably from northern Sicily.[46]

It may also be surmised that shell ornaments, ochre, brightly coloured pebbles, as well as a host of organic materials (such as skins and hides, perhaps highly decorated like pottery) were exchanged between the inhabitants of coastal plains, hilly hinterlands and interior zones, each of which had local products or specialities with which to tempt their neighbours. The range of exchange items (axes, millstones, flint, obsidian) in the ditched villages and the high quality of much of their pottery points to developed intra-regional exchange systems. Apart from their dietary role, domestic animals such as cattle, sheep and goat may also have served these communities in southeastern Sicily as a source of mobile wealth 'on the hoof'. The variety of goods, the geographical dispersion of raw materials and the different subsistence strategies dictated by nature imparted a certain stability and complementarity to these networks; no particular area seems unduly favoured and there was perhaps little chance for real monopolies to emerge. The balanced nature of exchange activity may also explain why the Neolithic in this area witnessed the development of elaborate material equipment, especially painted pottery and stone tools, and yet did not lead to major concentrations of power or the rapid onset of social inequality. Knowledge and use of a wide range of uncommon raw materials was also encouraged, which in turn must have generated an increasingly sophisticated technology, including high-temperature firing of pottery by the Middle Neolithic. This was followed by surprisingly early experiments with copper, attested by the slag from transitional LN-ECA (Diana-Spatarella phase) levels on Lipari, most likely imported from Sicily or Calabria.[47]

The impression gained is that Neolithic exchange was an inclusive and generalized phenomenon, implying a wide spectrum of frequent social interaction, albeit operating mainly through chain-like mechanisms between neighbours. Its economic or materialist significance was quite real, although this should not overshadow the social importance of interaction and communication of knowledge and ideas, which may also explain why archaic farming societies shared many characteristics over large regions. Accompanied by growing populations, this might also have provided more opportunity for conflict, while the proliferation of Neolithic figurines and a growing concern with cult activity could reflect an attempt to resolve the tensions. By the end of the period, it appears that those materials which were most sought after and distributed furthest were becoming increasingly linked with concepts of prestige, and were often being made into items of display and weapons, heralding forms of overt status enhancement that were more in evidence during the Copper and Early Bronze Ages.

Social and spiritual dimensions

One conventional approach to religion and cult is through the study of burials and manifestations of ritual symbolism in cave art and figurines. Neolithic graves are comparatively rare, while scattered finds of human bone in settlement ditches at Stentinello, Matrensa, Megara and Stretto, might suggest a lack of concern with formal burial, although these could represent secondary disturbances of nearby graves.[48] The latter sometimes took the form of pits: an example at Gisira, found within a Stentinello settlement, consisted of an elliptical hollow (2.3 x 1.6m) delimited by vertical slabs and paved with flat stones, containing a grinding stone with traces of ochre. Beside the pit was a large circular installation with a pebbled floor, covered by a layer of baked clay and traces of burning, perhaps a funerary hearth for offerings or sacrifices (fig. 35:3). Another solitary pit grave at Fontanazza (2.1 x 1.6m) contained a few human bones, traces of ochre and Stentinello pottery. Pits with single crouched inhumations at Vulpiglia may be slightly later in date; one contained a Serra d'Alto bowl. The same rite is found at Messina (Boccetta), where one of two

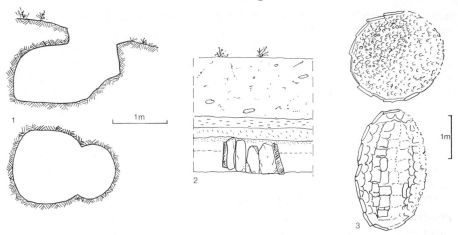

Fig. 35. (1) Castellazzo di Mazara chamber tomb; (2) Lipari cist grave; (3) Gisira pit grave and stone platform

pits lined with vertical slabs contained a whetstone and two flint blades. Likewise, simple pit graves containing single skeletons in a crouched position without grave goods are known from Apulian ditched villages. At face value, there is little to suggest social ranking, although the scarcity of burials in itself could mean that some selection criteria were involved.

Harder to assess is an isolated but more imposing structure recorded in 1930 near Calaforno, which consisted of an oval pit (Ø 1.80m and 1m deep) surrounded by large stones containing a few human bones, potsherds, a flint blade, a broken grinding stone, traces of red ochre and one incised sherd.[49] Doubts remain about the date, but this may have been a Neolithic shaft tomb; a form which is better known in the Early Copper Age.

Until recently, rock-cut tombs were thought to have been introduced in the Copper Age from outside the island, but new evidence suggests that this form of burial began during the Middle Neolithic.[50] At Castelluzzo di Mazara, three subterranean chambers (Ø about 1.6m), entered by a shaft, had been disturbed, but preserved fragments of trichrome and spiral-meander pottery (fig. 35:1). Likewise, rock-cut chambers first appeared in southern Italy during the Middle Neolithic and oven-shaped chamber tombs are also known from the Late Neolithic, when trench graves, cist graves and hybrid forms were widespread. Recent discoveries at the Boccetta stream (Messina) have revealed pit tombs and one example with stone slabs and stone artefacts, assigned to the Middle Neolithic.[51] Throughout the Italian Neolithic, caves were sometimes used for burial, often of juveniles and infants, and it would not be surprising if similar evidence were eventually found in Sicily.

One LN grave at Piano Conte on Lipari consisted of an oval pit in the volcanic tuff (1.20 x 0.60m), containing five fine red-burnished Diana bowls, clustered together in a little corner shaft (fig. 32:1-5). A solitary milk tooth suggests that the burial was, or perhaps included, that of a child. In Sicily, there are (unpublished) burials of this date at Biancavilla, Matrensa and Megara, where an oval pit was found holding a crouched skeleton and various Diana vessels.[52] A second grave at Piano Conte could be Late Neolithic or Early Copper Age: it consisted of a stone-lined cist (1.10 x 0.85m), containing a few plain sherds, obsidian flakes, traces of ochre and a tiny pedestal bowl (fig. 35:2). LN cist graves are also reported from near Paternò.[53]

Overall, the evidence is patchy and poorly published. The simplicity of EN pit graves with few or no grave goods, sometimes including red ochre, recalls Late Palaeolithic and Mesolithic traditions, although this is perhaps insufficient to prove real cultural continuity. Throughout southern Italy, concerns with ritual symbolism rather than status seem uppermost: magical and cosmological interests are suggested by the presence of ochre and the propensity to align corpses north-south, often facing east, perhaps to the rising sun. However, the main trend seems to be an increase in formal and initially single burials, and the provision of grave goods during the Middle-Late Neolithic, perhaps an indication of growing concerns with status and rank.[54] LN tombs in peninsular Italy sometimes have evidence for skull curation and multiple burial, a trend which anticipates CA developments, when rock-cut tombs were more common and burial rituals more elaborate.

Neolithic cult activities have been the subject of further study by R. Whitehouse (1992) who has combined several analytical and theoretical approaches (social, structural, ethnographic and psychological) in order to illuminate a complex world of ritual behaviour and symbolic meanings. In general terms, whereas Neolithic ritual in northern Europe focussed on prominent monuments, and in southeastern Europe on special artefacts, such as figurines, the context of ritual activity in southern Italy and Sicily was different. Here there appears to have been a subterranean dimension to religion, reflected in burials and caves, which were the focus of increasingly elaborate cults as societies grew in size and complexity, especially in the Late Neolithic and Copper Age. Greater interaction between communities may also have required more elaborate social controls, favouring an intensification of ritual behaviour.

Plainly, it is no straightforward matter to grasp the specific meanings of the many schematized wall-paintings, which are an important feature of the evidence, or to do justice to Whitehouse's work in a summary. However, there are clues in the context and content of certain visual symbols, which have suggested recurrent themes. Secrecy is one, perhaps associated with initiation practices and rites of passage, linked to male-dominated secret sects. Related to this is the persistence of a hunting iconography, while a third theme perhaps centred on unusual forms of water found principally in caves. It is suggested that such cults reflected various existential concerns: the growing importance of and need for ancestors as a guiding force, in which the caves and underground tombs provided a liminal context beween the world of the living and the dead; fertility and nature, as reflected in underground water, and perhaps including an element of womb symbolism; and the development of intermediary or part-human and part-spirit figures, sometimes represented anthropomorphically, suggesting a complex spirit world. With reference to social organisation, these cult activities may be appropriate to small-scale tribal communities divided mainly along lines of gender and age. By contrast, the more elaborate hierarchical structures of later middle-range societies (or chiefdoms) encouraged the development of ritual structures that were less concerned with underground and secretive cults, but required more conspicuous statements linked to assertions of power and authority (chapter 3).

There is always room for debate and for different theoretical perspectives in discussions about prehistoric belief systems. From an empirical standpoint too, thanks to the limited scale of excavations, it is likely that there is still much to be learnt. There is a small but growing number of anthropomorphic and animal figurines from domestic contexts, and the possibility of cult buildings in Neolithic settlements is not easy to assess. A shrine was probably present at Skorba on Malta.[55]

Not all Sicilian caves present evidence for ritual activities and the finds are often inconclusive or ambiguous in this regard. For example, scraps of pottery, animal bones and red ochre were brought into the Infame Diavolo cave (Palma di Montechiaro) on various occasions in the Stentinello-Diana periods, when fires were also lit, but the motives are uncertain.[56] Some caves, such as Uzzo, Corruggi and San Basilio, which were inhabited

Fig. 36. Painted figures in the Grotta dei Genovesi

during the Mesolithic, perhaps still served as temporary dwellings and shelters in the Neolithic, even if village life was now the norm. It was perhaps only certain caves, notably those of difficult access or with unusual features, that provided a focus for cult activity, as in the Copper Age.

One such example seems to be Antro Fazello at Monte Kronio, belonging to a system of karst tunnels, through which hot vapours emanate from a large underground spring.[57] Cult practices are documented here from the 6th century BC onwards, although they probably began in prehistoric times and were perhaps always associated with the curative powers of the hot vapours. Excavations have been restricted to narrow soundings, not all of which provide evidence for unusual cult activity. However, the EN levels provided large quantities of fragmented faunal remains, mainly from young caprines, comprising about 24% of the archaeological deposit and suggesting a sacrificial or votive practice. There is further evidence for ritual activity in the Copper Age (chapter 3).

Various cults of early historical times, concerned with natural phenomena, may have had Neolithic precursors. The LN and EBA deposits at the hot sulphurous fumaroles of Calcara on Panarea are otherwise hard to explain, while there are traces of MN and LN occupation in the vicinity of warm water and mud springs at the Salinelle of San Marco on the southern side of Etna. Bubbling mud springs at the lake of Naftia (Palike), mentioned in literary sources as a major cult centre of indigenous people (chapter 6), are associated with a long history of prehistoric occupation in the surrounding territory, perhaps already concerned with cult activity.[58]

The Grotta dei Genovesi on Levanzo (chapter 1) evokes another recurrent theme. This cave was revisited during the LN Diana phase and probably in the Copper Age, when the walls of the dark inner chamber were decorated once again, this time with a series of painted figures (figs. 36-38). Their date cannot be fixed precisely, but belongs probably in the 4th or early 3rd millennium BC. One group of about 30 figures covers a prominent panel of yellowish limestone in a frieze nearly 4m long and 1.50-2m above the floor. Another group occurs on darker rock below and others cluster nearby (fig. 15:A). Altogether there are nearly 100 individual figures in black (four red ones are usually regarded as Palaeolithic) and a few unrecognisable blobs. Most numerous are anthropomorphic forms with legs and arms apart and an elongated torso, suggesting a male gender. They vary from simple but plainly human forms to more schematized insect-like or bulbous motifs. Interspersed with them or in small separate groups are violin-shaped idols and wedge or dagger motifs. The former seem more schematically female than male and find parallels in the central Mediterranean with carved figurines, sometimes regarded as a female fertility divinity. Two examples were recently found in northeastern Sicily (fig. 44:5; chapter 3).[59] The remaining figures are of animals: three quadrupeds could represent pigs or boar, one a small dog, while three fish could be tuna or dolphin.

Fig. 37. Grotta dei Genovesi painted figures (longest about 31cm)

Darkness and secrecy are pervasive in this context. Despite the odd animal figure, there is no implication of a real scene or place being shown. The anthropomorphic figures seem to be evolving out of a human identity, perhaps towards reincarnation as animals, giving the impression of a transition to 'another' world, or a rite of passage. They may represent spirits or ancestors. In fact, there is evidence that many caves were associated with death and burial in the Copper Age (chapter 3), and similar figures appear on the wall of certain tombs in Sardinia.[60] In style and content the contrast with the earlier Palaeolithic engravings could hardly be greater.

Some caves have revealed their secrets only recently. The Grotta dei Cavalli near San Vito lo Capo is a large cavern with a broad entrance and a smaller chamber at the far end followed by a tiny cell-like niche.[61] The wall paintings are located in the small shadowy chamber, aptly named the chapel, except for a few anthropomorphic figures just beside its entrance from the main gallery (fig. 39). Two main groups appear on the right-hand wall, about 3m above floor-level (which was originally higher): the first combines dashes, concentric lines, circles with dots and hatched bands, rendered in two tones of red (probably ochre) and occasional black. It appears to be an abstract composition with a good deal of superposition, although certain motifs stand out and there is a suggestion of highly

83

Fig. 38. Grotta dei Genovesi painted 'idols' (longest about 12cm)

schematised zoomorphic or anthropomorphic forms, such as a quadruped with a dotted circular head near the centre. The second main group consists of dashes and figures, mainly anthropomorphic and male. Some are holding bows and hunting animals.

In style and content there is a marked contrast with the Grotta Genovesi figures and a much closer affinity with those in the famous Porto Badisco cave in Apulia, which can be dated approximately between the

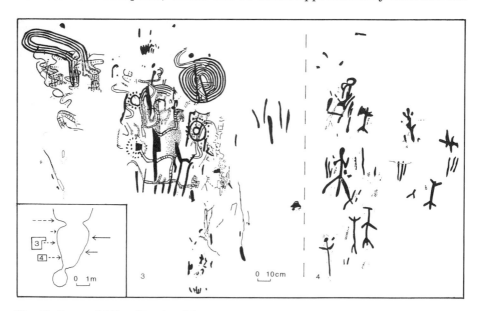

Fig. 39. Grotta dei Cavalli painted figures

Middle Neolithic and Early Copper Age. At Porto Badisco too, human forms occur as well as abstract motifs, frequently geometric or spiraliform, thought to represent more stylized versions of the former. There are several differences with the Grotta dei Cavalli motifs, but these should perhaps not obscure the recurrence of underlying themes: numerous male figures, bowmen, hunting and transformations into more abstract forms. The arrangement of paintings and the architecture of the cave, with its church-like plan, are especially evocative. A progression is easily envisaged from the relatively spacious and well-lit room, perhaps for larger assemblies or preparatory ceremonies, to a dimmer and more intimate inner chamber, perhaps for intitiates alone, marking the climax of a cult experience. Even the small dark cell at the end may have had a role in the proceedings. The transition from spacious to cramped and from light to shadow was perhaps a preparation for, or an accompaniment to, a spiritual journey from the familiar world outdoors to another world, revealed in mysteries and secret symbols.

3

New Territories and Tombs

Copper Age panorama

The scarcity of metal items in the Copper Age is a reminder of the somewhat arbitrary nature of this term, which embraces various assemblages and pottery styles between the 4th and 3rd millennia BC (table 1).[1] Three cultural provinces may be identified, albeit lacking precise boundaries: a) northeastern Sicily and the Aeolian islands, where painted wares are rare and the closest ties are with contemporary groups in Calabria and southern Italy; b) southern Sicily, where certain burial and ritual practices were current and local exchange networks linked various communities; c) the western provinces and the Conca d'Oro sites around Palermo, which have some features in common with the other two (fig. 40).

External forces and long-distance connections with eastern or western Mediterranean zones have often been cited as the main causes of cultural change during this period. However, the transition from more uniform and stable cultural patterns in the Late Neolithic, reflected in the wide distribution of Diana pottery and Lipari obsidian, to the more assertive regionalism and unsettled conditions of the Copper Age, probably occurred gradually as a result of several factors. The more consistent evidence for external links dates to a LCA phase (Malpasso) and to the Castelluccio period or Early Bronze Age, and is represented by certain stone, metal, bone and pottery artefacts, such as beakers, reflecting a growing interest in unusual raw materials and finely crafted items. This anticipates the more influential trans-Mediterranean relations of the 2nd millennium BC, but need not yet signal more than sporadic contacts due to trade and perhaps migrants. Greater mobility and periodic movements of small groups may have been encouraged by various changes: population growth and competition over land and resources; the proliferation of small settlement units; a shift towards pastoralism, mixed farming and a renewed interest in hunting; an uneven tenor of life in different territories; progress in boat-building and navigation; and perhaps growing social tensions, greater insecurity and an increase in armed conflict.

In addition, the elaboration of new ideologies and gender roles may be discerned in which males seem prominent, although warrior élites are not so conspicuous as in parts of Italy identified with Remedello, Rinaldone or Gaudo groups. Nevertheless, assertions of power by individuals and dominant groups are reflected in new material equipment, including weaponry, as well as funerary architecture, which evolved towards more complex and ostentatious forms in the Late Copper and Early Bronze Ages. Craft activities flourished, attested by fine pottery, while stone-working excelled in the production of pressure-flaked arrowheads, ground axes and mace-heads. Local copper ores were perhaps exploited on a small scale, stimulated by a growing appetite for prestigious raw materials, such as amber, jadeite and greenstones, traded over long distances and used mainly for display.

Less is known about settlements, which seem to have varied in size and importance, from small undefended hamlets in which much of the building material was probably of timber, to larger agglomerations surrounded by stone enclosure walls or ditches. New territorial divisions are implied and hierarchical relations between major centres and satellites may be suspected, although hard to delineate. During the Early Bronze Age, turreted walls and compounds appeared at sites near the coast, anticipating the prominence of these locations as centres of power and trade in the Middle Bronze Age. Subsistence patterns suggest diversification and a growing reliance on sheep and goat herding, secondary products and such related activities as spinning and weaving, although cattle were still present and hunting of deer and boar were also important (fig. 41). The use of animal traction and ploughing with oxen is quite likely on the basis of continental parallels, while limited evidence exists for the presence of equids by the Early Bronze Age.

Local originality, diversity and a propensity for innovation are hall-marks of this period. As regards social and economic changes, the Early Copper Age has more in common with the Late Neolithic than with the Late Copper Age, which anticipates several features of the Early Bronze Age. The distinction between these last two phases has become increasingly blurred. If only limited divisions by rank existed initially, a more articulated social order and new status concerns emerged in the Late Copper Age, for which the term 'chiefdom' is fashionable, although this label requires closer definition. The diversity of regional and island groupings also undermines generalisations. Left more to their own devices as Neolithic exchange networks were gradually superseded, small island communities could either stagnate or flourish: while the Aeolian archipelago experienced depopulation and a cultural and economic recession, Malta saw unprecedented and essentially unique developments in monumental architecture, associated with the temple culture. This was perhaps stimulated by internal pressures and a growing concern with status, more keenly tempered here than elsewhere by the need to maintain a community spirit within a constricted environment, while safeguarding the island's limited resources. In this insular laboratory, at a time of relative isolation between around 3500 and 2500 cal.BC, a kind of mystery religion developed with complex rites and powerful ideological and physical symbols, which may well have been more effective in maintaining social

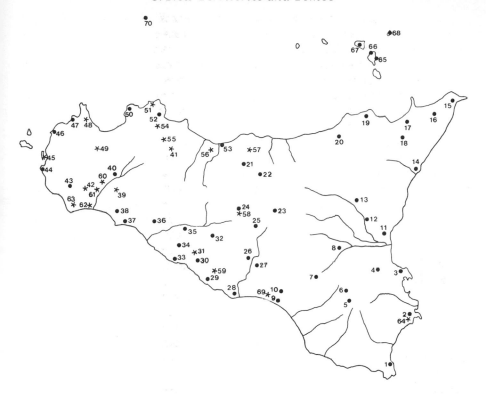

Fig. 40. *Copper Age (•) and Beaker (*) sites*: 1 G. Calafarina; 2 G. Conzo, Chiusazza; 3 Gisira; 4 Ossini; 5 Calaforno; 6 San Cono; 7 S. Ippolito; 8 Torricella; 9 Piano Notaro; 10 Settefarine; 11 Catania; 12 Trefontane; 13 Poggio dell'Aquila; 14 G. Monaci; 15 Boccetta; 16 Motta; 17 Pietro Pallio; 18 G. San Basilio; 19 Gioiosa Marea; 20 Alcara li Fusi; 21 G. Fico, Chiusilla; 22 G. Vecchiuzzo; 23 Realmese; 24 Marianopoli; 25 Caltanissetta; 26 Sommatino; 27 Riesi; 28 Casalicchio-Agnone; 29 G. Zubbia; 30 G. Ticchiara; 31 Serraferlicchio; 32 Malpasso; 33 Durrueli; 34 Busoné; 35 Capreria; 36 Ribera; 37 Kronio; 38 Tranchina; 39 S, Margherita Belice; 40 Ulina; 41 Villafrati; 42 Marcita; 43 Roccazzo; 44 Marsala; 45 Motya; 46 Erice; 47 Mocata; 48 G. Uzzo; 49 Segesta; 50 G. Puntali; 51 Carini; 52 Palermo Conca d'Oro sites; 53 Himera; 54 Torrente Cannizzaro; 55 Moarda; 56 G. Geraci, Puleri; 57 G. Chiusilla; 58 Cuti; 59 Naro; 60 S. Martino, Stretto, Cisternazza, Torre Donzelle; 61 Torrebigini; 62 Manicalunga; 63 Torre Cusa; 64 G. Palombara; 65 Lipari: acropolis; 66 Lipari: Piano Conte; 67 Salina: Malfa; 68 Panarea: Piano Quartara, Drauto; 69 Manfria; 70 Ustica: G. Azzurra

harmony and certainly less provocative than overt statements of individual power or wealth.

The elaboration of funerary ritual is a phenomenon encountered widely in the western Mediterranean at this time in diverse regional forms. Rather than the result of a radical new departure or of outside influences, the growing concern with funerary rites in Sicily can be seen as an organic process, already developing in the Late Neolithic, when some burials were provided with fine grave goods and more elaborate constructions, including subterranean chambers (chapter 2). The chamber tomb, which is so

	Sheep/goat	Cattle	Pig	Dog	Deer	Fox	Equid	Birds
COPPER AGE:	NR/MNI							
Grotta Chiusazza Ivc	55/6	20/4	6/3	1/1	6/2	1/1		
" Ivb	100/12	33/5	28/4	3/3	21/3	2/1		
" Iva	156/15	47/4	126/14	2/2	69/7			
Grotta Palombara	74	14	68	3	15	1		
Grotta del Conzo	55	32	60	1	11	6		
Lipari acropolis	2	3	1					
San Basilio I	12	2	24 (wild)			22		
Piano Vento	91	150	30	1	2			
EARLY BRONZE AGE:								
Grotta Chiusazza III	71/9	63/6	40/6	1/1	25/4			
Monte Casale	64/19	50/7	12/4	1/1	3/2		2/2(?)	
Valsavoia	129/10	161/10	43/6	4/2	3/1			
Fiumedinisi	23/7	15/3	17/5		37/6			
La Muculufa	4952/168	443/11	605/26	19/3	49/4			
Lipari acropolis	22	55	13					
Filicudi C. Graziano	133	48	31		1			2

Fig. 41. Copper-Early Bronze Age faunal samples. Number of remains/minimum number of individuals

characteristic of the island's later prehistory, provided a means of maintaining and reinforcing ancestral lineages, while perhaps imparting a sense of continuity through times of social and technological change. Designed to permit multiple burial, some tombs of the 3rd millennium BC were even re-used in the later Bronze and Iron Ages. Convenience aside, this reflects a strong endemic tradition, reinforced by a human landscape in which burial grounds were increasingly prominent. Potentially significant as territorial markers and symbols of power, they also provided a focus for cult activities and for specialists in ceremonial and magical formulae to promote social cohesion through ideological controls in a world of growing inequality and insecurity.

Overall, the cultural traditions, ideologies, subsistence regimes and more hierarchical power structures of the 2nd millennium BC were firmly rooted in the Copper Age. It cannot, however, be claimed that the 3rd millennium BC witnessed the emergence of such centralized and institutionalized hierarchies, associated with proto-palatial architecture and a high degree of craft specialization, as those encountered in parts of Greece and the Aegean. This could be due to several limiting or conditioning factors.

According to one line of reasoning, the absence of a direct stimulus from the older civilisations of Anatolia, the Near East or Egypt, which might have been provided by regular trade relations, was one relevant factor. This and other theories require a close analysis of the circumstances that led to the formation of regional centres or early states in the eastern

Mediterranean, which cannot be dealt with here.[2] However, despite certain similarities of climate and environment, there are also contrasts between the geography of Greece and the Aegean and that of Sicily and southern Italy, where environmental circumstances and pressures differed and were perhaps generally less intense. The potential for cereal production and stock rearing, which can be practised over much of Sicily, the relatively abundant sources of fresh water and the widespread opportunities for mixed arable and pastoral farming, combined with natural woodland resources, contrast with the more localised distribution of good natural resources in the Aegean. Vine and olive production in Greece would also have demanded a longer-term investment of labour, tying communities to specific territories. Opportunities for the accumulation of surpluses and wealth were therefore more concentrated at key locations and further encouraged by different forms of regional exchange, facilitated by easy maritime communications across the Aegean Sea.

Sequences and dates

The stratigraphies of several caves (Antro Fazzello, Palombara, Zubbia and Fontanazza) illustrate the transition to the Copper Age, but the best documented sequence is still that of the Grotta Chiusazza (fig. 42:A).[3] Here the Diana phase (level V) is followed by associations of painted (Conzo style), incised (Piano Notaro style) and dark burnished wares (levels IV/12-17), representing the Early Copper Age. Painted pottery (Serraferlicchio style) is subsequently more common (Middle Copper Age), succeeded by associations of LCA wares (Malpasso style, level IV/8-11) and by EBA (Castelluccio) material in layer III. Recent soundings in the Fontanazza I cave (Milena) have revealed a similar sequence, with Piano Notaro (layers VII-VI), Serraferlicchio (VI-III) and Malpasso pottery (V-I). In the late phase, monochrome Malpasso pottery was contemporary with various regional painted styles (San Ippolito, Naro, Partanna), which foreshadow Castelluccio wares (below). However, problems of definition remain: the different pottery styles may not all represent different periods, and the Middle phase remains the least well documented. In this instance a bipartite division between Early and Late Copper Age will suffice (table 1).

In the Aeolian islands, the Spatarella phase represents a local development from the Late Neolithic, followed by the Piano Conte (ECA) and Piano Quartara (LCA) phases. Painted wares are noticeably absent in the Aeolian sequence, although a few fragments, probably imports, and generic stylistic connections allow synchronisms to be postulated between Piano Conte and Serraferlicchio, and between Piano Quartara and Malpasso. In northwestern Sicily, the burials and cave excavations of the Conca d'Oro belong to different phases, but lack a reliable sequence of dating.

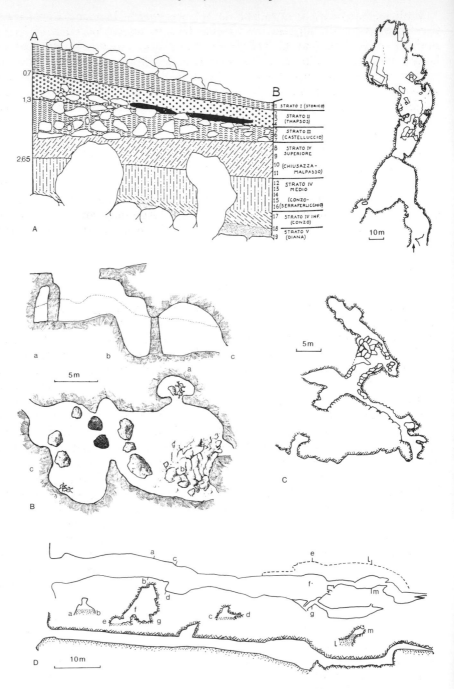

Within figure A, the stratigraphy labels:

1 STRATO I (STORICO)
2
3 STRATO II (THAPSOS)
4
5 STRATO III (CASTELLUCCIO)
6
8 STRATO IV SUPERIORE
9
10 (CHIUSAZZA-MALPASSO)
11
12 STRATO IV MEDIO
13
14
15 (CONZO-SERRAFERLICCHIO)
16
17 STRATO IV INF. (CONZO)
18 STRATO V (DIANA)
19

10m

5m

5m

5m

10m

Fig. 42. Caves: (A) Chiusazza section (tr. R) and plan; (B) Calafarina; (C) Infame Diavolo; (D) Vecchiuzzo

92

Radiocarbon dates are few and far between (table 4). Two samples from the Grotta Cavallo suggest that Piano Notaro ware was current in the mid-4th millennium cal.BC (3786-3380 cal.BC) and may partly overlap with Diana pottery. The most reliable dates for Maltese Zebbug contexts, traditionally synchronized with the Sicilian Early Copper Age (San Cono-Piano Notaro), fall between 4200 and 3600 cal.BC, which is earlier than might have been expected.[4] Radiocarbon dates are not abundant for the Italian Copper Age either, although a LN-ECA level in the Grotta Madonna (Calabria) has a date of 3639-3386 cal.BC. Moreover, the Rinaldone culture had started before 3000 cal.BC, while new dates from Conelle fall between about 3500 and 2900 cal.BC. For the later Sicilian Copper Age, it has been noted that Sicilian Piano Quartara pottery at the Brochtorff circle on Gozo can be dated by radiocarbon to the earlier 3rd millennium cal.BC.[5] In Sicily, therefore, the whole Copper Age may cover at least one thousand years until the onset of the Early Bronze Age (Castelluccio) at around 2500 cal.BC.

Funerary rituals

The persistence of LN traditions is visible in cave burials, pit tombs and chamber tombs. The latter are well documented in western Sicily, where many ECA burial grounds were probably sited on beds of softer rock, such as the crumbly calcarenite of Ribera or the marly gypsum of Piano Vento, in order to facilitate excavation.[6] Small subterranean tombs on flat or gently sloping ground were entered from above or from a contiguous vertical shaft (*pozzetto*) and sealed by a stone slab (fig. 43:A-D). More elaborate and possibly later versions of this design had two or three chambers leading off a deeper shaft, as at Uditore (fig. 43:E). Tombs set against a steeper slope more often had a side entrance (fig. 43:G-H), an arrangement which is characteristic of later periods (LCA-EBA).

One of the largest ECA cemeteries, near Ribera, with over 100 tombs, had been comprehensively ransacked by looters. Tranchina, Piano Vento and Roccazzo have respectively a total of 36, 27 and 44 tombs, although smaller clusters occur in the Conca d'Oro and elsewhere in western Sicily. There were fewer depositions per chamber in the early phases, when single burials predominated at Tranchina (33 out of 36 tombs) and Roccazzo, where skeletons were either placed supine or in a crouched position. By contrast, the Piano Vento, Uditore and Conca d'Oro burials more often contained between one and five individuals.

Funerary rites seem to have progressed towards collective or multiple burial, with the tombs developing in such a way as to facilitate periodic reopening, allowing new depositions to be added and existing ones to be rearranged. Most tombs were too small to accommodate more than one or two corpses at a time and the latest use is often represented by one or two articulated skeletons in the central area and disarticulated bones (of prior depositions) at the sides. Governing these associative burials was perhaps an ideology of lineage or kinship links.

Details of the ritual are known at Piano Vento, where an ECA settlement was established beside the old Neolithic site (chapter 2), which now became a burial ground. Several Copper Age tombs were dug through the floors of Neolithic dwellings; a similar superposition was encountered at Serra del Palco (below) and perhaps inspired by a sense of ancestral connections. Many chambers were damaged or had collapsed, but preserved their contents intact, while some depositions may have been in pits or shafts.[7] Four tombs had single inhumations, while the remaining 23 contained from two to five individuals, giving a total of about 70. The fully extended and articulated skeletons (20%) were mostly from single burials or representative of the last interments in collective chambers. Some tombs presented only rows of crania or long bones, which may have been taken from another place of primary exposure or rearranged within the tomb after reopening.

The demographic profile of the sample (tables 2-3) suggests that females were in the minority. Some double depositions consisted of males, while few tombs can be construed as husband-and-wife groups. Children may be under-represented due to the fragility of their bones. Rather than a cross-section of the population or classic family groups, the sample implies selection criteria favouring males and kinship patterns of a special kind. For example, there is a suggestion of consanguinity from similarities between two adult males in tomb 1. Also surprising is the high mortality rate, with only 12.5% of the population reaching the age of 30, although the males were of relatively high stature, robust build (by contrast with rather short females) and with good dentition, while chemical tests for calcium, strontium and zinc, imply a healthy meat and vegetable diet.[8] Some unfavourable circumstance, such as disease or warfare, may have been responsible for a rather high mortality rate, even by contemporary standards. It is also noteworthy that the zinc content (associated with a high protein intake) was generally higher in male than female bones and higher again in individuals from tombs provided with more pots.

Aside from a few painted or incised vessels, the Piano Vento tombs contained a rather monotonous series of small grooved cups and bowls, usually between one and eight examples per tomb, often positioned near the skull, although a few tombs lacked any (fig. 50:1-3). Traces of ash or burnt soil have suggested that food offerings were sometimes included. At Roccazzo, most single tombs had 2-3 vases and one or more stone blades or arrowheads, although one single deposition was accompanied by four decorated pots, shell beads, ochre fragments and a shark tooth. Notionally labelled the 'tomb of the shaman', this individual might have been distinguished by a special role in ceremonial activity, although small numbers of personal items are quite common in Conca d'Oro tombs, including shell and stone beads, perforated boar tusks and bone pins. There are no

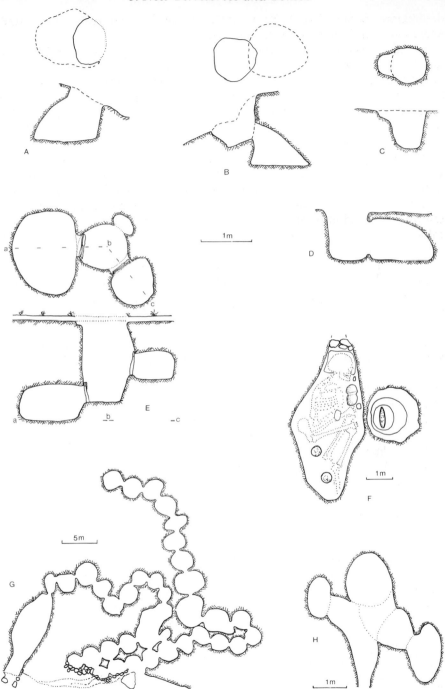

Fig. 43. Rock-cut tombs and pits: (A-B) Ribera; (C-D) S. Cusumano; (E) Uditore; (F) Busoné; (G) Calaforno, (H) Malpasso

obvious gender differences in the use of pottery, but stone implements seem more typical of male depositions at Roccazzo.

Red ochre was also identified at these sites, sometimes contained in vases, as at Uditore and Serra del Palco, but more often covering the tomb floor and the skeletal remains. In several cases the dust may have been sprinkled over corpses, staining the skeleton, or over the defleshed bones, when tombs were re-opened. Occurring naturally in parts of Sicily, ochre is recurrent in burials from the Upper Palaeolithic until the Copper Age. In addition to its function as a pigment, it is variously thought to have been a magical substance used in purification rites or offering ceremonies, perhaps symbolizing blood or a life-force, although it also helps to preserve organic material such as animal skins and has certain medicinal and antiseptic properties.

Social distinctions, therefore, are not easy to detect in ECA tombs and the rather subtle differences in the allocation of grave goods may imply contrasting roles or genders rather than institutionalized rank. However, there was often more to cemeteries than just the tombs. At San Cusumano, Uditore, Cozzo Busoné, Marianopoli, Serra del Palco and Piano Vento, rock-cut shafts or pits served additional ceremonial functions (fig. 43:C,F). Cylindrical shafts (usually 0.5-1m in diameter and depth) contained ashy soil, sherds and artefacts, including grooved axe-hammers at San Cusumano and Uditore. At the Mandria site of Serra del Palco, ECA funerary rites are implied by pits containing ochre-filled vases and seeds and by a small chamber dug into Neolithic levels, although lacking bones.

Of eleven shafts at Piano Vento, two had circular stone settings at the top and one held a large upright storage jar. The fill was generally rich in ash and charcoal, sometimes with burnt animal bones, sherds, small vessels, ochre and occasional figurines: one sizeable male figure of lightly baked clay, with arms outstretched and traces of painted lines perhaps represented the deceased, an ancestor or deity (fig. 44:1). The supernatural is further emphasized by a finely modelled and painted figurine of a four-legged creature, perhaps half-human, nick-named the 'centaur', pieces of which were found in two separate shafts, several metres apart (fig. 44:3). Evidently, part of the ceremony involved breaking materials before placing them in shafts along with burnt food offerings, perhaps funerary meals, which included bones of young cattle.

Jar inhumations may have begun in the Copper Age, although little is known about the bones found inside those at Marianopoli. Human bones were covered by large potsherds at Camaro, near Messina, in what was perhaps a funerary site with associated cult activity, represented by hearths and deposits of Piano Conte pottery.[9] Of special note is a 'violin' figurine of dark grey schist, possibly locally made, which resembles those painted in the Genovesi cave (chapter 2) and has widespread counterparts in the Aegean, particularly in the marble examples from the Cyclades of the late 4th-early 3rd millennium BC (EC1 phase) as well as in Anatolia (fig. 44:5). A second figurine has closer affinities with small bone pendants from Malta. These parallels are hard to explain: they may suggest diffuse, though perhaps mainly sporadic, contacts between these regions, and the existence of some commonly and widely held beliefs concerning burial ritual at this time.

As well as chamber tombs, pit graves were still current during the Early Copper Age, represented by the stone-lined shafts first recorded at San Cono and Piano Notaro (Gela), after which this phase is named.[10] One pit burial in Catania was subsequently enlarged to accommodate four depositions. At Cozzo Busoné, a hillock 15km northwest of Agrigento, EBA-MBA chamber tombs were found as well as natural rock crevices and man-made shafts containing what were probably votive offerings, dating from this period. A crouched adult inhumation in a pit grave with the head resting on a slab was accompanied by a large grooved hammer, a few vases and traces of ochre (fig. 43:F). The adjacent shaft contained a pebble figurine of phallic shape, but with female attributes pecked out and emphasized by red ochre. A second example from another shaft provides further evidence of the increasing degree of ritual symbolism associated with some burials (fig. 44:6-7).

Funerary rites and architecture probably evolved in stages through the Copper Age towards the often more crowded multiple burials and elaborate tombs, entered by a front door, of the Castelluccio culture. In the

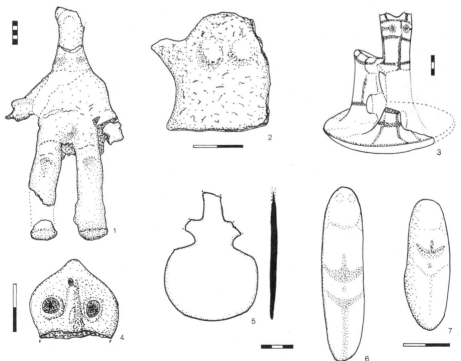

Fig. 44. Figurines: (1-4) Piano Vento; (5) Camaro; (6-7) Busoné

Conca d'Oro region, the old vertical-shaft tomb perhaps continued, while the appearance of larger chambers in the Late Copper Age is attested by a rock-cut tomb (Ø 2.70m), probably entered by a corridor, at Roccazzello (Mazara): the upper layer held two depositions and a lower layer had 16 individuals (table 2), four jars (Piano Quartara style), a long flint blade, several flakes, a few stone beads and a grinding stone.[11] An unusual burial at contrada Menta (Serra del Palco) consisted of disarticulated and partially burnt bones, including four skulls, placed in a rock-cut recess behind a wall. The limited burning of bones, which were probably already defleshed, suggests a secondary ceremony, perhaps a purification rite, rather than a cremation proper.[12]

Central-eastern Sicily has a mere handful of LCA tombs. At Malpasso they are set into the slope beneath the headland on which the settlement was probably located, and have a rather erratic design of adjoining chambers, containing several depositions, a few vases, flint and obsidian blades and one small metal ring (fig. 43:H). Much more elaborate is the veritable catacomb of 35 interconnected rock-cut chambers with three larger rooms (fig. 43:G), known as the Calaforno hypogeum (Ragusa).[13] Although found empty, a few sherds suggest first use in the Late Copper Age. In conception, this unusual agglomeration recalls the Hal Saflieni hypogeum in Malta, although the latter is altogether grander in design, with its allusions to local megalithic architecture. Rather than direct Maltese influence, this is more likely a case of shared interest in communal burial and lineage prompting the elaboration of essentially local building styles.

Towards the end of the Copper Age, as implied by associations with beakers and local painted pottery (Naro style), new evidence appears for the embellishment of tombs at various sites in western Sicily, clustered mainly between the Belice and Modione rivers.[14] These consist of roughly circular rock-cut chambers preceded by a corridor of variable length, with a rock-cut foundation, lined with upright stones or constructed entirely with dry-stone walling and orthostats. One of the first to be discovered, near Salaparuta, also preserved two large capstones across part of the corridor (fig. 45:A). Although partly rifled, this chamber contained dozens of disarticulated skeletons, fragments of local incised pottery in beaker style and plain grey wares, with additional inhumations and vases in the corridor. Similar tombs, with shorter corridors and one or two surviving stone pillars are known at Cisternazza, Torre Cusa, Corvo, Donzelle and Marcita. Two chambers at Marcita contained respectively at least 30 and 50 individuals, with similar kinds of pottery (Malpasso, Naro and Beaker), shell beads, axe pendants, boar teeth and flint blades. Tomb A at Donzelle (fig. 45:B) had a long corridor, an imposing entrance with pillars cut out of the bedrock and flagstones on the floor of the chamber.

From a structural point of view, these Belice tombs seem to be hybrid monuments, which combine the local tradition of rock-cutting with masonry additions. It is tempting to account for them in terms of contacts with other regions where a comparable tradition of 'megalithic' architec-

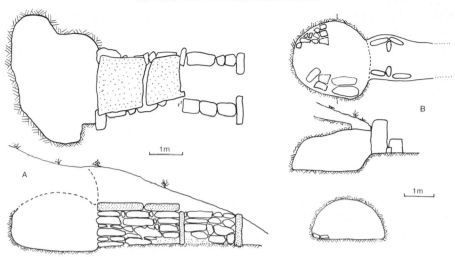

Fig. 45. Belice corridor tombs: (A) Salaparuta, contrada Pergola; (B) Torre Donzelle

ture existed, although this raises difficult questions about cross-cultural contacts, which recur in connection with Sicilian dolmens (below).[15] Hitherto, Sicily has seemed largely peripheral to discussions and surveys of the better-known megalithic remains in Malta, southeast Italy, Corsica and Sardinia. Nevertheless, the tomb corridors have affinities with those of a rather variable group of gallery graves, or *allées couvertes*, which are widespread in southern France from the Late Neolithic and recurrent in Sardinia during the Copper-Early Bronze Ages. The Sardinian parallels are the most compelling: long cist corridors are widespread in the island and sometimes combined with a rock-cut chamber in similar fashion.[16] Two close Sardinian parallels are those of Mesu Enas and Cucurru Craboni, the latter associated with Monte Claro and Bonnanaro wares, indicating a long period of use from the earlier 3rd millennium cal.BC. Contacts with Sardinia are also suggested by the presence of beakers (below).

Settlement landscapes

Systematic survey work is not very advanced for the evolution of the human landscape to be traced with much confidence and the patterns currently visible suggest marked regional variations. Piano Conte settlements in the Aeolian islands were located on the Lipari acropolis, the Diana plain and at a few upland sites, although the only settlements of any size were on the acropolis and at Serra Fareddu on Stromboli. Few structural features are known.[17] Finds of Piano Conte pottery are also reported in the northern foothills of the Peloritani near Barcellona (Messina). The situation is similar in the subsequent Piano Quartara phase, represented by scattered findspots, suggesting a period of sparse occupation after the Late Neolithic, perhaps due to changing alignments in exchange systems, the diminishing use of obsidian or some local environmental degradation after earlier occupation. The islands were also prone to periodic volcanic eruptions and earthquakes in recent prehistory, which may have created temporary set-backs in earlier times.[18]

By contrast, distribution maps in Sicily point to a variety of settlement locations and an overall increase in the numbers of LCA and especially of EBA sites (figs. 40 and 53) on inland hill-top plateaus throughout the south-central zone, and often nearer the coast in western regions.[19] A concentration of sites on the coastal plain and surrounding hills of the Conca d'Oro contrasts with an apparently low density along the Syracusan coast, where Neolithic ditched villages had once flourished. This is very like the situation on the Apulian Tavoliere, which seems to have been virtually abandoned at this time. Perhaps centuries of grazing, cultivation and clearance had contributed to the degradation of this area, now regarded as less productive than interior river valleys and hill country, which were better suited to an increasingly mixed economy that included pastoralism and hunting. Or perhaps the coastal plain now seemed too exposed; when EBA sites appeared here, they were often defended. Some inland sites, like San Cono, may have been established with an eye to local flint sources (below), while the attractions of the Hyblaean region must have included its springs and small rivers.

Many sites are recorded along the upper Simeto river in the Etna foothills and on terraces and hillocks flanking the Catania plain, often not far from Neolithic sites. The productive potential of this area is favoured by local hydrology, soil fertility and the proximity of Etna's forests. Although there is little evidence for direct continuity at individual sites from the earlier (Piano Notaro) to the later (Malpasso) phase, the pattern suggests fairly consistent occupation in this region, as in parts of western Sicily, where Neolithic and Copper Age finds are often contiguous, both on hill-tops and along river valleys.

Cemeteries are better known than settlements and the relationship between them is rarely visible.[20] At Piano Vento, very small circular structures (Ø 2-2.50m) with central posts were set into the slope just metres from the tombs. Traces of similar dwellings with Piano Notaro pottery are known on the summit of Monte Grande beneath EBA levels (below). Not far away, on the Rinollo hill near the Zubbia cave, at least two roughly oval huts (Ø 6.80 & 7.40m) with plastered floors, timber-frames and daub, were located within a rock-cut enclosure (33.60 x 27.60m), perhaps designed for the security of a few families and their domestic animals. Enclosure sites were recurrent in this region throughout the Bronze Age (below). The Roccazzo tombs, overlooking the plain near Mazaro, seem to correspond with nearby hut-floors on the flatter hill-top, suggesting a settlement of small groups of two or three houses, each with associated burials, spread over several hundred metres. Sizeable rectan-

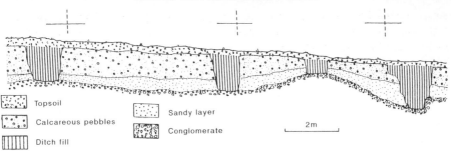

Topsoil

Calcareous pebbles

Ditch fill

Sandy layer

Conglomerate

2m

Fig. 46. Ditch sections at Heraclea Minoa

gular dwellings (12 x 6m) are evidenced by continuous bedding trenches and post-holes, associated with a smaller circular structure with two pits, perhaps for storage.

For the later Copper Age, small sections of curved stone walls at Serra del Palco and preliminary reports of circular or oval huts at Fiumedinisi and Poggio dell'Aquila (Adrano) represent all that is known of contemporary dwellings.[21] However, the existence of a ditched village has recently been documented at Eraclea Minoa, a pleasant coastal site near the Platani estuary. Four parallel ditches (1-1.70m wide and 0.40-1.40m deep) containing Malpasso pottery had been cut into the loose bedrock (fig. 46). At the bottom of one was a sunken pit with small animal or bird bones, perhaps a votive or foundation deposit.[22] The overall form and function of these ditches, like those of Neolithic date, remains to be established (defence, water storage or drainage, for example; chapter 2). There are a few parallels at this time in central and southern Italy for defensive ditches, although those at Conelle and Toppo Daguzzo are substantially bigger.

Caves

Caves account for a large proportion of Copper Age sites, which is due in part to what is sometimes irreverently called the *tradizione grottesca* of prehistoric archaeology, although this is destined to change with more surveys and excavations of outdoor sites. Nevertheless, over twenty caves with Copper Age finds are spread throughout Sicily.[23] Their purpose seems to have varied: temporary shelters, dwellings, burial-places, storage or working areas, as well as cult sites (already noted in connection with cave paintings in chapter 2) can be postulated. These functions could overlap or alternate over time, and some caves were probably used for either ceremonial or practical purposes by the inhabitants of adjacent open-air sites.

Examples of what were perhaps temporary shelters for seasonal use in the Peloritani mountains are the Grotta Lauro (900m asl), occasionally snow-bound in winter (with LCA ware), and the San Basilio cave (chapters 1 & 2), with Piano Conte and Serraferlicchio pottery. The percentages of wild animal bones in this and some other caves (fig. 41) suggest that they

101

were sometimes used by hunting parties. Further south, the Grotta dei Monaci (with Middle – LCA pottery), facing a steep gully, looks like an easily defended refuge. More convenient for habitation are several large lava-flow caves in the Etna region, which have provided material of Copper Age date, although EBA-MBA finds are most abundant and often associated with burials (Barriera, Novalucello and Marca caves). The earliest finds in the Grotta Basile (Catania) consist of Malpasso wares, associated with hearths and animal bones, which could be either of ritual or domestic significance. Orsi found traces of open sites in the environs of Etna caves, in which the presence of large jars, lithic debitage and raw clay, has suggested such uses as storage-places or workshops.

There are some indications of multiple functions over time. In the Chiusazza, Palombara and Conzo caves, occupation debris was mainly near the entrances and included pottery, spindle-whorls, stone tools and animal bones. Some of these large caves are invitingly cool in the summer. Hearths, faunal remains and a range of Malpasso pottery in the lower levels of the Grotta Ticchiara (Favara) could suggest a living-place, although the later (Castelluccio) levels were used for burial. More difficult to assess are the caves of Villafrati, Chiusilla and Vecchiuzzo, which all contained human bone, but were excavated with antiquated methods. In the Vecchiuzzo cave (83m long), hearths, ashy layers, animal bones and a wide range of pottery and lithic implements were more plentiful near the entrance, while the disarticulated human bones found in a jar behind a wall further inside, may suggest a separation of domestic and funerary areas (fig. 42:D). However, human bones from at least 16 individuals were more widely scattered than the excavators realized and may reflect complex rituals involving secondary selective burial.[24] Cult activity is also implied by strange deposits in wall-niches, one of which contained an incised bone, antler, boar tusk, knuckle-bones and a flint blade. Large jars found here and in the Monte Kronio caves may have been positioned in order to collect dripping water.

The Zubbia cave was perhaps used by the inhabitants of the nearby settlement at Rinollo (above). Here again, deposits in wall-niches, red ochre and fine lithic implements (arrows and a mace-head) imply cult activity. An ECA burial is suggested by the human jaw, Notaro pottery and finely worked arrowheads found in the Grotta Caprara, while Orsi discovered several ECA burials sealed against the walls in the Calafarina cave (fig. 42:B). Although he believed that the central chamber served as a dwelling, due to the presence of a hearth, it could be that the traces of burning and the cache of 20 unusually fine flint blades (up to 20cm long) were connected with cults and funerary ritual.

From the old publication of Serraferlicchio may be inferred the existence of a settlement with huts, a few chamber tombs and a contiguous cult site, represented by a natural rock fissure over 60m long and 1m wide, with concretions and stalagmites.[25] A mass of pottery came from the latter, including plain and fine painted wares (Piano Notaro, Piano Conte, Malpasso and Serraferlicchio styles) as well as pottery horns, chipped stone tools, basaltic grinding-stones, axes, bone implements and spindle-whorls. Although none of these artefacts necessarily signify a cult, the unusual context and the quality of much pottery suggests that offerings were made here over a lengthy period, reminiscent of the natural crevice deposits already noted at Busoné and recurrent in the Early Bronze Age (below).

Metal, stone and pottery

Until recently, the potential of Sicily as a producer of metal was not widely known.[26] However, metals are present in the Monti Peloritani, associated with crystalline schists containing sulphides of lead, copper, zinc, silver, iron, arsenic and antimony. Scattered deposits and easily accessible surface outcrops, most suitable for prehistoric extraction techniques, have been tentatively associated with local settlement patterns and exploitation from at least the Late Bronze Age (fig. 111). The main areas are in the vicinity of Barcellona on the northern foothills and Fiumedinisi on the southern slopes. Local extraction during the Copper Age is not proven, but hinted at by metal artefacts and possible traces of working at Fiumedinisi. Elsewhere in the island, where sources are lacking, at least re-smelting was probably practiced locally. A clay ladle with traces of burning and a socket for inserting a handle (fig. 51:15), found with a beaker in a cave at Villafrati, resembles a type of crucible used widely in the western Mediterranean at this time.[27]

In addition, the presence of metal slag in a transitional LN-ECA context on Lipari (chapter 2) and equally early evidence for the first use of copper in Italy and Sardinia, proves some knowledge of metal by the mid-4th millennium cal.BC, even though this did not lead to significant technological changes until later. Metal items seem to have been rare in Sicily before the Late Copper Age (Malpasso) and they did not replace stone tools until the Middle Bronze Age. The earliest finds consist of a few implements and ornaments, presumed to be unalloyed copper, although none have been

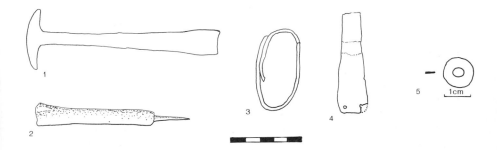

Fig. 47. Metal artefacts: (1) Chiusazza (2) Palombara (3-4) Chiusilla (5) Malpasso

scientifically analysed or sourced.[28] Given the presence of copper in the Peloritani, however, a distant origin is not necessarily implied. Stratified EBA metal finds are not very numerous either (below) and their contexts reveal little about the status of metal objects and those who used them, although some items have parallels outside Sicily. It is tempting to assume, in view of the prestige often associated with long-distance trade items and the scarcity of metal at this time, that the material was highly valued.

Aside from unidentifiable fragments, the main finds from LCA contexts include: a long-handled item, possibly a dagger with crescent-shaped pommel, from Grotta Chiusazza; a broken dagger from Grotta Chiusilla; an awl set in a bone handle from Grotta Palombara; a small ring or bead from a Malpasso tomb and another from a tomb near Boccadifalco (fig. 47). A sheet-metal fragment and a small decorated object come from a transitional LCA-EBA level at Fiumedinisi, while some thick-bladed axes are tentatively assigned to the Copper or Early Bronze Age on stylistic grounds (fig. 70:6,16-19). Generic affinities with simple copper objects in the Aegean and elsewhere have occasionally been noted for some of these items, but none are particularly compelling, by contrast with one or two closer parallels for Early Bronze Age artefacts (below).

Stone technology was still prevalent for making tools. The basaltic rocks exploited to make ground axes and millstones during the Neolithic continued to be used and exchanged in Sicily, while various greenstones were still imported, probably from Calabria (fig. 48:17-23).[29] There is clearer evidence now, especially from Conca d'Oro sites, for the use of highly polished jadeite and chloromelanite axes of probable Alpine origin, sometimes perforated for suspension. Various fine-grained stones were ground and drilled to make beads and pendants, including a V-perforated calcite button from Uditore, which may also suggest western Mediterranean connections, perhaps antedating beakers (below). Craftsmanship surpassed practical needs in the careful shaping and polishing of mace-heads, perhaps symbols of authority or status, known from several sites (figs. 48:19; 49:c). Shaft-hole axes with Italian parallels probably belong to this period too (fig. 49:a).

The use of local amber further emphasizes the interest in exotic and unusual materials. The Baltic variety (succinite) is known to have been traded widely in European prehistory, but Sicilian amber or simetite has only recently been characterized by spectroscopic analysis and shown to be distinguishable from both Baltic amber and African copal.[30] Finds of natural amber are recorded in southeastern Sicily, and the earliest certain evidence for its exploitation is represented by two finds (a small bead and a gem-like hemisphere) from a LCA tomb at Laterza in Apulia. Dark red amber-like beads are also known from an EBA tomb at Castelluccio and later contexts (chapter 4).

Obsidian was still widely used. Abundant in Piano Conte contexts on Lipari, its presence in LN and CA levels at Serra del Palco is fairly

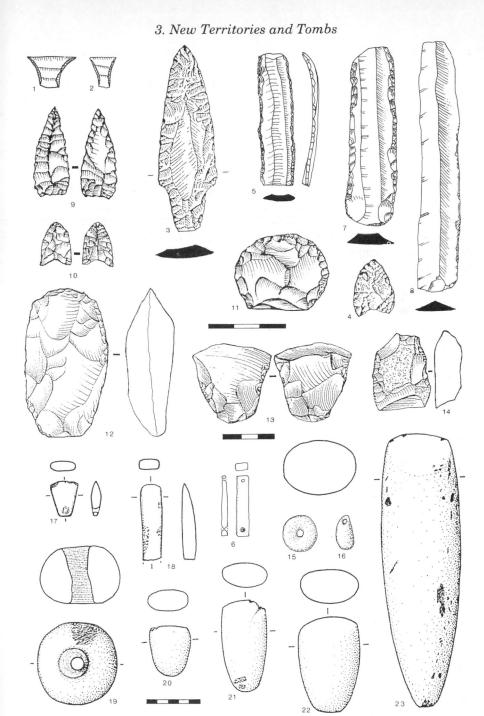

Fig. 48. Coppper Age-Early Bronze Age stone tools: (1-2) G. San Basilio; (3-4) G. Caprara; (5-6) La Muculufa; (7-8) Uditore; (9-10) Serra del Palco; (11) Mezzebbi; (12-14) Biddini; (15-16) Monte Racello; (17-23) Morgantina

105

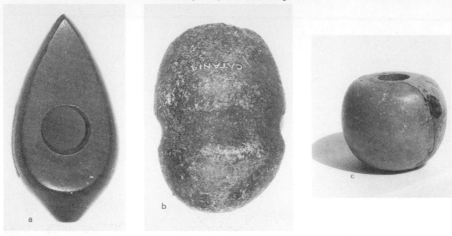

Fig. 49. (a) Ironstone axe, Aci Catena, L 10cm; (b) basaltic axe, Catania, L 13.2cm; (c) limestone mace, Conzo cave, H 5.5cm

constant (20-30% of all chipped stone). By this time, Lipari had largely replaced Pantelleria as the source of the material, although occasional artefacts of the latter still occur: more surprising is the discovery of two arrowheads in a CA tomb in southern France, far outside the normal distribution of this material, providing a glimpse of long-range contacts westward.[31] A few obsidian and flint geometric armatures of ancient tradition, associated with hunting, were still current, while larger flaked arrowheads appear with Piano Notaro pottery and are more common later (fig. 48:1-4,9-10). Even these, however, have precedents in Aeolian LN contexts. The Copper Age is also associated with the persistence of the Campignian tradition (chapter 2), the extraction of good quality Hyblaean flint from both open sites and mines, and with the appearance of nearby settlements (*villaggi-officine*) where the material was worked. Bifacial chopping tools (*tranchets* and *petits-tranchets*), probably for general clearance and agricultural work, are typical of this production (fig. 48:12-14), which generated huge quantities of debitage at certain settlements, such as San Cono. These traditions continued into the Early Bronze Age.

Much work remains to be done on ceramics, known mainly from old publications, in which unpainted wares were neglected, although they were probably in the majority, especially in domestic contexts. A gradual move away from LN red wares to darker burnished and incised ECA wares is discernible on the Aeolian islands (Spatarella phase) and in Sicily. As various styles overlapped in the Neolithic, several varieties were concurrent in the Copper Age: dark burnished ware (fig. 50:15), red and black painted or Conzo ware (fig. 50:16-17) and incised or Piano Notaro ware (fig. 50:9-11) occur in the earlier phases in southeastern Sicily. Some of the Uditore and Conca d'Oro incised wares (fig. 50:4,6-8) may also belong to

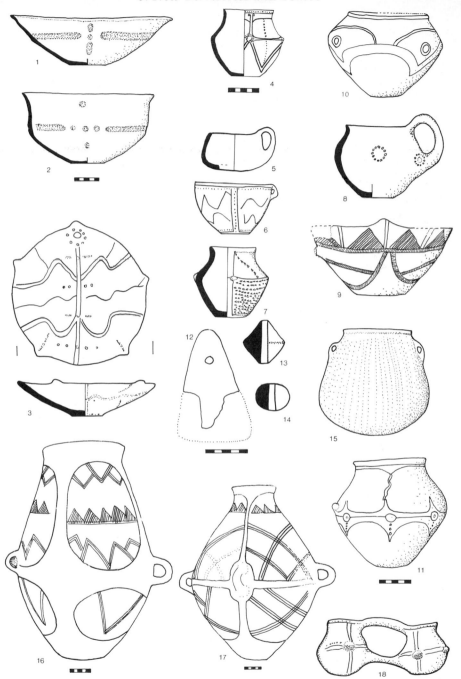

Fig. 50. Early Copper Age and Conca d'Oro pottery: (1-3) Piano Vento; (4,6-8) Uditore; (9) San Cono; (10-11) Gela; (5, 12-17) Chiusazza; (18) Valdesi

the Early Copper Age. The Piano Notaro round-bottomed bowls and open forms with incised motifs filled with red ochre or white substances and the jars with baggy bodies and narrow necks recall Neolithic traditions. Forms, techniques and standards of craftsmanship varied, from rudimentary small bowls to the large pear-shaped jars of the Conzo style.

The Serraferlicchio style of black-on-red geometric decoration (fig. 51:1,2,4-6), to which white was sometimes added, shows the persistence of painted wares in southern Sicily, which evolved through a succession of styles until the Early Bronze Age (San Ippolito-Naro-Castelluccio). Some LCA wares depart from older traditions: the Malpasso flat-bottomed cups, jugs and pedestal vases, perhaps reflect changes in cooking, eating and drinking habits, heralding those of the Early Bronze Age. Thin-walled tankards with elegant handles suggest more standardized and prestigious forms (fig. 51:11). Fine vessels were possibly trade items, although little is known about this.

The ceramic repertoire of the Copper Age also broadened to include items that mark new developments in subsistence and household economics: spindle-whorls, bobbins and loomweights, which began to appear at the end of the Neolithic, became increasingly common in subsequent periods, denoting a greater role for those secondary products, notably wool, derived from a subsistence regime in which sheep and goat were becoming more important. In the Late Copper Age appeared the first examples of pottery 'horns' set on a flat round base, which are also common in EBA-MBA domestic contexts (fig. 69:10). With no obvious practical purpose, they are usually regarded as phallic symbols, or even schematized figurines, used as domestic cult objects, although many are easily held in the hand and their flat bases might have been used to press down on some soft substance.

Parallels from the Aegean, Anatolia, Cyprus and the Near East have often been cited for Sicilian Copper Age pottery.[32] Taken singly, it may be countered that none are very significant. Mostly they reflect generic affinities between rather basic shapes of jars and jugs, or traits such as pointed handles and red burnish, while the wide diffusion of rather vague parallels in time and space increases the suspicion that some are coincidental: pointed handles are widespread in the western Mediterranean and red burnish recurs periodically almost everywhere from the Neolithic onwards. In the Late Copper and Early Bronze Ages, the similarities become slightly more frequent and specific: in particular, long-necked jugs with rounded bodies of San Ippolito and one from Gioia del Colle in Apulia may have Cypriot affinities (fig. 51:13), while clearer signs of at least sporadic contacts have been noted in connection with certain metal and bone items (below).

In seeking to explain this, it is hard to choose between movements of population, exchange or simply a low level of diffuse contacts filtered between neighbouring regions, as probably occurred during the Neolithic.

Fig. 51. Middle-Late Copper Age and Beaker pottery: (1-3) Chiusazza; (4-7) Serraferlicchio;
(8) Vecchiuzzo; (9-12) Malpasso; (13-14) San Ippolito; (15, 16, 17) Villafrati, Moarda, Segesta;
(18-19) Marcita; (20) Torrebigini; (21-23) western Sicily

The crossing of the Adriatic Sea by migrants is a possibility, although local continuity and the limited evidence available make a large-scale migration seem unlikely in the Copper Age. Trading links can be postulated at least between Sicily, Calabria and Apulia from movements of obsidian, albeit in much reduced quantity, Calabrian greenstones, amber and perhaps Alpine jadeite and metal. The movement of these materials was probably mediated by chain-like mechanisms, although more direct long-range contacts cannot be excluded and the speed of transmission was perhaps more rapid now than before.

A further problem is the lack of evidence for contacts in the Aegean. The case for some Cretan daggers being Italian imports is weak, while the presence of metals (silver, copper, tin) in Greece, Cyprus, Anatolia, and the Balkans, may have lessened the economic importance of Italy for the emergent complex societies in the Aegean or East Mediterranean.[33] Nor is there yet much sign of flourishing coastal or harbour sites in Sicily or southern Italy, which might be regarded as trading stations: the amount of material from Naxos, for example, is less than in preceding or succeeding periods. Nevertheless, it is likely that exploratory voyages were becoming more frequent, stimulated by a search for metals, other valuables and trading partners. More hierarchical social structures, progress in metallurgy, a growing appetite for exotic raw materials and fine craft products, especially in the eastern Mediterranean, may have encouraged the emergence of entrepreneurial groups, capable of undertaking maritime voyages, which anticipate more regular contacts between the Aegean and Italy from the beginning of the 2nd millennium BC.

The 'beaker connection'

There is stronger evidence for westward contacts in the mid-3rd millennium BC. Sicilian beakers mark the southeastern limit in the distribution of these distinctive vessels, which are widespread in northern and central Europe, Iberia and north-central Italy between about 2800 and 2000 cal.BC.[34] They first appear in LCA Malpasso-San Ippolito contexts, as in the Chiusazza cave, perhaps just before 2500 BC, although many of the old finds are not closely dated (fig. 51:17, 20-23). More recent discoveries show coexistence with local painted wares of the Naro style and with an EBA Castelluccio phase, at Manfria for example (below), probably prior to 2000 BC.

The distribution of Sicilian beakers is conspicuously biased towards northwestern zones (fig. 40), although further research in eastern areas might yet modify the imbalance. Nevertheless, this concentration is consistent with the broader Mediterranean distribution, encompassing the Tyrrhenian (but rarely the Adriatic) side of Italy, Sardinia, the Balearics and the Mediterranean shores of France, Spain and Morocco. It has often been supposed that Sicilian beakers derive from Spanish types, although there is no sure evidence that they represent actual imports, and since

North Italian finds have multiplied in recent years and a central European origin for the form now seems likely, the case for a direct Iberian link is not as compelling as it was. It could be that beakers spread across the southern Mediterranean through local contacts between neighbouring regions, but the lack of comparative material in northeastern Sicily, Calabria or Tunisia, if not merely due to lack of research, argues for more direct long-range maritime links. Typological comparisons are of limited help in view of the wide diffusion of different types, but there are associated elements in Sicily, including footed bowls (fig. 51:19), also found in southern Sardinia, which suggest communication between the two islands, doubtless by direct sailings across the shortest route (about 170 miles) between the Cagliari and Palermo regions.

Whether beakers imply movements of people, trade or even more diluted forms of indirect contact, is an old problem. In northern Italy, where beaker assemblages, including coarse pottery (the *begleitkeramik*), are sometimes distinguishable from indigenous contexts, the case for a population influx has been strengthened. Further south, there are concentrations of beakers in metal-rich areas, such as southern Sardinia or Tuscany, which has encouraged the idea of trade directed at areas endowed with valuable raw materials. There are no such obvious resources in western Sicily, although the putative crucible from Villafrati (above) hints at a link between beakers and metal-working in Sicily. It is noteworthy too that Sicilian beakers occur as single elements in local assemblages. Their shape and decoration was sometimes copied in a local idiom and influenced the zonal painted patterns of Naro and Partanna wares and local incised ware (of the Moarda style). Some fine painted beakers are undoubtedly local products (fig. 51:22-23). If the vessel itself was adopted as a prestigious item, connected with the fashionable diffusion of an alcoholic drink (perhaps a kind of fruity hydromel), as is sometimes maintained, then its appearance in Sicily could be seen as a result of long-distance trade that also included prestigious materials, such as jadeite axes, amber and metal goods.

However, the arrival of settlers cannot be ruled out, nor would it be incompatible with trading contacts. The association of beakers with the Belice tombs (above), which have Sardinian counterparts, is one possible indication of a population influx. A further dimension to the question, though inconclusive, is represented by the skeletal remains.[35] Studies of the cephalic index (length-breadth ratio) of skulls suggest that, prior to this time, dolicocephalic (long-headed) types were typical in Sicily. Individuals buried in the Chiusilla and Villafrati caves were primarily dolicocephalic, but also accompanied by brachycephalic (rounded) forms in the Late Copper Age, while the sample from a tomb at Stretto, associated with Naro ware, shows that brachycephalic forms were predominant (70%). These rather small and roughly dated Copper Age samples also include many variants or hybrid forms. A similar pattern occurs in Sardinia, suggesting that both islands had a population of somewhat variable

Fig. 52. Trepanned skull from Stretto

physical types at this time. On average, they were probably slightly shorter in stature than their continental counterparts. However, there is no scientific consensus regarding the significance of brachycephalization, which is sometimes thought to result from changes in lifestyle or stress. Although some authorities believe that a link with migratory movements is possible, it cannot at present be associated automatically with the arrival of 'Beaker folk'.

Among 20 or so skulls found in a Copper Age rock-cut tomb at Stretto was one of a brachymorphic adult male who had had a large bone disc (9.2 x 7.5cm) removed from the right parietal zone (fig. 52).[36] This is the first evidence from Sicily for trepanation, performed in this case on a living individual, who had survived for about a year afterwards. The cutting was probably achieved over several hours or possibly in stages over several days by a practised hand, who must have known how to stem an abundant flow of blood and avoid damaging the brain-covering membrane (*dura mater*), which would have quickly led to death. Whatever the reasons for trepanning – often surmised to have been a cure for tumours, headaches, insanity, or some aspect of a cult – it occurred sporadically throughout Europe and in Italy from the Middle Neolithic until the Bronze Age, although it was more common during the 3rd millennium BC in western Mediterranean regions, especially in Sardinia.

3. New Territories and Tombs

Early Bronze Age chronology

Although it was formerly dated from 1800-1400 BC, a longer duration has now been allocated to the period named after the site of Castelluccio, conventionally identified with the Early Bronze Age, on the basis of ^{14}C dates from La Muculufa and Monte Grande, which range from about 2500-1700 cal.BC (table 4). An extended chronology is also supported by the wide range and quantity of assemblages and sites, although the limited distribution of ^{14}C dates makes it hard to chart developments within the period and to distinguish chronological from regional patterns. A subdivision would now be desirable and it is here proposed to label the earlier phase 'BA1', from about 2500-2000 cal.BC, and the subsequent phase 'BA2', from about 2000 BC until the onset of the Middle Bronze Age around 1500 BC.[37]

Relative dates are indicated by several contexts.[38] In the Chiusazza cave, Castelluccio pottery lay between Malpasso (LCA) and Thapsos (MBA) layers (fig. 42:A). At Ramacca, a sounding revealed earlier layers with Serraferlicchio and San Ippolito (LCA) ware. At Serra del Palco, the typical EBA painted pottery in the older layers was gradually replaced by the unpainted pottery named after the northern sites of Rodì, Tindari and Vallelunga (henceforth RTV), heralding the development of MBA wares and suggesting a gradual transition. A similar development has been observed at Ciavolaro.

Cultural patterns initially resembled those of the Late Copper Age, with some persisting contrasts between southern (Castelluccio) and northern Sicily (RTV and Capo Graziano). The former is typified by rock-cut tombs and painted pottery with local traditions. There are suggestions of sporadic contacts with the eastern Mediterranean, but little evidence of regular links until the appearance of late MH (Middle Helladic) or LH I (Late Helladic) pottery, recently discovered at Monte Grande, which should allow the later BA2 stage to be synchronized with these periods of Aegean prehistory in the second quarter of the 2nd millennium BC.[39]

The Capo Graziano and RTV complexes in the Aeolian islands and northern Sicily reflect a slightly different cultural environment, closer to that of Protoapennine and Palma Campania assemblages in southern Italy. The first phase of Capo Graziano (CG1) is estimated to have begun by at least 2200 BC on the basis of affinities with EH III (Early Helladic) pottery and to have lasted for several centuries. A second phase, from roughly 1800-1430 BC, is associated with settlements in more defensive locations, which gradually evolved into the Milazzese (MBA) phase, when some new sites also appeared. There are no radiocarbon dates, although the later part of the second phase, from about 1600 BC, coincides with imported matt-painted and Late Mycenaean (LH I-IIA) ware (fig. 72).[40] Less well understood is the RTV complex in northern Sicily, known only from a few sites with plain dark and burnished wares, and now also being found at some southern Calabrian sites.

113

On Malta, the lack of continuity between the Tarxien Temple and Tarxien Cemetery phase has suggested a radical break, often associated with the arrival of immigrants, some of whose pottery was like that of Capo Graziano, although much rests on the interpretation of just three radiocarbon dates for the Cemetery phase: one (2563-2051 cal.BC) may suggest a sudden end to the temple culture within the 3rd millennium BC, while the others overlap at a later time (1732-1516 and 1683-1453 cal.BC), which would be easier to reconcile with a more gradual transition.[41] On Pantelleria, the Mursia settlement, which has parallels with Capo Graziano, was established by BA2, as implied by the earliest ^{14}C date (1683-1498 cal.BC). Overall, with the possible exception of some of the small islands, the pattern of development suggests a gradual evolution from indigenous CA traditions, represented by an early phase of the Castelluccio culture (BA1), which was most firmly rooted in southern Sicily, towards more mixed traditions with different burial rites, plain and incised pottery (BA2), which anticipate the MBA Thapsos and Milazzese complexes.

Castelluccio settlement and subsistence

Orsi's work in southeastern Sicily indicated that EBA sites were widespread and often on promontories or hills overlooking coastal plains and inland river valleys (fig. 53).[42] Systematic field survey by transects around Morgantina has shown LCA and EBA surface finds to be more numerous than those of other prehistoric periods and to occur in a variety of locations, from valleys to hill-tops. In the upper Simeto region on the western side of Etna, a pattern of settlement evolution has been postulated, characterized by numerous small sites, often less than 3km apart, in proximity with fertile soils at fairly low elevations, accompanied by a gradual increase in sites at higher altitudes (800-1100m asl), probably reflecting a mixed regime of arable farming and pastoralism. Surveys in central and western Sicily have also reported high percentages of EBA sites, frequently located on rocky promontories or slopes at higher elevations than other sites. They may be associated with light and well-drained soils, the greater potential for defence and for controlling lines of communication along valleys, and the additional attraction of upland woodlands and pastures. It used to be said that inland locations were favoured, but plenty of sites are now known along eastern and southern coasts.[43]

In fact, the patterns are hard to interpret. While they may denote an increasing population, the size and duration of sites are usually uncertain. Less than a dozen dwellings were found at Manfria and La Muculufa.[44] There were originally more at La Muculufa, but Manfria resembles a small settlement with no more than perhaps about 50 inhabitants (fig. 54:C). Larger communities can be postulated for Monte Grande, the Monti Tabuto and Racello complexes (if taken as an extended grouping) and possibly Branco Grande and Castelluccio, but estimates are hard to formu-

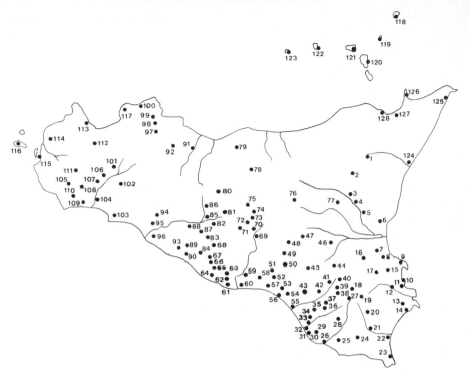

Fig. 53. *Early Bronze Age sites*: 1 G. Maniace; 2 Bronte; 3 Adrano sites; 4 Biancavilla; 5 Paternò; 6 Barriera; 7 Valsavoia; 8 Cava Cana Barbara; 9 Gisira; 10 Thapsos; 11 Predio Reale; 12 Castelluccio di Floridia; 13 G. Chiusazza; 14 Ognina; 15 Petraro di Melilli; 16 M. S. Basile; 17 Torrente Marcellino; 18 M. Casale; 19 G. Masella; 20 Castelluccio; 21 Cava Lazzaro; 22 Vendicari; 23 Calafarina; 24 Cava d'Ispica; 25 Caitina; 26 Maistro; 27 Donna Scala; 28 Ragusa; 29 S. Croce Camarina; 30 Canalotti, Torre di Pietro; 31 Branco Grande; 32 Capitina, Nipitella; 33 Alcerito Nuovo; 34 S. Croci; 35 Castiglione; 36-37 Monte Sallia, Tabuto, Racello; 38 M. Aranci, Calaforno; 39 M. Casasia; 40 Vizzini; 41 Licodia Eubea; 42 Poggio Biddini; 43 S. Pietro; 44 Palikè; 45 Caltagirone; 46 Torricella, S. Febronia; 47 Morgantina; 48 M.S. Mauro; 49 Valcanonico; 50 M. Bubbonia; 51 M. Lavania Nera; 52 Dessueri; 53 Sabuci; 54 Priolo; 55 Punta Vito; 56 S. Lucia, Mulino a Vento; 57 Manfria; 58 M. Priorato; 59 Suor Marchesa; 60 Casalicchio-Agnone; 61 M. Sole; 62 Muculufa; 63 Passarelli; 64 M. Grande; 65 Ragusetta; 66 Cignana; 67 Naro; 68 Canicattì; 69 Pietraperzia; 70 Gibil Gabib; 71 S. Cataldo; 72 S. Giuliano; 73 Sabucina; 74 Vassallaggi; 75 Cuti; 76 Assoro; 77 Centuripe; 78 Vecchiuzzo; 79 G. Chiusilla; 80 Vallelunga; 81 Marianopoli; 82 Montedoro; 83 Caldare; 84 Favara; 85 Milena; 86 Mussomeli; 87 Racalmuto; 88 S. Angelo Muxaro; 89 Serraferlicchio; 90 Agrigento; 91 Sciara; 92 Villafrati; 93 Monserrato; 94 Ciavolaro; 95 M. Sara; 96 G. Vancu; 97 Moarda; 98 G. Mastro Santo; 99 Boccadifalco; 100 Carini; 101 Pergole; 102 S. Margherita Belice; 103 Cannizzaro; 104 Serralonga; 105 Gattolo; 106 Stretto; 107 Torrebigini, S. Martino, Torre Donzelle; 108 Marcita; 109 Selinunte; 110 Torre Cusa; 111 Mokarta; 112 Segesta; 113 Uzzo; 114 G. Maiorana; 115 Motya; 116 Favignana; 117 G. Puntali; 118 Stromboli: San Vincenzo; 119 Panarea; 120 Lipari: Castello; 121 Salina: Serro dei Cianfi; 122 Filicudi: Capo Graziano; 123 Alicudi; 124 Naxos; 125 Boccetta; 126 Milazzo; 127 Rodì; 128 Tindari.

late. Specialized activities or adaptations can occasionally be inferred, such as flint-working at certain Hyblaean sites, while some larger sites perhaps had a wider range of subsistence, craft or ritual activities and were able to dominate larger territories.

New developments in monumental architecture are represented by turreted enclosure walls at certain sites, while increasingly hierarchical settlement patterns are perhaps also reflected by the larger tombs with porticoes, carved façades and antechambers, even though there is currently little corresponding evidence for any great elaboration of residential structures. Local élites do not seem to have erected such prominent buildings as those encountered in parts of the Aegean at this time. Nevertheless, certain 'proto-urban' features were developing locally before Mycenaean connections began to influence coastal sites (chapter 4). The larger and more formally structured plans of some MBA coastal sites (such as I Faraglioni and Thapsos phase 1) probably grew out of local traditions.

Subsistence strategies adapted to a variety of situations (fig. 41). The faunal sample from La Muculufa attests stock-rearing, based on sheep and goat (about 70%), pig (14%) and cattle (7%).[45] The relatively young ages of caprines point to meat consumption, although dairy products and wool were probably also important. Measurements of *tibiae* and *humeri* indicate a relatively short stature by comparison with Italian Neolithic and Bronze Age exemplars, perhaps due to rather poor local pasture. Domestic pigs were mostly killed in their second and third years. Cattle, numerically the least important and represented mainly by mature adults, were perhaps used for traction and milk products.

Elsewhere the picture differs. Cattle are better represented at some sites in eastern Sicily, such as Valsavoia, where local pastures were richer and there was a long-lived tradition of cattle rearing on the coastal plain. There is also more evidence for hunting at Fiumedinisi, due to the proximity of woodlands and forests on the slopes of Etna and the Peloritani. In coastal areas, fishing was undoubtedly important. Botanical evidence is much more limited. Plant remains from La Muculufa include oats, barley and wheats (*Avena*, *Hordeum*, *Triticum dicoccum* and *compactum*), horse-bean (*Vicia faba*), fruits (*Prunus*), mustard (*Sinapsis*), wild plants such as camomile and marigold (*Anthemis* and *Calendula*) and weeds associated with cereal cultivation (*Lithospermum*).

Site structures

In 1896, the first EBA hut was excavated on the promontory at Monte Racello: a rounded structure, about 3m across with a partly sunken floor and stone wall foundations flanked by a low internal bench. Two miles away, on a spur of the Sante Croci hill, traces of about 10 elliptical huts (Ø 6-7.5m) were identified, containing hearths, large storage vessels, painted pottery, grinding stones, flint and bone tools, spindle-whorls and terra-

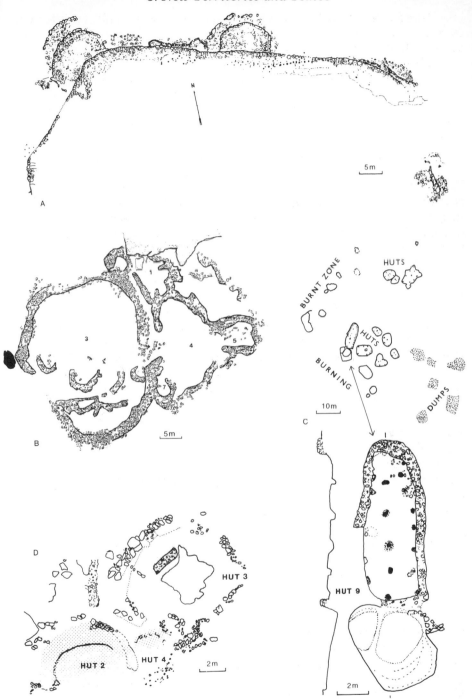

Fig. 54. Settlement structures: (A) Petraro; (B) Monte Grande; (C) Manfria; (D) La Muculufa

cotta horns. Elliptical huts with stone foundations were also found at Monte Casale (Giarratana) and Monte San Basile (Scordia).

Other EBA sites have been the subject of limited excavation.[46] For example, two settlement locations are recorded, nearly 700m apart, on the Serra Orlando ridge at Morgantina, consisting of quadrangular or oval huts with stone wall foundations, pits, ground and flaked stone tools, terracotta horns, bone points, spindle-whorls and bobbins. At Fogliuta (Adrano), a stone-lined pit and stone pavement were found in the space between three huts, one of which was a large elliptical building (Ø 15.5m) of neatly constructed stone walls, laid partly in a fish-bone pattern, with a floor of compacted sherds and pebbles, and three central post-holes. A kind of foundation offering may be represented by a deposit of miniature vessels set into the floor. A large circular hut (Ø about 8m) is known at Le Salinelle and part of an EBA settlement with circular huts and a large stone-lined storage pit or cistern was revealed beneath Iron Age houses on the plateau of Castiglione, 7km north of Ragusa, associated with chamber tombs on nearby slopes (below). A few miles away at Poggio Biddini, on a flat-topped hill overlooking the Dirillo, several huts with timber-laced walls have been discovered, as well as an oven, outdoor pits, bell-shaped silos or wells cut into the rock, an abundance of pottery, including large storage jars, lithic equipment, debitage from flint-working and animal bones of domestic and wild species (sheep/goat, pig, cattle, dog, deer, fox and wild cat).

A more extensive excavation in 1960 on a gentle slope beside the coast at Manfria, where Orsi had found groups of rock-cut tombs, 10km west of Gela, revealed two clusters of respectively three and six huts about 20m apart, surrounded by deposits of ashy soil, pottery, stone tools and animal bones over an area of about 60 x 45m (fig. 54:C).[47] Described as refuse tips, the latter may represent the remains of outdoor activities, such as flint-working, food preparation and perhaps pottery kilns. Stylistic affinities with LCA painted wares and the presence of a beaker suggest an early (BA1) date. The huts were mainly elliptical (Ø 3.75-5m), with one central and 4-5 perimeter post-holes, and a sunken floor covered with a plastered surface made from mixed calcite and sand. These forms and techniques of construction recurred subsequently throughout the Bronze Age. Two larger structures may have had different functions, perhaps as communal buildings or special residences: one (hut 7) contained a quantity of animal bones and another was a long building (hut 9: 3.25 x 9m) with central and perimeter posts, surrounded by a stone wall and flanked by a large kiln or oven (fig. 55).

A large coastal settlement was found by Orsi at Branco Grande, near Camarina, on a low spur on the sandy shore, where a substantial wall (W 2.5m, H 2m) of local beach stones was traced for about 100m along the southern edge of the site, which was thought to cover a hectare and consist of up to 30 or 40 huts (perhaps an over-estimate). Only a handful were

Fig. 55. Manfria hut 9 (L 9m)

excavated: elliptical structures (Ø 3.7-4.2m) with stone wall foundations, hearths, wood and daub superstructures, abundant pottery and flint implements. The lack of painted pottery and the analogies with the defensive wall at Mursia (below) might suggest a relatively late date (BA2).

Other coastal sites are little known.[48] Soundings at Ognina (chapter 2) revealed a mixture of plain and decorated pottery in both the Castelluccio and Capo Graziano styles, but little evidence for structures. At Thapsos (chapter 4), a curved wall nearly 200m long, with six semicircular bastions protruding on the seaward face, presumably guarded a village on its western side, which has yet to be revealed (fig. 75: fortification 2). Part of a similar construction was encountered at Naxos. A few miles to the north, the site of Timpa Dieri (Petraro di Melilli), first occupied in the Neolithic, was protected on one side by a steep bank of the Molinello river and on the other by a wall (1.5m wide) made of roughly quadrangular facing blocks, buttressed with two semicircular towers (fig. 54:A).

More sites with robust enclosure walls have come to light in recent years.[49] At Torricella, on the saddle of the Ramacca hill in the Catania plain, a curved drystone wall about 2m wide, was traced for 17m. Partly covering some earlier rounded huts, it was added in a second phase of occupation, possibly as a kind of enclosure rather than a fortification *sensu stricto*. Similar tracts of neatly built stone walls at Valsavoia indicate that this settlement consisted of two or more 'compounds', probably enclosing areas of 30m or more in diameter, with floor surfaces on the interior and exterior. The huts were largely of timber, wattle and daub. The settlement

119

extended over an area of at least 200 x 180m on a gentle slope beside a rocky outcrop in which Orsi found 43 rock-cut chamber-tombs, including several with multiple EBA burials. Numerous EBA sites and cemeteries (below) were placed on natural vantage points on the steep sides of the Cava d'Ispica, a picturesque canyon near Ragusa. One of these sites, Baravitalla, also had an enclosure wall with adjacent hut floors and hearths, attesting two occupation phases. The settlement at Santa Febronia was located on the promontory above the chamber tombs and may have covered three hectares, comprising round huts (Ø 4.8m) with stone foundations and an internal bench, perhaps delimited by an enclosure wall.

The appearance of enclosure walls invites comparisons with developments elsewhere in the Mediterranean between the 3rd and 2nd millennium BC, especially in Apulia, where substantial walls of several coastal sites are now dated in the early 2nd millennium BC (Protoapennine B).[50] This is sometimes explained in terms of local rivalries generated by population pressures or the desire to control prestigious resources and trade, although there are differences in the form and complexity of the Sicilian sites. Their function was probably not always defensive. Enclosure sites with residential and defensive features also occur elsewhere in the western Mediterranean at this time.[51]

For example, a series of enclosures has been found on the summit (260m asl) and on a gently sloping platform (200m asl) at Monte Grande, a limestone hill on the coast between Agrigento and Licata (fig. 54:B).[52] The main feature of the lower platform was a roughly oval precinct (no. 3: Ø 20 x 38m) made of large field stones, entered from the west and containing traces of floor-levels, terracotta hearths and hut walls (although some pre-date its construction). The eastern side gave access to a smaller adjacent precinct (no. 4) with two recesses (nos. 5 and 7), perhaps dwellings or working areas. Here too, terracotta hearths and floor-levels were found. A smaller enclosure (no. 1: Ø 14m) with recesses and a small circular room to the north could be reached by a narrow passage. More puzzling is a parallel alignment of large stones, like a trackway, leading to the top of the hill where it meets another curved enclosure wall.

The monumental layout and the presence of clay horns and figurines have led the excavator to postulate a sanctuary, used for special gatherings. However, there is also ample evidence for domestic activities from a range of typical EBA material: terracotta hearths, animal bones, millstones, large storage vessels, fine painted pottery, ground and flaked stone tools, spindle-whorls and loomweights. This may have been a residential site of compounds enclosing huts or shelters as well as open areas, perhaps for corralling livestock. Some ritual activities, such as feasting (below) or forms of worship could also have occurred. The presence of clay horns, figurines, some unusual models, possibly of huts (fig. 69:7), need not be surprising in a society where the sacred and the secular were not strictly divided. A more convincing case for a specifically ritual zone or a shrine might yet be made for the upper precinct (the so-called acropolis sanctuary, set above CA levels). However, the growing number of enclosure sites coming to light in earlier and later periods (such as Rinollo and Madre Chiesa) warns against according them all ritual or sanctuary status.

Sanctuaries have also been claimed at other sites. One is the flat plateau beneath the summit of Monte San Giuliano near Caltanissetta, where only fragmentary EBA floor surfaces survive beneath the Iron Age settlement, along with painted and plain RTV wares.[53] In one restricted area were found 22 figurines, suggesting a votive deposit (fig. 69:1-3; and below) or a focus of cult activity within a larger multi-functional site.

More information is available about La Muculufa, where a picturesque Miocene formation of limestone crags dominates the left bank of the Salso, 14km inland from Licata.[54] Excavations have revealed about 150 chamber tombs, crevice burials (below) and several circular huts, set on the terraced upper slopes (fig. 54:D). The walls had stone foundations, often flanked by a bench and a hard clayish floor on the interior, while the superstructure incorporated wattle matting, revealed by impressions of twigs, branches and wooden poles on chunks of straw-tempered daub, used for insulation and perhaps also for a decorative finishing touch. One hut had a contiguous outdoor working area with a millstone *in situ* and traces of exterior pathways and surfaces paved with small stones.

A few hundred yards away, on a scenic platform between vertical rocks at the edge of the crest, was the 'sanctuary', where a terrace wall was partly covered by deposits with a large quantity of pottery, lithic implements and small artefacts (including spindle-whorls), organic material, animal bones (notably of lamb and kid) and a human jaw bone. Within this area, traces of hearths were also found, suggesting that meals were prepared and consumed on the spot. Some of the finds also point to a special function: the proportion of painted wares is higher and the faunal remains include younger caprines than in the hut area. Special activities must have occurred here: the pottery, animal bones and hearths might suggest feasting or outdoor barbecues. Another possibility is a votive deposit. However, it requires a rather greater leap of the imagination to conclude that this was the centre of political and religious alliances for the whole region, a kind of prehistoric Delphi, as the excavators would have it.[55]

Funerary landscapes

Rock-cut tombs are the best known form of EBA burial, although depositions in caves, rock cavities and flint-mine galleries are recorded as well as stone cist graves, 'dolmen-like' structures and jar burials (figs. 56-61). Chamber tombs tend to cluster around the upper slopes of a promontory, hillside or rocky scarp, close to the settlement, and often command a view of a valley or plain. These were not modest tombs of convenience, but conspicuous ancestral monuments in a funerary landscape, possibly

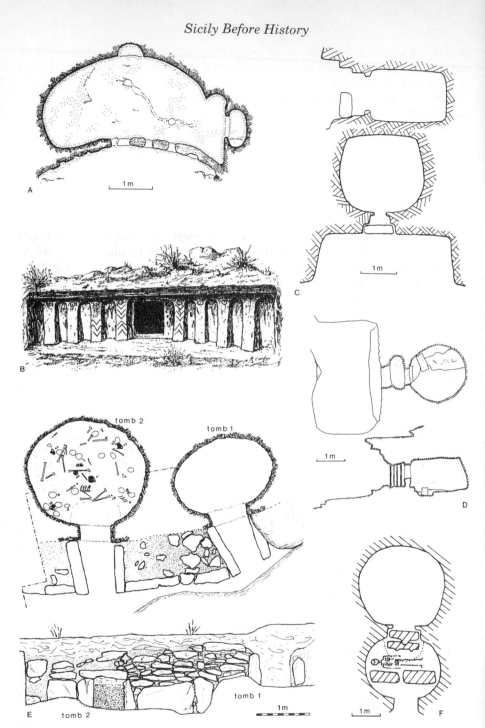

Fig. 56. Early Bronze Age tombs: (A-B) Cava Lazzaro; (C,F) Castelluccio; (D) Santa Febronia; (E) Paolina

affirming kinship ties, rights of residence and territorial control. They vary from small clusters to groups of over a hundred chambers, probably used over generations.

Most common in southern Sicily are rounded or roughly elliptical chambers with curved or flattened ceilings. They range from cramped cells in which one can barely crouch (Ø 1.20m, H 80cm) to more spacious rooms (Ø 2-3m, H 1-1.30m), entered through small rectangular doorways closed by a slab, a wall of masonry and rubble, or a combination of both. Quadrangular chambers (Ø around 1.75m) are slightly less common. The door slabs are usually plain, although several examples with carved figurative designs or bosses are known from Castelluccio (t.22,23,31,32,34), including two famous examples with anthropomorphic spiral motifs, one of which, at face value, is overtly sexual, although more complex issues of protection or regeneration may be implied (Figs. 59:A; 60). Spirals seem to have been widely associated in the western Mediterranean with funerary or metaphysical concerns.[56]

The main chamber was sometimes preceded by a small antechamber and a narrow entrance passage. More unusual features may include: a shallow rectangular hollow on the floor, sometimes holding a skeleton, or a circular shaft of uncertain function; a slightly raised platform resembling a funerary bed; and a semicircular or elliptical niche in the wall, also holding skeletons. Aside from more canonical designs are various irregularly shaped or very small chambers, possibly altered in the course of cutting due to inconsistencies in the natural rock.

An unusually large chamber at Ognina with a ceiling shaft and a very long corridor (4.2m) might also date to this period.[57] In a more common and elaborate version, the chamber was preceded by an open elliptical or quadrangular forecourt, several metres in diameter, also cut out of the rock, one side of which consisted of a curved or straight façade with the tomb door at its centre.[58] An expanded forecourt could also serve more than one tomb. At Santa Febronia, little steps led into these forecourts, which sometimes had a bench or other masonry structures, broken pottery (below) and a series of carved parallel grooves, resembling semi-columns, on the façade at either side of the tomb door (fig. 56:D). Chambers with façades up to 6m wide embellished in like manner are known in the Cava d'Ispica and in the nearby Cava Lazzaro (Modica). One of these had a symmetrical façade of semi-columns with engraved chevrons and circles, while another had pilasters and niches cut into the wall inside the chamber (fig. 56:A,B). An unusually grand example was provided with square rock-cut pillars, also encountered at Castelluccio, where they formed a porticoed vestibule (fig. 57). The elaboration of forecourts and façades, or the public aspect of these tombs, rather than the internal chambers which are often of fairly standard size, suggests the importance of external ceremonies for the living community; particularly, one suspects, on the occasion of re-opening in order to admit new burials.

Elaborate carvings and architectural motifs, including pillars, occur in

Fig. 57. Castelluccio tomb with pilaster vestibule (H pilasters about 130cm)

Fig. 58. Paolina tomb façade

other west Mediterranean rock-cut tombs, such as the *domus de janas* chambers of Sardinia, which have certain affinities with the Sicilian tombs just described. Architectural additions in the form of a short corridor or masonry doorway with covering slabs occur at Paolina, Castiglione, Biddini and Sante Croci in the Ragusa province. The entrances to two rock-cut chambers at Paolina consisted of large slabs joined to a dry-stone wall, presenting a masonry façade at least 13m long to the observer (figs. 56:E;

58). Doorways carved from single blocks were also found at Monte Sallia. The use of masonry most likely derives from the LCA tombs of the Belice group (above), although a local adaptation of megalithic traditions from the western Mediterranean cannot be ruled out. Continuing links with Sardinia could be claimed on the basis of the spiraliform motifs found on Castelluccio door-slabs and in some Sardinian tombs, such as Corongiu.[59] This may be another case of certain cult symbols being common to a wider Mediterranean province.

On flatter ground not far from EBA chamber tombs at Monte Racello, Orsi found two cist burials (Ø 1-2m) made of upright stone slabs, one of which had a U-shaped cutting and contained a single inhumation with a few undiagnostic sherds, perhaps originally covered by an earth mound (fig. 59:B).[60] Bone fragments and a flint scraper were found in the second cist tomb. If these burials were contemporary with the rock-cut chambers, which is not certain, they could be regarded as a survival of the old Neolithic and ECA custom of single burial, which is attested in various regional forms throughout the western Mediterranean, notably in Corsica, Sardinia, southern Italy as well as in Sicily. Their significance at this time is hard to assess, but might suggest individuals with a special status: another sign of the growing complexity and variability of EBA society.

The list of unusual built tombs should also include those from the Etna region recorded by Orsi inside a lava cavern at Biancavilla, consisting of circular shafts (Ø 1-1.50m, up to 1.80m deep) lined with stone blocks and probably covered by stone slabs, containing fragments of human bone and pottery.[61] Similar burials are known from the Grotta Maccarone, one of which held remains of a single inhumation with a metal axe, a stone pendant and five vases, while another had bones probably of one disarticulated individual, fragments of a sheet-metal cup (fig. 70:11), glass-paste beads and at least six pottery vessels. These single burials, perhaps reserved for individuals of high status, may represent a local development with antecedents in the Copper Age rock-cut shaft tombs.

In recent years, more examples of built or dolmen-like tombs have come to light.[62] A photograph of one near Petraro, taken just prior to its destruction, shows a large horizontal capstone supported by smaller stones. Although not associated with any artefacts, this structure more closely resembles Maltese dolmens, some of which are associated with EBA Tarxien Cemetery pottery. A slightly different type was recorded at Cava dei Servi, where a circular arrangement of six orthostats (1m high), forming a chamber (Ø 2m), contained disarticulated fragments of human crania and long bones (fig. 59:C). One or two further slabs may suggest that the roof was domed or covered. A sketch was made in 1926 of a similar structure at Polizzello, consisting of uprights, 1.10m high, enclosing a semicircular area in which a quantity of human bone had been deposited. Once again, it is unclear whether these structures were originally covered by a mound and there is no closely associated dating evidence, although Castelluccio pottery was reported in the vicinity of both monuments.

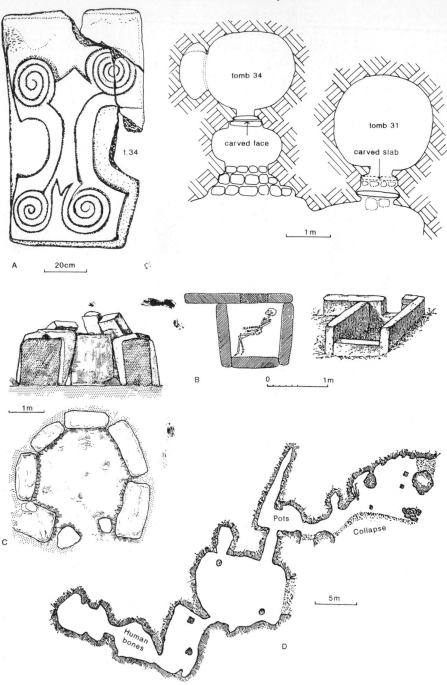

Fig. 59. (A) Castelluccio tomb 34 door slab and tombs; (B) Monte Racello cist tomb; (C) Cava dei Servi 'dolmen'; (D) Monte Tabuto flint mine

Fig. 60. Castelluccio tomb 31 door slab, H 1m

Dolmens are uncommon in Italy except in the Otranto area of Apulia, while more numerous parallels occur in Sardinia, Corsica, North Africa and Malta.[63] Like the Belice tombs (above), they raise difficult questions about the diffusion of megalithic burial monuments, aggravated by uncer-

127

tainties about chronology, variable designs and wide distributions. There are some indications that the more southerly European examples (in Apulia and Malta) are relatively late in date (late 3rd – early 2nd millennium BC) and lack local precedents of the 4th or early 3rd millennium BC, although this does not mean that they were all contemporary and later than their western European counterparts. However, only the latter can easily claim derivation from local traditions of megalithic burials. If a process of diffusion is postulated, therefore, it should be from west to east.

In the case of Sicily, this idea may draw some support from the appearance of beaker pottery and other LCA-EBA western links, notably with Sardinia (above). Geographical proximity might also suggest a link with the numerous but somewhat neglected Tunisian monuments, which are not closely dated. It has often been assumed that the Tunisian and Maltese examples derive from Apulia, although the latter has relatively few such monuments and is peripheral to their main distribution. In theory, the Sicilian, Maltese and Apulian examples could equally be seen in terms of a North African source of inspiration.[64] It is also questionable what kind of contacts, if any, need be sought in order to account for the spread of graves built of stone masonry: independent developments are possible or no more than a diffusion of ideas, without any influx of population. The small number of these monuments in Sicily, where they seem to be integrated within the local EBA cultural context of the southeastern region, warns against exaggerating their importance or reviving the old idea of itinerant megalith builders.

Natural caves and rock crevices were sometimes used for burial, although many of the large *caverne funerarie* described by Orsi at Monte Racello and Monte Sallia had been amplified by rock-cutting. At Sante Croci, recesses containing burials in various branches of a cave had been sealed by slabs, a practice with Copper Age precedents. Massed burials and one or two individual depositions were found in some of the flint mines at Monte Tabuto, evidently exploited as tombs once mining had ceased (fig. 59:D). Natural crevices at Ciavolaro and La Muculufa were also used as burial chambers. At Ciavolaro, a deposit outdoors near the crevice consisted of hundreds of vases, which may have accumulated as offerings.[65] In the cemetery at La Muculufa, there are indications of selective burning of human bones, provided with offerings that included bones of cattle, caprines, pig and deer. This may represent a first step towards cremation proper. Urn burials occur on Lipari and Malta at this time and there are grounds for believing that cremation urns were associated with some Apulian and Maltese dolmens.[66] More difficult to assess is the unpublished discovery of two skulls, of uncertain date, found underneath the floor of an EBA hut at Biddini (above).

Evidence for inhumation in large jars is scarcer, but growing. Three such burials are all that is known of a cemetery on the sandy shore beneath a Greek shrine at Naxos: single adult inhumations were found in one large jar (t.3) and in two jars placed mouth-to-mouth (t.1), possibly beneath a

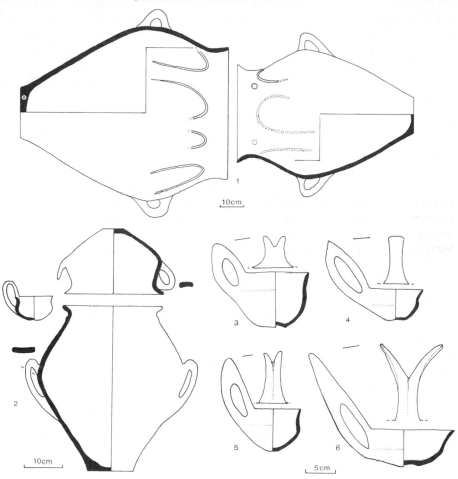

Fig. 61. (1) Naxos jar burial 1; (2) Naxos jar burial 2; (3-6) RTV style cups from Ciavolaro

mound of stones, while the milk teeth of a child were found in a smaller jar (t.2) covered by a bowl and accompanied by a dipper (fig. 61). Also difficult to date are a series of *pithos* burials (for adults) and smaller jars (for children) recently excavated at Milazzo and Messina, attributed to the RTV complex (perhaps BA2), although a MBA date is hard to rule out. This rite was recurrent in the Late Bronze and Early Iron Ages, although its origins are uncertain. Some authors regard it as a sign of settlers or cultural influences from Greece or even Anatolia, but since little is known about LCA burials and *pithoi* were already used in Copper Age cemeteries, the possibility of local development remains.[67] The overall variety and mixture of burial practices could easily be a result of local adaptations and social, rather than ethnic, distinctions.

129

Burial rites

Although a good deal of information exists, the fact that most rock-cut tombs were re-used or looted *ab antiquo* inhibits a detailed understanding of burial rites, which would benefit from more careful modern excavations. Tombs with collapsed ceilings or doorways concealed by a landslip often preserved the clearest picture of the internal arrangements, showing that the number and condition of skeletons could vary considerably. Nevertheless, skull counts often result in an under-estimate. In a few cases, Orsi recorded no more than 1-3 occupants per chamber, but more often 15-25 individuals and sometimes many more: there were over 50 in Monte Racello t.1 and Paolina t.2. One or two skeletons, probably the last depositions, were sometimes found in a crouched position in the centre of the chamber, while other skulls and disarticulated bones were scattered around the perimeter. In Castelluccio t.9, the skulls had been arranged on little mounds of bone. Water infiltration sometimes created a concretion of calcareous and ossiferous material up to 50cm deep. One such deposit in a large cave tomb (no. 9) at Monte Sallia was estimated to contain more than 150 individuals.

As in the Copper Age, therefore, burials seem to have been added over time, requiring alterations to make space for new arrivals. It would have been impossible to put more than one or two corpses simultaneously into small chambers. Orsi gained the impression that the grave goods of earlier burials had often been moved or broken by later depositions. It is also possible that some tombs served as ossuaries or places of secondary burial into which just a selection of bones were placed. The forecourts could also contain burials: in Castelluccio t.9, 22 and Cava Secchiera t.14, inhumations with grave goods had been laid out beside the tomb door; perhaps these were relatives or retainers of those inside, as Orsi suggested (fig. 56:F). In other cases, like S. Febronia, the cups, pedestal bowls and stone benches found in the forecourt have suggested offerings in a place that was used for a ceremony, perhaps a kind of wake.[68]

With the exception of the still little-known Etna shaft tombs, described above, in which the presence of individuals with metal items and small luxuries may suggest special status, an assessment of the chamber-tomb burials in social terms is obviously handicapped by the lack of specific associations between individuals and grave goods. The hypothesis of status differences rests largely upon contrasts in the scale and elaboration of certain tombs. Monumentality and greater labour requirements set some of them apart, although there are also signs that the latter had more grave goods: for example, Castelluccio t.9 and 22 were well furnished and Santa Febronia t.5 contained a dagger. These were perhaps the tombs of important groups or families. By contrast, smaller tombs and those of ill-defined shape tended to have fewer artefacts. At Monte Sallia, some of the larger grotto tombs with high numbers of skeletons contained little else.

3. New Territories and Tombs

In the rock-cut tombs, the grave goods consisted mainly of small personal items, such as beads and pendants of stone, bone, horn, boar tusk, shell, or copper; tools or implements, such as flint knives and stone axes; and pottery. Less common were obsidian blades, basaltic grinding stones and small metal objects (triangular daggers, points, ornaments, tweezers, possibly razors, wire, coil and sheet fragments). One bossed bone plaque (below) was found under a skull, and occasional finds of shark's tooth pendants, antler, tortoise shells, a bone spatula and pommel, pumice abraders and terracotta horns are recorded. The pottery rarely comprised more than six or seven vessels of painted wares (drinking cups and pedestal plates) and plain forms, sometimes used to hold food offerings, as attested by animal bones. Occasionally a large vessel was found near the tomb door. Personal ornaments and pottery were sometimes near the head, while long flint blades in the Castelluccio tombs were often beside or on top of the skulls. Rather than overt statements of personal wealth, these materials seem to reflect funerary conventions and perhaps only a subtle form of status symbolism. The pots may not represent individual possessions at all, although the numbers of ornaments and metal items exceed those normally found in domestic contexts.

Information about age, gender and physical characteristics is limited. Orsi believed that children and adults were often in the same chamber, as well as animal bones. A small family was suggested in some cases, but larger groupings or generations often seemed more likely, while clusters of tombs, such as those sharing the same forecourt, hint at special relationships or kinship ties. Recent anthropological studies are more illuminating.[69] Remains of 24 individuals from a crevice burial at La Muculufa comprised 12 adult males of young, mature and advanced ages, at least two of whom were tall (about 1.68m); six adult females of young and mature age; and six children (2-10 years old).

A larger sample comes from Castiglione, comprising disarticulated remains of at least 175 individuals from just seven tombs, holding between six and 48 skeletons (tables 2-3). A wide age range and a more balanced mixture of adult males and females were present. The mortality rates, highest between 20 and 40 years, but extending in several cases to around 50 years, are roughly consistent with other later sites and point to greater longevity by comparison with the Piano Vento sample. All tombs had one or two infant or child inhumations, but two in particular had high numbers of juveniles. Although the statistics are too few to allow certainty, it may be that age was a factor in tomb allocation. Medium-tall statures with considerable variation in the height of adult males and somewhat reduced sexual dimorphism were noted. Cranial features showed some similarities between individuals in the same tombs that might hint at genetic affinities, although the main impression was of a rather heterogeneous group. Dolicocephalic skull types predominated, but there were also brachycephalic and many intermediary forms. The adults were mostly robust

131

with signs of good musculature and teeth, although one case of vertebral deformity was found, along with occasional arthritis.

The Aeolian islands, northern Sicily and Pantelleria

In the Aeolian archipelago this was a time of expansion. New sites appeared in every island except Vulcano, initially on coastal plains (Piano del Porto, contrada Fucile, Calcara, Rinella, Diana), and subsequently on the Lipari acropolis, Serro dei Cianfi (Salina), San Vincenzo (Stromboli) and Capo Graziano (Filicudi), after which the cultural assemblage is named. The move to higher ground in a second phase is thought to reflect growing insecurity and a need for defence, although few contexts are

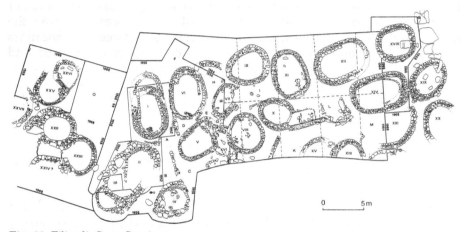

Fig. 62. Filicudi, Capo Graziano

Fig. 63. Filicudi, Capo Graziano hut

closely dated and neither San Vincenzo nor Serro dei Cianfi are naturally well defended.[70] The first phase is best represented at Piano del Porto (Filicudi) by a scatter of sherds around the bay and five huts, constructed of local beach stones and sometimes provided with little courtyards. Elsewhere, few buildings are known, although the contrada Fucile settlement on the outlying island of Alicudi was probably similar. By contrast, a dozen stone-lined pits at Calcara (Panarea) have suggested cult activity associated with the fumaroles, as in the Neolithic (chapter 2).

The second-phase settlement on Filicudi lies on a shelf (100m asl) on the western slope of Montagnola, but possibly extended over some higher terraces and the summit where one hut was found. Nearly 30 small elliptical stone huts have been excavated with sunken floors, outdoor hearths and rather plain pottery (figs. 62-64). An open space outdoors (17 x 7m) was paved with potsherds and small stones. Scattered over the nearby hillside and placed within natural crevices between the boulders of ancient rock-falls were sixteen separate deposits of small cups and bowls (e.g. fig. 64:21-22, 24-26), originally covered by stones. These were all that remained, due to the acidic soil, of what seem to have been inhumation burials, adapted to the peculiarities of the local volcanic terrain. Another group of small vessels in a similar position and some fragments of bone were found on the Lipari acropolis.[71]

Today, Filicudi seems a rather remote and rugged island. Unlike Lipari, it is not noted for any natural resources and it has little good drinking water. In early historical times, it was used mainly as pasturage by other islanders. However, conditions must have been easier in the Bronze Age when the inhabitants combined crop-growing, animal husbandry, fishing and shellfish collection. The soils of the narrow coastal belt are reasonably fertile and sheltered, and the nearby hillsides were perhaps terraced for cultivation, as in recent times. There is plenty of rough grazing for sheep and goat, which predominate in the faunal sample, although cattle and pig are also attested as well as marine molluscs and the odd deer and bird bone (fig. 41). Certain items had to be brought from other islands: obsidian blades and some pottery indicate Lipari as the main source. However, the use of native volcanic grits in much of the pottery implies local manufacture, albeit using imported clay. The later presence of Mycenaean sherds at the site (fig. 72) also suggests a redistribution of material from Lipari.

All the Aeolian sites have special characteristics, adapted to local conditions. On Stromboli, the huts occupied terraces near the shore at San Vincenzo and consisted of oval dwellings and smaller annexes, beside open activity areas where mortars and grinders were used. As on Filicudi, clay had to be imported. Some vases seem to have been made on Lipari, while others resemble Italian Apennine wares and perhaps came from Calabria. Lipari was able to support at least one large village in the harbour area as well as smaller hillside settlements, such as Castellaro and contrada Monte. The settlement in the Diana plain may have been the earliest, although the only recognizable structures are two quadrangular dwellings

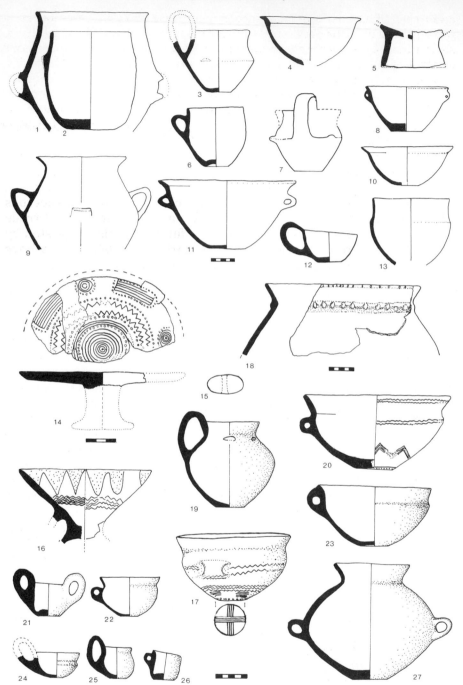

Fig. 64. Capo Graziano pottery: (1-13) Pignataro di Fuori, Lipari; (14-17) Lipari castello; (18-27) Filicudi, Capo Graziano

and about 30 tombs, providing evidence for cremation. The jars or urns were placed on their sides with a slab covering the mouth, sometimes surrounded by stones and accompanied by one or two small cups and bowls. A similar rite is documented at the Tarxien cemetery on Malta.[72]

Well over a hundred people could have lived on the Lipari acropolis where more than 20 oval huts (Ø 2.5-4.5m) were excavated in a relatively small area (fig. 81). One larger structure (dIV: 10.3 x 5m), set within an enclosure wall, stands out: it contained a range of pottery as well as numerous miniature vessels, which has encouraged the idea of a central cult building or shrine. Another unusual feature of the site was a large stone-lined pit, possibly a communal grain silo or a cistern (fig. 81:d1). The local potters stored imported clay in large pits and produced a wider range of vessels than their neighbours. Lipari was obviously a more prosperous island with more extensive trading contacts and the hub for local trade within the archipelago, as it is today. This function is also suggested by the EBA pottery recovered by divers in the harbour (fig. 64:1-13), perhaps the remains of a cargo destined for another island, although nothing remains of the boat in question.[73] Formerly prominent as a major source of obsidian, Lipari was now able to profit more from its location as a useful port of call in the lower Tyrrhenian Sea, as implied by the presence of Late Helladic pottery (fig. 72).

A new enthusiasm for island life is also reflected by the Bronze Age settlement of Mursia on Pantelleria, which is much further out to sea, beyond the normal range of vision from Sicily, and by the first phase of settlement at I Faraglioni on the island of Ustica.[74] Twice the size of Lipari, Pantelleria has evidence for what must have been a typical small-island subsistence regime: stock-rearing (mainly sheep and goat, followed by cattle and swine), fishing, crop-growing (the actual cultigens are unknown), shellfish-gathering and hunting of wild birds. The site occupied a natural terraced platform above the western shore, with a convenient docking place below, a spring and good, if rather dry, volcanic soils nearby (fig. 79:C). This already strong position was reinforced on the landward side by a formidable perimeter wall, 200m long, 7m high and 10m wide at the base, enclosing a large village area. About a dozen huts were excavated between 1966 and 1971, the first modern campaign since Orsi's work in 1894. Roughly elliptical structures, 5-9m long, sometimes subdivided,

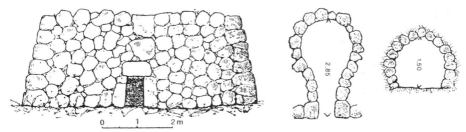

Fig. 65. Pantelleria sese

135

Fig. 66. Pantelleria sese entrance

their main features are solid walls of volcanic stones, occasionally bonded with clay, sunken paving slabs or hard earth floors, stone cists and terracotta hearths. They contained plain dark storage and cooking pots, mortars, grinders, millstones, obsidian tools, animal bones and simple domestic implements. Despite the obvious reliance on local materials, a few stone implements, copper and bronze fragments, and possibly some of the clay for pottery, were imported.

The superposition of structures and floor-levels suggests three occupation phases, interrupted by at least one destructive episode. Radiocarbon dates (from about 1700 to 1100 BC) and pottery types indicate an initial parallel development with the BA2 or RTV period in Sicily, Capo Graziano in the Aeolian islands and the Tarxien Cemetery phase on Malta, followed by MBA occupation and abandonment in the Late Bronze Age (chapter 4). However, many questions remain unsolved. The site may have been founded by settlers from Sicily although, with the exception of Ognina and perhaps Branco Grande, the assemblage has more in common with Malta,

136

the Aeolian islands and Ustica. The enclosure wall, though not closely dated, may suggest a need for defence, perhaps against an external threat emanating from Sicily, or even from Tunisia; unless it was an essentially symbolic artefact, proclaiming power and prestige, rather than practical concerns.

This was perhaps a rather self-reliant inward-looking community, not particularly interested in trade, an impression encouraged by the most distinctive prehistoric monuments of Pantelleria: the stone cairns of large volcanic blocks, called *Sesi*, first investigated by Orsi, who recorded 58 of them in the environs of Mursia. In a few cases, they contained scanty remains of inhumation burials and artefacts, suggesting use as tombs and coexistence with the Bronze Age village. They have an elliptical plan in the form of a truncated cone, up to about 3.5m in height and from 5-12m in diameter, enclosing chambers with corbelled ceilings, reached by a narrow corridor (figs. 65-66). The volcanic bedrock no doubt discouraged the creation of rock-cut chambers. Most prominent is the *Sese Grande*, nearly 7m high, with a domed roof on a large stepped base containing 11 chambers, which Orsi thought must have been the show-piece or mausoleum of local chiefs. In fact, little is known about these structures. Despite affinities with other Bronze Age buildings in western islands (such as Balearic *navetas*), comparisons only serve to highlight differences in form and function and to remind one of the potential of relatively small and autonomous Bronze Age societies to develop distinctive stone monuments of their own.

Malta at this time (Tarxien Cemetery phase) also presents analogies with Capo Graziano and RTV complexes and an influx of population has been postulated to account for the appearance of cremation, the use of monochrome incised ware and the demise of the remarkable local traditions associated with the temple culture. The precise source of any immigrants is still not obvious, although the appearance of dolmens in the island had suggested South Italy. However, the discovery of Sicilian dolmens and coastal sites, such as Ognina, where similar monochrome and incised pottery occurs, strengthens the hypothesis that any settlers came, or included groups, from southern Sicily.[75] Whether this took the form of a sudden mass invasion or a gradual influx into an island already underpopulated or in decline for other reasons remains unclear, as noted above. From this time onward, however, cultural evolution in Malta stayed more closely in step with Sicily.

Why did these scattered island groups have more in common with each other than with the Castelluccio culture in Sicily? Part of the reason may be chronological. They belong mainly to a 2nd-millennium (BA2) phase, when painted Castelluccio pottery was becoming less common and being replaced by monochrome (RTV) wares, even in southern Sicily, for example at Ciavolaro, Serra del Palco, Branco Grande and Ognina. Moreover, the LCA tradition of rock-cut tombs was not so easily adapted to the geological conditions of northeastern Sicily, where rock-cut cemeteries seem to be rarer and smaller, or to the small islands, where they are often entirely absent.

Bernabò Brea has argued that the Aeolian Capo Graziano communities arrived as immigrants from Greece and were initially quite distinct from their counterparts in Sicily and South Italy.[76] Some generic and more specific parallels between Capo Graziano and Early Helladic pottery as well as other aspects of the assemblage have been noted. However, it is also apparent that Aeolian groups were not so different from their contemporaries in northern Sicily and in southern Tyrrhenian Italy (represented respectively by the RTV and Palma Campania complexes). The idea of a mass migration seems to derive largely from a synthesis of diverse elements dating over a long period of time and their ascription to a single event. Alternatively, these affinities could result from an increasing frequency of diffuse or multi-directional contacts and exchanges, probably mainly between western Greece, the Balkans and southern Italy, which anticipate the more directional long-distance trading contacts of the Middle Bronze Age.

From Palermo to Messina and down the eastern coast at least as far as Naxos, plain and dark burnished pottery is also found at this time, as well as evidence for mixed burial rites including rock-cut chambers (Rodì), cremation (Milazzo) and single inhumation in jars (Milazzo, Messina, Naxos). Castelluccio pottery is rare in this zone, although some contexts, like the Vallelunga rock-cut tomb, combined painted and plain wares of Castelluccio and RTV type.[77]

Northern Sicily is less well known and the origin of Capo Graziano and RTV groups is obscured by the lack of evidence about the Late Copper Age in this region. Nevertheless, the RTV complex probably derived essentially from local LCA groups (Conca d'Oro II and Piano Quartara): the pottery maintained the tradition of plain and burnished wares even if cremation and jar burials represent a new development (below). In fact, Capo Graziano incised pottery is present in northern Sicily and its origins may lie in the local Conca d'Oro, Moarda and Beaker styles. An alternative thesis, therefore, would be that the Aeolian Capo Graziano culture was an insular offshoot of a North Sicilian regional complex, albeit one enriched by contacts with southern Italy and Greece. The overall relationship, therefore, would not be so unlike that of earlier periods, when a considerable degree of cultural homogeneity characterized this southern Tyrrhenian zone.

Internal and external relationships

Most categories of EBA artefact production denote continuity from the Late Copper Age, although the rich material culture of this period has yet to be fully exploited in research, which has been handicapped by uncertainties about chronology. In particular, the evolution of EBA painted pottery and a distinction between regional styles and temporal variations

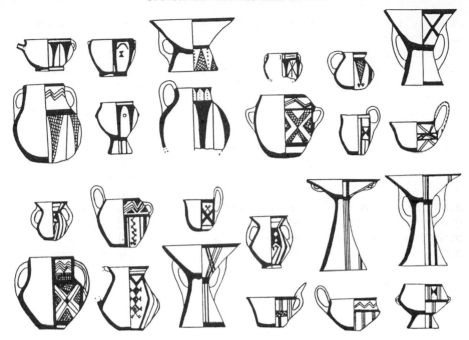

Fig. 67. Early Bronze Age painted pottery from sites around Etna, not to scale

still needs to be clarified. As a working hypothesis, three stages of Castelluccio wares in eastern Sicily have been proposed: a so-called 'protocastelluccio', resembling and perhaps contemporary with LCA San Ippolito and Naro styles; a mature phase, best represented in the Hyblaean region; and a late phase, with simpler decoration and changes in shape. A slightly more detailed scheme has recently been suggested for sites around Etna, although they are largely unpublished (fig. 67).[78]

The best known assemblage is from La Muculufa, where the decorated ware reflects an early stage of evolution from LCA traditions and includes vessels of San Ippolito and Naro type, as well as a few pieces resembling Malpasso and Moarda or Beaker styles (fig. 68:1-5).[79] Painted ware accounts for neary 50% of the assemblage and consists mainly of black motifs on a red, or occasionally yellow, brushed-on slip. Pedestal bowls, pitchers, dippers, jars and cups are common, decorated with a wide repertoire of geometric motifs, such as hatched bands, triangles, zig-zags, wavy and straight lines, checkerboards, metopal designs and occasional figurative allusions to eyes and faces. The finesse of execution varies, with considerable elaboration apparent on drinking cups and some jars.[80] Petrographic study has shown that local clays were used, tempered with grog and decorated with a manganese paint, probably also obtained locally. Less attention has been paid to EBA plain wares, which include large ribbed storage jars, partitioned vessels, strainers and a wide variety of cups, jugs

Fig. 68. Early Bronze Age painted pottery: (1-8) La Muculufa; (9-13) Monte Tabuto and Monte Racello; (14-15) Monte Sara

and jars, some of which may be no different from those typically labelled 'RTV' types. One widespread form, which seems more characteristic of the BA2 phase, is an elegant dipper or cup with a high forked handle (fig. 61:3-6).

It has been claimed that Castelluccio pottery was closely related to the EH and MH matt-painted wares of Greece and the Aegean.[81] However, there are few specific and chronologically relevant similarities. Only one rather simple vase from La Muculufa has a possible EH II counterpart, while several other correspondences between widespread simple geometric motifs could well be coincidental. Moreover, the overall formal and decorative repertoire in Sicily seems so firmly rooted in local LCA traditions as to preclude a significant external source of inspiration, although this does not rule out occasional imports and influences before the documented presence of Aegean pottery. A surprising variety of imported pottery at Monte Grande suggests that more regular contacts with the eastern Mediterranean were established during the 16th or possibly 17th centuries BC.[82] Preliminary reports of analyses by R. Jones note the presence of lustrous decorated and fine orange wares, matt-painted, Aegina gold mica and Cypriot wares, as well as some coarser and larger vessels, probably used for transportation, from various Aegean and eastern Mediterranean sources. One local resource that may have been traded at this time is sulphur, for which there is some evidence of local extraction.

Cult artefacts are suggested by terracotta horns already current in LCA sites (above) but more common in EBA domestic contexts, as well as later (fig. 69:8,10). Some examples from La Muculufa have schematic arms or a pebble inserted at the apex, while the putative hut-model from Monte Grande might instead represent a group of schematized figures (fig. 69:7). The lower part of figurines may also be recognised in some incomplete items, one of which contained sockets for additional insertions (fig. 69:6,9). Another variety, known from Palermo and Ramacca, probably represents a female figure, with crossed bands painted on the chest (fig. 69:4-5). To these may be added disc-shaped painted pottery plaques from Manfria, which resemble Maltese (Tarxien Cemetery) types.[83]

Less schematic in form are 22 figurines from Monte San Giuliano, between 2.5 and 9.5cm long, some of which are of red burnished pottery with traces of black painted lines on the surface (fig. 69:1-3). Six are identified as female, two male and the rest uncertain or possibly children, in view of their smaller size and the absence of breasts.[84] The modelling of sexual features and the apparent differentiation between adults and children has encouraged the view that they represent human figures or ex-votos rather than divinities or supernatural beings.

While there is little evidence for any sudden change in the quality or quantity of metal-working, the range of metal products was certainly growing (fig. 70).[85] Short triangular daggers from Monte Racello and Santa Febronia were of copper with 7-10% arsenic or antimony, which could have been made in Sicily. Various pointed implements and ornaments are

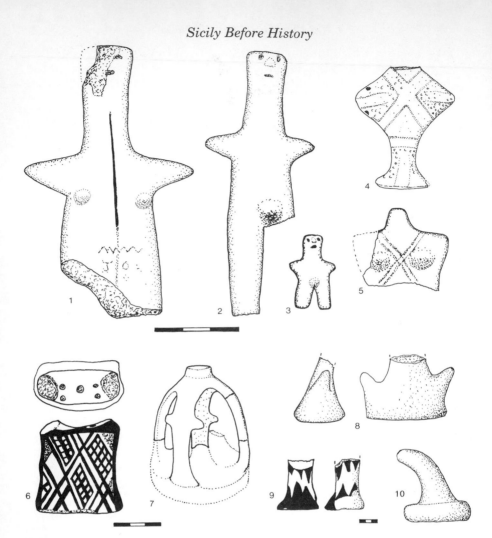

Fig. 69. Clay figurines: (1-3) Monte San Giuliano; (4) Palermo; (5) Ramacca; (6) Cava Lazzaro; (7) Monte Grande; (8-10) La Muculufa

known, while axes probably served as convenient exchange items. Some forms suggest long-distance trade. Close comparisons can be drawn between a spearhead (fig. 70:1), reputedly from Monte Venere (Taormina) and various EBA Aegean or more typically Anatolian types with parallel slots and 'rat-tailed' tangs, datable between about 2500 and 2300 BC. A curved piece of iron from a Castelluccio tomb, which now appears to be the earliest artefact of this metal from the western Mediterranean, may represent a trade item, as also the pieces of a bronze cup from a shaft burial in the Grotta Maccarone (fig. 70:2,11). By contrast, two fragments of so-called 'scale-balances' (fig. 70:4,6) could easily be local ornamental forms.

142

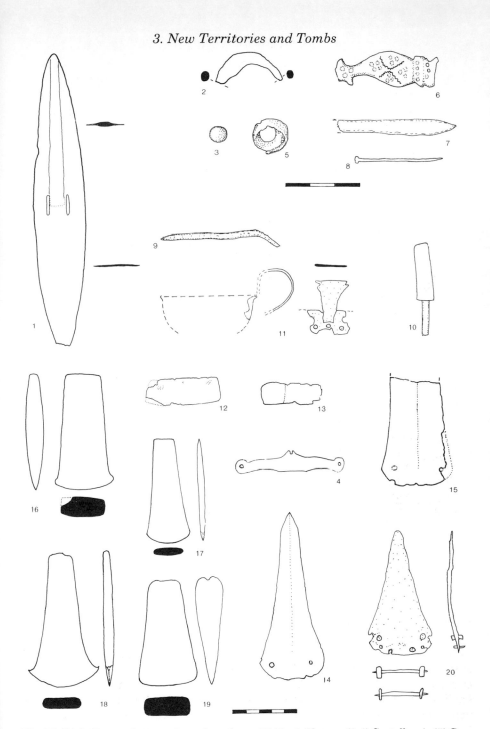

Fig. 70. Early Bronze Age metal artefacts from: (1) Monte Venere; (2-4) Castelluccio (5) Cava Cana Barbara; (6) Fiumedinisi; (7-10) Lipari acropolis; (11) Grotta Maccarone; (12-15) Monte Racello; (16-19) Sporadic; (20) S. Febronia

143

Further indications of long-distance links are provided by bossed bone plaques (fig. 71).[86] About 20 Sicilian examples are known from burials as well as domestic contexts, made from cut long-bones, probably of cattle. One piece from La Muculufa probably belongs in the BA1 phase. Up to 16cm long, though mostly incomplete, they present a row of bosses that were sometimes well polished and finely incised with alternating circular, volute, stellar and geometric motifs, flanked by reticulation. They may have been kept or worn as amulets, while some of the motifs could be highly schematized representations of female attributes (eyes, breasts, navel, vulva), as first suggested by J.D. Evans, although not all can be accounted for in this way and some have alternating crosses or only plain bosses. The latter most closely resemble single examples from Apulia, Malta, Lerna in Greece, and four specimens from Troy.

There is no reason to doubt that the Sicilian examples were made locally, but the wider distribution is puzzling. It has sometimes been thought to reflect the arrival of migrants from the eastern Mediterranean, although it is not clear that the Greek (early Middle Helladic) or Trojan examples are any earlier in date, and it could equally be argued that any movement went in the opposite direction. Moreover, whatever their symbolic function, such finely crafted items may have been exchanged along with other prestigious materials between regions.

It appears, therefore, that more complex and far-flung multi-directional exchange relationships developed and intensified in the course of the Early Bronze Age. At the local or inter-regional level, many traditional utilitarian items, such as ground stone axes, stone beads and ornaments, millstones, flint and obsidian moved between neighbouring communities, as indicated, for example, by the abundance of basaltic axes from Etnean or Hyblaean sources or the wide diffusion of small, probably Calabrian, greenstone artefacts. The movement of domestic livestock along river valleys and of secondary products, such as textiles, probably played an important role in these local transactions. As in earlier periods, variations in the natural environment may have lent additional symmetry and stability to these local networks.

Another sphere of exchange included more unusual, often non-utilitarian and prestigious materials, such as the Sicilian amber, which reached southern Italy, small jadeite pendants of northern peninsular origin, metal goods and probably other finely crafted and small luxury items. These long-distance movements would have required maritime transport and gravitated towards larger centres, especially those nearer the coast. The existence of inter-regional networks and a knowledge of prior contact probably encouraged the development of more regular long-range contacts during the later BA2 phase with Greece and Aegean, where more hierarchical societies were now evolving. The imported pottery of late Middle Helladic or Late Helladic I type (fig. 72) in the lower Tyrrhenian region (the Phlegrean islands in the Bay of Naples, the Aeolian islands) and

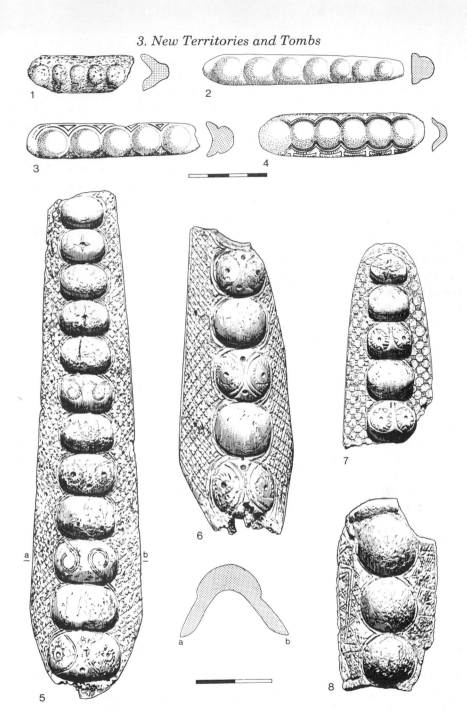

Fig. 71. Bossed bone plaques from: (1) Malta; (2) Lerna; (3) Troy; (4) Apulia; (5-8) Castelluccio

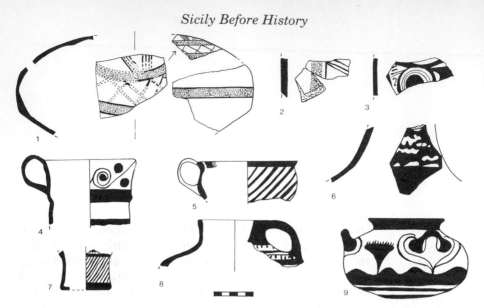

Fig. 72. Aegean pottery from Capo Graziano layers on Lipari and Filicudi: (1,2,6) matt-painted; (3,8) LM I (?); (4,5,7,9) LH I-II

southern Sicily anticipates subsequent relations between these areas and the Mycenaean palace centres.[87]

The social and political structure of EBA society was, therefore, variable and evolving. On the one hand, dominant groups were bolstering their authority with reference to family lineages, reflected by elaborate chamber tombs and more typically masculine statements of power and status, such as fine weaponry. At the same time, leaders maintained a close association with cult activity, reflected in the pre-eminence of burial grounds and the continuing elaboration of funerary ritual. These were traditional trappings of authority. Further dimensions were represented by more overt and practical statements of power, such as well-defended sites with turreted walls. Territorial controls and shifting alliances might also have been negotiated through local exchange networks. Moreover, the potential of metal as a means of accumulating wealth was beginning to be realized. Even if the extent and regularity of long-distance contacts were probably not yet sufficient to bring about radical local changes, the control of valuable and exotic raw materials, items of fine craftsmanship and contacts with eastern Mediterranean and Aegean groups were already providing an opportunity for local leaders to wield greater power and influence.

146

4

Interaction and Trade

The Middle-Late Bronze Age setting

The Middle Bronze Age (MBA) is a period of no great length according to the traditional chronology (about 1425 to 1250 BC), which nonetheless saw significant transformations in social and economic organisation. Settlements differed greatly in scale and function, while more elaborate tombs and buildings appeared in urbanized settings along with sophisticated craft products. Centralisation, social stratification and craft specialisation are key factors in these developments, which also characterize the earlier part of the Late Bronze Age (LBA) until approximately 1050 BC.[1] Pottery, metal and ornamental items imported from Greece, the Aegean and Cyprus, or resembling contemporary forms in these regions as well as in Italy and Malta, attest the existence of networks that permitted a diversity of goods to flow in greater quantities and over longer distances than before. Identifying the origins of these goods and raw materials is an increasingly international and scientific area of research, although much of the evidence in Sicily awaits examination. One may hope that a shipwreck with its cargo of this period will eventually be found in Sicilian waters.

Trading links with the Mycenaean world, for which the foundations had already been laid in the BA2 phase (chapter 3), were influential now, intensifying concurrently with the expansion of palace economies in the Aegean.[2] It was from about the middle of the 2nd millennium BC, therefore, at a time when early forms of state organisation were maturing in the eastern Mediterranean, that Sicily assumed a more prominent position as a bridge between east and west. External contacts stimulated the local economy, while encouraging the emergence of socially stratified communities in a 'proto-urban' environment of sites with a special interest in maritime trade. These could have been a major force for change: serving as regional centres for the collection of resources from the hinterland and the redistribution of trade goods, while promoting those with access to status-enhancing goods, their collaborators and clients.

Two cultural and geographical zones can be distinguished: the Milazzese sites of the Aeolian islands, Ustica and northern Sicily, which have counterparts in Calabria; and the Thapsos sites in the Syracusan region and southern Sicily (fig. 73). Both derive from pre-existing cultural complexes (Capo Graziano, RTV and late Castelluccio). The Milazzese zone had closer links with southern Tyrrhenian Italy (in its MBA Apennine

147

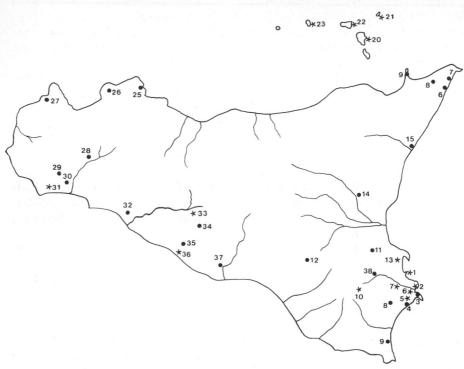

Fig. 73. *Middle Bronze Age sites (•); with imported Mycenaean (LH IIIA-IIIB) or Cypriot pottery (*)*: 1 Thapsos; 2 Syracuse; 3 Plemmyrion; 4 Ognina; 5 Matrensa; 6 Cozzo del Pantano; 7 Floridia; 8 G. Chiusazza; 9 G. Calafarina; 10 Buscemi; 11 Lentini; 12 Caltagirone; 13 Molinello; 14 Paternò; 15 Naxos; 16 Messina; 17 Paradiso; 18 Rometta; 19 Milazzo; 20 Lipari: Castello, Urnazzo; 21 Panarea: Milazzese; 22 Salina: Portella, Serro dei Cianfi; 23 Filicudi: Capo Graziano; 24 Ustica: I Faraglioni; 25 G. Ferraro; 26 G. dei Puntali; 27 G. Mangiapane; 28 Monte Castellazzo; 29 Marcita; 30 Case Pietra; 31 Erbe Bianche; 32 Scirinda; 33 Milena; 34 Caldare; 35 G. Ticchiara; 36 Cannatello; 37 Madre Chiesa; 38 Pantalica

phase) and maintained earlier traditions of settlement types and craft production. Single inhumations in jars with modest accoutrements predominated in northern Sicily, whereas chamber tombs with richer furnishings characterized southern sites, which more conspicuously display the changes in social and economic organisation noted above. However, within southern Sicily, settlements could range from small rural sites inland to larger coastal centres of innovation and trade, like Thapsos.

Dating depends partly on Mycenaean (Late Helladic: LH IIIA-IIIC) pottery, which provides links with historical chronologies in the eastern Mediterranean by means of cross-dating (fig. 74).[3] Radiocarbon dates are still too few to support an independent dating system. One ^{14}C date (1373-1114 cal.BC) from a MBA layer at Capo Graziano on Filicudi, associated with LH IIIA:1 ware, partly overlaps with the pottery chronology (roughly 1390-1365 BC), while another ^{14}C date (1213-1011 cal.BC) from a MBA context on Lipari is lower than would be expected from asssociations with LH IIIA:2 pottery (about 1365-1335 BC). Radiocarbon dates from Milazzese and later contexts on Ustica fall mainly between about 1450 and 1000 cal.BC (table 4).

In the Aeolian islands, Portella (Salina) and the upper (Milazzese) layers of Capo Graziano have a little LH IIB pottery and more of LH IIIA:1. These contexts may date between about 1440 BC and 1365 BC. By contrast, imported LH IIIA:1-IIIB pottery at Punta Milazzese (Panarea) and on Lipari suggests a slightly longer and later duration from about 1390 BC down to a certain point within the LH IIIB period (1335-1185 BC). The end of the MBA phase on Lipari is conventionally dated around 1250 BC since most of the imported pottery in the succeeding Ausonian I levels is LH IIIB and because the assemblage is of Italian LBA 'Subapennine' type, associated with an invasion of the Aeolian islands by their eponymous founder, Liparus, and the Ausonians (chapter 5).

In southern Sicily, a gradual transition from Early to Middle Bronze Age seems to have been underway before 1500 BC, as suggested by a ^{14}C date for a MBA hut at Madre Chiesa (1740-1462 cal.BC). In the Italian peninsula, the period is associated with Apennine assemblages and dated between about 1600 and 1300 BC. In Sicily, the date of 1500 BC may be taken as a convenient approximation for the beginning of the period, pending further radiocarbon dates, which may require it to be raised (table 1). A narrower conventional dating for southeastern Sicily (1400-1250 BC) is based only on the presence of LH IIIA and a few LH IIIB imports in Thapsos chamber tombs, which could represent a secondary phase. There are also some indications from tombs (e.g. Cozzo Pantano t.9) that local Thapsos wares were still current alongside violin-bow and arched fibulae: forms known in the Aegean during the 12th century BC (LH IIIC). The scarcity of LH IIIC imports suggests a decline in contacts with Greece during the 12th century BC, which may have ceased by about 1050 BC.

In Sicily, the MBA-LBA transition is less clear-cut than in the Aeolian islands. It used to be associated with the emergence of large sites inland,

Mainland Greece	
ca.1600 BC	LH I
ca.1500 BC	LH IIA
ca.1440 BC	LH IIB
ca.1390 BC	LH IIIA1
ca.1365 BC	LH IIIA2
ca.1335 BC	LH IIIB
ca.1185 BC	LH IIIC
ca.1065 BC	Submycenaean
ca.1015 BC	

Fig. 74. Simplified Mycenaean pottery chronology

such as Pantalica, according to Bernabò Brea, who defined the Pantalica I (or North) culture (1250-1000 BC) as the successor of Thapsos. However, some of the material from Pantalica tombs resembles that of Thapsos. A painted vase of Mycenaean type from Pantalica tomb 133N (fig. 92:14) is only roughly dated to the LH IIIB-C period and might be earlier. That Pantalica and Thapsos were partly contemporary during the 13th and 12th centuries BC is likely, although Pantalica and some other sites inland (Dessueri, Cassibile) expanded markedly in the Late Bronze and Early Iron Ages (chapter 5).

Sites and buildings

Information from old excavations, biased towards cemeteries in the south-eastern region, and more recent work, which has begun to correct the imbalance, suggests that southern Sicilian sites of the 14th-12th centuries BC fall into several categories, as exemplifed by the following:

(a) a harbour site and trading emporium, with extensive residential and funerary structures (Thapsos);

(b) seaboard sites, some of which might have been similar to the preceding, though known mainly from tombs or limited excavations (Ognina, Plemmyrion, Syracuse, Naxos, Cannatello);

(c) smaller sites on or near the coastal plain, often occupying low-lying promontories, represented mainly by tombs (Matrensa, Molinello, Cozzo Pantano, Floridia) and settlements in the foothills overlooking the coast (Madre Chiesa, Scirinda);

(d) hill-top settlements inland (Monte Castellazzo, Sabucina, Mokarta);

(e) large cemeteries on promontories and hill-tops (Caltagirone, Pantalica), which lasted for most of the Late Bronze Age and denote a major centre;

(f) smaller possible satellite communities within the territorial orbit of the preceding (Rivetazzo);

(g) caves (Chiusazza, Calafarina, Barriera) used as occasional shelters, cult or burial places.

The largest settlement is Thapsos on the Magnisi peninsula in the Gulf of Augusta: a low-lying limestone promontory, 2300m long and up to 800m wide, connected to the mainland by a narrow isthmus, providing a sheltered leeward anchorage and beaching place (fig. 75).[4] Covering an area of about 1000 x 300m, the residential quarter lay on the slightly higher western side, just 20m above sea level, while much of the adjacent zone was occupied by burial grounds. This is a complex site with several phases, including traces of EBA occupation (chapter 3), where the buildings survive to a height of only 40-50cm in a shallow deposit.

The first MBA settlement phase consisted of round or subcircular huts (over a dozen have been uncovered), spread over an area of about 600 x

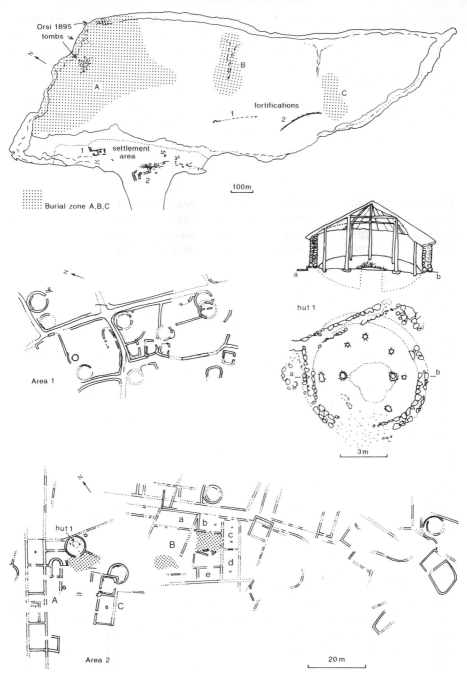

Fig. 75. Thapsos

151

200m. In the northern zone (fig. 75: Area 1), they were often accompanied by a separate rectangular room located inside spacious compounds forming urban plots, delimited by a rough grid of narrow pathways. In the central zone (Area 2), at least one round hut was set beside a wider thoroughfare (Ø about 3m) on a NW-SE axis, linked with side-passages. The round huts are of local type, 6-8m in diameter, made of roughly-shaped stone blocks, fitted with small stones and preserving traces of internal wall-plaster and a plastered floor. In many cases, the entrances faced south and a low stone bench flanked the inside wall. Hearths and cooking platforms of baked clay and pebbles were sometimes located near the middle, while one structure had two stone plinths and a ring of holes for upright timbers, probably supporting a conical thatched roof (fig. 75: hut 1).

A few Mycenaean sherds (LH IIIA:1-IIIC) are reported from the habitation zone, but the stratified pottery consisted mainly of storage vessels, pedestal basins (fig. 76), cordoned jars and open forms, some of which resemble early Borg in-Nadur wares of Malta (below). There are also similarities with some local pottery in the tombs, which included more jugs and bowls, associated with Mycenaean wares (figs. 90-91). Phase 1 is assigned approximately to the 15th-14th centuries BC.

To a slightly later moment (phase 2) belongs a more elaborate rectangular complex, located on the western edge of the lane opposite hut 2, known as complex B (fig. 75: Area 2,B). This consists of rectangular rooms (a-e), 7.5-10m long, in a U-shaped arrangement enclosing a central court with a cobbled floor. Local pottery found here included a large pedestal basin (in room C) with a vertical handle incised with birds and bosses (fig. 76:2). About 30m to the southeast was a rectangular structure with projecting lateral walls, a feature reminiscent of simple Mycenaean megaron houses. West of complex B, lay four joining rectangular rooms (complex A; fig. 75: Area 2,A) on the edge of an open cobbled area provided with a well, possibly contemporary with complex B. Although these elaborate buildings are not closely dated, stratigraphic considerations and the nature of the local pottery suggest that phase 2 was not much later than phase 1 and that the earlier round huts were perhaps still in use: a date in the 13th or 12th centuries BC has been suggested.

The first and probably the second phase is also represented by chamber tombs in the north, central and southern zones (A,B,C) and possibly by jar burials in the central area (below). In addition, tracts of a perimeter wall almost 300m long (fig. 75: fortification 1), aligned with the natural scarp on the western side of the settlement, may have served to delimit or defend the central habitation quarter, with its more elaborate rectangular complexes. Remains of later date (phase 3) are scattered widely in the upper deposits of the site, represented by sporadic LBA or EIA finds (Ausonian, Cassibile and Maltese Borg in-Nadur and Bahrija forms) and by later rectangular buildings, such as Area 2 complex C (chapter 5).

It is often said that Mycenaean contacts affected not only local craft

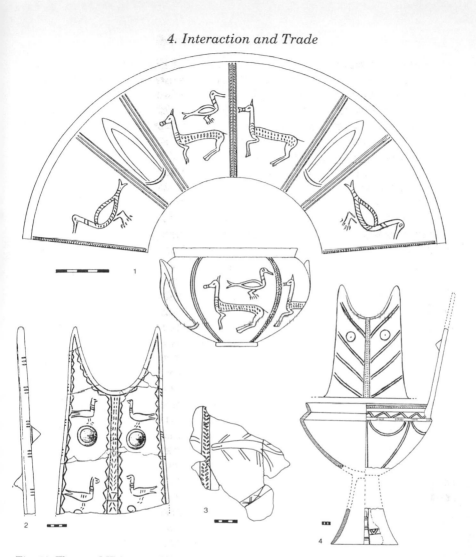

Fig. 76. Thapsos MBA incised pottery

production, which is readily demonstrable, but domestic and funerary architecture at Thapsos, which is more difficult to assess. Recent work has shown that the first phase already possessed an orderly layout of round huts within compounds, delimited by a network of pathways, that need owe nothing to outside influences. Similarly agglomerated structures on Ustica and Panarea (figs. 79:A;83) suggest an indigenous urban phenomenon in which plots and enclosures had an important defining role. However, the courtyard complexes (A and B) of the second phase have encouraged comparisons with Mycenaean and eastern Mediterranean settlements. The association of adjoining rooms with open courts and intersecting passageways, creating a roughly orthogonal plan, is reminiscent of some urban sites in the Aegean and eastern Mediterranean coastal towns, such as Ugarit in Syria, Enkomi and Kition in Cyprus, although the evidence from Thapsos is much more limited in quality and quantity and the correspondences are too generic to allow any specific source of origin or inspiration to be identified. Affinities have also been noted between some structures at Thapsos and the rectangular plan of Mycenaean megaron houses, entered through a vestibule created by projecting side-walls. It is possible that, without replicating a specific site or model, ideas were absorbed from outside and applied within the context of a pre-existing settlement, which was already growing in prestige and economic importance as a result of long-distance trade. In fact the 13th-12th centuries BC saw new developments in urban planning over a wide area of the central and eastern Mediterranean.

Thapsos was perhaps not the only urbanized site associated with a harbour on the east coast. Little is known about Syracuse until later periods (chapter 5), but sporadic traces exist of MBA-LBA occupation layers as well as chamber tombs, one of which contained Cypriot and Mycenaean wares and a cylinder seal of eastern Mediterranean type.[5] Comparable sites may have existed on the southern coast. Round structures to which rectangular buildings were attached, associated with local as well as Mycenaean (LH IIIA:2-IIIB) and Cypriot pottery, have been found at Cannatello (Agrigento), probably a coastal trading centre for traffic following the southern coast into the western Mediterranean via the Sicilian channel.[6]

A few miles away on the foothills bordering the coastal plain, Madre Chiesa resembles a simpler rural site, with half a dozen small round huts and one larger building, possibly an open compound. Further west, on the limestone promontory at Scirinda, an initial Thapsos phase with large round huts was succeeded by rectangular structures, dated between the 13th and 12th centuries BC. On Monte Castellazzo, dominating the upper Belice valley, only one round hut with Thapsos pottery survived, yet sufficient to show that inland hill-tops were occupied, as also indicated by surface finds from Mokarta (near Salemi) and between Monte Iato and Monte Maranfusa. Apart from strategic advantages, these locations are generally less susceptible to landslips than the lower slopes and valley sides. All the known structures had stone wall foundations except for a round hut (Ø 8m) at Erbe Bianche, represented by a ring of 30 post-holes.

Sabucina, a prominent hill overlooking the Salso river, has traces of at least 15 circular huts scattered over several hundred metres on the sloping ground beneath the summit.[7] Many had suffered from hillside erosion and others were probably destroyed by urban expansion in the 7th-5th centuries BC (chapter 6). They are mostly from 3.5-7m in diameter, sometimes with small semicircular or rectangular annexes, floors cut into the rock and stone walls built up against the slope in regular courses, surviving up to 1.6m in height. In places, the walls are represented by circular bedding trenches with post-holes. Thick ash and charcoal deposits suggest a thatched and wooden roof. However, none are fully published and some buildings must date to a later phase (chapters 5 & 6). The finds included red burnished and handmade coarse ware, notably pedestal basins, strainer jugs, storage jars, as well as millstones and stone moulds for casting daggers, roughly datable between the Thapsos and Pantalica I phase (1250-1000 BC). Two round huts may have held potters' kilns. The habitation area is also interspersed with several large chamber tombs, thought to be Bronze Age in origin, although their contents were mostly disturbed and they had been re-used in Archaic times. Quantities of animal bone raise the possibility of a cult function.

Pantalica has over a thousand rock-cut chamber tombs spread over steep slopes in several large groupings (fig. 77; and below). This is a famous prehistoric site, located in the Hyblaean hills and linked to the coastal plain by 20km of winding gorge through which the Anapo flows on its way to the harbour at Syracuse.[8] It consists of a vast limestone promontory surrounded on three sides by precipitous canyons (known as *cave*). At a certain time, although possibly not until the later Iron Age, the narrow western approach was barred by a large rock-cut ditch backed by a wall. Access is also possible up a steep path on the northeastern slope. The gently sloping summit is an eroded wind-swept place, with only pockets of thin soil. However, just below the highest elevation on the southern side is a building with several rooms and a vestibule (the so-called *anaktoron* or 'palace'), which has often been thought of as the residence of the local ruler (fig. 78).

In the largest room (fig. 78:A; 8.5 x 8m), which presents an impressive prospect of 'megalithic' quadrangular blocks, Orsi found evidence of metal-working and kitchen activities: an ash deposit with animal bones, fragments of stone moulds (two for casting axes), LBA red ware and the base of a large jar, while fragments of bronze implements, perhaps destined to be melted down, came to light outside. Mixed with these finds throughout the building were numerous fragments of roof-tiles of late antiquity. A recent sounding nearby produced a few sherds of MBA type and some Iron Age fragments. The flat ground on the western side was occupied by a forecourt, with traces of a cobbled floor, possibly part of a precinct. Three parallel walls were located on the southern side: one on the edge of the plateau, provided with a trapezoidal tower, delimited the forecourt and was probably for defense. Two others further down the slope could have been for terracing purposes. The whole complex must have resembled a fortified acropolis, clearly visible from surrounding hills, perhaps serving as a place of refuge in times of danger.

For a century it has been widely accepted that this was originally a LBA or MBA structure that was re-used in late antiquity. Affinities have been noted with Mycenaean buildings, such as the Oil Merchant's house at Mycenae with its adjoining rooms beside a corridor, or the citadel at Gla, located on the edge of a plateau and joined to a defensive wall. However,

Fig. 77. Pantalica North cemetery

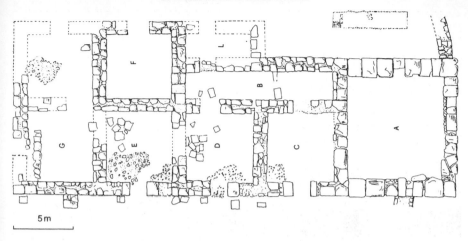

Fig. 78. Pantalica 'anaktoron'

the lack of a clear stratigraphy, the mixture of material from inside the building and the presence of mortar in many of the walls imply extensive re-structuring in later times. Serious doubts regarding the antiquity of the whole structure have recently been expressed by A. Messina, who has noted that the megalithic construction and the overall layout would be consistent with a large Byzantine fortified farmstead (or *kastellion*) of the 9th century AD.[9] As a result, and pending further study, the building can no longer be regarded with much confidence as a Bronze Age palatial residence.

Island worlds

A distinctive tradition of settlement architecture evolved from EBA tradi-tions during the Milazzese period on Pantelleria, Ustica and the Aeolian islands. The MBA inhabitants of Capo Graziano occupied oval stone dwellings like their predecessors. On Panarea, the eroded cliff-edged promontory of Punta Milazzese preserved about 24 mainly oval huts (Ø 4-7m), often provided with an annex, forming units of two or three rooms, surrounded by narrow winding passages and open areas (figs. 79:A,B; 80).[10] Associated with a few LH IIIA-B sherds were quantities of kitchen and storage pottery, most abundant in the annexes, which no doubt served as storage or domestic activity areas, complementing the indoor chambers. One quadrangular hut (no. 16), set slightly apart, contained more abun-dant material and Mycenaean pottery: it may have differed in function although there is nothing to indicate its specific nature, for example as a cult place or a special residence. The contemporary settlement on the Lipari acropolis, where 19 huts have been revealed, is quite similar, although few of the mostly oval rooms have annexes (fig. 81). Two huts

157

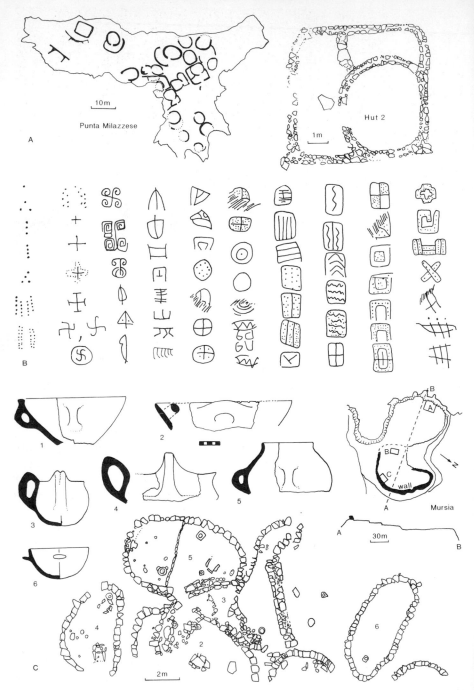

Fig. 79. (A) Panarea, Punta Milazzese; (B) Milazzese potters' marks; (C) Pantelleria, Mursia plan and local pottery

158

Fig. 80. Panarea, Punta Milazzese hut 1

stand out here: one small chamber (gIV) could represent a storage or specialized function, while one building with straight walls (gXII) is noticeably larger than the rest. If the total number of dwellings was originally closer to 40 or even 50 at both of these sites and 3-5 persons are allowed per unit, village populations in the order of 120-250 may be estimated.

On nearby Salina, a line of ten round huts, no more than 4m in diameter, and scanty traces of others, had their floors and walls cut into the steep slope of a rocky crest overlooking the shore at Portella. Despite the presence of one Mycenaean vessel and a fine necklace of glass-paste, amber and stone beads in one hut (F), this resembles a smaller, rather defensively sited island community, less concerned with trade than with subsistence: fishing, tending sheep and goat, and spinning.

The Faraglioni settlement is more imposing (figs. 82-84). Located beside sea-cliffs on the northern coast of Ustica, 70km north of Palermo, it began as a collection of apse-ended dwellings and a possible cult chamber (phase 1) and subsequently developed into an agglomeration of subcircular or quadrangular rooms with open courtyard annexes, intersected by narrow passageways (phase 2).[11] Many rooms have a low bench, grinding-stone and a round terracotta hearth-slab set into the floor (fig. 83). The pottery is a local version of Milazzese, with fewer peninsular (Apennine) influences, typified by a limited range of jars, bowls and cups, including many oval platters, perhaps used for leaching acorn flour (fig. 82:7).[12] A single Mycenaean sherd (LH IIIB-C) was found in a surface stratum. Stone moulds for casting a simple axe or blade and an ingot fragment

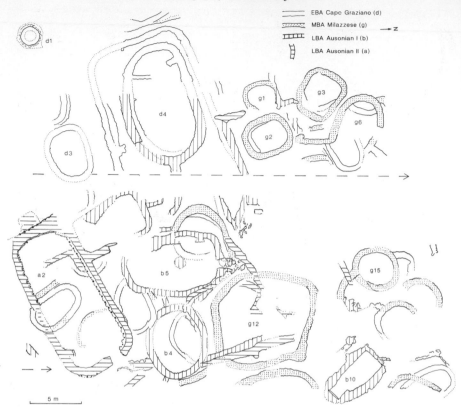

Fig. 81. Lipari acropolis: areas I-III EBA-EIA levels

imply limited metallurgical activity, but metal finds are scarce and obsidian blades were probably still being used.

The second and third phases are associated with the erection and periodic modification of a massive perimeter wall which is most imposing on the landward side, constructed of large stone blocks (the largest near the base), provided with ten projecting semicircular towers, enclosing the roughly elliptical settlement area (fig. 84). Since parts of the internal zone were free of buildings, an initial inflated estimate of 300 huts has been radically revised to no more than about 20 or so courtyard structures per phase, which may suggest a population of no more than about 100 people.[13] Defence was clearly a matter of concern and may well reflect the troubles and incursions which led to the destruction of all the Aeolian Milazzese sites in the 13th century BC. However, floor deposits overlying the phase 2-3 buildings and several radiocarbon dates show that occupation continued into the Late Bronze Age, as it did on Lipari. Caprines and cattle predominate in the faunal sample, with fewer pigs and surprisingly small numbers of fish or bird bones (fig. 96). A small island in a rather outlying

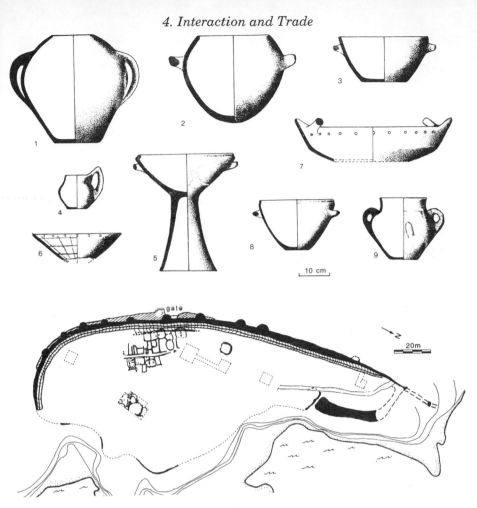

Fig. 82. Ustica, I Faraglioni plan and local pottery

position with fertile if rather dry soils, Ustica was undoubtedly capable of supporting a small community, but one that was probably less frequently visited and perhaps, with little to offer in exchange, was less interested in trade than contemporary Aeolian groups, who were more closely integrated by local exchange networks.

The inhabitants of I Faraglioni had more in common with another outlying community on the island of Pantelleria, where the village of Mursia had been occupied since the Early Bronze Age (chapter 3).[14] Several ^{14}C dates combined with stratigraphic and stylistic considerations indicate that Mursia was still inhabited during the Milazzese period and then abandoned in the Late Bronze Age: hut 3 in zone A (1375-1133 cal.BC) has a stone bench, millstone, terracotta slab set in the floor and a series of

161

Fig. 83. Ustica, I Faraglioni (1990)

vessels, including platters, which are very similar to those of Ustica and other Milazzese sites (fig. 79:C).

Burials

The cemeteries of the Syracuse region once provided the bulk of evidence for this period and many sites are still known only from tombs. By contrast, the Aeolian islands lack evidence for burial. In Sicily, two funerary rites are documented: multiple inhumations in rock-cut chamber tombs, and burials in large jars, both of which have EBA antecedents. Thanks to Orsi's work, a good deal is known about rock-cut tombs, although the available records are schematic by modern standards. Jar burials are much rarer.

Thapsos had three main clusters of tombs beside the residential quarter (fig. 75). They are most numerous in the northern area, with smaller groupings in southern and central zones, where some new chambers have been discovered recently, as well as jar burials. About 300 chamber tombs are recorded, about 15% of which preserved burials in whole or in part. Plainly, many of them were originally richly furnished and much has been lost. Remains of about 20 jar burials are known, perhaps a fraction of the original number, none of which preserve contents except for occasional bone fragments. Other cemeteries in the region are smaller, perhaps representing minor settlements, although many tombs have probably

Fig. 84. Ustica, I Faraglioni, perimeter wall

disappeared: about 60 are recorded at Cozzo Pantano, 50 at Plemmyrion, 35 at Molinello, and a dozen at Matrensa. In addition, numerous empty chambers are scattered over limestone outcrops and escarpments in south-ern Sicily, for which the documentation is either scanty or non-existent.

While no different in principle from earlier rock-cut tombs, the elabora-

163

tion of certain features sets some MBA tombs apart. There are essentially two main types with optional additional features:

– Type 1a: a large subcircular or circular chamber, with a flat or domed ceiling (fig. 85:A), located on flat terrain and entered from a vertical shaft (*pozzetto*).
– Type 1b: a more elaborate version of the latter, with a small anteroom between the main chamber and the shaft; additional features of both types may include a step down into the main chamber, large niches in the wall and a low bench around the perimeter. Rectangular cuttings were occasionally recorded on the ground outside the entrance shaft, with broken stone bases set into them, possibly the remains of stelae or grave markers (e.g. Plemmyrion t.2 and 10).
– Type 2a: a subcircular or circular chamber with a narrow corridor (or *dromos*) cut out of the bedrock and widening into a rectangular or trapezoidal forecourt in front of the tomb door (fig. 86). Sometimes a dividing wall of blocks or pillars framed an additional doorway (fig. 85:B) or formed a cornice and a partially roofed vestibule with benches (e.g. Thapsos t.3, 23 and 28).
– Type 2b: like the preceding, but with antechambers (fig. 85:D,G); additional features of both types include a recessed doorway, niches and a low bench around the edge of the main chamber; the ceiling may be almost flat or markedly arched, reminiscent of an Aegean beehive tomb or *tholos* (e.g. Molinello t.2 and 4; Cozzo Pantano t.9, 11, 13, 16 and 23).

Thapsos tombs with other features or more erratic shapes, sometimes caused by irregularities in the bedrock, are not unusual. In one case (t.41), the inside wall was buttressed by blocks laid in the manner of a dome or vault. Double interconnecting chambers are also recorded (t.6), and in one case (t.26) a trench containing four skeletons had been dug into the floor. Tomb 5 contained a funerary couch with headrest carved out of the rock on which three skeletons rested. Two simpler and smaller chambers (t.43 and 47) set slightly apart from the more elaborate tombs were more roughly-cut and packed with skeletons, but few grave-goods (fig. 85:C). Such variations within the cemetery might imply differential status (below).

A detailed analysis is inhibited by various factors: the topographical distribution and full range of tomb types is not known; most had been robbed in whole or in part; the burial rite often seems to have entailed re-arranging or removing earlier burials to make room for new ones; some tombs were re-used in historical times, though later burials were usually distinguishable; few skeletal or other organic remains have been kept and detailed illustrations of internal stratigraphies and arrangements of finds are lacking; since few intact tombs have been excavated in recent times, we remain heavily dependent on Orsi's observations.

Only inhumations are recorded, although occasional cremations might

Fig. 85. MBA-LBA rock-cut chamber tombs: (A-D) Thapsos; (E-F) Pantalica; (G) Molinello; (H) Milena

Fig. 86. Thapsos tomb entrance

have escaped notice.[15] The number of deceased per chamber could vary considerably: typically between two and six, although several with over ten and occasionally as many as 50 are recorded (Thapsos t.D and 10). Most were laid on the floor of the main chamber, while the niches sometimes held one or two individuals, and occasional depositions were found in the small antechambers or forecourts (Cozzo Pantano t.10, 13 and 23). Pottery sometimes found broken in the forecourts and corridors could have been formally deposited, as in some EBA tombs, or simply reflect subsequent re-use or interference.

It appears from a few Thapsos tombs (t.1) that the deceased were placed with legs bent and heads against the wall or bench, perhaps originally in a sitting position, with a series of cups and bowls to hand. They were no doubt fully clothed and wearing personal ornaments; some rings were still in place on phalanges. Although some tombs had been disturbed, Orsi thought that the large pedestal basins were originally placed in the centre and that an attempt had been made to represent a convivial gathering, with the participants arranged in a circle, each able to dip a cup or bowl into a pedestal vase. The circular tombs with low benches, reminiscent of contemporary huts, and the pedestal basins and plates, recurrent in domestic contexts, give the impression of an underworld banquet arranged for the deceased.

As in earlier periods, these were perhaps family or lineage tombs, but little can be said about age and gender relationships. Artefacts specific to the sexes are not easily distinguished, although certain ornaments, such as glass-paste beads or gold bracelets, perhaps belonged to females, while men had bronze weapons, including daggers, sometimes worn on the chest (Milocca t.1). Rapiers were perhaps broken as demanded by ceremony or concerns with liminality (fig. 94:1,2). Records exist of organic items, including tortoise shells (Plemmyrion t.20) and food offerings, whereas spindle-whorls and other weaving items are rare (Thapsos t.7) by contrast with LBA-EIA tombs.

At Pantalica, over a thousand tombs honeycomb the limestone cliffs (fig. 77), although records of interments exist for only about 100. The majority date after about 1250 BC and they vary greatly in plan (chapter 5). However, one large subcircular chamber (N133, Ø 2.68m) and some oven-shaped examples are early types (fig. 85:F). The largest rectangular or quadranglar tombs (e.g. NW22, Ø 3.15m; NW38, Ø 3.80m), entered by a corridor, held several inhumations and an abundance of goods (fig. 85:E). Small oven-shaped chambers (*tombe a forno*) contained only one or two individuals (e.g. NW23). Despite prior disturbance, a wide range of material was recovered (figs. 92,93): occasional gold and silver ornaments (N37, N62), fine bronze items, such as the violin-bow fibula and mirrors, as well as various utensils (daggers, knives, razors, needles) and a mixture of handmade and fine wheel-made pottery, including 'table' wares (cups, plates, *askoi*) and transport or storage jars (amphorae). Most conspicuous are the large pedestal basins, which could assume monumental proportions (fig. 93). The range of vessels in some tombs might reflect a wealthy household, or a funerary banquet service in which the basins on stands had a special role, as at Thapsos.

Funerary customs, like domestic architecture, have been thought to reflect external influences in this period, although rock-cut chamber tombs can be traced far back in Sicily and the Aegean respectively and both the design and the burial rite of Sicilian MBA tombs have strong local roots. In fact, some architectural features, such as long corridors with masonry additions, which once suggested Mycenaean influences, can now be seen to have local precedents in the Sicilian Early Bronze Age. Nevertheless, certain affinities between MBA tombs can be observed: couches and cist-graves in the floor of some chambers, long corridors with forecourts, corbelled masonry, stone grave-markers, arched and pointed ceilings, sometimes culminating in an indentation, reminiscent of a *tholos*. The large rectangular tombs of Pantalica also have Mycenaean counterparts, although these need not indicate any direct contact.[16] There are similarities in the burial rite too: multiple depositions over time, placed in chambers and corridors, requiring periodic re-opening of tombs; allusions to drinking or feasting; an emphasis on certain kinds of pottery, personal ornaments, utensils and the presence of clay models (below). Taken separately these affinities are not especially significant and could be coincidental, but together they fit with a wider scenario in which processes of interaction transcended the economic sphere and may have involved a convergence of ideologies; this question is discussed further below.

Elsewhere in Sicily, many chamber tombs can be assigned to the Thapsos or Pantalica I periods, although the examples from hill-top sites inland tend to be simpler in form, lacking the elaborate forecourts and details of Thapsos, no doubt because they were adapted to steep terrain and perhaps because they served smaller rural communities, less affected by innovations occurring in coastal areas. Further west, along the Platani valley, however, are numerous small clusters of tombs, which include well-finished circular chambers, with concentric recesses around the

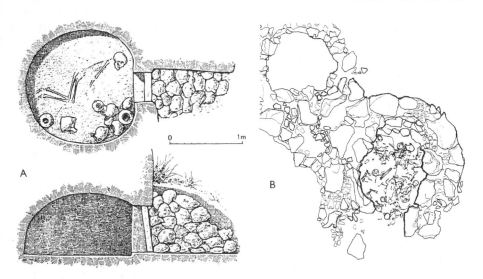

Fig. 87. (A) Dessueri LBA rock-cut tomb F54; (B) Le Salinelle LBA built tomb

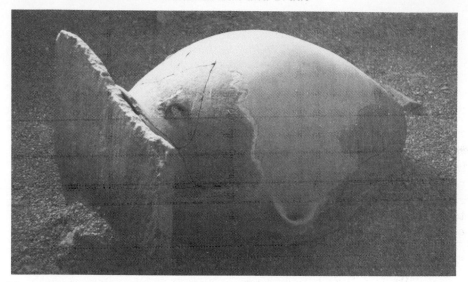

Fig. 88. Milazzo MBA jar burial reconstruction, Lipari Museum

doors, internal benches or funerary couches and domed ceilings. Good examples are known at Milena (fig. 85:H), which contained Thapsos wares and items of Mycenaean type (LH IIIB or IIIC). At Caltagirone, several hundred tombs in groups of up to 50 or more consisted of circular, elliptical and oven-shaped chambers as well as some fine single and double chambers, which stood out on account of their large size (Ø 2.20-2.75m), circular plan and arched ceilings.[17] This cemetery probably expanded at a slightly later date (roughly 13th-11th centuries BC) than that of Thapsos, while the Dessueri cemetery seems to have been used throughout the Late Bronze Age (fig. 87:A). By the end of this period it was more common for tombs to contain fewer or just single inhumations.

Some of the chambers at Sant'Angelo Muxaro, spread over three kilometres around the hillside, could date from the Late Bronze Age, although many of them were empty or re-used over a long period of time. Their contents belong primarily to the Iron Age (chapters 5-6).[18] One group of 55 tombs excavated by Orsi included small chambers with truncated, conical and domed ceilings (Ø usually 2-3m). In their midst is the exceptional Grotta di Sant'Angelo: a vast rock-cut double chamber, with a surrounding bench and possibly a funerary couch. The first chamber (Ø 8m and 3.20m high) dwarfs all rivals, while the second has a carved indentation at the apex, like the Milena tombs. Both had long since been emptied of their contents and were at one time adapted to make a chapel.

Much less is known about jar burials, probably single inhumations (or *enchytrismoi*), only parts of which have been found at Thapsos and tentatively assigned to the Middle Bronze Age. They provide a puzzling contrast with the chamber tombs; perhaps used by a different social group within the community. In northeastern Sicily, they appear to be more common: at Milazzo (podere Caravello) and Messina, several dozen large storage jars (for adults) and amphorae (for children) were placed sideways with the mouth sealed by a stone slab, and possibly buried under a mound of earth and stone (fig. 88).[19] This rite, which derives from local precedents, persisted into the Iron Age (chapters 3 and 5).

A recent discovery points to the existence of alternative forms of burial chambers, perhaps dictated by the presence of tough volcanic rocks: at Le Salinelle (Paternò), an oven-shaped tomb with a funerary platform was built entirely of lava stones and contained at least six disarticulated individuals with LBA pottery of Pantalica North type (fig. 87:B).[20]

Production and consumption: pottery, metal and luxury goods

Pottery and metalwork figure prominently in discussions of trade and interaction and yet much relevant material in Sicily's rich museum collections is not well known or published. New studies are needed, combined with scientific analyses of the composition of both metal and ceramic artefacts aimed at determining their provenance.[21] Mycenaean pottery in Sicily comes mainly from coastal sites near Syracuse and from the Aeolian islands (fig. 89), although finds from central-western areas are now increasing. This is partly due to the concentration of archaeological research in these areas. Nevertheless, despite an uneven state of knowledge, the large sample from Thapsos can be taken as an indication of its prominence as a place where foreign imports were relatively abundant. Fewer examples of Mycenaean ware have been found inland, although a juglet from Pantalica, a stirrup-jar from Buscemi and more recent finds from the Platani valley, show that their distribution was not exclusively coastal

	PJ	Al	Ju	SJ	Ky	Cu	Go	Bo	Pi	Am	Mu	Kr
SE SICILY												
Thapsos	14	7	3	1		1	1	1				
Cozzo Pantano					1							
Floridia		1										
Matrensa	2											
Molinello	1											
AEOLIAN ISLAND												
Filicudi			1	1								
Panarea	5	1	1					1	1?			
Lipari	3		3		4	10		5		2	1	2

Fig. 89. Mycenaean LH IIIA-B pottery type nos. (Piriform jar, alabastron, jug, stirrup-jar, kylix, cup, goblet, bowl, pithos, amphora, mug, krater) from Sicilian chamber tombs and Aeolian settlements

Fig. 90. Mycenaean (LH IIIA-B) and Cypriot LBA pottery from Cozzo Pantano (1), Thapsos (2-10, 12), Floridia (11) and Milena (13): (1) kylix, (2) goblet, (3) piriform jar, (4) alabastron, (5) cup, (6) stirrup-jar, (7) Cypriot base-ring jug, (8) Cypriot white shaved ware jug, (9) jug, (10) spouted jug, (11) alabastron, (12) piriform jar, (13) krater

(fig. 73). Sites such as Thapsos, Cannatello and possibly Syracuse may have acted as redistribution centres, supplying their hinterlands.

Whereas Mycenaean imports in the Aeolian islands, where MBA tombs are unknown, are all from domestic contexts, the Sicilian finds are mainly funerary. The extent to which Mycenaean pottery was used in Sicilian residential contexts is uncertain: small quantities are documented at Thapsos, more is now reported from Cannatello, but local pottery predominates at all sites. The frequent occurrence of Mycenaean vases in burials is significant, particularly at Thapsos, where one tomb (t.D) contained almost as many Mycenaean as local forms. Piriform jars are most common, followed by *alabastra*, both of which may have contained unguents, or possibly honey (fig. 90). Small stirrup-jars, most likely used for perfumed oils, are less common, but occasionally found along with goblets, *kylikes*, cups, truncated stemmed bowls and jugs (fig. 90). Overall, there is a combination of small storage vessels and table wares, selected as appropriate and perhaps prestigious items for funerary use. Many of these vessels are also characteristic of LH IIIA-IIIB burials in Greece, although there is a lack of Mycenaean figurative pottery in Sicily by contrast with some other areas, such as Cyprus.

The Aeolian sample, represented mainly by fragments from habitation contexts, includes similar kinds of painted wares, although cups and bowls are better represented as well as larger forms and plain storage or transportation vessels.[22] A large stirrup-jar of a kind often used for olive oil or wine was found underwater at a possible shipwreck site beside a treacherous stretch of coastline near Capo Graziano on Filicudi. On Lipari, one Milazzese hut (αIII) contained a phi-shaped figurine, an item commonly found in Mycenaean burials and houses, which has encouraged the idea of Mycenaean residents here. Recognizable vase shapes (mainly LH IIIA:1) include the goblet, alabastron, piriform jar, mug, *kylix*, various jugs, cups and bowls. Preliminary reports from Cannatello note the presence of large storage jars of Late Cypriot type, comparable with finds from Antigori in Sardinia.[23]

New studies are encouraging a reassessment of production centres and trade. The first clay analyses of Mycenaean pots in Italy have already shown that some were local imitations of their painted Mycenaean counterparts and therefore can no longer be regarded as long-distance trade items.[24] Local production of 'Mycenaean' vessels is particularly well attested at some sites in southern Italy, where the imitations may far outnumber the imports. In Sicily, a painted amphora (with LH IIIB-IIIC parallels) from Milena tomb A has been identified as a local product, whereas a krater from tomb B (closer to LH IIIA:2-IIIB types) was most likely imported (fig. 90:13). Visual inspection has suggested that a painted vase in Mycenaean style from Pantalica was made locally (fig. 92:14), and the same may be suggested for three base-ring juglets and three bowls of Cypriot type from tombs at Thapsos and Syracuse (figs. 90:7; 91:3).[25] However, much of the Mycenaean material and at least one Cypriot white shaved ware juglet from Thapsos (fig. 90:8) have the appearance of imported ware. It may be that local imitations were more common at sites inland, where imports were less abundant.

Many of the Mycenaean pots in Italy were once thought to be Rhodian in origin, although research by W. Taylour (1958) pointed to several provenances; a conclusion reinforced by recent studies, although there is growing evidence for a Cypriot connection. However, it is difficult to identify a single dominant source or source of inspiration for the Sicilian material. This may result from the diffuse nature of Bronze Age trade, the mixed cargoes of ships or the multiplicity of contacts. In fact, many vessels

Fig. 91. Thapsos local pottery

from the Thapsos tombs are common forms, which were traded widely not only in the Aegean but to Cyprus, the Near East and Egypt, especially within the period from about 1370 to 1330 BC (LH IIIA:2).

Fired at high temperatures, these wheel-turned decorated vases were technically superior to local handmade wares but did not replace them. However, local vases adopted some of their features and also began to be made on the wheel. Vessels inspired or influenced by Mycenaean shapes include local versions of piriform jars, the cylindrical pyxis and possibly some deep bowls, dippers, tubular-spouted and narrow-necked incised jugs, which also recall Cypriot forms (e.g. fig. 91:3,4,7,14,17). The Pantalica and Caltagirone LBA tombs contain further examples: collar-necked jars at Caltagirone, which have Mycenaean (LH IIIB:2-IIIC) equivalents; strainer-jugs, which were widespread from LH IIIC, and popular in Cyprus, perhaps used to serve a herbal drink; the Pantalica amphorae, which resemble Mycenaean (LH IIIC) belly-handled amphorae, and Pantalica askoi, which have generic Mycenaean and Cypriot affinities (e.g. fig. 92:1-4,7,10).

The finer local wares were decorated mainly by incision, burnishing or applying cordons. Pedestal plates with festoons in relief and segmented patterns of incised vertical lines on jugs and basins suggest a knowledge of Cypriot base-ring wares (figs. 91:2; 92:6). A monumental pedestal basin from Pantalica with vertical ribbing and a lustrous red finish (fig. 93) may well allude to metal forms, just as Mycenaean monochrome wares often imitated bronze vessels. Incised birds, animals and fish on local Thapsos wares (fig. 76) were probably inspired by similar figures on bichrome pottery from Cyprus or the Near East. The origin of the local geometric style of painted wares that persisted throughout the Late Bronze and Iron Ages in Sicily and southern Italy may derive from the practice of copying Mycenaean vessels of the LH IIIB and IIIC periods.

Potters' marks, which were already current in the Capo Graziano phase, are particularly common on Aeolian Milazzese vases and represented by 69 different engraved signs, about 25 of which occur more than once (fig. 79:B).[26] The meaning of the various symbols is difficult to assess: the use of dots could have a numerical significance, while the more elaborate graphic signs seem more likely to denote ownership or manufacturers' marks. Their diffusion within the Aeolian archipelago might be linked with the absence of good clay sources and the unusually intensive exchange of ceramics between the various island communities. For example, the marks may have been a means of reminding the user of the manufacturer's identity and the source of the item for which some return was due.

Links with Malta are suggested by certain vessels from Thapsos, including bowls with raised handles, pedestal basins with line-and-dot motifs (fig. 91:20-21), globular jugs and by some forms at other southern Sicilian sites, which are matched at Borg in-Nadur, where there is also a Mycenaean (LH IIIB) sherd. It is unclear whether such vessels represent

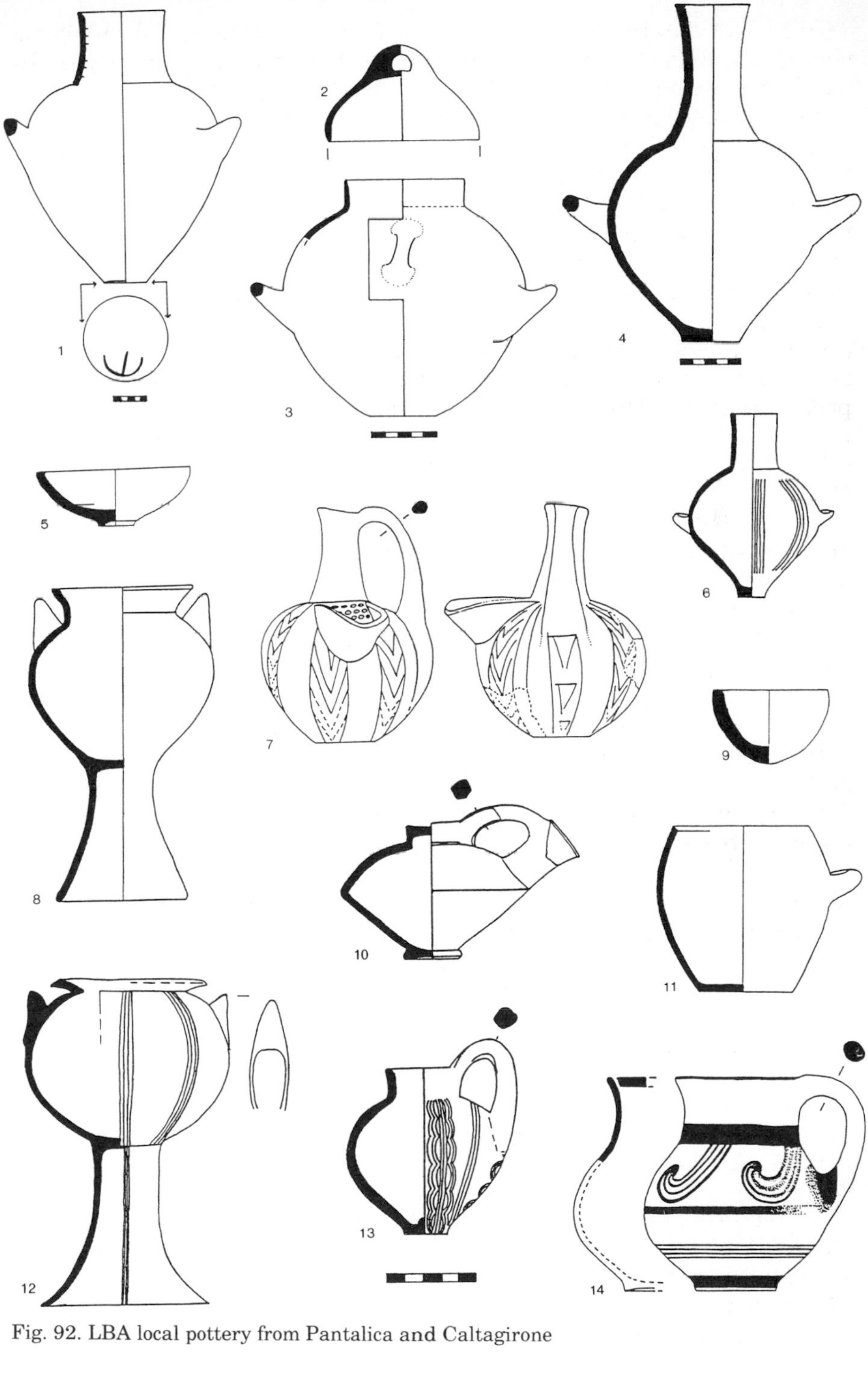

Fig. 92. LBA local pottery from Pantalica and Caltagirone

imports to Sicily, as sometimes assumed. If they are simply local products, they may reflect no more than a shared style common to both islands at this time, encouraged by increased contact.[27] In fact, it is more likely that Sicily was the main exporter of materials to Malta, which may have included metal items, rather than vice versa. Contacts with Malta intensified in the Late Bronze and Early Iron Ages (chapter 5).

Notwithstanding the influence of Mycenaean and Cypriot wares, the overall impression conveyed by Sicilian pottery is of distinctive styles generated by local preferences which maintained independent traditions. This is especially evident in the pottery from Aeolian Milazzese settlements, which is more closely related to South Italian Apennine wares and included imports from that area. In western Sicily, plain handmade ware seems to predominate. Pedestal bowls or chalices are common from this time on, but there is little evidence for wheel-made painted wares. In eastern Sicily too, local pottery accounts for the bulk of production and includes some remarkable vessels, which must have been of special significance, such as monumental pedestal basins, recurrent in both domestic and funerary contexts (fig. 76:2,4). Their vertical forked handles, decorated with circular and triangular motifs seem vaguely anthropomorphic, representing a face or mask or, in some cases, a branching tree.

Metal-working between the 14th and 12th centuries BC is characterized by increased production, a wider range of forms and refinements in quality. In part, this reflects growth in demand due to the appeal, versatility and potential of metal as a convenient way of accumulating wealth in a concentrated form and as a material for trade. The earliest bronze hoards, such as that from San Mauro (Lentini), date from this period, while the new emphasis on metal prestige goods also reflects the promulgation of an élitist ideology. Technological advances are attested by items with a high tin content, sheet-bronze, gold and silver jewellery and two small pieces of iron rod in a Thapsos tomb, which were probably imported. Several forms, especially luxury objects and ingot fragments, are either imports or imitations of Aegean and eastern Mediterranean types.[28] On the other hand, evidence for local continuity in metal production is provided by traditional forms such as axes.

One conspicuous weapon of the Thapsos period is a rapier, represented by examples up to 74cm long with a short tang, three rivet-holes and a raised midrib (fig. 94:1-2). These are elegant, but rather delicate items, perhaps more suitable for display than real combat, although a long sword from Caltagirone was sufficiently well-alloyed with tin (12%) to be practical. Shorter weapons are also known. They are probably not imports or copies of early (LHI-II) Mycenaean rapiers, which have a slightly different hilt design, although they could have been loosely inspired by Mycenaean or Levantine counterparts. Of the shorter daggers, which include miniature forms from burials of Pantalica and Dessueri, one or two examples with a broad blade, squared shoulders and a T-shaped pommel, can be compared with the Aegean F-class, of the 13th-12th centuries BC (fig.

Fig. 93. Pantalica tomb NW38, pedestal basin, H 1.08m

94:12). However, most of the utilitarian short swords and daggers of this period (the Thapsos-Pertosa group), with their triangular arrangement of rivets, are found throughout Sicily as well as in southern Italy and need owe nothing to outside influence. One similar example from the LBA shipwreck of Ulu Burun in southern Turkey could well be a western, possibly Sicilian, export.[29]

Various Sicilian bronzes have widespread parallels in the central Mediterranean and belong within a typological family (or *koiné*) of the 13th-12th centuries BC: these include the violin-bow and early arched fibulae, one-edged knives, shaft-hole axes and various small utensils, such as chisels (fig. 94:10,11,20).[30] Their place of manufacture is uncertain, but it would not be surprising if many were local products, albeit imitations of Mycenaean or eastern Mediterranean forms. The bronze mirrors from Pantalica (fig. 94:18) are sometimes thought to have a Cypriot source, although they also have parallels with Cretan and mainland examples of LH IIIB-IIIC. A stronger case for a Cypriot origin exists for the sheet-bronze bowls from Milena and Caldare, which are almost identical to examples from Enkomi (fig. 94:6,7,9).[31] Fragments of another were found by Orsi in a Thapsos tomb.

Gold and possibly silver ornaments from the Thapsos tombs mainly take the form of small biconical or annular necklace beads, probably imports, albeit of uncertain origin. The gold and silver finger-rings with oval bezels, sometimes incised with coil, fish and eye motifs, from Pantalica, Dessueri and Caltagirone (fig. 94:16,17,19,23) are not easy to date and have only generic parallels in the Aegean or eastern Mediterranean; local manufacture from imported raw materials is hard to rule out. One of the wealthier single burials at Pantalica (t.N37) of about 1200 BC, contained probably a young female, accompanied by a pedestal basin, jug, bezel ring, gold bracelet, three tiny gold beads, fragments of thin gold plate, a bronze mirror and violin-bow fibula (fig. 94:10,22,23). Colourful biconical and disc-shaped glass-paste beads, usually regarded as trade items, are plentiful in the Thapsos tombs, although it would be rash to exclude local manufacture for the amber beads from several MBA-LBA tombs (fig. 95).[32] Techniques of jewellery manufacture as well as metalworking could have been quickly learned and practised. On the other hand, a cylindrical seal-stone recently discovered together with Mycenaean and Cypriot pottery in a tomb at Syracuse undoubtedly represents an import.

Despite centuries of plundering, it is not surprising that most of these finds are from tombs. Metal objects and valuables are unlikely to be discarded in habitation contexts. The ingot fragments from Thapsos and Cannatello may encourage the idea of centralized control over metallurgical activity, as was the case in Mycenaean and East Mediterranean palace economies, although casting moulds are widespread in Sicily and occur with other evidence of metallurgy in dwellings of the Milazzese group (Panarea, Filicudi, Ustica) and at sites inland (Sabucina). The smaller

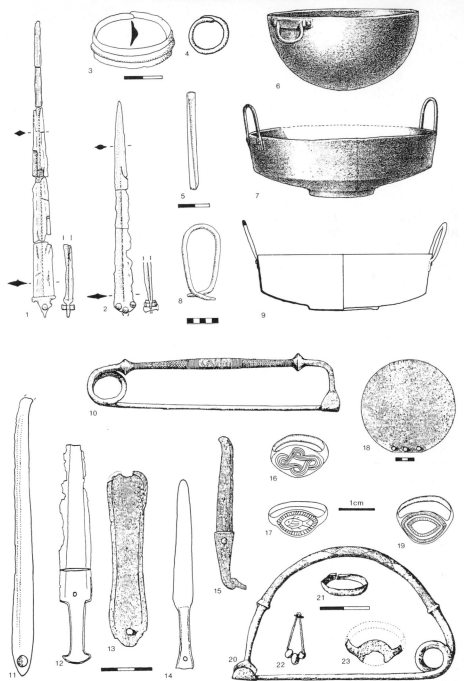

Fig. 94. MBA-LBA metal types: (1-2) Plemmyrion; (3-5, 8) Thapsos; (6-7) Caldare; (9) Milena; (10-18, 20-23) Pantalica North tombs; (19) Caltagirone

179

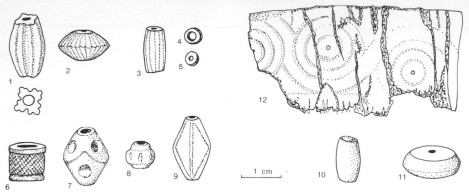

Fig. 95. (1-9) Glass paste beads from Thapsos and Plemmyrion; (10-12) amber beads and bone comb from Plemmyrion

communities were at least involved in recycling, trade and local casting. As demand increased, so too must the incentive to mine local deposits. It would be surprising if native sources of copper in the Peloritani (chapter 5; fig. 111) had not been exploited at this time.[33]

International systems and regional trends

Long-distance maritime trade was a seasonal activity (April-October) in the Mediterranean even in Roman times and Bronze Age boats, which probably had a rather shallow keel and a square sail, would have been profoundly influenced by winds and currents.[34] The latter vary at different times of year and are affected by temperature and weather changes. In the Ionian basin, the early summer currents and the prevalence of the Levant and Scirocco winds generally facilitate crossings from Greece to southern Italy. Likewise, the early spring currents (April-May) in the Tyrrhenian basin tend to favour sailings northward up the coast of Italy. For most of the summer, however, the prevailing Tyrrhenian currents lead clockwise from eastern Sardinia to central-southern Italy and down to Sicily, while the Ionian currents often favour a return sailing to Greece from southern Italy between August and November. These currents would be consistent with voyages westward in the spring and a return to the Aegean in the late summer. From the far western Mediterranean, currents tend to move eastward along the North African coast towards Sicily from Gibraltar for much of the year, although they are rather weak along the Tunisian coast and the pattern can be inverted between June and August. It is also possible that Sicily was approached via the Libyan and western Egyptian shores, where new evidence for Mycenaean trade has been found at Marsa Matruh.[35] A rough idea of the time required for certain journeys may be obtained from classical sources, which suggest that the voyage from the Aegean to Sicily could take up to two weeks, although the narrow stretch from Corfu to Brindisi could be crossed in about nine hours, while the circumnavigation of Sicily often took about one week.

Among the western lands, Sicily must have been of special importance in Bronze Age relations with the Aegean and the eastern Mediterranean, not least for geographical reasons: the voyage along its upper eastern coast is obligatory for boats entering the Tyrrhenian Sea through the Straits of Messina. Well-watered, fertile and with good landing places, the south-eastern shoreline is more welcoming than Calabria's mostly rugged coastline. Thapsos and Lipari must have been strategic ports of call, conveniently placed to provide services and hospitality and to serve as a base for onward voyages. Mycenaean pottery in south-central Sicily may also suggest the existence of an alternative route along the southern coast and perhaps on to Sardinia via the Sicilian channel and North African coast, foreshadowing the pattern of Phoenician settlement centuries later.

Sicily itself must also have been a worthwhile destination on account of its own resources (amber, alum, pumice, rock-salt, sulphur-based products, metal) and as a place where goods from further afield might be obtained, perhaps saving the need for longer sailings westward. The importance of the island as a supplier of goods in a world hungry for metals and trade items of all kinds has probably been underestimated, even though it lacked the metallurgical wealth of Sardinia, Tuscany or Spain. The special relationship with Sicily may also have been facilitated by a long tradition of contacts, extending back to the Early Bronze Age, its strategic location and insular status, and the ability of Sicilian communities to maintain overland, inter-island and coastal trading links.

Paradoxically, more is known about local exchange networks in the Neolithic and Copper Age than later. To what extent indigenous MBA communities engaged in maritime trade is hard to judge, although it seems likely that this period witnessed new initiatives and growing confidence in their ability to undertake long-distance voyages and to carry larger cargoes, thereby laying the foundations for expanding maritime commerce in the western Mediterranean during the later Bronze and Iron Ages. Diverse though not entirely separate mechanisms or spheres of exchange probably existed, both local and long-distance in scope: the former concerned mainly with a more generalized distribution of local commodities, and the latter with valuables and prestige items that accumulated at major centres. Transactions with foreign mariners probably occurred mainly or even exclusively at coastal emporia, like Thapsos in Sicily or Scoglio del Tonno in southern Italy.[36] From such favoured locations, a certain amount of material would have moved through local distribution systems to hinterland sites.

Access to the more sophisticated foreign craft goods evidently stimulated indigenous production and the emulation of exotic items, as shown by the appearance of local versions of Mycenaean pottery. Imported pots and other goods, whose value was enhanced by a distant origin and a long sea voyage, probably gained the status of prestige goods in Sicily, encouraging demand which could best be satisfied by initiating production locally. Greater uniformity in the style of metal products could equally have stemmed from a desire to facilitate exchange transactions by greater standardization, as reflected by the widespread adherence to established forms of metal ingots. A growing appetite for luxury items as well as raw materials was accompanied by the spread of new techniques, such as sheet-bronze working and the use of the potter's wheel. New styles of weaponry and probably of warfare were emulated. In sum, long-distance trade stimulated the regional economy while raising expectations and standards on the part of local consumers and producers, encouraging the emergence of local craftsmen capable of manufacturing the high-quality goods found in wealthy tombs. In such a context of increasing internationalism, there would have been greater opportunity for the absorption of outsiders, especially at sites like Thapsos, and for craftsmen themselves to become more mobile.

Since economic and social concerns are usually entwined in pre-market exchange systems, the flow of raw materials as well as luxury items can be viewed as a response to both practical and ideological demands: the social and symbolic purpose of luxury objects was to stress the links between privileged groups who participated in and promoted international trade, while enhancing their status with prestige goods and gifts. Their special concern with valuable raw materials and luxuries must have involved centralized authorities on both sides capable of organizing production for exchange (surplus) and maritime trade relationships, with their necessary guarantees of sponsorship, protection and access. The increasing importance of this trade may therefore account for the growth of stratified and centralized communities with urbanized structures in Sicily at this time.[37] The Mycenaean initiative in pursuing links with Sicilian communities and the ability of the latter to participate in and sustain increasingly complex social and economic structures, were determinant.

Settlement hierarchies with residential structures of varying size and complexity and funerary ritual give the impression of unequal consumption, as might be expected of a society (a 'complex chiefdom') in which status was marked by items of adornment, exotic objects obtained by long-distance trade, examples of fine local craftsmanship and large or more elaborate burial chambers. In the LBA tombs of Pantalica, despite the shortcomings of the evidence, unequal concentrations of grave goods and the presence of some large richly-furnished tombs support the idea of a stratified society. Moreover, distinct clusters of tombs within cemeteries, corridors linking separate chambers (Pantalica) and niches in tomb walls (Thapsos), suggest the persistence of Sicilian traditions of kinship links, through which status was perhaps inherited or reinforced by funerary ritual; access to an ancestral tomb representing a claim to and a legitimation of status. This old tradition was destined to change in the Iron Age.

Storage facilities are also noteworthy, represented by large *pithoi* and jars, which are consistent with two other aspects of a more complex social organisation: provisioning for larger communities, which include greater numbers of individuals (whether craftsmen, traders or élites) who are not directly involved in food production and need to be supported; and production of surpluses for trade. As regards local subsistence and trade, the caprine and cattle bones from Thapsos could also represent a mobile resource linking coastal and hinterland communities (fig. 96).[38] It is not clear whether olive-growing, viticulture and wine-drinking had begun, although jugs and narrow-necked vessels are common. More centralised forms of land ownership and intensified food production techniques might be expected to have developed, accompanied by greater control over subsistence activities, land and resources.

Finally, even if the Mycenaean palace centres were larger, more elaborately structured, economically powerful and sophisticated in terms of craft production, than contemporary Sicilian societies, one may be wary of interpreting relations between them in terms of colonisation, dominance or the one-sided perspective of a core-periphery model. The idea of a Mycenaean colonisation, resembling that of Greek colonisation at the beginning of the historical period, finds little support, while the Mycenaean homeland was probably too far away to have been able to exert any effective territorial control in Sicily. Relations with the island were close,

	Sheep/ goat	Cattle	Pig	Dog	Deer	Equid
MIDDLE BRONZE AGE						
Grotta Zubbia	23/5	4/2	4/2		4/1	
Comiso Muraglie	23/6	14/3	5/2			
Grotta Chiusazza	44/8	55/7	37/6	3/3	283/18	
Thapsos pit 1&2	118/17	101/8	95/11	6/2	15/4	
Lipari Milazzese	32 (NR)	39	20			
Filicudi C. Graziano	21 (NR)	7	8			
I Faraglioni	874/40	938/21	165/12	3/2		
LATE BRONZE AGE						
Lipari Ausonian I	26 (NR)	22	25			
Lipari Ausonian II	41 (NR)	158	70		1	
LATE BRONZE-IRON AGE						
Morgantina	52/5	68/5	31/7	2/1	57/6	4/1
Fiumedinisi	28/7	55/5	18/4	2/1	46/8	2/1

Fig. 96. MBA-EIA faunal remains. Number of remains/minimum number of individuals

but even at Thapsos and Pantalica the rather eclectic mixture of foreign influences and their tendency to shift towards a new identity, points to a different cultural environment which, at least in part, followed its own agenda and generated its own aesthetic values.

Myths of precedence

Were it not for the absence of written documents, the evidence for this period would stand comparison with some cultures of early historical times. The archaeological record for the 9th-7th centuries BC denotes little more sophistication or complexity as regards settlement design, technology or craft production. Yet despite potters' marks and perhaps some indirect knowledge of the accounting systems and records of Linear texts used in the Mycenaean world, this MBA-LBA society was non-literate and has left no records of language, names, numerical systems or mythology. The only possibility, discussed from time to time, is that one or two legends concerning Sicily and the origins of its inhabitants, recorded by later Greek writers of the historical period, contain a vague recollection or folk-memory of a time when Mycenaean contacts with the island had actually taken place.

This is plausible in theory, although wide gaps remain between possible interpretations of fleeting written notes, colourful anecdotes and archaeological evidence or, put another way, between those more willing to credit the relevant stories with some historical basis and those with a more sceptical outlook. In fact, the proper context for an evaluation of the legends is that of their formation or diffusion in early historical times. Few scholars today maintain that they have documentary value and most are wary of circular arguments in which archaeological remains 'support' the factual basis of legends, which are then used to explain material evidence in pseudo-historical terms. Nonetheless, there exists a lengthy bibliography of erudite but inconclusive speculation, not only in Sicilian historiography, concerning the stories of Greek mythological figures arriving in the island prior to the arrival of Greek settlers proper: Daidalos' flight from Crete to Sicily, the supposed wanderings of Herakles and Odysseus in the island and the arrival of refugees from Troy have been discussed periodically for more than a century by classicists, philologists, local historians and archaeologists.[39] Their assessments have ranged widely from outright dismissal as mythological inventions of the historical period to a sometimes surprisingly literal acceptance as memories of Bronze Age contacts, colonisations or military expeditions.

Most attention has been given to the Daidalos story. By contrast, the exploits of Herakles in the western Mediterranean as recounted by Diodorus (IV.24) are redolent of myth and propaganda.[40] Herakles' tour of Sicily led to various trials of strength with local heroes in the Lentini region, but was apparently designed as a civilizing or Hellenizing mission, which has justly aroused suspicion and led the critics to regard it as a politically motivated literary device, a kind of 'myth of precedence', intended to justify Greek colonisation and expansion in the island. Of course, if the Chalcidian settlers at Lentini really did have some knowledge or memory in folk-tale of Mycenaean contacts with eastern Sicily, this would certainly have lent greater appeal and potency to the story in the context of later Greek colonisation.

The Minos story is more elaborate and compelling, although still encapsulated in no more than a few lines by Herodotus (VII.170) and somewhat embroidered by Diodorus (IV.78). It tells essentially of the flight of Daidalos, an Athenian inventor at the court of Minos, from Crete to Sicily, where he was protected and given employment by a local Sicilian king, whose name was Kokalos, the ruler of Camicus. Soon after his arrival in Sicily, Minos himself and a Cretan expeditionary force followed in pursuit, intending to recapture him, which led to a lengthy siege by the Cretans of the Sicilian stronghold at Camicus. However, the siege failed and, according to one version, Minos was treacherously killed by the daughters of Kokalos, while bathing, but given burial locally in a sumptuous tomb, described by Diodorus, and thought by some scholars to echo the temple-tomb at Knossos. Herodotus implies that the events took place before the Trojan War and states that the Cretans attempted to return home but eventually settled in Apulia.

The historical basis and potential Bronze Age origins of the saga seem impossible to vindicate. One interesting observation is that Minos' ignominious death in Sicily and the implied fiasco of the Cretan expedition shed little credit on the Greeks and might therefore suggest an origin in an indigenous oral tradition (or in some anti-Cretan propaganda). Pugliese Carratelli has argued that the name Kokalos resembles a word in Linear B script, a connection discounted by others, and that the story reflects Mycenaean rather than Minoan contacts with Sicily, after the decline of Minoan power in the Aegean. Through a mist of romantic legend, the story has continued to work on the imagination of some scholars and still sustains the idea of a Mycenaean connection with Sicily that could have involved some ill-fated expedition or a thwarted attempt at territorial control. However, those who have looked to archaeological evidence for some tangible support have had to be content with rather limited permissible conclusions based on Mycenaean or Cypriot material in the island, while noting that there is no sign of specifically close relations with Crete.

By contrast, the sceptics point out that Minos and Daidalos are no more than legendary or semi-legendary figures; the latter a mythological or symbolic personification of Archaic arts and crafts, whose presence was also inferred in Sardinia and Egypt by Greeks of the colonial period in support of their Hellenocentric world view, which promoted the idea of ultimately Greek inspiration for the achievements of non-Greeks in architecture and sculpture. It is no surprise to find that several building and engineering works in Sicily were associated with the name of Daidalos in

Greek tradition. In effect, the story has come to occupy a marginal position in the minds of most archaeologists.

There remains the reference to Camicus which may be grounded in reality. The town was evidently situated in the territory of Agrigento and still existed in Roman Republican times (Strabo VI.273). Its location has often been debated by local historians and topographers: once thought to be the ancestor of Caltabellotta (which is more likely Triocala), others would identify it with Sant'Angelo Muxaro (chapter 6), if only on the grounds that the archaeological finds, notably the large chamber tombs, imply that this was an important site during the Late Bronze and Iron Ages. However, there are other possible candidates and the question remains open.

The links between myth, history and archaeology are no less tenuous in the case of the Odyssey. A tradition had already developed in antiquity that various episodes in Homer's epic poem occurred in Sicily, although there is precious little in the work itself from which to infer actual locations in the west. Nor does it shed much real light on the Mycenaean world, despite certain archaic elements. Nevertheless, Homer obviously knew something about Sicily: Odysseus set sail from *Sikanie* (XXIV.307), an old name for Sicily also noted by Thucydides (VI.5) and Herodotus (VII.170), before arriving in Ithaca, where his aged father, Laertes, was assisted by a Sicilian servant-woman (XXIV.211,366,389), referred to as Σικελὴ γρηῦς (ἀμφίπολος), possibly a bought slave. The association with slaves recurs when the suitors mock Telemachus, advising him to ship his dinner guests off to Sicily for a profit (XX.383), the implication being that Sicily was also a place where slaves were kept, and that to send someone there might simply mean to get rid of them.

Perhaps Homer was once again merely projecting contemporary (8th-7th century BC) information back into the heroic past. However, these references are at least a reminder of another aspect of Bronze Age trade, very difficult to discern archaeologically, but possibly quite real. The Linear B texts, which are the only authentic written document for this period, contain several references to servants or slaves, often female and both privately-owned or belonging to a palace. It appears that some of these women were foreigners, purchased or captured in lands on the edge of the Mycenaean world, such as Anatolia. Good evidence for this comes from tablets at the palace of Pylos in the western Peloponnese, a site also mentioned in the Odyssey. No firm conclusions are possible, but Sicily is no further from Pylos than Anatolia and there is at least one archaeological link between them, represented by an amber bead with a Sicilian provenance from a tomb at Vayenas.[41] One other possibility, as yet difficult to prove, is that the presence of generically western (but probably Italian) coarse pottery, notably from Late Minoan III contexts at Kommos and Chania in Crete, and of certain Italian metal types at other localities in the Aegean, is a reflection of the actual presence of immigrants or slaves.[42]

5

Realignments in Protohistory

Iron Age chronologies and connections

The Early Iron Age (EIA) is conventionally dated between about 900 BC and the foundation of the first Greek settlements in eastern Sicily in 734 BC (table 1). In Italian terminology, it succeeds the Final Bronze Age (*Bronzo Finale*, 1200-900 BC) and, like the latter, falls within the broader designation of *Protostoria*. The early phase (*prima età del ferro*) is distinguished from a second phase (*seconda età del ferro*), which is contemporary with the initial period (734-650 BC) of Greek colonisation (chapter 6).[1] In Sicily, the Early Iron Age has been named after the Pantalica III (or South) complex: the later chamber tombs found by Orsi in the southern cemetery at this site in the Hyblaean hills (below). Iron was more common now than before, although utilitarian products were mostly of bronze. The term Iron Age, therefore, is a conventional one and the date of 900 BC for its beginning is only a convenient approximation since there is no clear break coinciding with the spread of iron-working at precisely this moment. In fact, several sites discussed in this chapter, such as Mulino della Badia (and Madonna del Piano), Dessueri, Morgantina and Cassibile, date from the Final Bronze Age (probably from a rather late stage of the latter) in conventional terminology, but lasted well into the Iron Age.

Declining contact with the Aegean after about 1200 BC hinders effective cross-dating during the centuries which coincide with the Greek Submycenaean, Protogeometric and Early Geometric periods.[2] An historical calendar begins with the foundation of Greek colonies, but the Sicilian cultures of the preceding centuries are dated by an internal sequence. Much rests on the stylistic evolution of a few artefacts, such as bronze fibulae, generally limited to tombs. Although the relative sequence of development is reasonably clear, period subdivisons and real dates have been the subject of several revisions and unresolved controversies. The situation would be clearer if more ^{14}C dates were available, if securely dated imports from the Aegean were found in local contexts and stratigraphic sequences were better known.

I have argued that the Pantalica II (or Cassibile) phase (traditionally about 1000-850 BC) lasted longer than the standard chronology assumes. Sites such as Thapsos, Cassibile and Dessueri could still have been occupied well into the 8th century BC, while the recent discoveries of indigenous buildings on Syracuse could represent the remains of native

187

dwellings abandoned in the 8th century BC due to the arrival of the first Greek settlers.[3] Similarly, the Iron Age (Ausonian) settlements at Lentini and Morgantina must have lasted until the arrival of Greek settlers in the 8th and 6th centuries BC respectively. Many of the Pantalica III (or South) tombs, hitherto dated between the 9th and 8th centuries BC, would be better dated in the early colonial or Finocchito period (734-650 BC).[4]

Despite continuity of tradition and of occupation at some locations, various features of the Early Iron Age contrast with those of earlier times. In eastern Sicily, the last phase of occupation at Thapsos signals a break with the earlier urban layout; the chamber tombs of the Cassibile phase tend to be more uniform than their predecessors, suggesting transformations in social structure; the relatively new settlements of Mulino della Badia, Morgantina and Lentini, characterized by so-called Ausonian assemblages, paralleled on Lipari, share features with contemporary groupings in southern Italy, especially in Campania and Calabria. The similarities include forms of domestic architecture, burial practices and craft products, or features of the socio-economic and ideological spheres, and possibly extended to aspects of ethnicity, such as language.

Inspired by references in ancient literary sources to the movements of Sikels and other groups (Ausoni, Morgeti), it is widely believed that immigrants from continental Italy entered Sicily during the Late Bronze and Early Iron Ages. Archaeologically, they are associated with the expansion of Ausonian complexes, although certain features of the Ausonian sites point to a separate and distinctly Sicilian identity, due to local adaptations. Cultural changes occurred as a result of both local and external forces. Western Sicily has more evidence for continuity in pottery styles and burial practices. However, new excavations at Dessueri and Scirinda have revealed rectangular huts with ceramic assemblages that closely resemble the Ausonian complexes of eastern Sicily. In addition, the Maltese Bahrija complex has close affinities with Ausonian Sicily; the main influences at this time, like the metals which they accompanied, were undoubtedly coming to Malta from Sicily rather than vice versa.

Iron Age communities seem less hierarchical than their predecessors and suggest a somewhat devolved arrangement of large village-based groupings, possibly with more egalitarian social structures, less concerned with prestige goods and status-enhancing luxuries from distant sources than with local craft production for general consumption. They might be described as 'simple chiefdoms' or even 'tribal' entities, although these labels risk equating them with Neolithic societies, which were very different in character. Although we know little about their political organisation, Iron Age society was one of articulated social roles, probably based on factors such as age, gender, handicraft skills and physical prowess. The presence of warriors, weavers, potters, metalworkers and traders can at least be inferred. Moreover, this was a time of technological

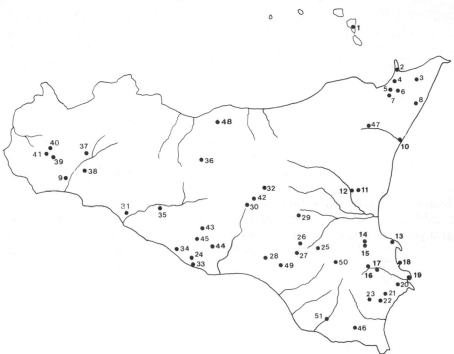

Fig. 97. LBA and EIA sites and hoards: 1 Lipari; 2 Milazzo; 3 Rometta; 4 Pozzo di Gotto; 5 Longane; 6 Piano Cannafé; 7 Pietro Pallio; 8 Fiumedinisi; 9 Stretto; 10 Naxos; 11 Paternò; 12 Pietralunga; 13 Punta Castelluzzo; 14 Lentini (Metapiccola, San Mauro); 15 Carrube; 16 Pantalica; 17 Rivetazzo; 18 Thapsos; 19 Syracuse; 20 Cozzo Pantano; 21 Cassibile; 22 Avola; 23 Noto; 24 Boccazza; 25 Mulino della Badia-Madonna del Piano; 26 Caltagirone; 27 Monte San Mauro; 28 Dessueri; 29 Cittadella-Morgantina; 30 Sabucina; 31 Scirinda; 32 Calascibetta (Carcarella); 33 Castellazzo di Palma; 34 Cannatello; 35 Sant'Angelo Muxaro; 36 Valledolmo; 37 Monte Finestrelle; 38 Santa Margherita Belice; 39 Timpone Pontillo; 40 San Ciro; 41 Mokarta; 42 Capodarso; 43 Canicattì; 44 Campobello di Licata; 45 Naro; 46 Spaccaforno; 47 Malvagna hoard; 48 Gratteri hoard; 49 Niscemi hoard; 50 Vizzini (Tre Canali) hoard; 51 Castelluccio hoard

innovation and intensification of local production, particularly evident in metal-working.

The 'Dark Age' epithet which is applied to contemporary Greece would therefore be misleading for Sicily, although there are analogies with the Aegean, where profound social changes took place at about the same time. One reason for social change may be the decline of trade with the Aegean at the end of the Mycenaean period. The MBA-LBA social system, in which local élites were sustained by access to external sources of power and ideology, could have been undermined when communications began to break down, encouraging new forms of political power and movements away from the old centres, whose former preeminence was no longer justified. In terms of socio-political evolution, one may be reminded that

Fig. 98. Lipari acropolis hut a2 (L about 16m)

centralized and relatively complex 'chiefdoms' do not necessarily develop into early states.

New relationships were also being formed towards the end of the Bronze Age between Sicily, southern Italy and the western Mediterranean due to economic and perhaps political realignments, encouraged by changes to international trade networks following the disruption of links with the Aegean. The demise of palace economies in Greece did not prevent the expansion of metal-working and trade within the western Mediterranean and may even have democratized commercial activity by loosening centralized controls. Regional styles in metal-working flourished throughout Italy in the 10th and 9th centuries BC, while the relationship between eastern Sicily and Calabria became closer, doubtless facilitated by cultural affinities between 'Ausonian' and Calabrian groups. Long-distance contacts allowed metal goods to move between Iberia, Sardinia, Tyrrhenian Italy and Sicily. By the Early Iron Age Sicily had returned to a western sphere of interaction.

Settlements and domestic architecture

EIA site locations show considerable diversity (fig. 97). At one end of the scale are deposits in rock-shelters and caves, such as Punta Castelluzzo and the Grotta Chiusazza, which may represent no more than temporary shelters used by transhumant shepherds.[5] There is little evidence for the use of caves for burials or cult activities. The more complex, multi-faceted sites were probably those at certain coastal locations, which were still

190

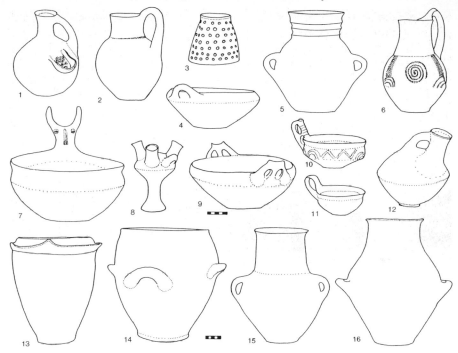

Fig. 99. Lipari, Ausonian II levels, LBA-EIA pottery

occupied: Syracuse, Naxos and Thapsos, provided with good natural harbours, no doubt retained a maritime role at this time, as suggested by the
persistence of Maltese connections with Thapsos. The same applies to the
Lipari acropolis, where some buildings, such as the large Ausonian I hut
(a2) probably continued in use (figs. 81 and 98) and the pottery shows only
a gradual stylistic evolution (fig. 99).

However, there are signs of a break in continuity and a change in the
layout at Thapsos (phase 3), where circular or courtyard buildings (phase
1-2) were replaced by quadrangular structures and there is little evidence
for burial.[6] Two contiguous rectangular rooms, respectively 10m and 7m
long, had a low bench around the inside wall and different activity areas,
suggested by a cluster of large storage jars and pottery at one end,
scattered loomweights, deer antler and a more open space with millstones
at the other end (fig. 75:Area 2,C). While the overall urban plan remains
obscure, the rectilinear design of these buildings suggests a more regular
layout, perhaps encouraged by the flatter coastal terrain, by comparison
with inland hilltop sites. The finds include coarse wares, plumed vessels,
carinated cups and storage jars, similar to those of the Metapiccola hill at
Lentini and the Cittadella of Morgantina (fig. 100:4,9), as well as various
cups, jars and pedestal bowls matched in the later Borg-in Nadur and
Bahrija horizons on Malta (fig. 100:1-3,5-8).

191

According to Thucydides (VI.3), the indigenous inhabitants of Syracuse were evicted by Greek colonists. Potentially one of the most informative Iron Age settlements in Sicily, but known only from limited soundings beneath the layers of the Greek colony, it evidently extended over the highest ground (subsequently the acropolis) near the middle of the island of Ortygia: sections of at least five huts have emerged in the vicinity of the Athenaion and Prefecture, typified by curved stone walls with internal benches, coarse kitchen wares, fine plumed and geometric painted wares and large storage jars.[7] A rock-cut tomb located about 2km away (on Via P. Orsi), containing at least five inhumations, local painted ware, bronze elbow and serpentine fibulae of the 9th, or possibly early 8th, century BC, could represent the burial area of the Ortygia site or of another as yet unknown indigenous settlement on the adjacent mainland.

Far from these exposed coastal sites were sizeable hilltop villages overlooking inland river valleys. Several had already appeared in the Late Bronze Age and more emerged subsequently, persisting into historical times when they still represent a characteristic feature of indigenous settlement patterns (chapter 6). Many took advantage of defensive positions and opportunities offered by the confluence of diverse habitats: hilly and wooded hinterlands in which wild game was still plentiful as well as pasture and arable land on rolling hills and river valleys. For example, a string of settlements extended along the southern side of the Catania plain, following a natural line of communication inland. Similar patterns can be found in earlier periods, but the growing importance of these sites at the end of the Bronze Age may also be due to a decline in the central-place functions and prestige of coastal sites, which had formerly enjoyed a privileged role in long-distance trade.

At Lentini and on the Cittadella of Morgantina, the settlement probably

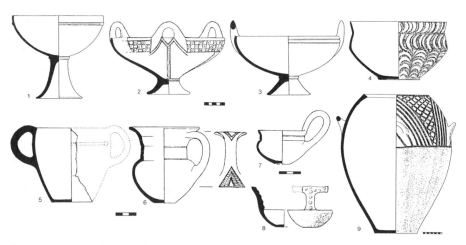

Fig. 100. Thapsos LBA-EIA pottery

192

consisted of several clusters of houses, without a close-knit urban layout, streets or central public buildings.[8] Several rectangular 'long-houses' are known, each constructed according to similar criteria, in the tradition of later prehistoric dwellings in many parts of western Europe (fig. 101:B,D). They had sunken floors, often cut into the bedrock and covered with a tough lime plaster, a low bench along the inside walls, and a combination of dry stone masonry, sometimes plastered with clay on the inside, timber posts, and a wattle and daub superstructure. Projecting doorways can be inferred at Lentini and Lipari. Solid, relatively spacious, and well insulated against summer heat or winter cold, they were evidently built to last (several floor-levels are common), rather than to impress.

The largest houses were substantial buildings (up to 20 x 4.5m), sometimes subdivided. On the Cittadella, there were well-furnished units with the requisites of domestic life and shelter (fig. 101:E): one or two hearths, consisting of broken potsherds and baked clay surfaces, centrally located; two or three terracotta cooking-stands, beside a domed oven, occupying a corner intended for preparing food, with millstones nearby; an uncluttered space around the central hearths, perhaps for sleeping; and a storage zone with large jars placed on paving stones at one end. Aside from abundant pottery, the finds included loomweights, spindle-whorls, metal-working equipment, stone, metal and bone tools, and antler. Leaving aside comparisons with the urban complex (phase 1-2) at Thapsos, Iron Age houses were as well or better equipped than the ordinary dwellings of the previous period. They may reflect an overall improvement in the living standards and material wealth of the community as a whole.

Until recently, it was believed that western Sicily maintained separate traditions derived from the Thapsos-Pantalica MBA-LBA phases. However, this view is changing as excavations reveal more evidence for EIA buildings which resemble those of eastern Sicily and Lipari.[9] For example, a long-house at Scirinda (fig. 101:C) with central post-holes and an internal bench, contained plumed and coarse wares of Ausonian type. Subdivided quadrangular structures with similar pottery are known at Dessueri (Monte Maio), dated between the 11th and 9th century BC (although they could be 8th century BC). Rectangular dwellings with timber-laced walls, rock-cut floors and similar pottery succeeded the LBA round huts at Sabucina (chapter 4), where they probably represent the last phase of prehistoric occupation, and are also known at Piano Vento. Similar structures are encountered on Malta: elliptical dwellings (7.5 x 3.5m) at Borg in-Nadur, with internal benches, hearths and sunken floors covered by a tough lime plaster, could date to about this time (fig. 101:A).[10]

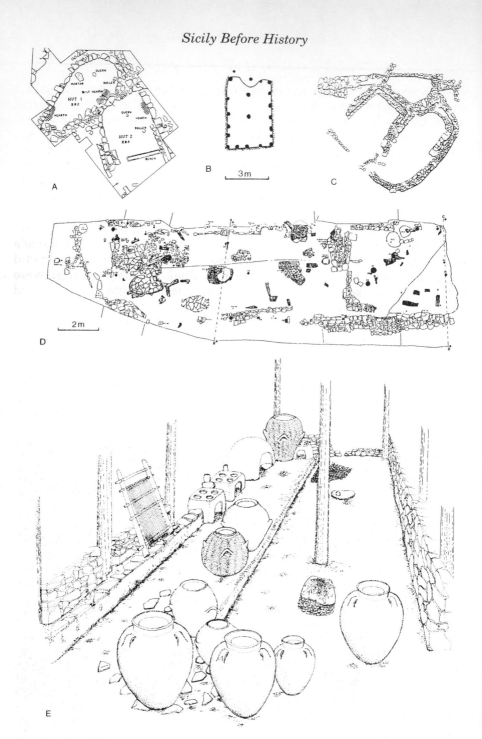

Fig. 101. LBA-EIA house plans: (A) Borg-in Nadur; (B) Lentini; (C) Scirinda; (D-E) Morgantina trench 31

Burial practices and social structure

The diversity of burial practices in Sicily, sometimes encountered at the same site, presents a challenge for interpretation. Two main types of cemetery are known: those with the traditional rite of inhumation in a rock-cut chamber tomb, and those with various combinations of single inhumations in jars (*enchytrismoi*), trench graves (*fossae*) and cremations. The earliest cremation cemetery is probably that of Milazzo, which resembles a LBA urnfield of Italian 'Protovillanovan' type (fig. 102). Probably slightly later in date (LBA or Ausonian II) is the cemetery of Piazza Monfalcone on Lipari in which both jar burial inhumations and cremations occur (fig. 103).[11] Apart from separate burial grounds, usually located on the slopes or near the valley bottom beneath the settlement, a few burials within the inhabited zone are documented, for example at Morgantina and on Lipari, where the remains of some individuals, possibly children, were deposited in bucket-shaped vessels (*dolia*) placed upright in the ground just outside the houses.

A major source of information is the cemetery of about 340 tombs at Madonna del Piano, where various practices are encountered.[12] Most burials (about 175 examples) consisted of single inhumations in trench graves dug into the earth, sometimes lined with stone slabs, and covered by a mound of earth or stones, perhaps visible as a grave-marker (fig. 104:A-C) The deceased were supine, probably clothed, and wearing such items as fibulae and rings. Other grave goods, such as a pot or metal

Fig. 102. Milazzo, LBA cremation urn burial reconstruction, Lipari museum

Fig. 103. Lipari Piazza Monfalcone, LBA jar burials

implements, were generally located by the head or around the body. Almost as common (about 137 examples) were single burials in large storage jars (*pithoi*) placed on their sides with the mouths sealed by a pottery vessel or slab and covered by stones (fig. 104:D). In these cases, the grave goods were found mixed among the bones. Smaller jars (*dolia*) were sometimes used as burial containers, probably for children. In addition, one example of a stone sarcophagus is recorded. Cremations, by contrast, were rare (nine examples), represented by a pottery urn, sometimes with the mouth covered by a bowl, placed upright in a shaft that was lined and covered with stones. Any tomb goods were usually beside the urn within the shaft. However, at least one cremation (tomb 61) was identified in a *pithos*.

Some doubts remain as to why certain people were inhumed in jars, others in trench graves, while a few were cremated. The different forms of burial were spread throughout the cemetery and there was no obvious difference between the contents of the jars or *fossae*, betraying social or gender distinctions. Some of the cremations may be slightly earlier in date than the fossa graves (9th century BC), but there is little reason to doubt that mixed practices subsequently coexisted. One explanation might be that separate clans, community traditions or even ethnic groups were reflected in the cemetery, perhaps used by more than one local settlement. The trench graves and cremations in particular have suggested the presence of immigrant groups, or at least the adoption of practices from

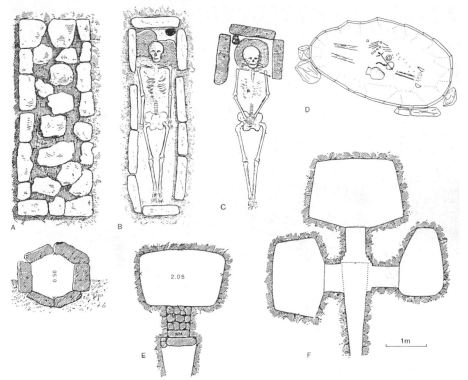

Fig. 104. EIA burial types: (A-D) Mulino della Badia-Madonna del Piano; (E-F) Cassibile

continental Italy, whereas the jar burials have local precedents in the Sicilian Bronze Age.

However, although skeletal studies are lacking, it seems more likely that the different rites were partly determined by age-group. The small size of many pottery containers and of bones found inside them suggests that they were for children. By contrast, the trench graves seemed to contain adults. In the Archaic period, it was sometimes the case that children and younger people were placed in jars, and this might derive from an EIA tradition. The proximity of certain burials to each other may also reflect kin relationships or family groupings, as in a modern cemetery. Tomb 121b, for example, possibly contained a mother and child, represented by a small jar burial resting on the bones of an adult (provided with a needle) in a trench grave.

Certain variations in the number and kinds of burial objects, notably bronze ornaments (fig. 105), also seem explicable in terms of gender. On the basis of the greater quantity of dress ornaments (fibulae, rings, bracelets, combs, buttons) it is tempting to infer that some of the 'wealthier' tombs were female. Moreover, sets of utensils (knives, awls, needles, spindles and spindle-whorls) in a few of these graves suggest an association between women and spinning, or textile manufacture, a recurrent feature of Italian Iron Age burials. The presence of textile equipment in fairly well-furnished adult tombs may also signify rank. Harder to explain are some burials containing little bronze bells and tubes, possibly musical instruments, or jingling dress ornaments: perhaps females endowed with a special status. There is no sign of inferior female rank in terms of grave goods. In fact, adult male tombs generally seem to be poorer, with only a fibula and a 'razor', an implement which resembles a palette and may have served a funerary purpose.[13] Children's burials, with an occasional exception, were generally poorly furnished: perhaps status was acquired in adulthood, rather than inherited at birth.

It has been estimated that female burials outnumbered male by almost 3:1, although this calculation could be misleading if more of those with few or no grave goods, omitted from the equation, were in fact male.[14] Children or young persons seem to account for about one-third of the cemetery, but there is no evidence for infants. It seems that burial was reserved for individuals of a minimum age, whereas infants may have been placed in the jars found in residential zones.

Cremation was a more restricted practice (less than 4% of tombs), although not exclusive to either sex. Several cremations held items like those of inhumations and five of them are reckoned to have been female on the basis of spindle-whorls and other ornaments. Grave goods accompanying cremations also varied in quantity. One of the wealthiest (tomb 26), presumed to be male, included a set of bronze weaponry: a short sword with sheath, spear, greaves, a possible leather corselet (or helmet?) sewn with buttons, four bronze rings, a fibula and a strainer-spouted jug (fig. 105:1-5).

The combination of a spear and short sword suggests a loose style of fighting or skirmishing that required ease of movement, reminiscent of Homeric combat, which perhaps started with an exchange of javelins and concluded with a *mêlée*. Iron Age weaponry seems generally better designed from a practical standpoint than that of earlier periods, as reflected by a wider range of sturdy defensive and offensive arms from burials and hoards (below). Some warriors may have been mounted, as suggested by horse-bits (fig. 115:3) and possibly the greaves, although the nature and extent of warfare is hard to gauge. Perhaps the ownership of large flocks and herds led to rustling and raiding, while the population movements thought to characterize this period provoked territorial conflicts. Nevertheless, only half a dozen or so burials at Madonna del Piano contained weapons: a much lower proportion than that of many south Italian sites, such as Torre Galli.[15] The militaristic dimension should therefore not be exaggerated.

The existence of another cremation and inhumation cemetery near Santa Margherita Belice of the 8th-7th centuries BC shows that burial grounds of this kind were probably widespread amongst indigenous groups.[16] These rites continued during the early historical period and must

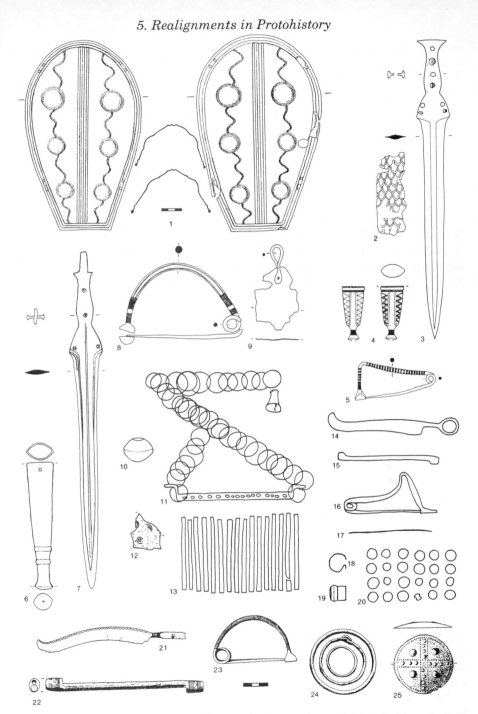

Fig. 105. Grave goods from Madonna del Piano: (1-5) cremation tomb 26, probably male; (6-9) cremation tomb 196, probably male; (10-20) jar burial 5, probably female; (21-25) various tombs

have seemed quite familiar to the first Greek settlers, especially those from Rhodes and Crete, where mixed rites of cremation (usually adults), inhumation in jars (generally children) and even in chamber tombs were also practiced (chapter 6).

At Pantalica, Dessueri, Cassibile, Carcarella and other sites, especially in southern Sicily, the traditional rite of inhumation in a rock-cut tomb persisted (fig. 104:E,F). The later tombs were characterized by growing uniformity in size and grave goods by comparison with the Thapsos and Pantalica North periods.[17] The Dessueri and Carcarella tombs were mostly circular in plan, from 1.50-2m in diameter and about 1m in height, and rarely contained more than four depositions, sometimes of adults and children together, or couples, while some individuals were buried alone, or added later (fig. 87). This suggests small family groups. Likewise, in western Sicily, there was nothing monumental about the Mokarta tombs: modest rock-cut chambers of circular or elliptical plan in which the deceased (from 1-7 individuals) were accompanied by one or two vases but few luxuries, except for some tiny glass paste beads, and very little metal, represented by an occasional arched fibula and ring. Vessels were sometimes found in the corridor, perhaps reflecting some additional ritual outside the chamber proper (see chapter 6). The Cassibile tombs were mostly quadrangular (Ø 1.50-2m), with relatively modest grave goods: one or two plumed plate-stands, jugs and bowls, bronze fibulae, rings, buttons and belt-hooks, or small implements, such as knives and razors (fig. 106). Except for the recurrent plate-stands, these items are similar in style to those of Mulino della Badia, suggesting a move away from the conspicuous consumption of earlier times.

A puzzling aspect of funerary practice is the mixture of rock-cut tombs and jar burials within the same region, and sometimes near the same site. Lentini is an interesting case (fig. 107; and chapter 6).[18] The deceased from the Metapiccola settlement may be represented by jar burials recently discovered in the Pozzanghera valley below. However, on the adjacent San Mauro hill and in greater numbers at Cugno Carrube, just 2km away, small rock-cut tombs of about same period have been found. Most of the Carrube chambers had been disturbed, but probably contained between 1 and 3 skeletons, sometimes couples, accompanied by a small number of personal ornaments (fibulae, curved knives), spindle-whorls, vases and small bronze tubes, not unlike those from *enchytrismos* and *fossa* burials.

The main contrast, therefore, was in the form of grave and the number of deceased: rock-cut tombs with multiple depositions and jar burials with a single individual. Lacking skeletal studies, age differences are unclear, while status or class differences are equally hard to discern, since the grave goods were all relatively modest. It could be argued that chamber tombs were more prestigious because they required greater effort to construct, although some of the larger chambers used or re-used at this time probably date from an earlier period, and could therefore have been merely tombs of convenience. There remains the possiblity that, rather

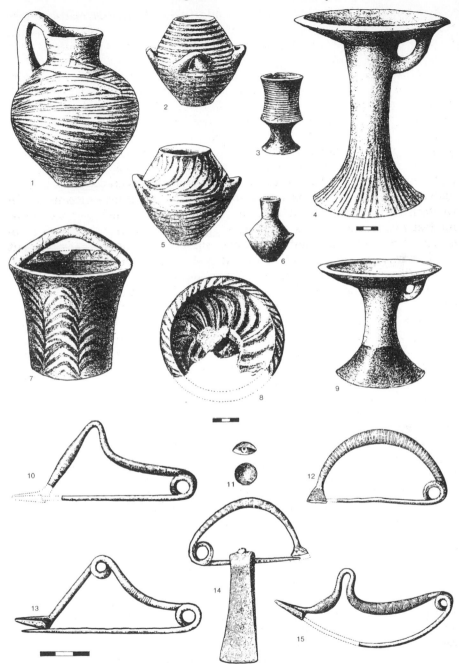

Fig. 106. Cassibile grave goods

than social or ethnic differences, these contrasts denote no more than the existence of different local traditions or preferences: an old tradition of rock-cut tomb burial, firmly rooted in southern Sicily; a more scattered tradition of jar burial of EBA origin; and a more recent LBA custom of cremation and trench-grave inhumation of peninsular derivation, adopted by some groups, especially in central-northern Sicily.

Aside from this problem, most differences between the various categories of Iron Age burials may be accounted for in terms of gender, age and role. In general, they sustain the impression of a shift towards a more egalitarian society. Against this, perhaps, is the cremation of Madonna del Piano (tomb 26) which stands out on account of its weaponry. Does this betray the existence of a warrior élite? Cremation is obviously a very different procedure, more like a sacrificial consecration, and the burning of a body, perhaps someone who excelled or died in battle, might have been a mark of particular respect in this case. Even so, there remain several otherwise unremarkable cremations in the cemetery and it is debatable whether we are in the presence here of a restricted élite, or merely of armed individuals with a special role as protectors of their fellows, from whom they were not otherwise socially distinct.

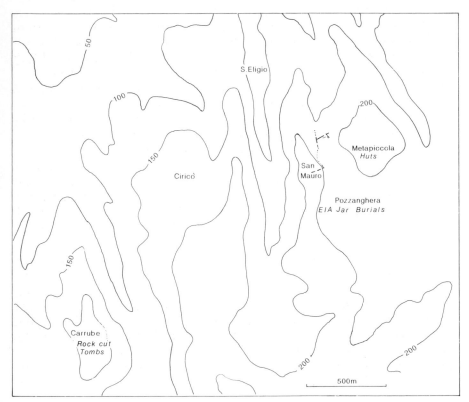

Fig. 107. Lentini plan

It is also possible that ideology changed at the end of the Bronze Age so as to renounce or disguise status affiliations in death, which was now regarded as the leveller of real inequalities among the living. The existence of lower-class dependents or serfs denied access to these cemeteries, or of a privileged clique whose burials have yet to be found elsewhere, cannot be ruled out entirely. Obviously, it is even harder to identify actual forms of political leadership on the basis of the available data, and it would be rash to assert that these communities were acephalous. Some kind of social differentiation is bound to have existed. However, as it stands, the evidence could suggest that whether through the individual prowess of petty chieftains (with reference to warrior cremations), or through the collective authority of elders or village councils (with reference to the overall homogeneity of settlements), or some combination of these, leadership at this time was along the lines of *primus inter pares* and was not associated with conspicuous personal wealth.

Crafts, subsistence and trade

If warriors, weavers or spinners may be so characterized by their funerary accoutrements, while many other burials are entirely anonymous, various craft activities can be inferred in domestic contexts. Pottery falls into various classes (fig. 108). Handmade vessels are abundant and most likely the product of non-specialist labour and individual households. They often take the form of bucket-shaped vessels (*dolia*) with lightly burnished orange-brown surfaces and blackened patches from uneven firing, sometimes simply decorated with raised cordons or provided with basic lug-handles. Along with conical milk-boilers (fig. 99:3) and in conformity with a widespread tradition of the European Bronze and Iron Ages, they can perhaps be associated with the dairy products of a pastoralist society. Of superior quality are wheel-made or possibly mould-made burnished wares: ubiquitous drinking cups and bowls with a single raised handle, sometimes modelled with bosses and horns (figs. 99:7; 109). Various bowls and broad flat dishes were used for cooking and sometimes placed directly on the hearth.

Fine wheel-made plumed and geometric painted wares are represented by amphorae, suitable as storage and perhaps trade items. These required a selection and preparation of clays, a potter's wheel and careful firing, suggesting the existence of craft workshops with skilled artisans, although perhaps not full-time specialists. Plumed pottery usually had a slipped and burnished surface, painted with bands of reddish-brown semicircular motifs, reminiscent of basketry. Geometric patterns consisted mainly of broad concentric triangles and linear bands, occasionally combined with plumes. Incised symbols on the bases may represent ownership or workshop marks.

The huge pedestal basins of Thapsos and Pantalica seem to have been

203

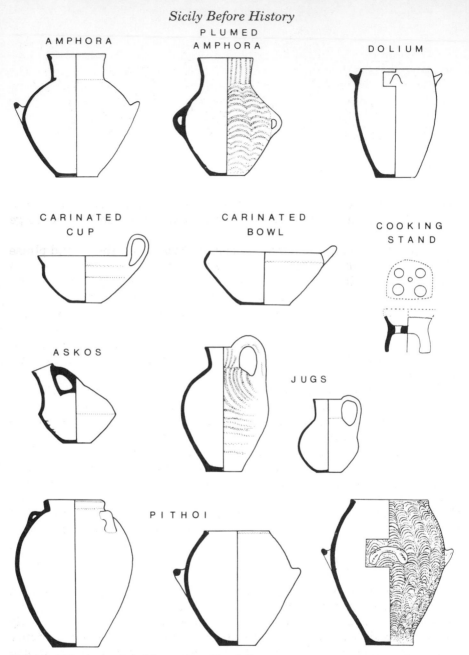

Fig. 108. EIA pottery from Morgantina, Cittadella

substituted by more modest pedestal plates (fig. 106:4), while the metallic red wares of Pantalica gave way to darker oranges and browns, although the amphora shape persisted and various jugs, cups and storage jars were still produced. The styles had changed but the technical advances of

Fig. 109. Carinated cups from Morgantina, Cittadella

MBA-LBA potting had not been lost. The overall impression is of diversified levels of production with regional stylistic variations and a wide range of forms.

Incised wares were uncommon in eastern Sicily until the second phase of the Iron Age, although some fragments from Ausonian sites attest an earlier local origin, paralleled in southern Italy. On stylistic grounds, the Sant'Angelo Muxaro pottery of central and western Sicily (fig. 142) seems to derive from the incised ware of Thapsos and Pantalica, while certain shapes resemble those of Cassibile. However, the elaborate development of local incised ware occurred later with the Polizzello and so-called Elymian styles of western Sicily and Finocchito in the east (chapter 6).

Well-shaped and evenly fired, large storage jars (*pithoi*), frequently over a metre high, were used as burial containers in cemeteries, such as Madonna del Piano, as well as for storage. They were sometimes distinguished by incised marks on the handles, perhaps a reference to their contents or makers (fig. 110). Clay sources are relatively common in Sicily so that pots might seem unlikely trade items, unless they were particularly finely made and decorated, or used to transport other substances. The handsome painted amphorae may belong in this category, whereas the largest *pithoi* were most likely made locally. In this case, the potter could have been an itinerant artisan serving more than one community. However, there is little to suggest that painted vessels were other than utilitarian, and widely available in domestic contexts: perhaps a sign of greater equality of consumption.

Information about cereal agriculture is scant and mainly indirect: lava millstones were traded widely, and grain impressions on baked clay are known. Barley is documented in the early colonial period and was probably cultivated widely in the Late Bronze and Iron Ages. Slender evidence exists for grapes, though probably of a wild variety (chapter 6). Some changes in agricultural practice are suggested by new implements resembling hoes and pruning-hooks (fig. 113:6,10,12), possibly a reflection of increasing arboriculture.[19] Caprines, cattle, pig and deer dominate faunal assemblages and a little evidence exists for equines and dogs (fig. 96). A faunal sample from EIA Syracuse collected by Orsi consisted mainly of

205

Fig. 110. Storage jars from Morgantina, Cittadella trench 31

cattle (more than 20 individuals), followed by caprines, pig, deer (about 8 individuals), with slight evidence for equids (teeth only), large quantities of land and marine molluscs and some fish bone.[20] Ausonian groups evidently practised a combination of plough agriculture and diversified stock-raising, supplemented by hunting and gathering of wild species as well as coastal fishing.

Bone, horn and antler from domestic species and deer were turned into buttons, combs, awls and handles, while hides and skins, which are eminently suitable trade items, were no doubt processed. The ubiquitous spinning and weaving materials (spindle-whorls, loomweights, combs and needles) suggest that many Iron Age households had a loom, testifying to the importance of manufactured goods derived from a diversified subsistence base. Woollen textiles frequently contribute greatly to trade in communities where the men are predominantly concerned with plough agriculture and pastoralism, while the women spin and weave.

In sum, the Iron Age household was both a destination for the various products of skilled artisans and a producer of goods for local consumption and probably for exchange between neighbouring communities. Some craft activities, such as textile production, were perhaps organised cottage industries, and the larger villages probably had their own skilled potters. More specialised activities, including those of prospectors, scrap metal merchants and smiths are implied by the increase in metal-working, described below. Metallurgical equipment and stone casting moulds have been found in domestic contexts on the Cittadella, a sign that members of the local community participated in production. At most sites, which were too far from primary sources to have been involved in mining, this must have taken the form of collecting, recycling and recasting objects that were broken or no longer required. The main source of metal consisted of hoards, although some primary copper circulated in the form of plano-convex 'bun' ingots during the 8th century BC.[21] If Iron Age society was decentralized by comparison with that of the previous period, as claimed here, it seems likely that metallurgical activity would have been organised or sponsored by a collective rather than by an élite group.

The quantity and variety of metal objects in contemporary hoards and burials emphasize the importance of metal goods in local economies throughout the western Mediterranean. Extraction of raw material must have intensified everywhere and even minor sources were probably now thought worth exploiting. An increase in settlements known from surveys in metal-bearing regions of the Peloritani suggests that local groups here were engaged in extracting ores from natural veins near the surface (fig. 111). Recent metal analyses, though still at an early stage, and the widespread use of bronze in the island cast doubt on the idea of a complete reliance on external sources of the raw material.

The distribution of supplies and finished items must have altered as a result of social and economic changes. Exchange relations were realigned towards metal-producing areas of Italy and the western Mediterranean, especially Sardinia, Tuscany and perhaps Calabria. The Aegean and eastern Mediterranean probably no longer provided reliable clients for raw materials, nor much of an inspiration for metal-production in the West after the 11th century BC, even though some items, such as the fibulae of Greece and southern Italy, still shared several traits; sporadic contacts doubtless persisted, but of secondary importance by comparison with western links.[22] Moreover, social changes following the demise of the

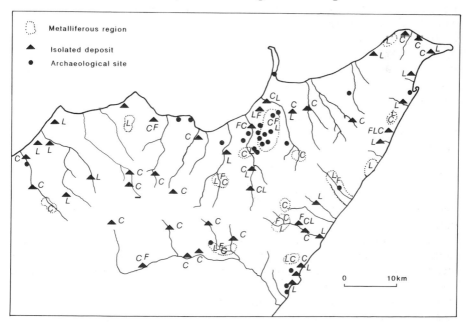

Fig. 111. LBA-EIA sites and areas with metal sources: C = copper; F = iron; L = lead

207

Mycenaean palaces were encouraging a wider and different use of metal goods, which were no longer valued so much for exotic connotations and showy effects as for utilitarian criteria, durability and efficiency. In Sicily, delicate rapiers had given way to daggers, knives and spears; axes were tested with various hafting arrangements; new agricultural tools and implements appeared; violin-bow fibulae, once accessible to a small minority along with mirrors and jewellery, were replaced by more widely available bronze personal ornaments, especially arched and elbow (Cassibile) fibulae. A wider range of metal goods was being produced than before (figs. 112-115).

Regional styles of bronze-working evolved throughout Italy towards the end of the Bronze Age, perhaps due to the emergence of increasingly self-sufficient groups, all of whom had access to supplies and were in possession of the technological know-how to satisfy their own manufacturing needs. At the same time, there are many similarities between Sicilian and southern Italian metal goods, which probably reflect down-the-line inter-regional trade as well as more diffuse forms of cultural interaction, including movements of population, perhaps of metal-workers in particular, encouraging the spread of technical information and metal-working practices. Long-distance maritime links also allowed materials to move over considerable distances. As a result, hoards and burials contain various implements and weapons that are matched in peninsular Italy, Sardinia, southern France, Iberia and occasionally in northern Europe.[23] This is worth remembering when considering the nature of local society at the time of Greek and Phoenician colonization (chapter 6) and contradicts the notion, sometimes expressed by ancient historians and a few archaeologists, that indigenous peoples, by contrast with Greeks and Phoenicians, were incompetent mariners or somehow 'thalasso-phobic'.

Pottery also provides evidence for long-distance contacts. Several vessels from Thapsos (phase 3) resemble forms of Bahrija, after which the last period of Maltese prehistory is named, although it is unclear whether these are of Maltese origin (fig. 100:1-3,5-8). Much of the Bahrija complex, including carinated cups, bowls with inturned rims and even domestic architecture, can be derived from that of later Ausonian Sicily. An influx of settlers in the Late Bronze or Early Iron Age, perhaps linked with the expansion of Ausonian groups throughout Sicily, is a possibility.[24] Nevertheless, Maltese craft production still had distinct features, such as elaborate incised wares, with only generic parallels in southern Italy, but little painted ware. Trading contacts were perhaps maintained along lines already established in the Borg in-Nadur period (chapter 4). One further suggestion has been that Malta supplied textiles to Sicily in return for metals, although spindle-whorls are ubiquitous in Sicily at this time and there is no real evidence that Malta was a major centre of textile production. Logic would suggest that the incentive to trade rested mainly with the Maltese, although the only readily identifiable imports from Sicily are a small number of bronze objects and probably a few fragments of painted

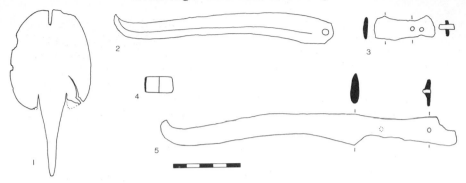

Fig. 112. (1-2) Cassibile, bronze razor, knife; (3-5) Madonna del Piano, iron knives and ring

or plumed ware. It cannot be taken for granted that external contacts were always friendly or welcome in Malta: Borg-in Nadur was provided with a massive defensive wall and sites like Bahrija occupy well-defended hill-tops. A real harbour site with an open outlook has yet to be found on the island.

The appearance of Sardinian Nuragic ceramics in Ausonian II layers on Lipari is further proof of westward links across the Tyrrhenian Sea.[25] Well-endowed with metal ores, Sardinia was a major producer of copper in the Early Iron Age, exporting some of its products to central Italy, and perhaps to Sicily too. Examples of western bronzes, including a spatulate razor (fig. 112:1) and certain kinds of axes (fig. 115:4), possibly of Iberian or southern French origin, may have come to Sicily via Sardinia. Sicilian exports are harder to identify, but probably include the plumed vessels at Pontecagnano in Campania, dated between about 850 and 750 BC, perhaps containers or items shipped with metal goods or by-products of trade. However, the southern-style ceramics produced locally at Osteria dell'Osa (Lazio) could reflect the presence of immigrants. Various forms of diffusion were undoubtedly at work. Glass-working was certainly known in Italy in the post-Mycenaean period and beads of glass-paste, amber, rock-crystal and other attractive hard stones still circulated widely. One of the Lipari Monfalcone tombs contained an unusually large number of them.[26]

While bronze was abundant, iron occurred only sporadically, at first in the form of small objects, such as rings and knives in burials and even more rarely in hoards, probably not earlier than the 10th century BC.[27] Seven rings and two curved knives at Madonna del Piano (fig. 112:3-5) seem to be mainly from female burials with relatively abundant tomb goods, which may suggest that they were items of special value. It appears that iron technology did not develop fully before the historical period in Sicily, as was generally the case in the western Mediterranean. However, the production of one-edged knives with bronze rivets and perhaps steeled blades shows an awareness of the functional potential of this metal and some progress beyond a preliminary stage of working. Moreover, iron objects are certainly under-represented in museum collections due to poor preservation and are beginning to be found more frequently as a result of careful excavation techniques.

Once attributed to early Phoenician traders, a more likely alternative would be that these iron artefacts reflect trade or shared technical knowledge between indigenous societies in the western Mediterranean, perhaps especially with Calabria, where similar items occur in EIA graves. There are suggestions of iron-working in southern Italy as early as the 11th century BC. Unusually early finds of iron in Sicily (from EBA and MBA contexts of the 2nd millennium BC) have been noted in previous chapters. Even if the latter were imports from the Aegean or Cyprus, it is possible that experiments in local production soon followed. The fact that iron rings and knives from Madonna del Piano resemble their counterparts in bronze points to local manufacture.

Hoards

The deliberate accumulation of metal which began towards the end of the Middle Bronze Age, became more common during the Late Bronze and Iron Ages and persisted into historical times.[28] Sicilian hoards are often incomplete and lack information about their find circumstances. Unlike some hoards in central-northern Italy and northern Europe, there is little evidence for ritual or votive deposition with no intention of recovery in contexts such as lakes or rivers. As a result, explanations tend to be rather prosaic. Those consisting of miscellaneous broken implements found in or close to settlements are often regarded as founder's hoards, connected with the activities of a craft workshop, or as the pooled resources of a community. Old and broken objects were evidently removed from circulation like scrap metal in order to be recycled locally or to be exchanged within a wider trade network. Sets of finely finished goods are often regarded as merchant's hoards, while the enormous Mendolito hoard of slightly later date could have been accumulated in the form of cult-offerings or votives.

The large LBA hoard (75 kilos in total) found in an Ausonian building on Lipari could be regarded as the collectively assembled wealth of the local community.[29] It consisted of an unusually wide range of mainly broken items, probably from many different sources, which could only have been obtained by long-distance maritime trade: daggers, swords, spearheads, axes, razors, ornamental and miscellaneous fragments, including parts of ox-hide ingots, which had been tightly packed into a large sealed jar before being deposited, probably hidden, below the floor of one of the largest dwellings (hut a2; fig. 98). The circulation of metal was evidently carefully controlled here. Much smaller, but of similar date, are the Biancavilla, Cannatello, Malvagna and Gratteri hoards, consisting mainly of axes. Prominent in hoards, but entirely absent in

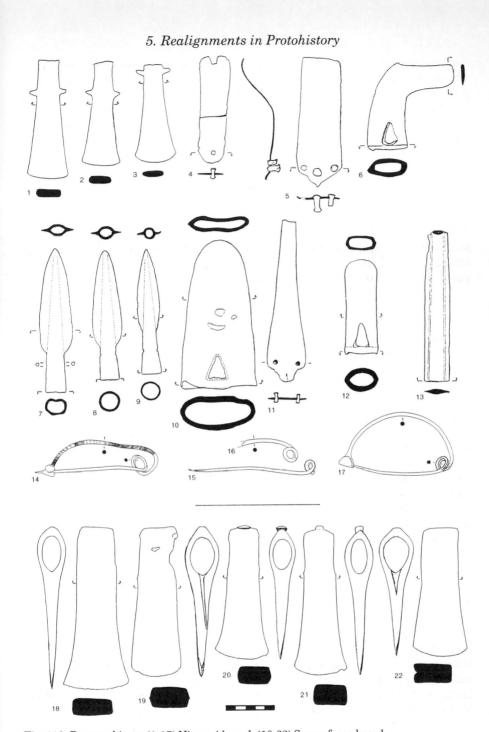

Fig. 113. Bronze objects: (1-17) Niscemi hoard; (18-22) Spaccaforno hoard

211

burials, axes had a special role as a medium of exchange, perhaps due to a universal recognition of their utility. Like ingots, they are conveniently compact, hard to damage, easy to weigh or test, and free of elaborate stylistic features. The Spaccaforno hoard consisted entirely of axes (fig. 113:18-22).

Some hoards of the 10th-9th centuries BC are difficult to categorize due to the mixed nature of their contents. For example, the Niscemi hoard contained five spearheads, five flat axes, three daggers, four socketed tools, one razor and six fibulae pieces, some in good condition and therefore potentially useful or exchangeable as finished objects, and others broken or damaged, which were probably destined for re-casting (fig. 113:1-17). The little Noto Antica hoard of socketed tools and axes in good condition might have belonged to an artisan, while the Modica and Vizzini hoards (fig. 114), consisting of broken spears, daggers, axes, fibulae and ingot fragments, seem intended for re-smelting. Likewise, the large hoard (about 30 kilos of bronze) of similar date, found at Castelluccio di Ragusa, which included a heterogeneous collection of tools, ornaments and weapons, including finished, unfinished and broken objects and stone moulds, looks more like a founder's hoard, or the collected wealth of a small community (fig. 115:1-12).[30] The style of certain items in this hoard is matched by forms known in Italy, Sardinia and Spain.

The Polizzello hoard was found in a jar at this site, which is also known from Iron Age chamber tombs and a later settlement (chapter 6).[31] It contained mainly axes and ingots, some of which may be dated within the 8th century BC (fig. 115:13-20), as well as incrustations from iron artefacts that had disappeared. Metallographic tests and microanalyses of a selection of the objects have revealed details about composition and working-techniques, well suited to the function of the different objects. The cutting-edge of a spearhead (fig. 115:18) and an axe had been hardened by cold-hammering and in other cases by annealing and cold-hammering (fig. 115:20). Sulphur-rich and iron-rich inclusions suggest that the primary copper employed in the alloy came from sulphur-based minerals and that two bun ingots were composed largely of primary copper, taken directly from its source. One axe (fig. 115:17) had a high tin content (9-11%) and other items had a relatively high iron content, implying advanced methods of copper extraction by smelting and then adding silicates and ferrous minerals as a flux, followed by refining in a crucible. By contrast, the low grade of iron found in one socketed axe of central Italian (S. Francesco) type (fig. 115:20) would support the hypothesis of an actual import from that region.

Although dating to the early colonial period (chapter 6), three other hoards deserve mention. That of San Cataldo (fig. 134) is the only one composed entirely of decorative objects (mainly rings and bronze vessels), all intact, perhaps recently made and destined to be sold. Second, the

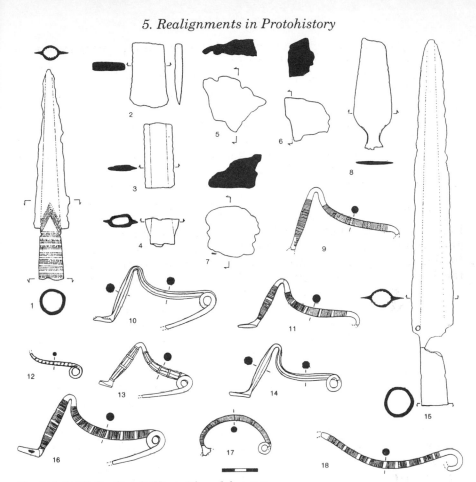

Fig. 114. (1-18) Tre Canali (Vizzini) hoard, bronzes

sizeable hoard from Giarratana (over 200 kilos of bronze) consisted mainly of ingot and unrecognizable metal fragments, as well as fibulae pieces, and was probably deposited in the late 8th or early 7th century BC. Finally, the massive hoard from Mendolito di Adrano (fig. 133), the largest in Sicily, consisted of about 900 kilos of bronze, including unworked metal and ingot fragments, and over 1,000 objects (spears, sheet bronze pieces, axes, razors, ornamental items).[32] A date in the second half of the 7th century BC has recently been proposed for its deposition on the basis of a miscast pyramidal arrowhead, although most of the objects are earlier and include tripod fragments and other prestigious and possibly votive items of Greek style, datable in the late 8th or early 7th century BC (fig. 133:7-9). It was found in a large *pithos* on the edge of an indigenous town, about which little is known, not far from Adrano on the slopes of Mount Etna. The hoard is also of interest since it might have been associated with a sanctuary, like others known in Greece and

213

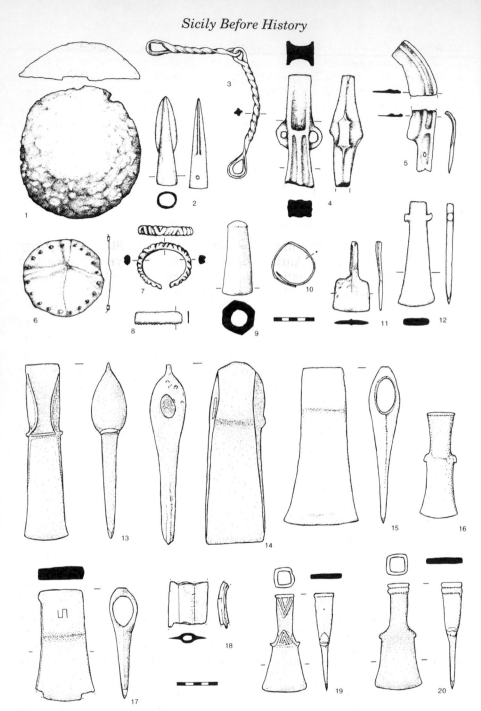

Fig. 115. Bronze objects: (1-12) Castelluccio hoard; (13-20) Polizzello hoard

the Aegean during Archaic and earlier times, which provided protection and an ideological focus for accumulating metal items in the form of gifts to a divinity. In the case of Mendolito, historical sources indicate that the cult of a local warrior-god, Adrano, whose origin seems pre-Greek, had a special association with this region of the volcano, and was assimilated or equated by the Greeks with their own Hephaestus, god of fire and metallurgy (chapter 6). This at least encourages the idea, although still difficult to prove, that a connection between metallurgical activity and local cults or sanctuaries had antecedents in late prehistoric contexts.

Ethnicity and historicity

Thucydides, Philistus, Hellanicus, Diodorus, Dionysius, Strabo and Pliny (with frequent reference to Antiochus, a 5th-century BC Syracusan writer) all refer to movements of native peoples from peninsular Italy to Lipari and Sicily prior to the arrival of Greek settlers in the 8th century BC.[33] They mention three groups in particular: the *Ausoni*, *Sikeloi* and *Morgetes*. While none of these authors provide reliable details about the scale or date of these migrations or invasions, it has often been assumed that considerable numbers were involved and that they took place at various times during the protohistoric period. Philistus and Hellanicus placed the arrival of Sikels in Sicily three generations before the Trojan War, while Thucydides believed this event to date about three hundred years before the foundation of Greek colonies in Sicily.

Modern scholarship has attempted with varying degrees of success and conviction to seek confirmation of these legendary or semi-legendary accounts in the archaeological evidence. Taking 1180 BC as an approximation for the date of the Trojan War and allowing about 30 years for each generation, Bernabò Brea noted that the date of 1270 BC could be proposed for the arrival of groups from peninsular Italy on Lipari.[34] In this case, archaeology and literary tradition find some common ground insofar as the excavations on Lipari have revealed an assemblage which shares many features with those of contemporary southern Italy (in its Subapennine – Protovillanovan phases). The later Thucydidean date of about 1030 BC is thought possibly to reflect a second wave of settlers associated with the transition from the Ausonian I to II period and the Pantalica I to II (Cassibile) phases in Sicily. The name Ausonian was given to the LBA culture of Lipari on the basis of a tradition related by Diodorus (V.7), describing the emigration from peninsular Italy to Lipari of its eponymous founder, Liparus, son of Auson, leader of the Ausoni, an Italic people from the region of Campania or Calabria.

Greek writers also made passing reference to foundation stories associated with Lentini and Morgantina, which are essentially variations on the same theme of Italic settlers (Morgetes and Sikels) entering eastern Sicily and establishing settlements there. Once again, the mythology is at least broadly consistent with the archaeological evidence from these sites, which share certain characteristics with Lipari and contemporary assemblages in Calabria and Campania, and may therefore be described as belonging within the Ausonian cultural tradition. Although attested by inscriptions of much later date (see chapter 6), the Sikel language, which stems from an Italic root, could also derive from the cultural ties formed at approximately this time. In fact, the term Ausonian is now widely used as a convenient archaeological label for broadly similar LBA and EIA assemblages on Lipari and in Sicily, although this does not necessarily imply that these are the archaeological remains of a single ethnic or tribal group.

In support of the literary tradition, it may be said that the references to Italic settlers entering Sicily in the protohistoric period are not easily dismissed (like some other legends described in chapter 4) as a propagandistic invention of Greek colonial historiography. The stories of local heroes or eponymous settlement founders such as Liparus, Auson, Xouthos and Morges, bear no reference to Greek traditions or territorial claims in Sicily. They are more likely to represent the remains of an oral tradition of local origin. Modern scholarship has generally accepted that settlers spread through central Sicily in the course of the Late Bronze and Iron Ages, and that their progress is charted not only by the emergence of new Ausonian sites, such as Lentini, Morgantina and Madonna del Piano, but by changes to pre-existing traditional sites of the Pantalica culture. In fact, the latter show changes in their assemblages between the 11th and 10th centuries BC: Caltagirone was perhaps abandoned due to the foundation of Mulino della Badia nearby, Pantalica has few tombs of this period, and Cassibile seems to have developed with modified burial customs, perhaps as a result of this Ausonian influence.[35]

The causes of such movements, perhaps comprising no more than small bands or tribal splinter-groups, may be sought in Italy, where some authors have regarded the spread of Protovillanovan traditions in terms of population movements extending down the peninsula. More recently, it has been suggested that an invasion of the Aeolian islands in the 13th century BC was inspired by increasingly hostile relations between native southern Italian communities and the rather different 'Mycenaeanized' Aeolian groups of the Milazzese culture.[36] In northern Sicily, however, the evidence for a destructive advance and for hostile relations with peninsular groups is less clear and it is harder to assess how much is due to the arrival of settlers and how much to more diffuse contacts or trade. The point needs to be made, however, that there is ample evidence for economic links and trade and for a gradual mixing of local insular and peninsular traditions in the Iron Age, giving rise to distinct regional cultures. Moreover, social and economic changes set in motion at the end of the Bronze Age may have encouraged a basic convergence in ideology over a wide area. This is not to deny that the Iron Age saw periodic movements of population; perhaps these too were partly the result of the looser social and political structures of the time.

In a very general way, the apparently complex ethnic map of the island just prior to Greek and Phoenician colonisation, which is implied by early written sources, finds an archaeological reflection in the wide variety of Iron Age craft traditions and burial customs, which seem less uniform than those of contemporary Italy. However, it does not seem possible to distinguish with any accuracy or confidence between Ausonians, Morgetians or Sikels on a purely archaeological basis, and there have been few credible attempts to do this in recent times. Even the tradition related by Thucydides and Diodorus that Sicily was once divided into eastern and western cultural zones, inhabited by two contrasting and even antagonistic ethnic groups, the Sikans and the Sikels, is difficult to reconcile with the archaeological evidence currently available. However, some authors have pointed to the more conservative and traditional assemblage of Sant'Angelo Muxaro in the west, derived from local MBA precedents, as characteristic of the Sikan sphere and an earlier ethnic substratum, by contrast with the Ausonian sites of eastern Sicily, generally associated with Sikel groups.

Emblematic of the difficulties inherent in the attempt to match archaeological material with ethnic or tribal epithets mentioned by later Greek writers is the vexed question of the Elymians, recorded in various Greek and Latin sources as a native group inhabiting the far west of Sicily.[37] They are variously described as related to their Sikan neighbours, or as Italic or even Anatolian in origin. The latter seems quite unlikely, whereas some local inscriptions of the 6th-5th centuries BC suggest a generic affinity with Italic languages, which is not inherently surprising. However, the Early Iron Age in western Sicily is still little known, while attempts to define a regional group on the basis of incised pottery has become increasingly problematic: incised wares are simply too widespread to correlate with the supposed geographical locus of any one tribal group. The more elaborate incised pottery style of western Sicily, for which the term 'Elymian' is rather misleading (since it is essentially the later geometric incised ware of Sant'Angelo Muxaro) dates primarily between the 7th and 5th centuries BC and partly reflects relations with Greek settlers (chapter 6). Nor does the recent hypothesis of an emigration from Apulia to Sicily, based on relatively minor resemblances in pottery styles, seem particularly compelling.

6

Indigenous Peoples in the
8th and 7th Centuries BC

From prehistory to history

The 8th century BC was a time of rapid transformation in the western
Mediterranean, caused in part by movements of settlers and by the
foundation of the first Greek and Phoenician towns: new centres of power
that were destined to play a major role in the historical and cultural
development of the region prior to absorption within the Roman Empire.
Their establishment signals the transition from 'prehistory' to 'history'
and the emergence of new areas of discussion, concerned not least with the
critical evaluation of written sources, although these provide only limited
information about the 8th-6th centuries BC.

Prehistoric and classical archaeologists may claim areas of special
interest in this period: the former because of the fact that, while the first
Greek settlements were still establishing themselves and growing in size
during the 8th and 7th centuries BC, the majority of the island's population
consisted of indigenous people, descended from those represented by the
archaeological evidence described in the preceding chapter. It was not
until even later, in the 6th century BC, that the effects of Greek colonisation, essentially a coastal phenomenon, were fully felt in the interior
territories of the island. While the foundation of Naxos, Syracuse and
other Greek settlements in the 8th century BC is regarded as the beginning
of an 'early colonial' period, elsewhere in Sicily this same period is still
known as the later or second Iron Age, or the Finocchito phase, after a
large indigenous site in the Hyblaean hills.

Several histories were now unfolding concurrently. First, that of the
Greek colonies, concentrated initially in eastern coastal regions (fig. 116).
The literary and archaeological evidence for their formation, rivalries,
political, socio-economic and artistic development, have been discussed in
many works and are of only partial relevance here. Second, the Phoenician
presence in western Sicily, centred on Motya, represents a branch of
Phoenician expansion across the southern and western Mediterranean,
although this is a history with no autonomous literary tradition. Likewise,
its relevance here is limited to the question of pre-colonial contacts and
early relations with indigenous groups. The society of indigenous people,
encompassing the largest territory within the island, is relatively less well

219

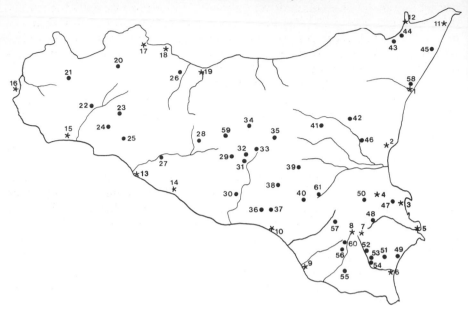

Fig. 116. *Greek and Phoenician settlements (*) and indigenous sites (•), 8th-6th centuries BC:*
1 Naxos; 2 Catania; 3 Megara Hyblaea; 4 Lentini; 5 Syracuse; 6 Helorus; 7 Akrai (Palazzolo);
8 Casmene (Monte Casale); 9 Camarina; 10 Gela; 11 Zancle (Messina); 12 Mylai; 13 Heraclea
Minoa; 14 Akragas (Agrigento); 15 Selinus; 16 Motya; 17 Panormus (Palermo); 18 Solunto;
19 Himera; 20 Monte Iato; 21 Segesta; 22 M. Castellazzo; 23 Entella; 24 M. Adranone; 25
Caltabellotta; 26 Mura Pregne; 27 S. Angelo Muxaro; 28 Polizzello; 29 Vassallaggi; 30 M.
Saraceno; 31 Gibil Gabib; 32 Sabucina; 33 Capodarso; 34 Terravecchia di Cuti; 35 Calas-
cibetta cemeteries; 36 Butera; 37 Dessueri; 38 M. Bubbonia; 39 Morgantina; 40 M. San
Mauro; 41 Centuripe; 42 Mendolito; 43 Longane; 44 Pozzo di Gotto; 45 Fiumedinisi; 46
Paternò; 47 Villasmundo; 48 Pantalica; 49 Avola; 50 Ossini; 51 Noto; 52 Tremenzano; 53
Finocchito; 54 Giummarito, Murmure; 55 Modica; 56 Castiglione; 57 M. Casasia; 58
Cocolonazzo; 59 Marianopoli; 60 Giarratana hoard; 61 San Cataldo hoard

known archaeologically. Apart from occasional references to contacts with
Greek settlers, information about the indigenous culture before the 6th
century BC is essentially archaeological, unaided by texts or inscriptions.
The main concern of this chapter, therefore, is with the indigenous world
at a time when its identity can still be distinguished, albeit changing as a
result of contacts with its new Greek and Phoenician neighbours.

The relationships between these groups must have been complex and
varied, sometimes pacific, sometimes violent, and profoundly affected
their development. In recent years, a more flexible approach has emerged
to questions of cultural interaction in an attempt to understand its subtle
and reciprocal dynamics, which resulted in radical changes to indigenous
communities and perhaps also, though less obviously, to the character of
western Greek and Phoenician towns. Critical assessments of research
traditions have suggested that a process of change, which is frequently
termed 'Hellenisation' or acculturation, has often been seen as uni-directional

and coloured by the colonial experiences of modern states, which were different from those of antiquity. Nevertheless, it is undeniable that the outcome of this interactive process, which extended over several centuries, was the transformation of the indigenous culture. Only the initial stages of the process are traced in this chapter.

Despite certain refinements in craft production (notably of jewellery, glass and some pottery), the technological disparity between the first settlers and the indigenous peoples whom they encountered in Sicily is not comparable with that of many colonisations of recent history. Of all the foreign lands settled by Greeks, Sicily must have seemed one of the least different from their own, presenting similarities of climate and vegetation within a rural landscape of settled agriculture, pastoralism and villages. One may be wary of underestimating the effect of indigenous peoples on their Greek neighbours and the degree of interaction between them, as well as the tendency to pre-judge the circumstances of the late 8th and 7th centuries BC in terms of the later and more familiar historical situation of the 5th and 4th centuries BC. On the other hand, the influence of the Phoenicians on local peoples in Sicily was slighter and more circumscribed in territorial terms (by contrast with other western Mediterranean islands, such as Sardinia).

One question that sometimes arises is whether indigenous people can be distinguished from Greeks or Phoenicians using archaeological and often only funerary evidence.[1] For example, when both local and imported goods are found in burials it can be hard to tell whether the deceased was a Sicilian Greek who adopted local customs or a local who adopted Greek ones. Whatever the answer to such difficult questions about ethnic identity, the main point is that the societies in question were not homogeneous and that their boundaries were porous. The literary sources distinguished between *Sikeliotes*, Sicilian-born Greeks, and *Sikeloi*, indigenous inhabitants, but these terms were probably often blurred and reflect a Greek viewpoint. The situation is still ambiguous in subsequent centuries when Greek religion, language and social customs were widespread. Ethnic identity, which artefacts cannot always reflect and which may embody racial (or biological), linguistic or other idiosyncratic cultural traits, is partly a state of mind.

It was noted in the last chapter that there is no obvious correlation between EIA assemblages and the apparently complex map of indigenous groupings in the island, sometimes described in the literary sources as Ausonians, Sikels, Sikans, Morgetians or Elymians. Not enough is yet known about the native languages or dialects of Sicily to distinguish between ethnic groups. The surviving 'Sikel' and 'Elymian' inscriptions, dating from the late 6th century BC, resemble each other and have affinities with Italic (Indoeuropean) languages, such as Oscan and Latin. They also indicate that the adoption of writing and the Greek alphabet in indigenous contexts, such as Mendolito and Montagna di Marzo, only occurred long after the foundation of Greek colonies.[2] It is also noteworthy that in the mid-5th century BC, 300 years after the arrival of the first settlers, the concept of native identity was still sufficiently potent in parts of the island to find a champion in the Sikel leader, Ducetius, and a just cause in the rebellion fomented in central Sicily against Greek dominion, or at least against the hegemony of the coastal cities. The indigenous language was still current at this time, although the communities of central Sicily that supported Ducetius were substantially Greek from the point of view of material culture.

Greek foundation dates

Historical dates for the foundation of the first Greek colonies in Sicily can be extrapolated from the well-known passage at the start of the sixth book of Thucydides, which provides the following sequence: Naxos (734 BC), Syracuse (733 BC), Lentini (729 BC), soon followed by Catania (729 BC), Megara Hyblaea (728 BC) and Gela (688 BC). Zancle (Messina) was perhaps founded soon after Naxos. Most of these colonies were established within a space of time that is too narrow to be accurately subdivided by archaeological (or at least pottery) chronology. The earliest material at many of these sites is currently represented by pottery of LG I (Late Geometric) style, of about 750-725 BC (fig. 117).

Much past debate about chronological precedence has been fuelled by the existence of literary sources that contradict Thucydides, who probably made use of the Sicilian history of the 5th-century logographer, Antiochus of Syracuse. The reliability and merits of Thucydides' version by comparison with those of Strabo, Ephorus, Polyaenus or Eusebius have been discussed frequently. While none of the ancient authors are free of bias, Thucydides has provided the most connected and complete single account of events, even though that does not mean that it has to be trusted absolutely.[3]

In fact, several uncertainties remain. One long-standing debate, which has only recently attenuated, concerns the relative position of the founda-

Foundation dates (Thucydides)	MG pottery <750	LG pottery 750-700	EPC pottery 720-680	MPC pottery 680-650	LPC pottery 650-610	EC pottery >610
Naxos, 734		•	•	•	•	•
Syracuse, 733	•	•	•	•	•	•
Lentini, 729		•	•	•	•	•
Catania, 729		•				
Megara, 728	?	•	•	•	•	•
Gela, 688		•	•	•	•	•
Selinus, 628				•	•	•

Fig. 117. Foundation dates (Thucydides) and Greek imported pottery in Greek colonies

tion of Syracuse and Megara, which stems from the comment by Strabo (VI.1.2) that Naxos and Megara were the first two foundations in Sicily, not Syracuse. For a time, this seemed to be supported by the presence at Megara of early LG I pottery. However, this pottery has now been found at Syracuse too, in the form of 'Thapsos' cups and other early forms, so that the archaeological argument for the priority of Megara over Syracuse has collapsed.[4]

Another discrepancy exists between the Thucydidean chronology and a slightly higher one based on Diodorus. The calculation of foundation dates using Thucydides rests on his assertion that Megara existed for 245 years prior to its destruction by Gelon of Syracuse, an event datable independently to 483 BC, a valuable chronological reference point for Greek Sicily, which implies a foundation date of 728 BC for Megara. According to Thucydides, the Megarians founded their sub-colony of Selinus in western Sicily exactly 100 years after Megara itself, giving a foundation date of 628 BC for Selinus. An alternative date for the foundation of Megara can be reached following Diodorus (XIII.59.4, based on Ephorus or Timaeus), who states that Selinus was founded 242 years before its destruction by the Carthaginians (in 409 BC), which would give a foundation date of 651 BC for Selinus. With reference back to Thucydides, a foundation date 100 years earlier could then be postulated for Megara, at 751 BC. Naxos, regarded unanimously by ancient writers as the first Sicilian colony, would date from 757 BC, which would place the foundation of the first Sicilian colonies at about the same time as Pithekoussai (modern Ischia) or Cumae, described by Strabo (V.4.4) as the first Greek settlement in Italy. Since early LG I pottery and even some MG pottery is now known from Sicilian sites (below), this is theoretically possible on archaeological grounds, although most authors are reluctant to combine the separate accounts of Thucydides and Diodorus in order to produce an earlier date.

Greek contacts before colonisation

A vast literature exists on the reasons for Greek colonisation of the western Mediterranean and the character of early Greek colonies.[5] The question is often prefaced with a review of the first evidence for renewed contacts between Italy and the Aegean after the period of late Mycenaean trade, sometimes discussed under the heading of 'pre-colonisation', although the use of this term has become contentious in recent years. The background knowledge of local communities and geography obtained by outsiders as a result of early trading contacts would obviously have been helpful in establishing the potential for settlement, although it may be advisable to distinguish between trade, organised by a relatively restricted class of people with essentially commercial aims, and emigration, motivated by different circumstances and needs, notably that of obtaining land for settlers. Different views about colonisation are to some extent

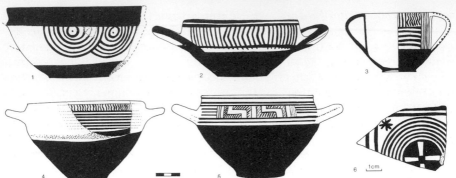

Fig. 118. (1-5) Villasmundo, pendent semicircle skyphos, chevron skyphos, LG kyathos, Aetos 666 kotyle, 'Thapsos' cup; (6) Syracuse, MG amphora sherd from Fusco

influenced by different views about the nature of the economy of the time. Nevertheless, a sharp distinction cannot always be drawn between trading ventures and migrations, at least in the middle years of the 8th century BC when both were happening concurrently. In addition, the distinction between mercantile and agricultural colonies can be over-stated. Although Pithekoussai was a Greek foundation with strong commercial interests it obviously provided a home for settlers, while the so-called agrarian colonies of eastern Sicily were mostly located by natural harbours and also developed extensive trading activity. Naxos, the earliest colony, was placed on a rather narrow stretch of volcanic coastline with an adequate harbour, beside a mountainous hinterland.

The main archaeological evidence for links prior to the foundation of colonies currently consists of a small quantity of pottery. Villasmundo, located at a bend in the Marcellino river only 8km from Megara Hyblaea, is an important site in this regard, known primarily from about 150 rock-cut chamber tombs, some of which date from the Early Bronze Age, although most are Iron Age.[6] The shape of the chambers and the rite of multiple inhumation are typical of indigenous Iron Age practices (below), while the grave goods included pottery and personal ornaments of local tradition as well as scarabs and numerous locally-made vessels decorated in Greek geometric style dating mainly to the second half of the 8th century BC: bowls, amphorae, jugs, cups and kraters. The site was probably abandoned in the course of the 7th century BC.

Of special interest are Greek imports of an early type, such as the *skyphos* (cup) decorated with pendant semicircles (fig. 118:1). This form was current in the 9th century BC, although some examples were still being used in the middle or late 8th century BC, and the Villasmundo cup, which is from a disturbed tomb (t.65), is more like the later types.[7] A *skyphos* with chevron decoration of Euboean-Cycladic type (t.10), has parallels in MG II (later Middle Geometric) production, from about 775 to 750 BC, although it may be that a few were still in circulation at a slightly

224

later date (fig. 118:2). Another small cup of about the mid-8th century BC (t.4), generally associated with the first years of the colonies, is the Corinthian Aetos 666 *kotyle* (fig. 118:4). Likewise, Thapsos cups with panel decoration (fig. 118:5) and other imitated LG I (750-725 BC) wares can more obviously be linked with the first settlers. While some of these materials from Villasmundo could pre-date the nearby Greek foundation of Megara Hyblaea (Thucydidean date of 728 BC), the margin of error in pottery chronologies and the possibility that rather archaic forms, like pendant semicircle cups, persisted for longer than has been recognised, prevents absolute certainty. Some sherds from Megara Hyblaea could even belong to the late phase of MG II production.[8]

It is also noteworthy that a MG belly-handled amphora of Cycladic type was found by Orsi in the early colonial Fusco cemetery at Syracuse (fig. 118:6). On stylistic grounds, this piece should antedate the foundation of Syracuse and its presence here is therefore surprising, although it might have survived until a late date and been brought to Sicily as an antique.[9] Likewise, tripod fragments from the Mendolito hoard (fig. 133:7-9) cannot safely be regarded as pre-colonial imports, even if made in the early 8th century BC, since the same hoard contained items of later date.[10] Elsewhere in Sicily, there are no imported or locally imitated items that necessarily pre-date Greek coastal foundations, although LG I cups from Modica, Cozzo della Tignusa, Castelluccio (Ragusa) and sites in the vicinity of Catania and Paternò show that imports reached indigenous sites at an early date.[11]

As regards literary evidence, a passage quoted below (Thucydides VI.2.6), mentioning the arrival of Hellenes 'in large numbers' might suggest that some were already present, perhaps as traders who had forged links with local people and begun to settle. It is also worth considering that the establishment of a new settlement could have been a gradual process and that years may have passed before such sites grew sufficiently in size and status to merit recognition.[12] The foundation dates might refer to some defining moment or formal occasion in their formative phase, but not necessarily to the year in which the first boat-load disembarked or the first stake was driven into the ground.

The Phoenician zone

The date of the first Phoenician contact with Sicily is as vexed a question as the broader one of the earliest Phoenician expansion in the western Mediterranean. When and why this began and the manner in which it developed affects understanding of several important matters: the role of long-distance trade during the so-called Dark Age, its effects on local Iron Age groups and significance as a precursor of colonisation proper. The controversy has focused on archaeological and literary evidence and has flourished wherever agreement is lacking between them. If the literary sources were once most influential in shaping interpretations, modern

Fig. 119. Bronze 'smiting-god' bronze figurine dredged from the sea-bed near Sciacca, H 35cm

research relies increasingly on archaeological evidence, which is constantly expanding and being re-evaluated.

In fact, some aspects of the literary tradition have also been reassessed and the old controversy between the advocates of high and low chronologies for Phoenician settlement in the western Mediterranean has been largely superseded.[13] References to a very early (12th-century BC) colonisation of Spain (Cadiz) and North Africa (Utica) occur in suspiciously late sources, such as Velleius Paterculus (I.2.3), Pliny (XVI.216) and tracts of the *De Mirabilibus Auscultationibus* (Pseudo-Aristotle 134). These probably derive from attempts by certain Hellenistic scholars to rationalise strands of Homeric tradition and the exploits of Herakles (mythological ancestor of the Phoenicians) in the western Mediterranean in times beyond recall. Of greater relevance are references by Timaeus and Thucydides to a Phoenician presence in the west prior to Greek colonisation. Timaeus (reported by Dionysius of Halicarnassus I.74) implies a foundation date for Carthage in the late 9th century BC (traditionally 814-813 BC), while Thucydides believed that Phoenicians were present in Sicily before Greek settlement got under way (before 734 BC). Thucydides is quite explicit and all the more difficult to dismiss as he credits Greece's rivals with precedence:

> Phoenicians, too, had settlements all round Sicily, on promontories along the sea coast, which they walled off, and on the adjacent islets, for the sake of trade with the Sicels. But when the Hellenes also began to come in by sea in large numbers, the Phoenicians left most of these places [*emporia*], and settling together lived in Motya, Soloeis [*Solunto*] and Panormus [*Palermo*], near the Elymi, partly because they trusted in their alliance with the Elymi and partly because from there the voyage from Sicily to Carthage is shortest (Thucydides VI.2.6).[14]

From an archaeological perspective, however, there is little to suggest even Phoenician contacts with Sicily during the Early Iron Age, let alone settlements or emporia all around the coasts. It is possible that there was some memory in Greek tradition of Cypriot and Levantine contacts with sites such as Thapsos in the late Mycenaean period, but the last phase of occupation at Thapsos, though still little known, suggests a changed environment of local (Ausonian) character (chapter 5). The notion that Phoenicians were resident here as traders amidst the indigenous population is purely hypothetical. Certain materials have been said to reflect Phoenician trading links in the 10th-9th centuries BC but, on close inspection, the arguments are carelessly constructed (chapter 5): the iron finds from Madonna del Piano could easily be local products, like the elbow (Cassibile) fibulae. The strainer-spouted jugs certainly resemble Cypriot and Levantine forms, but they do not require a Phoenician link since they were first used in the island when Mycenaean and Cypriot contacts were prevalent.[15] More compelling, at first glance, as an authentic example of Levantine contact in the pre-colonial period, is the bronze statuette of a

Fig. 120. Motya cemetery, Phoenician vases, early 7th century BC

smiting-god, dredged from the sea between Selinus and Sciacca (fig. 119). However, its date is controversial: formerly attributed to Mycenaean or eastern Mediterranean contacts during the Middle Bronze Age, G. Falsone recently concluded that, despite an 'archaic' appearance, such items were produced well into the 1st millennium BC and are known from 7th-century BC contexts.[16] The Sciacca figurine could have come to Sicily in early colonial times.

Despite such inconclusive strands of evidence, it may be that contacts were maintained between the eastern and western Mediterranean at a much reduced level of frequency after the period of regular long-distance trading during the Middle Bronze Age. A process of gradually increasing pre-colonial contact can draw some support from the wider Mediterranean context: Near Eastern links, however slender, were maintained with some areas of the Aegean after the 11th century BC, and Phoenician craft-products appear with a certain frequency in the Aegean from at least the 9th century BC.[17] In the western Mediterranean, the Euboean settlement on Pithekoussai had strong Phoenician links in the mid-8th century BC, which was doubtless preceded by a phase of familiarisation. Claims for 9th-century BC Phoenician links have been made for Sardinia, which has a greater range of evidence than Sicily, although bedevilled by chronological uncertainties.[18] While local societies must have been the protagonists in maritime trade within western regions during the 10th and 9th centuries BC (chapter 5), a Phoenician presence in Sicilian waters may be hypothesized for a time prior to the foundation of Pithekoussai, perhaps around 800 BC. Plainly, this date can be no more than conjectural at present, and may need to be raised if new discoveries permit.

The first sure evidence for Phoenicians in Sicily comes from their settlements in the west of the island. Indeed there is no discrepancy between Thucydides' account and the archaeological evidence from Motya, the main Phoenician centre in Sicily, where the earliest datable material has been found in the necropolis: Greek imported pottery of early Protocorinthian and Subgeometric type, assigned to about 720-710 BC, associated with Phoenician pottery (figs. 120-121).[19] Occupation from the Copper-Middle Bronze Ages is attested, although there is no sign that Motya was inhabited when Phoenician settlers arrived. As Thucydides implies, the Phoenician foundation may have been prompted by an increase in the numbers of Greeks arriving in eastern Sicily and by the desire to safeguard Phoenician interests in the island which, like the others claimed by Phoenicians in the western Mediterranean, could play a useful commercial and strategic role in an expanding trading network. The definition of a Phoenician zone in western Sicily and of a Greek zone in the east suggests an essentially contemporaneous process of settlement, albeit one dictated to the Phoenicians by the more aggressive territorial ambitions of their Greek counterparts.

Located on a small island offshore, Motya seems emblematic of a Phoenician foundation as described by Thucydides. The 7th century BC witnessed the urban expansion of the site, although little is known about its monuments or layout until the 6th century BC, by which time it had emerged as a major centre, occupying the whole island and surrounded by defensive walls. Greek fine wares, luxury goods of eastern style, including items of jewellery, faience, alabaster, scarabs and amulets, as well as pottery and bronze items of late Villanovan and Etruscan type (fig. 122:2,4) from the cemetery attest wide-ranging commercial links during the late 8th and 7th centuries BC. Clearly, maritime trade was a key element in the economy of the site.

Thucydides also implies that good relations and an alliance existed with the neighbouring Elymi, which contrasts with the notices of recurrent

Fig. 121. Motya cemetery, Phoenician beaker and Protocorinthian cup, early 7th century BC

229

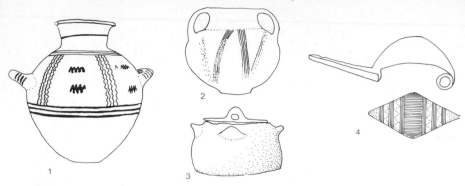

Fig. 122. Motya cemetery and tophet finds: (1) geometric amphora; (2) incised jar; (3) cooking ware; (4) navicella fibula

confrontations between locals and Greeks in eastern Sicily. This encourages the view that Phoenician colonisation was less threatening to indigenous people, perhaps because it placed more emphasis on trade than taking over land, whereas Greek settlements in eastern Sicily were bent on controlling and owning at least the surrounding *chora*, considered essential to the function and prosperity of the emerging *polis*. In the case of Motya, the nature of the relationship with the adjacent mainland is hard to assess on archaeological grounds, but during the early years it may have involved alliances with local people, or concessionary territorial rights, which would have allowed essential agricultural produce of the hinterland to be exchanged for craft products and luxury goods from the settlement.

A relationship of this kind could explain the presence at Motya of pottery with painted motifs in local style, such as geometric amphorae (fig. 122:1). Though obviously suitable containers for foodstuffs, these were sometimes used or re-used as urns in the early cemetery and sacrificial burial ground (*tophet*). While clearly owing something to Greek LG styles of decoration, they are typical of indigenous production in Sicily, and those found on Motya could have come from native sites nearby, if they were not made by Phoenicians. Another kind of pottery found on Motya, possibly associated with indigenous people, is the plain handmade cooking ware, which resembles local types and might represent the adoption of local cooking techniques or even the presence of some indigenous people at the site. Aside from economic interaction, therefore, some closer social contacts between locals and settlers can at least be countenanced at Motya, although the evidence is still rather slender.

From the complementary standpoint of Phoenician products in local sites, much remains to be clarified. Indigenous sites of the 8th-7th centuries BC are little known and it is not surprising, therefore, if only a few items can as yet be ascribed to Phoenician contacts. The gold bowls (fig. 123) and rings in Orientalizing style (fig. 142) from tombs at Sant'Angelo Muxaro are possible candidates, although some doubts remain as to

Fig. 123. Sant'Angelo Muxaro gold bowl (Ø 14.6cm)

whether these are imports or local imitations of Phoenician types.[20] Scarabs with pseudo-hieroglyphs in local tombs at Finocchito (fig. 129:22) must have been imported, and some local red-slipped jugs (*oinochoai*) from Sant'Angelo Muxaro could have been loosely influenced by Phoenician wares, although it is surprising that more common Phoenician forms are not represented here. Phoenician trading links with Greek colonies are suggested by faience containers, Egyptian-style vases and idols, scarabs, lamps, alabastra, red-slip, Cypriot and glazed wares, for example at Syracuse, Zancle and Gela, but here too the overall quantities are neither large nor comparable with the much more abundant Greek imports at Motya.[21] Moreover, Greek as well as Phoenician merchants may have traded all these materials. More information is available from later western sites: Punic transport amphorae reached native strongholds such as Monte Maranfusa and Monte Castellazzo in the Belice valley in the 6th-5th centuries BC, and Punic influences, including chamber tombs, have been detected at Monte Adranone, from the late 6th century BC. In the early 4th century BC this site seems to have become a Punic garrison, but in the Archaic period Greek imports are predominant, while the main trading and cultural links in this region emanated from Selinus.[22] Whatever their political affiliations, alliances or friendships may have been, the fact remains that the majority of indigenous people in western Sicily adopted Greek, not Phoenician, cultural traditions during the 6th century BC.

Literary sources and political relations

Aside from chronology, the literary sources make occasional reference to relations between early settlers and indigenous people.[23] Especially noteworthy are the circumstances which led to the foundation of Megara Hyblaea. Having been preceded by the Euboean settlement at Naxos and the Corinthian foundation at Syracuse (according to Thucydides), the Megarians tried unsuccessfully on various occasions to establish their own base in what was evidently becoming a hotly contested region. After a brief stay at Thapsos, where their leader Lamis died, the Megarians founded a settlement at Megara, with the consent and help of a local ruler:

> In the fifth year after the settlement of Syracuse, Thucles and the Chalcidians, setting forth from Naxos, drove out the Sicels in war and settled Leontini, and after it Catana. The Catanaeans, however, chose for themselves Evarchus as founder. About the same time Lamis also came to Sicily with a colony from Megara and settled in a place called Trotilus, beyond the river Pantacyas; but afterwards, having removed from there and joined the settlement of the Chalcidians at Leontini, he was a little later driven out by them, and then after colonizing Thapsus met his death. His followers were expelled from Thapsus and settled then at a place called Megara Hyblaea, since Hyblon, a Sicel king, gave up [*betrayed?*] the land to them and led them to the site (Thucydides VI.3-4).[24]

Hyblon is the only recorded name of a native leader before the 5th century BC, which has encouraged some speculation about the location of his territory or capital, perhaps known as Hybla. There have been two main suggestions: one proposing an identification with Pantalica, which was certainly one of the largest indigenous sites in southeastern Sicily; and another in favour of Villasmundo, a smaller site, but a possible candidate, since it is nearer Megara.[25] The implication of friendly relations between Hyblon and the Megarians also fits with the archaeological evidence from the Villasmundo tombs. Albeit highly compressed, Thucydides' account implies a somewhat disorganised scramble for land, riven with rivalries and quarrels, giving rise to unstable and even unlikely alliances between Greeks, or between Greeks and locals against other Greeks: not surprising, perhaps, in a context of competing claims by small political entities with individual allegiances and ambitions, lacking the structure and organisation of a nation state with an established 'colonial policy'. Indeed, apart from conflicts with the Phoenicians, which periodically induced a sense of unity, the subsequent history of Sicily was dominated by rivalries and struggles between various cities for hegemony.

Meagre though it is, the literary evidence is sufficient to indicate that initial contacts between Greeks and locals varied considerably from formal alliances or concessions, as in the case of Megara, to outright hostility, as at Syracuse and possibly Naxos. Provided with fresh water, natural defences and the best harbour in Sicily, Syracuse was bound to be contested. Thucydides (VI.3) speaks of the eviction of the native inhabitants (although one might speculate that there was at least a preliminary phase of contacts), encouraging the view that the Dorian Greeks pursued a more aggressive form of territorial expansion at the expense of the locals than their Chalcidian neighbours. This is also suggested by the rapid extension of Syracusan dominion over the surrounding territory, probably beginning with a sub-colony at Helorus, a few miles to the south, before 700 BC.[26] The end of native autonomy in the hinterland was signalled by the establishment of a fortified outpost at Akrai (662 BC), which probably marked the culmination of a military campaign. The large indigenous centres of Finocchito and Pantalica have little evidence for occupation after 650 BC, by which time their populations must have dispersed, perhaps inland, or have been incorporated into lowly ranks of serfs (*killyrioi*) working the lands of the colonies.

Inevitably, perhaps, even relations that were initially friendly, if only as a matter of expediency on the part of incomers who still had much to gain from local support, deteriorated as the new settlements grew in size and strength. The situation at Lentini provides an interesting glimpse of the strains that could soon develop between the parties, although the written sources are not without contradictions: Thucydides, quoted above, states merely that Chalcidian settlers established themselves at Lentini (728 BC) after driving out the Sikels, and that the Megarians joined them for a while, before being forced in turn to seek a new home elsewhere. A more complex sequence of events is recounted by Polyaenus (V.5), who believed that the Chalcidians initially settled alongside the indigenous inhabitants. Theocles, the Chalcidian leader, having made some formal declaration of friendship to the locals, subsequently invited the Megarians to join him, somewhat perfidiously, on condition that they expel his Sikel cohabitants on his behalf. A night-time attack was staged, and the Greeks took over.

These literary snippets need not dominate an assessment of archaeological evidence from these sites, which is more helpful in shedding light on complementary aspects of cultural or socio-economic interaction. However, this more colourful anecdote denotes a souring of relations in the late 8th century BC, which is also suggested by the pattern of occupation at other sites in the hinterland of Greek settlements, described below. First, however, it is worth noting that some new light has been shed on the character of the colonial foundations themselves.

Greek colonies with native people?

Centuries of re-building and the practical difficulty of finding the deepest levels intact (frequently now under modern towns) have obscured the early years in the life of many Sicilian Greek towns. Nevertheless, over 2,000 graves of the 7th-6th centuries BC (there are rather few of the 8th century BC) have been excavated in the cemeteries of Megara, Syracuse and Gela and more evidence for settlement structures has come to light in recent years. New research by G. Shepherd has challenged the old idea that the colonies were closely modelled on their mother towns in the Greek homeland. Despite many similarities, the burial rites of these three cities do not precisely reflect those of their place of origin, notably Corinth, Megara Nysaea, Rhodes and Crete.[27]

For example, whereas rock-cut trench graves (*fossae*) were most common in Syracuse, the monolithic sarcophagus was the norm for adults at Corinth; while the early burials at Megara in Sicily were mainly cremations and inhumations in pottery vessels, these are not found at Megara in Greece; inhumations outnumber cremations at Gela, but adult cremation was more common in Rhodes and Crete. There are also several contrasting aspects of child burials. Although the divergences are mainly of a statistical nature and do not represent radical departures, they nevertheless signal a move away from homeland practices, implying that the Sicilian colonies were less tied to or constrained by the cultural norms of the mother country than has often been thought. It has also been suggested that the burial practices of Gela, Syracuse and Megara Hyblaea reflect mutual emulation and possibly competition through a display of status, as seen for example in the use of grand sarcophagi.

At first glance, there is no sign of indigenous people. There are no rock-cut chamber tombs with multiple burials and the use of sarcophagi seems more typically Greek (fig. 124:1). On the other hand, the burial practices of Greek settlers cannot have been unfamiliar to local peoples. Although the chamber tomb was predominant locally, trench graves, jar burials, cremations and even sarcophagi were known. Iron Age burial rites varied in both Greece and Sicily where attitudes to burial, or at least to the kind of receptacles used for the deceased, were probably more flexible than has generally been allowed and were not determined by ethnic origin (chapter 5). Is it possible, therefore, that some of those interred in the new cemeteries were not Greek settlers but local people? This has rarely been admitted in the past. Dunbabin believed that the Sicilian colonies were 'pure Greek', that the Greeks in Sicily jealously guarded their identity, and even doubted whether Greek men married indigenous women, despite the fact that there were probably more men than women among the early settlers. In reality, it is impossible to be so categorical, while the literary evidence is of limited help on this matter.[28] Greek writers could have ignored or been reluctant to admit the presence of local people, especially if they were mainly women.

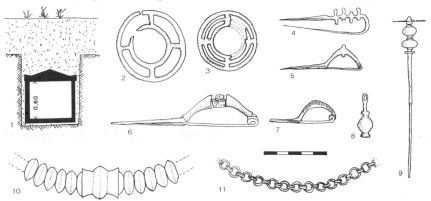

Fig. 124. (1,2,4-11) Syracuse, Fusco cemetery sarcophagus and examples of personal ornaments; (3) wheel ornament from Megara tomb

Of course, local people may well have adopted Greek habits in a colonial
setting and Greeks moving into territories outside the colonies may have
adopted local customs. While it is impossible to identify indigenous people
in colonial burial grounds with absolute confidence, certain aspects of the
funerary rite point to different or changing identities, influenced by the
local cultural environment. In particular, associations of certain grave
goods occur, especially personal ornaments, that are more consistent with
local customs. For example, at Syracuse some tombs (about 14% of the
total) contain several depositions, often couples, but occasionally adults
and children, suggesting a family group. This is practically unknown in
Corinth, but is typical of indigenous traditions. Corinthian burials
generally contained fewer grave goods than those of Syracuse, often no
more than an iron dress pin, a form which was not used hitherto in
Sicily, although it is very frequent in the Fusco cemetery (fig. 124:9). If
more tombs could be found of the first generation of settlers, it is
possible that evidence of indigenous traits or partners would be more
apparent.

However, for an ostensibly Greek cemetery, fibulae are well represented at Syracuse: several dozen were found (but probably less than the
true number, since some were fragmentary) and it is noteworthy that
these often accompanied multiple depositions.[29] A common variety had the
bow decorated with bone and amber, perhaps obtained locally (fig. 124:6).
They were probably designed in the western colonies, but they could
equally have been made by indigenous people and were evidently worn by
them, since they occur in native cemeteries. A type with knobs on the bow
more obviously derives from indigenous serpentine fibulae (fig. 124:4).[30]
Several tombs of the early 7th century BC at Syracuse contained multiple
burials and an unusual quantity of bronze ornaments: chains, beads,
globular pendants, wheel ornaments, fibulae, pins, and even a terracotta
spindle-whorl (t.129). This is consistent with an indigenous burial rite

(chapter 5) in which women of a certain rank were provided with a range of bronze personal ornaments (fig. 124). During the first decades of Greek settlement, similar items were found in rock-cut chamber tombs at sites further inland.[31]

It is possible, therefore, that a significant minority of local origin was resident at Syracuse in the early years of the colony, most probably women, who at least maintained some of their traditions of dress. Moreover, the fact that these burials occur in monolithic sarcophagi or trench graves, accompanied by fine pottery, would suggest that they represent individuals who enjoyed full or at least normal status in the community. It is also noteworthy that such a claim can be made for Syracuse: pre-eminent among the colonies, responsible for the destruction of a native settlement on the same site and the eviction of its population according to Thucydides, and associated with an aggressively expansionist policy at the expense of indigenous people in the territory. If locals were admitted here, then it is likely that they were also present at Megara, which was politically weaker and, judging by the Hyblon reference, probably better disposed towards local peoples. In fact, there are several graves at Megara, and at least one at Naxos (below), which would be consistent with the presence of local women.[32]

According to Thucydides, Gela was founded by Rhodians and Cretans in 688 BC, although discoveries of early Protocorinthian pottery indicate that settlement may have begun before 700 BC.[33] Gela has various burial rites in its early years: inhumations in monolithic stone sarcophagi (later replaced by terracotta boxes) or under tiles, jar burials (especially for children) and cremations. These practices undoubtedly reflect homeland traditions and perhaps the influence of neighbouring colonies, although it is worth recalling that child inhumation in jars was also known locally in the Iron Age. The 7th-century tombs are poor in grave goods, so that few personal ornaments are visible, although indigenous pottery traditions are represented by the large plumed jars used for some child burials in the Borgo cemetery (fig. 136:6). These *pithoi* are almost identical to those of about the same date at the nearby indigenous site of Butera (below).

Local pottery recurs in other colonial settings. On the northern coast at Mylai (modern Milazzo), founded in 716 BC by Chalcidians from Zancle, cremation was prevalent in the early years of the colony, which is consistent with the Euboean background of the settlers. However, cremation was also the main practice of earlier indigenous communities at this site, where the early colonial burial ground has some burials in jars and bucket-shaped *dolia* of local type.[34] Here is another possible case of integration between people of Greek and local origin.

The layout and design of the earliest buildings in the colonies is also noteworthy.[35] In the mid-8th century BC, towns in Greece such as Megara and Corinth consisted of loosely agglomerated dwellings with their burials nearby, which had sometimes gravitated naturally around good land or sources of water, often as a result of choices made in earlier periods. They

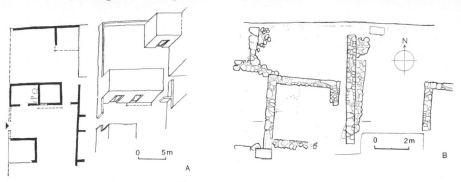

Fig. 125. Early colonial dwellings at (A) Megara and (B) Syracuse

do not show evidence of the formal urban plan of later towns, with areas dedicated respectively to dwellings, public spaces and monuments. It is significant, therefore, that the late 8th and early 7th-century BC dwellings at Megara and Syracuse were arranged in quadrangular plots, probably within larger block divisions (fig. 125), just as the surrounding land or *chora* was probably divided into units for cultivation. This could reflect a relatively egalitarian allocation to various families encouraged by the new surroundings in which homeland traditions of social class and land ownership were no longer being reinforced by long-established divisions of space. It would follow, as often remarked, that the colonising experience was itself a factor in the creation of a new attitude to urban living.

By the late 8th century BC, Megara, Syracuse and Naxos had quadrangular buildings surrounded by narrow trackways or lanes, with a roughly rectilinear layout. After about 650 BC, a more elaborate plan evolved, which nevertheless respected the original one. However, the dwellings of the first settlers were modest in size (about 4 x 4m) and no more advanced in the materials and techniques of construction than those of indigenous people: they utilized roughly hewn stones for the wall foundations, perhaps surmounted by mud-brick, while the roofs were probably thatched, and some had an internal bench around the wall, a feature characteristic of Iron Age dwellings in both Sicily and Greece. A row of contiguous rooms with doors opening onto a narrow passageway (W 2.5m) has been found at Syracuse, which contrasts with the layout of the Iron Age settlement at Morgantina or Lentini, although the latter were probably adapted to hill-top locations. If a precursor or parallel for the urban geometry of Syracuse or Megara were to be sought in the indigenous world, the best candidate would be Thapsos, another coastal site on fairly level ground, where the buildings of the second and, of greater relevance, the third phase (chapters 4-5) consisted of rectilinear units of adjacent (and more spacious) rooms, flanked by lanes or courtyards.[36] The first Greek settlers knew little if anything more than the locals about building techniques.

Local histories in eastern Sicily

Regional settlement patterns changed markedly in the course of the 8th and 7th centuries BC as a result of Greek colonisation. The occupation history of many indigenous sites can be linked with the development of the coastal towns and their territorial expansion, although the patterns and processes varied from one region to another. Particular contrasts may be noted between coastal communites, those in the hinterlands within easy reach of Greek colonies and those further inland, where local traditions lasted longer.

There is no reason to believe that eastern Sicily was only sparsely populated at the time of colonisation or that its inhabitants were already concentrated at just a few places inland, as sometimes stated. Some large centres of population existed in the Hyblaean hills, such as Pantalica, but the foothills beside the coastal plain also have clusters of chamber tombs, especially in places where limestone escarpments are cut by rivers, creating deep canyons. Although many tombs are undated, the cemeteries near Villasmundo, Cassibile and Avola, where 8th-century material has recently been found, show that these were characteristic settlement locations.[37] Good harbours or landing-places (Syracuse, Punta Castelluzzo, Naxos, and probably Thapsos) were also occupied during the Early Iron Age (chapter 5), which further undermines the idea that the coast was semi-deserted or that local peoples were only '*inutilement présent*'.[38]

An initial effect of Greek settlement in this region may have been to encourage local people to move inland. This may be inferred from the presence of several small centres in the Hyblaean hills, such as Noto Vecchia, Tremenzano, Cozzo delle Giummare, Grotta del Murmuro and from the large number of 8th/7th century BC tombs at Finocchito, located

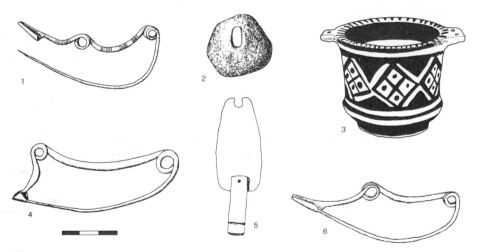

Fig. 126. Late 8th-early 7th century BC: (1-3) Pantalica South tomb 6: serpentine fibula, amber bead, beaker; (4-6) Butera: fibulae and razor

on the slopes of a limestone hill in the middle Tellaro valley, about 35km southwest of Syracuse.[39] The inhabitants of some of these smaller sites may well have moved to Finocchito in the later 8th century BC. A similar phenomenon is encountered at Pantalica, which has relatively few burials of the Cassibile period, but a considerable number in the South cemetery, some of which are datable to the late 8th-early 7th century BC (figs.126:1-3; 130).[40] The expansion of population at certain sites suggests forms of synoecism (the coming together of small communities at larger centres), caused by insecurity as well as other factors: one economic incentive for the creation of these central places may have been the provision of easier access to trade goods from new and correspondingly centralized markets; politically too, there must have been advantages in conducting negotiations with the more unified entities, represented by the emerging Greek *poleis*, from the comparative security of an indigenous stronghold. Similar forces probably operated in western and central Sicily, where many large indigenous sites developed on hill-tops commanding river valleys and natural lines of communication inland.

In proximity to Lentini and Megara, many indigenous sites survived and may even have flourished in the late 8th and early 7th centuries BC, before either being abandoned or changing in character. Early Greek imports at Villasmundo suggest exchanges with Megara, perhaps based on a mixture of political, economic and even social transactions, such as intermarriage. Mindful of the literary reference to territorial concessions by Hyblon (above), we may infer an initially cordial relationship here, but the site seems to have been abandoned in the course of the 7th century BC. Lentini lies not far from the coast in an area of renowned fertility, where the sedimentary formations of the Hyblaean hills encounter volcanic lithologies and are traversed by several stream valleys on the southern edge of the Catania plain, the largest alluvial basin in Sicily. Its history of occupation can be reconstructed from scattered findspots and patchy research over the last century.[41] Prior to the arrival of Greek settlers, several clusters of dwellings on neighbouring hills used various cemeteries on the slopes and valleys below (fig. 107): Ausonian huts on the Metapiccola hill, jar burials in contrada Pozzanghera, scattered chamber tombs and sporadic finds on the adjacent hills of San Mauro, Carrube and Ciricò (chapter 5). The layout is reminiscent of Iron Age Rome. Little is known about residential areas, but there is plenty of indigenous pottery from San Mauro which could date to the later 8th century BC, when Greeks and locals were perhaps living together on this hill.[42] The 8th/7th-century chamber tombs provide an interesting mixture of local and Greek traditions (below).

The evidence from other indigenous sites in the region (such as Ossini and Cozzo della Tignusa) is again mainly funerary, but the pattern is not dissimilar. It has been suggested that Lentini adopted an expansionist policy at the expense of its neighbours in the course of the 7th century BC and that the Chalcidian settlements soon proved to be

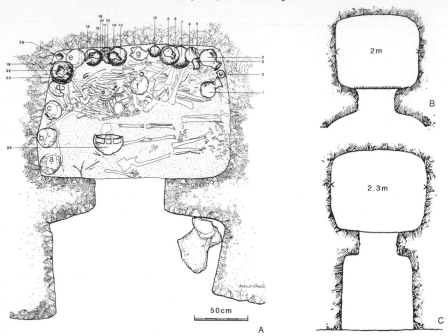

Fig. 127. Chamber tombs: (A) Villasmundo; (B-C) Licodia

no less aggressive or ambitious in their desire to acquire new territory than their Syracusan neighbours.[43] Deteriorating relationships are undoubtedly reflected by the appearance of fortification walls at native sites inland during the 6th century BC (for example, at Mineo, Palike, Monte Balchino, Monte San Mauro, Civita and Mendolito). Greek imports and local pottery production are well attested at Ramacca during the 7th century BC, but the site may have been destroyed soon after 600 BC, and was subsequently resurrected as a substantially Hellenized settlement.[44] However, it would be exaggerated to infer a state of endemic ethnic warfare between Greeks and natives. The conflicts between rival Greek cities were equally fierce and the main contention must have been over land.

Information about most of these sites is limited to burials. The quadrangular chambers of Villasmundo were sometimes arranged in rows, presenting an extended façade. Some had antechambers or small forecourts, where pieces of human bone were found and coarse pottery that may have been used for ceremonial offerings. Single tombs could be used for several depositions, sometimes over twenty, which required pushing the earlier remains to the rear in order to make space for newcomers, or covering over the earlier burials (fig. 127:A). Apart from those items of possibly pre-colonial date noted above, much of the pottery consisted of bowls, cups and amphorae of local design, decorated in LG style. However, indigenous funerary traditions persisted here.

At Lentini, the burials of the late 8th and 7th centuries BC occur in the rock-cut tombs along the Sant'Eligio valley (Orsi's San Aloe). Over 100 are estimated to exist, although only a few dozen preserved any contents. Here too the majority were quadrangular chambers with flat ceilings, sometimes provided with narrow rock-cut benches or wider funerary couches and preceded by a vestibule. Some examples were over 2m in diameter. The deceased numbered mainly between one and three and were accompanied by a few personal items, such as spindle-whorls, beads, an iron knife and a good quantity of pottery. Imported forms were greatly outnumbered by local geometric production that combined traditional shapes, especially amphorae and bowls, and Greek Geometric styles (fig. 128).

It is generally assumed that these were tombs of indigenous people: the funerary rite and accoutrements reflect local traditions, although the chambers are slightly more elaborate and the quantity of pottery larger than in the Early Iron Age. Where, then, are the tombs of the Greek settlers? According to historical sources (above), there was a period of coexistence between locals and Greeks at Lentini, and no separate and more obviously Greek burial ground has yet been found. It could be argued, therefore, that these tombs represent the mixed burials of locals and incomers during the period of cohabitation. If this is correct, it would appear that the Greeks initially adopted many aspects of indigenous burial practices, but that later generations abandoned them, since the

Fig. 128. Local geometric vases and bronze ornaments from Lentini (1-5) and Licodia (6-9)

burials of the 6th-5th centuries BC, notably single trench graves, are essentially Greek in form.

Almost nothing is known about the residential area at Finocchito, except for the remains of a turreted fortification wall, guarding the naturally weakest approach from the North.[45] However, the cemetery is one of the best documented in the southeastern region. The tombs consist of small rock-cut chambers of traditional type: occasionally elliptical in plan, but more frequently quadrangular and with a flat ceiling (Ø around 1.75m, H around 0.90m). The small doorway was sealed by a slab, held by a cross-bar and a rubble covering, sometimes preceded by a short corridor. Several groupings were arranged in rows on natural terraces around the hillside; a total of 570 has been calculated, which is a conservative estimate, although most were found empty or partially despoiled. The dead were usually placed on their backs with the head sometimes resting on a raised ledge, probably clothed, wearing ornaments such as fibulae, rings and beads. A cremation urn may be represented by an amphora (tomb 80), as occasionally noted at other sites of this period. The majority of undisturbed tombs contained just one or two individuals, although up to 10 are recorded. A living population of several hundred seems likely.[46]

At face value, the rather standardized chambers and repetitive rite could suggest that the local population was not highly ranked, although the often incomplete finds and the emphasis on certain kinds of grave goods may be obscuring differences in wealth, status and role. For example, weapons are conspicuously absent in most indigenous tombs at this time, but common in contemporary hoards. Judging by the abundance of personal ornaments and the recurrence of spindle-whorls, many tombs included women or couples (fig. 129). A small set of pottery vessels, consisting of bowls, jugs, *oinochoai*, *askoi*, *pyxides* and an occasional amphora, was often placed at the feet or shoulders of the deceased, perhaps in observance of a ritual that required a set of vessels for offerings or as a symbol of a funerary meal.

The tomb goods, especially pottery, denote increasing contacts with Greek colonies during the main phase of occupation (about 730-650 BC). Metal jewellery consisted of bronze and iron rings, chains, beads, serpentine and later styles of fibulae, examples of which were also found in the colonial cemeteries (above), although these items are consistent with indigenous tradition: notably the considerable quantity of bronze dress ornaments worn by indigenous women, which seems to be typical of the Italic world. If certain dress items were adopted from the Greek colonies, they were adopted selectively. For example, there is a striking absence at native sites of the Corinthian dress pins found in many of the Syracuse tombs. On the other hand, small luxuries and novelties, such as scarabs and ivory plaques (fig. 129:22,30), were imported from coastal sites.

Syracuse and its sub-colony at Helorus, located at the mouth of the Tellaro river, were well-placed to trade with Finocchito, reached by follow-

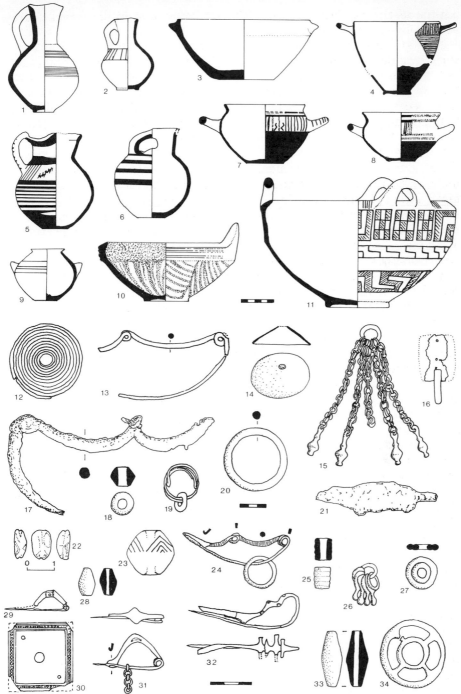

Fig. 129. Finocchito grave goods

ing the river valley. It is not immediately obvious what the local inhabitants were offering in return, although the fertile and well-watered Hyblaean region was noted by ancient authors for a wide range of agricultural products, as well as honey, skins and textiles. The abundance of spindle-whorls and loomweights indicates textile production and ownership of flocks, while Iron Age faunal samples (fig. 96) show that, in addition to sheep, goat, cattle and pig, there was wild game (boar and deer) still available, implying the existence of woodlands and their associated resources. The lack of archaeobotanical evidence may encourage the view that the indigenous subsistence economy was more concerned with stock-keeping than cultivation, while the agrarian regime of Greek coastal settlements concentrated on cereal cultivation, with vines, olives and fruit trees. However, this requires further archaeological investigation. Although the loss of control over the coastal plains may have been a serious blow to indigenous sites in the Syracusan hinterland, it may have stimulated trade in subsistence produce: possibly domestic animals from the hinterland in return for craft products from the coastal centres.

Changes in craft production are visible at all the indigenous sites of the region. Greek vases, whether imitated locally or imported, became ubiquitous. Those from Finocchito show that Corinthian styles were most familiar to local people, no doubt due to the proximity of Syracuse, whereas indigenous sites further north show a greater awareness of Euboeo-Cycladic styles of decoration, favoured in Chalcidian colonies, and different style zones are also visible in western regions (below). Geometric patterns and vase-shapes were copied by local potters, who were used to making wheel-made pottery, albeit decorated in a more carefree manner. Several local shapes, such as jugs and amphorae, were not so different from Greek equivalents and continued to be used, while new forms also developed that were only loosely inspired by Greek styles, such as deep bowls with incised decoration (fig. 130). Of equal or greater interest perhaps were the contents of the vases, the association with wine-drinking (below) and the access to a wider range of craft products and exotic trade items.

The presence of jugs and amphorae in burials had local precedents, since these forms often occurred in LBA tombs and a single jug was sometimes placed in graves at Mulino della Badia. However, one form of Greek origin that now gained widespread popularity was the juglet with trifoliate rim or *oinochoe* (e.g. fig. 129:5). It is not certain whether vines were cultivated locally prior to the 8th century BC. The only grape-pip known from an Iron Age house at Morgantina resembled a non-cultivated variety (*Vitis sylvestris*), and the use of strainer-jugs may suggest that some other brew was preferred in Sicily, perhaps a herbal drink, or mead. However, wine was probably fast becoming an important commodity and the same may be true of olive oil, although the extent of olive cultivation (if any) prior to this period is also uncertain. Imported oil amphorae (Attic SOS, Euboean and Corinthian A forms) are found in the Greek colonies from the late 8th century BC and at indigenous sites from the late 7th century BC, when the first wine amphorae (East

Fig. 130. Pantalica South tomb 86, incised bowl

Greek) also appear, for example at Butera and Monte San Mauro. The importance of wine is more clearly evidenced in the 7th century BC by the presence of Greek-style drinking cups, such as Protocorinthian *skyphoi* (fig. 129:4), and in the 6th century BC by the proliferation at indigenous sites of transport amphorae and Ionic *kylikes*.[47] These cups were frequently included in wealthier burials, reflecting the emergence of a local élite that was acquiring the habit of drinking *graeco more*, with its etiquette of convivial banqueting or *symposia*, widespread in Greek and Italic funerary symbolism.

Communities further from the coast were slower to adopt Greek customs. About 30km southwest of Lentini, the local chamber tombs of Licodia (fig. 127:B,C) began to include imitations of Greek pottery styles and imported Protocorinthian wares in about the mid-7th century BC.[48] This site was regarded by Orsi as emblematic of a gradual process of local acculturation, giving its name to the Licodia Eubea complex, but the ancient town probably lies under the modern one and its cemeteries have been ransacked. Beyond the immediate grasp of Syracuse, the Ragusa area remained a stronghold of indigenous culture, as represented by chamber tombs at Modica, Castiglione and Monte Casasia, located on the southern promontories of the Hyblaean hills.[49] A few imports arrived in this area in the late 8th century BC, for example at Modica, while the Castiglione chamber tombs, dated from the early 7th century BC, include late Protocorinthian ware, local geometric amphorae and bowls in the Licodia and Finocchito styles. These communities subsequently estab-

245

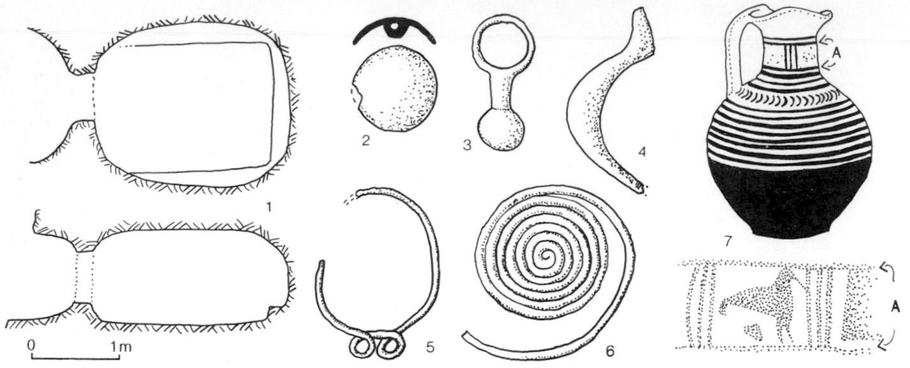

Fig. 131. Cocolonazzo tomb 5, LG *oinochoe* (7) and local bronzes (2-6)

lished formal and probably friendly relations with Camarina (founded in 598 BC) and must have been prominent among those indigenous groups known to have joined the latter as allies in the ill-fated campaign against Syracuse in the later 6th century BC.

Noteworthy here and at other sites nearby are rock-cut trench graves, datable from the early 6th century BC, containing mainly local wares. Rather than an indigenous practice, they are generally thought to represent the adoption of a Greek burial form, although the presence of several individuals (sometimes adults and children) in a single grave may be a local custom. A few miles away on a hill-top above the upper Dirillo valley, the 7th-6th-century BC necropolis of Monte Casasia consisted of traditional round or quadrangular chamber-tombs entered by a vertical shaft or a corridor. More is known than usual about the skeletal remains from these two sites (tables 2-3). The burial population of at least 133 individuals from Monte Casasia included a high proportion of adults (72%), although children may be under-represented due to lack of preservation. Adult males (62.5%) appear to be more common than females (35.4%) and the lifespan statistics suggest greater longevity by comparison with earlier periods, with 29% aged between 40 and 50, and 21% over 50. Average statures of 164.33cm for males and 153.94cm for females are slightly higher than the Castiglione sample, but lower by comparison with the local EBA population, especially in the case of females (by about 6cm). More illuminating comparative studies of contemporary Greek and native populations may soon be possible.

The evidence from northeastern Sicily is less abundant. Naxos, universally regarded as the earliest Greek foundation in Sicily, located beside the bay on Capo Schisò, had a pre-existing Iron Age settlement. Not enough has been revealed to judge whether local people were evicted or absorbed by the new settlement, although one burial (t.72) of a young woman may represent a local woman on the basis of dress ornaments.[50] It is hard to see how Naxos, surrounded by mountains, could have survived or prospered

246

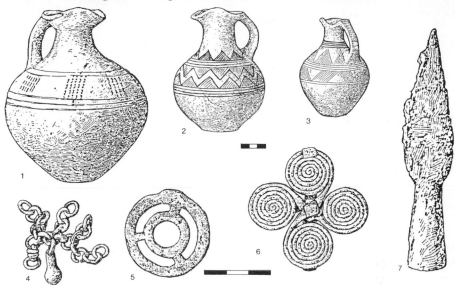

Fig. 132. Pozzo di Gotto, local vases, bronzes and iron spearhead, late 8th – early 7th century BC

without some understanding with local people. The nearest indigenous site is only 4km away and has a commanding view of the coastal plain from the rocky crests of Cocolonazzo (near Taormina). Several rock-cut chamber tombs were excavated here by Orsi, datable to the late 8th century BC: mainly quadrangular rooms, with a low bench and vestibule (fig. 131). The funerary rite and materials are mostly in the local tradition, while the pottery shows the influence of LG decoration and includes some imports (fig. 131:7).[51] The pattern of occupation is a familiar one: a period during which a local group maintained their traditions, while trading with their new neighbours, but with no evidence of continuity into the 6th century BC.

Burial customs further north before Greek settlement were mixed. Lipari and Milazzo had jar inhumations and cremations, Fiumedinisi has traces of Iron Age settlement and *dolium* burials, possibly contemporary with Greek colonisation, while rock-cut chamber tombs were used at Rodì and Pozzo di Gotto. The latter are similar to those at Cocolonazzo and probably belong mainly to the early colonial period.[52] Cremated remains in an amphora from a chamber tomb at Pozzo di Gotto point to a further combination of rites. Iron spearheads were found and various personal ornaments: iron fibulae with copper wire decoration, bronze spiral fibulae and a variety of small rings, beads, chains and spiral ornaments, typical of indigenous dress (fig. 132:4-7). Much of the pottery reflects the persistence of local traditions, although the prevalence of *oinochoai* and incised decoration in bands and metopes (fig. 132:1-3) suggests a knowledge of LG styles and affinities with communities in Calabria, where similar materials and burial rites occur at Canale and Ianchina.

247

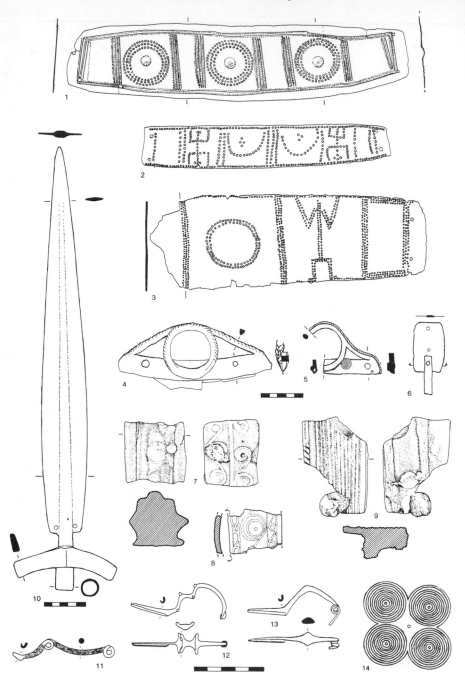

Fig. 133. Bronzes from the Mendolito (Adrano) hoard, late 8th-7th century BC

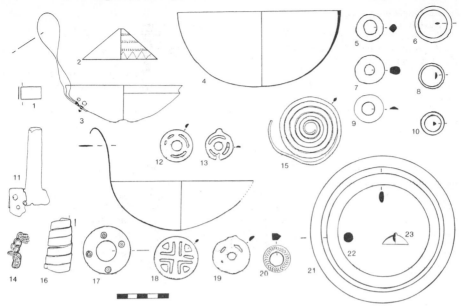

Fig. 134. Bronzes from the San Cataldo hoard, late 8th-7th century BC

Recent research suggests that local groups exploited copper sources in the Peloritani mountains (chapter 5). Metal might have constituted an item of exchange with coastal communities in this region, although proof of this is still lacking. However, large metal hoards of this period, notably that of Mendolito (Adrano) and San Cataldo (chapter 5) illustrate the persistence of traditional indigenous dress forms (serpentine fibulae) and the vitality of indigenous metal-working in the 7th century BC (figs. 133-134). Overall, it appears that local people in northern Sicily maintained their cultural identity for longer and with fewer alterations than their cousins in southeastern regions, probably as a result of several factors: the more rugged nature of the terrain and the presence of fewer Greek settlers, perhaps less inclined to pursue such an expansionist policy inland as that of Syracuse and other towns.

Regional patterns in central and western areas

Elsewhere in the island, more information is available from indigenous strongholds on inland hills. Further from Greek coastal colonies, which were established at a slightly later date in southern and western Sicily, the history and character of these sites is often different from those noted above, since many survived and preserved local traditions well into the historical period. Their development followed a recurrent trajectory: villages of loosely aggregated dwellings expanded in the later 8th and 7th centuries BC, while undergoing changes in craft production, due first to

249

trade and then probably to increasingly direct contacts with *Sikeliotai*, which led to more profound changes in local customs, reflected in new settlement plans and designs of individual buildings as well as burials during the 6th century BC. However, details of the earlier phases (8th-7th centuries BC) are only beginning to emerge. The challenge remains to clarify the nature of different settlements at each stage of what must have been a complex process of interaction and change, with reference not only to craft production, burial practices and architecture, but also to neglected questions of subsistence and economic organisation.

Several indigenous sites lie in the hinterland of Gela, initially the main Greek colony in southern Sicily. The expansion of Geloan territorial claims may well have caused the abandonment of Dessueri (chapter 5), where recent excavations have revealed traces of settlement on Monte Maio, probably still occupied in the 8th century BC.[53] Literary sources suggest that there were early conflicts with local people ('Sikans') in this territory and that one of the first Geloan military conquests inland was a native centre called Omphake, thought to be either Dessueri or Butera.

Unlike Dessueri, however, Butera seems to have reached a *modus vivendi* with the nearby colony, which was only 15km away.[54] The settlement occupied the summit and lower terraces of a rocky outcrop, where small quadrangular stone-built dwellings of the 7th century BC have been found, containing plumed storage jars. As customary, the cemeteries were

Fig. 135. Butera, tomb 167 pottery, late 8th – early 7th century BC

250

spread around the lower slopes and plain below. The earliest tombs are rock-cut chambers with two or three inhumations, accompanied by a considerable quantity of bronze personal ornaments, including serpentine fibulae (fig. 126:4-6) and a mixture of local Iron Age pottery (notably plumed jugs) and painted *oinochoai* (fig. 135). A date in the late 8th or 7th century BC seems likely, contemporary with the first settlers at Gela (perhaps prior to the Thucydidean date of 688 BC). During the 7th century BC, various burial rites were practised at Butera: jar burials (fig. 136:1-5), containing inhumations of babies or children, although one or two held cremations; urn burials in amphorae, generally representing cremated adults; and a few inhumations in simple trench graves.

More unusual are two contiguous rectangular rooms or precincts (nos. 138-9) with a low stone wall, resembling shrines, entered by a doorway on the narrow side (fig. 136). Built into the wall of no. 138 was a large stone-lined cist, covered with a slab, containing several burials: a plumed jar with cranium fragments and half-burnt bones; a painted amphora with some mixed bones; and a large jar with cremated remains and five whole skulls. An amphora in the adjacent precinct contained three adult skulls. A similar rite of head-removal (*akephalia*) is attested in some other tombs in which the unburnt skull had been removed and placed in an urn with cremated remains. This is thought to reflect the local adoption of a Greek custom, with precedents in Crete, after the foundation of Gela, where a similar practice is attested, and possibly the presence of Greeks at Butera.[55] However, the situation is ambiguous: if the rite is of Cretan inspiration, the plumed *pithoi* and personal ornaments (iron serpentine fibulae, bronze chains and beads) are consistent with local traditions as is the habit of multiple burial, attested by the various ossuaries.

Overall, Butera resembles a provincial satellite with an indigenous substratum and an increasingly mixed population living within the orbit of Gela. It may have been granted limited political autonomy, but was undoubtedly closely tied, not least by trade, to the nearby colony. Like other provincial centres of indigenous origin, which adopted some customs of the colonies in the course of the 7th century BC, these places may have exerted considerable influence in surrounding territories. As communities where the native language was probably prevalent and with more obviously mixed cultural traditions than the colonies, they would have been well placed to act as secondary centres and markets, and to deal directly with indigenous and rural populations further inland. To the latter, they could offer the attraction of markets in which the produce of the land could be exchanged for quality craft items and luxuries emanating from coastal centres and ultimately from maritime trade.

Spread over five summits near Caltagirone, in what were known as the Heraean hills, at the watershed of two river valleys leading alternately east to Lentini or south to Gela, the site of Monte San Mauro has evidence for continuity of occupation from at least the Early Iron Age.[56] Sporadic

Fig. 136. Butera, precinct tombs and burial *pithoi* from Butera (1-5) and Gela (6)

finds recovered since Orsi's day imply the existence of an indigenous settlement, recently shown to consist of elliptical huts with internal benches, dated to the 8th and early 7th centuries BC, recalling those at Morgantina. One structure, with some evidence of destruction by fire, lies partly beneath a Greek shrine (which Orsi mistook for a local '*anaktoron*'). In the late 7th or early 6th century BC, the style of buildings began to alter, although the urban layout makes no pretence of an orthogonal plan with streets of regular width, which would have been hard to adapt to the

252

sloping hillside. A long-house with an internal subdivision and curved lateral wall could also reflect the persistence of local traditions.

As usual, more profound changes occurred in the early 6th century BC, when new clusters of houses with a tripartite structure of Greek design appeared. Their contents, however, illustrate domestic concerns not unlike those of earlier Iron Age dwellings: large storage vessels, terracotta cooking bases and abundant loomweights. The main concessions to modernisation, or Hellenisation, seem to be represented by roof-tiles, terracotta 'bath-tubs' and fine drinking wares (Ionic cups and a black-figure krater). Likewise, the cemetery points to a mixture of local traits (inhumations in plumed *pithoi*) and innovations (burials in imported amphorae of diverse origin).

Botanical remains from two *pithoi* provide an indication of local cultivation: barley (*Hordeum distichum* and *vulgare*), spelt (*Triticum dicoccum*), vetches and beans (*Vicia ervilia, Vicia faba, Lathyrus*). These species probably had a long history of indigenous use and may have been more characteristic of native subsistence strategies inland, although it is not known whether olives and vines were also significant locally. It is possible that the latter were mainly produced by coastal or Greek communities and that subsistence patterns also reflected different cultural traditions. Little can be said about the the environmental implications, although a period of alluviation, associated with the erosion of land in the Gornalunga valley near Morgantina, occurred at some time between the 8th and 4th centuries BC, either as a result of climatic change or, perhaps more likely, as a result of human activities, such as clearance.[57] This might have been encouraged by a growing emphasis on cereal agriculture inland, foreshadowing the role of central Sicily as a major grain-producing region.

A few miles to the west lies Monte Bubbonia, another indigenous settlement that was probably still independent during the 7th century BC when some Protocorinthian imports arrived and local potters began to adopt geometric motifs. The bulk of the material found so far dates from the 6th century BC, by which time the character of the settlement was being transformed and Greek influence was increasingly strong, as reflected by shrines, votive terracottas and a changing urban layout.[58]

Further inland, indigenous traditions survived slightly longer, as is exemplified by cemeteries in the vicinity of Calascibetta.[59] The earliest, Carcarella, consists of inhumations in rock-cut tombs of the 10th-9th century BC (chapter 5) and a few of the 8th-7th century BC, contemporary with many others at the nearby cemetery of Cozzo San Giuseppe (fig. 137). Here too the persistence of local customs is seen in the use of rock-cut tombs and traditional items of dress, albeit accompanied by the adoption of painted *oinochoai*. Greek imported pottery was present by the mid-7th century BC, when Protocorinthian cups appeared, followed by increasing numbers of Ionic cups (*kylikes*) in the 6th century BC. These imports need denote little more than indirect trade between neighbouring indigenous

Fig. 137. Rock-cut tombs at Cozzo San Giuseppe (Realmese)

groups, in this case gravitating mainly towards the Chalcidian zone (Lentini and Catania), and to a lesser extent southwards to Gela.

Access to new craft items provoked changes in fashion and local craft production even in these internal areas of Sicily. Nevertheless, there is a risk of reading too much into changing pottery styles or the presence of Greek imports. Judging by burials, neither the ideologies nor the daily customs of local people in central regions altered significantly during the 7th century BC. It is debatable whether they had yet acquired more than a superficial familiarity with the customs of coastal towns or whether their interest in the latter extended much beyond certain prestigious or useful materials that could be obtained by trade. It is only after the mid-6th century BC that more profound changes are witnessed locally, as reflected in the necropolis of Valle Coniglio (mid-6th/5th century BC). Even in this case, however, the indigenous rite of burial in chamber tombs continued, as it did throughout central Sicily. The prominence given to Greek pottery and artefacts in many of the older publications has perhaps also contributed unduly to an impression of profound acculturation at indigenous sites in the 6th century BC.

Morgantina presents a similar picture. Chamber tombs were current between the 8th and 5th centuries BC. Three tombs of EIA tradition could belong to the late 8th or early 7th century BC (fig. 138). Their plans became more elaborate during the 6th century BC through the adoption of certain architectural embellishments, such as pitched ceilings, couches and built

254

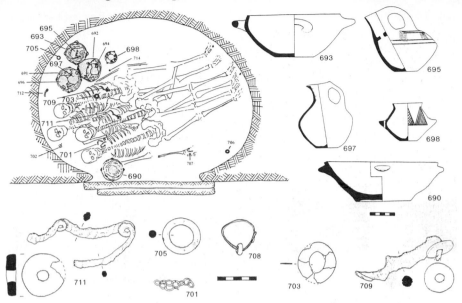

Fig. 138. Morgantina tomb 6, probably late 8th or early 7th century BC

façades.[60] At the same time, trench-graves, tile-tombs, sarcophagi, jar inhumations, cremation urns, wooden coffins and earth graves appeared in the same cemetery. The diversity of funerary ritual in this area during the 6th century BC is also evident at Rossomanno, where similar forms of burial are attested as well as a rite of decapitation, reminiscent of Butera.[61] Here again the skulls had been removed and some placed in bowls of local type, carefully arranged beside urns, which presumably contained the cremated post-cranial remains.

Such elaboration of burial ritual may be explained in terms of hybrid practices stemming from new cultural influences or settlers in the area, although the persistence of the indigenous rite of inhumation in a rock-cut chamber tomb is significant. If there was an influx of Greek settlers in the 6th century BC at Morgantina, as seems likely, some of them may have adopted indigenous burial practices. The monumentalization of certain tombs and the unequal quantities of grave-goods may be taken as assertions of growing differences in status and wealth, especially during the 6th century BC. From an ideological or psychological standpoint, the proliferation of complex rituals at this time might also have represented a way of maintaining cultural identities while negotiating new relationships between different groups and classes; perhaps a recurrent feature of periods characterized by rapid social and political change.

The evidence from the habitation quarter at Morgantina also reflects substantial changes only from about the mid-6th century BC, when Greek shrines, architectural styles and a new urban layout appeared on the

Cittadella hill. Prior to this date, the local community had received some Greek imports (a few Protocorinthian and numerous Ionic cups, for example) and potters had imitated geometric styles. However, the traditional plumed pottery as well as some storage and cooking wares of indigenous design continued. Even the earlier Iron Age house-designs (chapter 5) with timber-laced walls, wattle and daub, clay hearths and benches, probably persisted during the 7th century BC.

To the northwest of Gela were many other indigenous hill-top centres with which the colony soon established contacts, facilitated by a natural thoroughfare along the Salso river.[62] At Monte Saraceno (Ravanusa), which was already occupied before the foundation of Gela, architectural changes occurred under Geloan influence in the late 7th century BC, probably due to forms of acculturation rather than any military conquest. Sabucina was inhabited continuously from the Late Bronze Age (chapters 4 & 5) and not abandoned at the end of the Pantalica I phase in favour of the neighbouring hill of Capodarso, as formerly believed. Traces of quadrangular subdivided dwellings are recorded in the late 7th century BC, probably reflecting early Greek house designs or a mixture of indigenous and Greek. The associated material includes local and imported late Protocorinthian ware. More obvious signs of Greek influence appeared in the mid-6th century BC, when the settlement assumed a fully agglomerated, albeit irregular plan, clustered behind the fortification wall, with evidence for cult activity in the so-called hut-shrines (below).

Further from the coast in west-central regions were several redoubtable bastions of indigenous culture, such as Polizzello and Sant'Angelo Muxaro, two sites which have returned to prominence thanks to recent excavations.[63] The hill (or *Montagna*) of Polizzello dominates a stretch of the upper Platani river near Mussomeli and consists of a flat platform, where a residential quarter was located, just beneath the summit (877m asl) or acropolis (fig. 139). Several groups of rock-cut tombs were set into the steep surrounding slopes, especially on the northern and western sides, consisting of sub-circular, oven-shaped chambers or quadrangular rooms with short corridors, holding multiple depositions and grave goods, often found in superimposed layers, which attest periodic re-use in the 7th and 6th centuries BC. Especially noteworthy is the occasional presence of crouched inhumations just outside the tomb door and the discovery nearby of children's trench graves and jar burials, as well as various installations for funerary rituals, including a circular stone platform or altar, votive deposits containing animal bones, small stone-built precincts for jar burials and a cult-room or shrine with a bench (fig. 139:C): a further indication of the real complexity of indigenous burial rites at this time. The grave goods consisted mainly of fine local incised and painted wares (fig. 139:D), associated with imported small luxury items, such as scarabs, and bronze fibulae, razors and beads. Evidence for cult activity is discussed below.

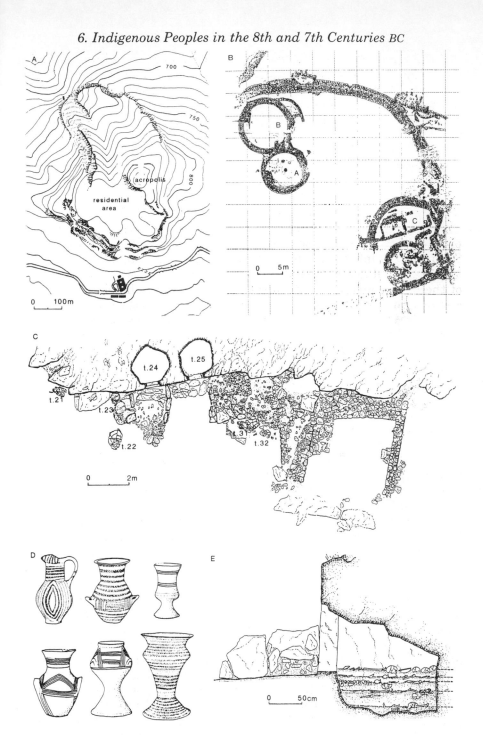

Fig. 139. Polizzello: (A) site plan; (B) acropolis buildings; (C) east necropolis; (D) local pottery; (E) tomb 25 section

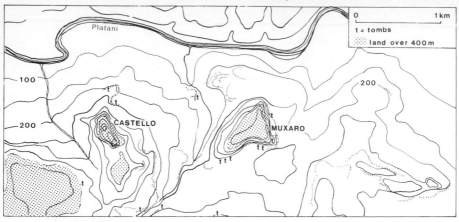

Fig. 140. Sant'Angelo Muxaro

Sant'Angelo Muxaro in the middle Platani valley is associated by some scholars with Camicus, the capital of Kokalos (chapter 4).[64] The cemetery consists of several clusters of tombs around the slopes of a rocky outcrop on the south side of the river (fig. 140), while traces of the habitation site, perhaps also consisting of various clusters of dwellings, have been found on the neighbouring hill. A few tombs may date back to the Middle or Late Bronze Ages, but the best known are a series of large chambers with collective burials and an abundance of grave goods datable mainly to the 7th and 6th centuries BC (fig. 141). Aside from the spectacular Grotta di Sant'Angelo (chapter 4), there are several very large sub-circular chambers, up to 4.60m in diameter and 3m in height. Intact tombs usually had a mass of human bone on the floor, the result of periodic re-opening to admit new arrivals: Orsi counted three dozen skeletons in one and a recently excavated chamber contained at least 45 individuals.

The pottery cannot be assigned to specific individuals, and the recurrence of certain vessel shapes (36 jugs and 23 plate-stands in tomb IV for example) suggests a selection of grave goods, perhaps with only one or two vessels and few personal ornaments (such as an iron fibula) per person. However, some chambers had a raised rock-cut bench with a headrest and step. Tomb VI, excavated in 1931, had two individuals laid out on this funerary bed, with one skull resting on a carved wooden headrest and a finger-bone still bearing a chunky gold ring with an engraved wolf (fig. 142:5). Raised above the mass of skeletons on the chamber floor, this was clearly a case of special treatment, perhaps accorded to a distinguished ancestral couple, the head of a family or clan. Tomb A, excavated in 1976, had a concentration of vases on the floor beside a stone bench (fig. 141:A). Slightly different burial customs evidently prevailed in this region, which resemble the older MBA-LBA practice of large-scale collective burial.

Greek settlers came later to this part of Sicily. In the 7th century BC, the nearest colony was Gela, about 70km away over hilly terrain. Selinus

258

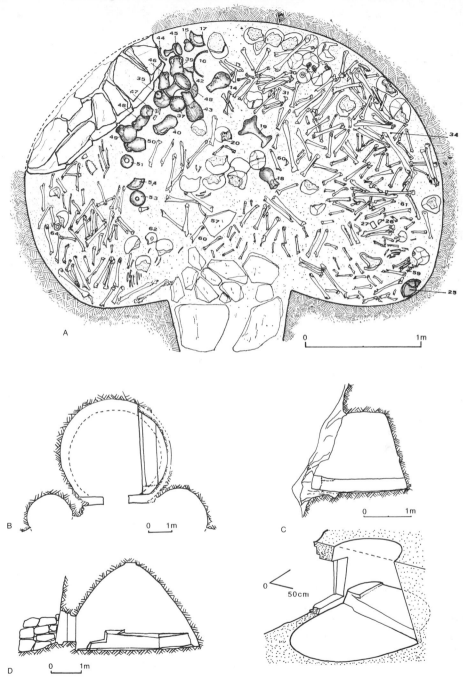

Fig. 141. Sant'Angelo Muxaro tombs

259

Fig. 142. Sant'Angelo Muxaro pottery (1-4,6-8) and gold ring (5)

was almost as far in the other direction and was not founded until 628 BC (Thucydidean date), followed by Agrigento (Akragas) in 580 BC. It is not surprising, therefore, that local traditions predominated at Sant'Angelo Muxaro until at least the mid-6th century BC. From a stylistic point of view, local pottery of the 8th-7th centuries BC inherited much from the Pantalica II period, such as plate-stands and incised decoration (fig. 142), while undergoing elaboration and refinements, probably loosely influenced by Greek pottery styles (geometric incised decoration and painted *oinochoai*). Some finely painted jugs suggest Geloan influences, while the two gold rings and four gold bowls (fig. 123) in Orientalizing style known to have been found at the site could also have come from Gela, or possibly from the Phoenician zone further west (above). Datable to the 7th or early 6th century BC, they suggest some form of exchange with a local élite, perhaps led by emissaries from Gela. Greeks bearing gifts at this time may well have been assessing local strength or preparing the ground for their sub-foundation at Akragas, only 20km away.[65]

Further west, the pattern was also one of lofty indigenous settlements overlooking river valleys inland, such as Monte Castellazzo, Monte Adranone and Monte Maranfusa, which betray encroaching Greek influence in

Fig. 143. Mendolito hoard, bronze sheet plaque

the course of the 6th century BC, mainly from Selinus (above).[66] Little is known about their Iron Age phases, although new evidence is now emerging at Caltabellotta, where a large circular building (Ø 10m) of indigenous tradition, dating from at least the 7th century BC, continued to function into the late 6th century BC, when local incised ware was still being produced. Of about the same date are five circular or subcircular huts on a flat promontory at Montagnoli, 4km from the mouth of the Belice.[67] The largest (hut 1: Ø 10m), in the tradition of earlier dwellings, had a stone wall foundation flanked by an internal plastered bench, a thatched roof supported by a circular arrangement of postholes, and much evidence of daub with wattle and timber impressions. The finds included local incised, plumed and geometric painted ware, associated with a Corinthian Sub-geometric cup (7th century BC) and evidence for a second phase of use in the 6th century BC.

Indigenous cults and iconographies

A striking feature of the archaeological record in the 6th century BC is the abundant evidence for the spread of Greek cults to indigenous sites,

261

Fig. 144. Bronze sheet with repoussé decoration from Terravecchia di Cuti, L 24cm

witnessed by the appearance of shrines with votive depositions, architectural terracottas and figurines in Greek style. This is a sure sign of the adoption of Greek ideas within the indigenous world, a phenomenon encountered over much of southern Italy at this time. A wide acceptance of Greek customs and a continuing process of acculturation in the 6th and 5th centuries BC is also attested by the use of writing at indigenous sites, represented mainly by short inscriptions using Greek letters, some of which prove the persistence of the Sikel language.[68] The embarrassment of riches for the study of Archaic cults, contrasted with the lack of comparable evidence for indigenous Iron Age practices, encourages a preliminary generalization: that the elaboration of cult practice and its physical manifestations in the form of shrines and cult objects was encouraged by the development of more complex social and political formations, essentially early states, in which religious practices were developing into a form of state institution. For the indigenous societies of the Early Iron Age, the sense of the sacred was doubtless no less important and diffuse in everyday life, although the main context of ritual was that of the cemeteries, in keeping with a long-standing tradition.

However, evidence is now coming to light of cult buildings within indigenous settlements, such as Sabucina and Polizzello, where the 'hut-shrines' probably represent a fusion of indigenous and Greek cults, dating from at least the 7th century BC.[69] The large size and circular form of these buildings, which are reminiscent of local MBA-LBA huts, was perhaps specific to cult practices at this time. Those at Sabucina contained votive deposits consisting mainly of 6th-century BC materials: black-figure pottery, local geometric ware, a clay goat figurine, Greek goddess terracottas, a model of a Greek-style shrine and abundant pig bones. A series of more elaborate cult buildings within an enclosure surrounding what appears to have been a large sanctuary area has been found on the summit of Polizzello (fig. 139:B). In the northeastern zone, this consisted of two adjacent circular structures entered through a projecting portico, with a bench around the inside wall, a paved floor, a circular stone installation near the centre (of A), presumably surmounted by a conical thatched roof. The original function and date of construction are uncertain, but there is no doubt that by about the mid-7th century BC both rooms were provided with numerous votive pits containing ashy deposits, burnt animal bones and a range of unusual artefacts: local incised and painted pottery, bone and amber beads, horn, shells, astragali, bronze ornaments, spindle-whorls, loomweights, iron implements and two bronze figurines, including one of an offering-bearer. In the southwestern zone was a semicircular building enclosing a quadrangular structure with a circular clay platform covered by ash deposits and animal bones, and another round shrine (D) with a wealth of finds, including some of later date (silver fibula and Late Corinthian ware).

The finds from such places reflect the encroachment of Greek materials and possibly Greek practices. Votive offerings in pits and the sacrifice of small animals are consistent with chthonic rites of Greek tradition, although it is possible that there were similar indigenous practices, which would have facilitated the incorporation of Greek materials or a form of religious symbiosis. However, the extent to which these cults represent the continuation or modification of local customs will remain uncertain until good evidence of pre-Greek cults, preferably of the 9th century BC, can be found.[70]

Burials are an obvious point of reference in discussions of indigenous religion, although there may be much in burial practice that is practical or habitual. The persistence of inhumation in rock-cut tombs points to continuity in funerary ideology, while the main differences over time occurred in the grave goods, the number of deceased per tomb and the type of chambers. Explanations for these are usually sought in terms of age and rank, kinship links or changing social structures (chapter 5) rather than religious beliefs, although it is often said that inhumation in a chamber tomb, accompanied by a selection of artefacts, reflects the idea of a survival of the spirit within the tomb chamber. On the other hand, it could be argued that the chamber tomb was only a temporary or liminal residence and that the final destination was another less tangible one, reached once the corpse had decomposed sufficiently to lose its material reality. The act of cremation suggests a more direct form of consecration to the spirit world, which dispenses with the slower process of decomposition, although this rite probably represented only a different route to the same destination. In fact, both cremations and inhumations were provided with grave goods and there are cases of cremations inside chamber tombs.

Noteworthy too is the lack of a separate iconography of funerary materials, despite the selection of certain kinds of grave goods, such as juglets, bowls, small luxuries or items of prestige. However, funerary or ritual

Fig. 145. Incised vessels from: (1) Entella; (2) Polizzello; (3) Naro

surrogates may be represented in LBA and EIA tombs by miniature vessels and bronzes, sometimes also encountered in caves in peninsular Italy. The concept of votive offerings was probably important and widespread. Rare examples of broken weapons in MBA-LBA tombs, such as snapped blades, might indicate ritual destruction to prevent their use by spirits, while miniature metal axe-pendants (fig. 106:14) suggest the persistence of a very old tradition of amuletic devices, represented by stone axe-pendants in EBA graves.[71]

In a recent survey, R. Peroni noted that several decorative styles are recognizable in later Italian prehistory, rather than a specific or universal artistic style encompassing different media.[72] The same applies to Sicily, where regional decorative traditions are visible on pottery or bronze artefacts, some of which may be traced back to the Early or Middle Bronze Age, although there are many similarities with groups in southern peninsular Italy, which further emphasize the close cultural links between Sicily and the peninsula during the Late Bronze and Iron Ages. Stylistic motifs can also shed light on ideologies and cults, although it is often difficult to distinguish cult symbols from ornamental motifs, particularly in the absence of a strong realistic or figurative tradition in later Italian prehistory.

It may be that there was no perceived need to portray divinities in Iron Age religion or that, if such images did exist, they were rare or made of perishable materials, such as wood. Horned cup-handles with facial features (fig. 99:7) are one of the few examples of a figurative motif modelled in the round. They are widespread in the central and southern Italian Late Bronze Age and are still found in late Iron Age contexts in Sicily, while horned animal heads are suggested by the cordon decorations on certain indigenous amphorae of the 7th-6th centuries BC in western Sicily (fig. 145; below). The persistence of cattle as symbols in a society concerned with stock-rearing is easily rationalised, although these objects reveal little in themselves.

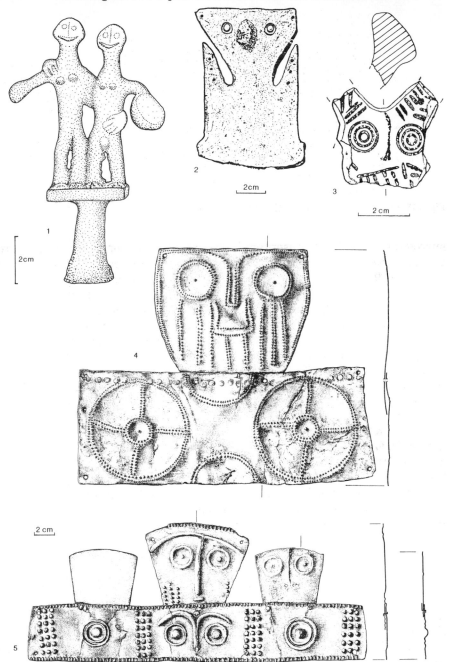

Fig. 146. (1) Bronze figurine from Vizzini; (2) Segesta, cup handle, 7th century BC; (3) Monte Castellazzo incised handle, 7th-6th century BC; (4-5) Syracuse region, bronze sheet appliqués, 7th century BC

265

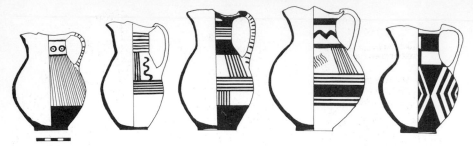

Fig. 147. Painted *oinochoai* from Sabucina, 7th-6th century BC

During the 8th and 7th centuries BC there was an increase in figurative work. Nine of the 107 sheet-bronze appliqués, possibly belts or girdles, from the Mendolito hoard had repoussé decoration of schematic human figures and one face (figs. 133:2,3; 143). From a stylistic point of view, the figures with raised arms can be derived from an Italic tradition, well represented on Villanovan pottery urns for example and often thought to represent a divinity. Stylized faces or masks recur on similar bronze plaques from Terravecchia di Cuti, Sabucina and the Syracuse region, dated to the late 7th or early 6th century BC, perhaps worn by indigenous warriors for apotropaic or protective reasons (figs. 144; 146:4,5).[73] The breasts on one example from Terravecchia suggest a female personification; otherwise the sex is unclear. Human faces or anthropomorphic allusions occasionally appear on amphorae, jugs and cup handles from western sites (figs. 145; 146:2-3), which may cleverly combine curved and geometric motifs in such a way as to suggest faces and horned animals: perhaps an intentionally ambiguous personification of a divinity with both human and animal traits.

In western Sicily, local incised and painted decoration flourished in the 7th and 6th centuries BC, often juxtaposing Greek or geometric motifs in an original and unconventional way. This is characteristic of a substantial territory extending from Sant'Angelo Muxaro to Polizzello, Marianopoli and Butera, which can be distinguished on grounds of style from the Licodia complex in eastern Sicily.[74] In particular, the geometric *oinochoai* of Sabucina illustrate a lively use of eye-motifs, ladder, panel and metopal decoration, in which Corinthian and Rhodian models are apparent, while the influence of Geloan workshops is perhaps uppermost (fig. 147). The strength and persistence of local craft traditions is more obviously apparent in the long-lived production, from the 8th to the 5th century BC, of fine wheelmade wares decorated with a wide variety of incised motifs ('Elymian' wares). That Greek influence is sometimes detectable, for example in the use of certain metopal arrangements, in no way detracts from the striking originality of this production.

Also noteworthy are the two painted figures with flamboyant hats on an *oinochoe* from Polizzello: possibly warriors holding shields, separated

Fig. 148. Painted *oinochoe* from Polizzello, late 7th-early 6th century BC

by an elaborate spiraliform design, perhaps influenced by motifs on Corinthian pottery, although usually thought to represent an indigenous product (fig. 148). An amphora from Naro shows an incised figure mounted on a horse and similarly capped, accompanied by birds and a bull. If parallels are sought, then the broad-brimmed hats point to an indigenous iconography, widespread amongst native Italic peoples at about this time, as exemplified by the Etruscan 'cowboy' of Murlo, the Capestrano warrior (middle Adriatic) and the Certosa situla (Po valley). There are also many indications that birds were of symbolic importance in Italic cults, prior to their well-attested role in Etruscan divination.

An indigenous aesthetic and ideology may also be reflected in a number of bronze figurines.[75] Most of these lack an archaeological provenance and are therefore difficult to date, although some are from inland sites, which were originally indigenous strongholds. Their manufacture probably only began in the later 8th century BC, stimulated by an acquaintance with Greek bronze figurines, and in some cases they reflect Greek styles, although this is often ambiguous. For example, individuals with outstretched arms holding a bowl or some other item (often missing), categorized as offering-bearers, are known in both Italy and Greece, especially from shrines and votive deposits such as that on the Polizzello acropolis (above). Small animal figurines, mostly bovine, are also widespread, whereas a trident model from Polizzello, perhaps a schematic idol or divine triad, has no obvious parallels. Another type shows a couple arm-in-arm: the one from Vizzini has a smaller male figure (the deceased?) holding a bowl, perhaps for a libation or offering, beside a slightly larger female figure, possibly a divinity (fig. 146:1). Couples in similar poses occur in funerary contexts in Iron Age Italy, especially in Calabria, while some of the elaborate Sardinian *bronzetti* show a male warrior supported by a larger female, perhaps a goddess. Only two of the five Sicilian examples, from Catania and Centuripe, have known contexts, of surprisingly late date (4th-3rd century BC), which could suggest a long-lived tradition.[76]

Aside from archaeological evidence, there have been attempts to extrapolate information from historical sources, although the main problem is that by the time Greek writers came to describe local cults, the latter had already altered and been adapted to resemble Greek practices.[77] Judging by archaeological evidence, the most popular cult in central Sicily in the 6th and 5th centuries BC was that of Demeter and Persephone, whose myth symbolizes growth, decay and regeneration. Ostensibly Greek, the cult nevertheless appealed to the indigenous substratum of the island's population in the 6th century BC, perhaps because it resembled some local counterpart, or simply because it was well-suited to the agricultural environment of central Sicily. Assimilation, however, is claimed in the case of Adranon, probably an indigenous god of fire with warrior-like attributes, or a personification of Etna, where his cult was centred. He was naturally associated by the Greeks with their own Hephaestus.

The literary evidence suggests that one of the most important and durable cults in Sicily was that of the *Palikoi*, twin brothers born of Thalia, a local nymph, and Zeus. They were associated with the bubbling gaseous springs near the ancient town of Palike near Mineo in east-central Sicily, which were renowned for their miraculous and oracular powers and venerated as a place of exceptional importance, as transpires from the account by Diodorus (XI.89). Like other cults for which an indigenous origin seems likely, such as those connected with rivers or springs, it was associated with unusual natural phenomena. The shrine was still regarded as a place of sanctuary during the slave revolts of the 2nd century BC, although it had long since been Hellenized, and doubts remain as to the form of the cult in earlier times. Traces of prehistoric occupation (mainly Palaeolithic, Neolithic and Early Bronze Age) have been found nearby, although no evidence of Iron Age activity survives, nor much of the classical period. It is noteworthy, nevertheless, that the shrine assumed great symbolic importance as a focus of Sikel nationalism during the turbulent years of the mid-5th century BC, when Ducetius chose a nearby location for a new settlement named Palike. Strategically located in the heart of 'native' territory, the shrine must have been a natural rallying point for the uprising, to which it could lend the appropriate support of an indigenous cult.

Tables

1. Simplified chronological scheme for Sicilian prehistory

PERIOD	YEARS BC	SICILY	
		PHASE	KEY SITES
UPPER PALAEOLITHIC	35,000	Aurignacian	Fontana Nuova (?)
	25,000	Gravettian	
	18,000	Early Epigravettian	Canicattini/Niscemi (?)
		Evolved Epigravettian	San Corrado (?)
		Final Epigravettian (1)	Acqua Fitusa/ Giovanna/ San Teodoro (D-C)
		Final Epigravettian (2)	San Teodoro (B-A)/ Genovesi 3
MESOLITHIC	9000	Sauveterrian/ Castelnovian	Uzzo/Genovesi 2/ Perriere Sottano
		SICILY	AEOLIAN ISLANDS
		KEY SITES/ASSEMBLAGES/STYLES	
EARLY NEOLITHIC	6000	Impressed ware/ Stentinello (?)	Castellaro Vecchio
MIDDLE NEOLITHIC	5000	Stentinello/Trichrome/ Serra d'Alto	Trichrome/Serra d'Alto
LATE NEOLITHIC	4000	Diana	Diana/Spatarella
EARLY COPPER AGE	3500	San Cono/Piano Notaro/ Piano Vento	Piano Conte
LATE COPPER AGE	3000	Serraferlicchio/Conca D'Oro/Malpasso/Beaker	Piano Quartara
EARLY BRONZE AGE (1)	2500	Naro/La Muculufa/ Castelluccio/Beaker	Capo Graziano 1
EARLY BRONZE AGE (2)	2000	Castelluccio/Rodi-Tindari-Vallelunga	Capo Graziano 2
MIDDLE BRONZE AGE	1500	Thapsos/Cannatello	Milazzese
LATE BRONZE AGE	1200	Pantalica North/ Caltagirone	Ausonian 1-2
EARLY IRON AGE (1)	900	Mulino della Badia/ Cassibile/Morgantina	Ausonian 2
IRON AGE 2	734	Finocchito/Sant'Angelo Muxaro/Butera	

2. Age classes from Palaeolithic-Archaic period burials

	0-10 (yrs)	11-20	21-30	31-40	41-50	50+	Uncertain age (adult)
S. Teodoro (Palaeolithic)		1	3	1	2		
Uzzo (Mesolithic)	3	1	6		2		
Piano Vento (ECA)	7	16	19	5	1		
Roccazzello (LCA)	2	4	6	4	1	1	
Castiglione (EBA)	16	5	21	15	7	3	
M. Casasia (Archaic)	12	2	17	10	21	15	4
Castiglione (Archaic)	11	2	7	7	6	2	14

3. Average statures from Palaeolithic-Archaic period burials

Site	Sex	Pearson	Manouvrier	Trotter & Gleser (B)	Trotter & Gleser (W)
S. Teodoro (Palaeolithic)	M				
	F	162.3	164.2	161.2	
Uzzo cave (Mesolithic)	M			161.6	
	F			152.9	
Piano Vento (ECA)	M				171.9
	F				146.2
Stretto (LCA)	M		161		
	F		151		
Castiglione (EBA)	M	163.7	163.9		
	F	155.9	157.03		
M. Casasia (Archaic)	M	164.3	166.6	167.6	
	F	153.9	156.7	157.8	
Castiglione (Archaic)	M	162.3	160.8	164	
	F	151.1	150.8	155	

Tables

4. Radiocarbon dates

Site	Context	Lab No	^{14}C Age BP	1σ cal.BC
Acqua Fitusa	Epigravettian	F-26	13,760±330	14,959-14,550-14,109
Gr. Giovanna	Epigravettian	R-484	12,840±100	13,436-13,230-13,003
Gr. Perciata	Epigravettian	F-27	11,960±330	12,102-11,690-11,308
Gr. Genovesi	Epigravettian	F-19	11,710±295	11,764-11,410-11,094
Gr. Genovesi	Epigravettian	R-566	11,180±120	11,034-10,890-10,737
Gr. Genovesi	Epigravettian	F-18	10,175±300	9541-9020-8576
Gr. Genovesi	Epigravettian	F-20	10,110±300	9923-9170-8903
Gr. Uzzo	Tr.G,9	P-2736	10,070±90	9964-9410-9133
Gr. Genovesi	Epigravettian	Pi-119	9694±110	8940-8630-8422
Gr. Uzzo	Tr.C,3	P-2558	9300±100	8426-8290-8139
Gr. Uzzo	Tr.A,16	P-2557	9180±100	8340-8110-8079
Gr. Uzzo	Tr.A,7	P-2556	9030±100	8090-8040-7975
Perriere Sottano	Level 53	UtC1424	8700±150	7937-7700-7540
Gr. Molara	Grave	OxA-534	8600±100	7697-7570-7506
Perriere Sottano	Level 60	UtC1355	8460±70	7538-7500-7437
Gr. Uzzo	Tr.F,16-18	P-2735	8330±80	7483-7420-7267
Gr. Uzzo	Tr.F,13-14	P-2734	7910±70	6998-6700-6605
Gr. Uzzo	Tr.F,7-9	P-2733	6750±70	5711-5635-5558
Gr. Uzzo	Tr.W,15	UD-165	6720±80	5648-5626-5534
Stretto	US46	Rom291	6630±120	5640-5535-5427
Stretto	US76	Rom292	6260±110	5330-5234-5074
Gr. Cavallo	A/17	Rom432	6200±80	5238-5215-5059
Piano Vento	A10-IV	A-4474	6130±90 BP	5226-5131-4941
Gr. Cavallo	A/16	Rom431	5990±80	4997-4928-4788
Stretto	US15	Rom290	5690±100	4714-4527-4408
Monte Grande	P-8-III	A-5723	5485±60	4365-4349-4264
Lipari acropolis	AO,y	R-366a	5200±60	4211-3998-3977
Piano Vento	II-A9, Tomb 9	A-4473	5040±120	3990-3878-3701
Lipari acropolis	AP	R-180	5000±200	4000-3785-3544
Gr. Cavallo	A/9	Rom430	4925±80	3786-3761-3643
Lipari Diana	XXI	R-182	4885±55	3775-3694-3638
Piano Vento	II-III, B10	A-4472	4840±200	3926-3642-3370
Gr. Cavallo	A/2-3	Rom429	4755±75	3640-3580-3380
La Muculufa		A-3957	4080±180	2885-2590-2364
Gr. Zubbia	S89/2		4010±55	2590-2538-2469
La Muculufa	Hut 3 p-hole	A-6547	3990±60	2574-2471-2508
La Muculufa	EBA	A-3953	3810±120	2457-2260-2038
Piano Vento	Tomb 15		3805±90	2399-2268-2046
La Muculufa	EBA	A-5283	3790±60	2292-2200-2129
La Muculufa	EBA	A-3967	3730±90	2276-2070-1976

4. Radiocarbon dates (contd)

Site	Context	Lab No	¹⁴C Age BP	1σ cal.BC
Monte Grande	F/G-17/IV	A-5724	3700±65	2267-2072-1977
La Muculufa	EBA	A-5284	3680±100	2199-1987-1916
La Muculufa	EBA	A-3959	3640±80	2132-2010-1887
La Muculufa	EBA	A-3964	3610±120	2134-1940-1772
La Muculufa	EBA	A-3956	3600±100	2120-1940-1776
I Faraglioni		A-6523	3560±55	1949-1887-1778
Monte Grande	N/O-13-II/III	A-5722	3495±45	1886-1818-1744
Madre Chiesa	MBA hut 1(J30-II)	A-4730	3310±110	1740-1605-1462
Mursia	EBA hut 1,A,Ib-7	R-671	3280±50	1683-1569-1498
I Faraglioni	MBA	A-6522	3135±65	1443-1407-1316
I Faraglioni	MBA	A-7885	3120±70	1436-1401-1270
I Faraglioni	MBA	A-7887	3085±60	1413-1340-1263
I Faraglioni	MBA	A-7884	3055±55	1397-1310-1219
Mursia	MBA-LBA hut 3	R-670a	3010±50	1375-1279-1133
Capo Graziano	MBA hut VIII	R-369	3000±50	1373-1281-1114
Mursia	MBA-LBA Ivbc-4	R-668a	2990±50	1371-1225-1112
I Faraglioni	MBA	A-7886	2985±55	1296-1246-1119
I Faraglioni	MBA	A-7888	2950±55	1258-1149-1038
Mursia	MBA-LBA hut 1,A	R-669a	2930±50	1288-1153-1051
Madre Chiesa	MBA hut 1 (J30-IV)	A-4731	2900±90	1290-1107-939
Lipari acropolis	MBA hut VII	R-365a	2900±50	1213-1107-1011
I Faraglioni	MBA	A-7889	2885±55	1126-1029-942
Mursia	hut 4,IV-f3	R-673	2830±50	1079-982-924
Lipari acropolis	LBA hut aII	R-367	2820±50	1076-975-906
Morgantina	LBA-EIA hut 31a	St-2471	2810±100	1112-930-831
Morgantina	LBA-EIA hut 31a	St-2473	2785±100	1029 (910) 820
Lipari acropolis	LBA hut aII	R-367a	2770±50	1004-964-835
Morgantina	LBA-EIA hut 31c	St-2474	2750±100	999-870-807
Morgantina	LBA-EIA tr29-6B	St-1339	2695±70	904-820-802
Morgantina	LBA-EIA hut 31a	St-2493	2685±100	913-820-793
Lipari acropolis	LBA zone BR	R-181	2555±50	799-789-597

Notes

Introduction

1. For a survey of antiquarian traditions, see Leighton 1989b (with references).
2. Orsi's life and work was the subject of many contributions in the commemorative volumes: *Archivio Storico per la Calabria e la Lucania*, 5 (1935); *Annali dei Musei Civici di Rovereto*, 6 (1991); also Leighton 1986; La Rosa 1985 (with further references); and with reference to Greek and Roman times, see, for example, Wilson 1990, 1-17.
3. Bernabò Brea 1957. See also n. 2. Tusa 1992 is a longer survey, with references to many smaller sites.
4. Contrasts further discussed by Evans (1977).
5. Agnesi et al. 1997 for a recent geographical survey (with references); and with reference to Greek and Roman times, see, for example, Wilson 1990, 1-17.
6. Braudel 1972.
7. In this regard, Momigliano (1979, 179) noted a casual remark, which is an emblematically negative modern definition: 'To be a Sicilian is not to be a Neapolitan'.
8. Perhaps one of several factors which has led to a bias within archaeology departments in British and American universities towards Aegean and eastern Mediterranean prehistory, despite the enormous opportunities for research in the western Mediterranean.
9. Space restrictions prevent the presentation of a full bibliography. I have given priority to recent or major works in which more references can be found. Likewise the selection of illustrations and discussion of material and sites is limited to those which seem especially significant and are well-published (the main limiting factor). Fuller distribution maps with more sites and longer bibliographies can be found in *Prima Sicilia* (pp. 635-43), *Early Societies* (pp. 189-211) and Tusa (1992). Most new discoveries in Sicilian archaeology are noted in *Archaeological Reports* (e.g. Wilson 1996). In general, I have concentrated on Sicily itself, rather than the surrounding small islands, while reference to the Maltese archipelago is limited to matters which more directly concern relations with Sicily.

1. Early Faunal and Human Populations

1. Bonfiglio & Piperno 1996; Leighton 1996a, 10 (with references).
2. For a summary with references, see Bonfiglio & Piperno 1996; Agnesi et al. 1997.
3. Alimen 1975; Shackleton et al. 1984.
4. Surveys by various authors in the volume edited by Guidi & Piperno (1993).
5. Chilardi 1993-94, 1349; 1997.
6. Bertolani Marchetti et al. 1984.
7. Costantini 1989 (with further references).
8. From a vast specialist literature on endemism in Mediterranean islands, for example: Masseti & Vianello 1991; and the Sicilian exhibition catalogues: *Ippopotami di Sicilia. Paleontologia e Archeologia nel Territorio di Acquedolci* (Messina, 1989); *La Sicilia prima della storia* (Palermo, 1990).
9. Kotsakis 1979; Burgio 1997, with references.
10. Bonfiglio & Piperno 1996, with references.
11. See n. 8.
12. See n. 5.
13. The Cypriot evidence is discussed by several authors in *Journal of Mediterranean*

Archaeology 9 (1996). Fedele (1988, 63) has noted that traces of burning were found on some pigmy elephant bones in the Spinagallo cave in Sicily, which are not easily explained.

14. Gliozzi & Kotsakis 1986.

15. Bonfiglio & Piperno 1996, 25 (with reference to work by Orsi and Vaufrey).

16. For recent discussions: Palma di Cesnola 1994; Bonfiglio & Piperno 1996; Piperno 1997a.

17. E.g. Bianchini 1971; Palma di Cesnola 1994 (with further references); Tusa 1993-94, 1493-1503; Venezia & Lentini 1994.

18. For surface collections in the Catania region attributed to the Lower Palaeolithic, see for example Broglio et al. 1992; Piperno 1997a (with references). Emblematic of the difficulties is the fact that a preliminary Aurignacian dating for Perriere Sottano was subsequently revised (to Mesolithic) following excavations: Aranguren & Revedin 1992.

19. For a summary, see Guidi & Piperno 1993.

20. There is a considerable literature, primarily of antiquarian interest now, on cave explorations before 1940 (Pianese 1968; Tusa 1992). See also Laplace 1966, and more recent surveys by various authors (Bietti et al., Segre & Vigliardi) in the volume: *Actes du Colloque internationale 'La position taxonomique et chronologique des industries à pointes à dos autour de la Mediterranée européenne, Siena 1983. RSP*, 38 (1985). Also Martini 1997. For specific sites and studies: Vigliardi 1968 (San Teodoro); 1982 (Grotta dei Genovesi); Bianchini & Gambassini 1973; Martini & Sarti 1973 (Acqua Fitusa); Bernabò Brea 1973 (Coste di San Corrado, Grotta Giovanna, Pedagaggi, Rosolini); Cardini 1971 (Grotta Giovanna); Zampetti 1990 (Riparo Castello di Termini Imerese); Di Geronimo et al. 1981-92 (Pedagaggi); Venezia & Lentini 1994; Tusa 1993-94, 1493-1503 (Belice sites).

21. Gioia 1984-87; Chilardi et al. 1996. Others, such as Palma di Cesnola, have expressed reservations about an Aurignacian date (Bonfiglio & Piperno 1996, 26, with references).

22. Martini 1997, 119 (with references).

23. Zampetti 1989.

24. Bernabò Brea 1965a, 17.

25. For a recent survey: Aranguren & Revedin 1996. The main sites are: Grotta dell'Uzzo (e.g. Tusa 1992; Compagnoni 1991; Tagliacozzo 1993; 1994, with further references; Piperno 1997b); Perriere Sottano (Aranguren & Revedin 1992); Grotta dei Genovesi (Vigliardi 1982); Grotta Corruggi (Bernabò Brea 1949); Riparo della Sperlinga di San Basilio (Cavalier 1971; Biddittu 1971).

26. Costantini 1989; Costantini & Stancanelli 1994 (for a broad summary).

27. Tagliacozzo & Piperno 1993.

28. Avellino et al. 1990.

29. Muzzolini 1989.

30. The correlation between radiocarbon dates and the stratigraphy is not precise enough to separate the last Mesolithic layer from the first Neolithic. Layers 14-11 in trench F have been discussed as a single unit and yet doubts remain about the date of layers 11-12, often referred to, perhaps rather misleadingly, as 'transitional', and about the significance of a single einkorn seed from a late Mesolithic or transitional (mixed?) level. See n. 26 and chapter 2.

31. See, for example, Borgognini Tarli in Guidi & Piperno (1993), for a summary.

32. Graziosi 1947.

33. Fabbri 1993.

34. Borgognini Tarli et al. 1993; Canci et al. 1995. Two Uzzo burials (U1 and U4) have aminoacid racemization dates of around 8600 and 9500 BP respectively.

35. For a general survey, see Graziosi 1973. Major sites include: Grotta dei Genovesi (Graziosi 1950; 1953; 1954; 1962; Vigliardi 1982); Grotta Giovanna (Cardini 1971; Segre Naldini 1992); Grotta Addaura (Bovio Marconi 1953; Blanc 1955; Graziosi 1956); Grotta Niscemi (Bovio Marconi 1954-55). The figurative scenes have frequently been the subject of comment in works on Palaeolithic art. For recent discussions with further references: Zampetti & Mussi 1991; Pluciennik 1994.

36. Vigliardi 1982, 123; Mezzena 1976 (for an early date). Bovio Marconi (1953, 15) on Spanish and North African affinities.

37. Mezzena 1976.

38. With the exception of Pluciennik (1994, 53), who suggests non-synchronous fragments of narrative or myth.

39. For the figurative motifs of Grotta Racchio and linear marks in the Isolidda, S. Rosalia and Armetta caves, see Mannino 1962; 1978. Caves with figurative or linear motifs are also illustrated in Graziosi 1973: Grotta della Za Minica, Grotta dei Puntali, Grotta delle Giumente, Grotta Giglio, Grotta di San Teodoro, Riparo Armetta. See also Bernabò Brea 1973 (Coste di San Corrado); Cavalier 1971, 17 (Sperlinga di San Basilio); and Tusa 1992, 117-20 (Grotta dell'Uzzo) and further references.

40. Graziosi 1954; Cardini 1972; Whitehouse 1992, 168-70.

2. The First Farming Societies

1. Ammerman & Cavalli-Sforza 1984.

2. See the useful survey by Cipolloni Sampò in Guidi & Piperno (1993).

3. A controversial ^{14}C date from Coppa Nevigata was once used to argue for an earlier start to the Neolithic in Apulia, around 7000 cal.BC. Most authors now accept that the earliest reliable dates for the Tavoliere sites are later: Whitehouse 1994a, 88.

4. Ammerman 1987, 345.

5. Lewthwaite 1986; 1990.

6. After F. Braudel, this expression was used by Vallet (1984-85, 141) to describe indigenous people in Sicily at the time of Greek colonisation (chapter 6).

7. Most recent discussions (for example in *Premières communautés paysannes en Méditerranée occidentale*, CNRS, Paris, 1987, edited by J. Guilaine, J. Courtin, J. Roudil and J-L. Vernet) have considered evidence in Apulia, for which Tinè emphasizes the importance of colonisation, in the tradition of Childe and Bernabò Brea, whereas Whitehouse, Tusa (1996a; 1997a) and others stress local adaptations. For Petraro, see Voza 1968.

8. Cassoli et al. 1987; Tagliacozzo 1993.

9. Costantini & Stancanelli 1994. Despite claims for an early date in the 7th millennium cal.BC (Costantini 1989) these charred seeds seem to be dated 5648-5534 cal.BC (by UD-165). The significance of a single grain of *Triticum monococcum* in layer F-13 remains uncertain.

10. Villari 1995; Tagliacozzo 1993, 168. More surprising are a few equid bones from Megara and Matrensa, resembling both domestic horse and ass (*Equus caballus* and *asinus*). Doubts persist about this association, perhaps a result of infiltration from later deposits.

11. In general, see Bernabò Brea 1987; Tusa 1992; 1996a; 1997a.

12. Ammerman & Bonardi 1985-86, 221; Tinè 1971.

13. E.g. Aldridge, in Ammerman 1985 (Acconia); Morter 1994 (Capo Alfiere).

14. Orsi 1890; 1912b.

15. Tusa 1992; Procelli 1983, 46.

16. Tinè 1971; Tinè et al. 1994 (with references).

17. Tusa 1992; Ammerman 1987, 345.

18. E.g. Whitehouse 1994a, 87.

19. Troja et al. 1996.

20. Bernabò Brea (1987, 354) regards this ware as a sign of settlers on Lipari from eastern Adriatic regions. However, most of the Aeolian Neolithic pottery can be matched in Sicily and southern Italy and it may be only a matter of time before closer parallels for this pottery are also found in Italy or Sicily.

21. Cavalier 1979.

22. Malone 1985.

23. Brown 1991, with references.

24. Ammerman 1987.

25. Di Stefano 1983; Cultraro 1988.

26. Orsi 1890; 1912b; Tinè 1961.

27. Orsi 1921; Vallet & Villard 1960.

28. Orsi 1900b, 208.

29. Bernabò Brea 1966.

30. Whitehouse 1994b (with subsequent discussion sessions and further references).

31. Tusa 1993-94, 1503-8; Cottignoli 1995; Grimaldi & Scaletta 1997.

32. Bernabò Brea 1966.
33. Spigo 1984-85, 866.
34. Castellana 1985-86; 1987a; 1995 (with further references).
35. La Rosa 1987.
36. Johns 1992, 409; see also Tusa 1997a; Bernabò Brea 1987.
37. Aeolian Neolithic settlements are described in several articles and monographs. Principally: Bernabò Brea & Cavalier 1957; 1960; 1980; Cavalier 1979; Bernabò Brea 1987 with more references; Cavalier & Bernabò Brea 1993-94. For a comparison with Malta, Evans 1977.
38. Evans 1971, 208-12; Trump 1966; 1995-96.
39. Radi 1972.
40. Mannino 1991 (Ustica).
41. See Williams-Thorpe 1995; Nicoletti 1997, with bibliography.
42. Cavalier 1979, 109-26; 1990. Another flow at Acqua Calda on the north of Lipari was probably also used.
43. Ammerman 1985; Ammerman & Polglase 1993, with references; Genovese 1978, for Stentinello sites near Barcellona.
44. Francaviglia 1988. For Holocene chipped stone industries, see Nicoletti 1990; 1996.
45. Leighton & Dixon 1992; Leighton 1992, with references.
46. Williams, in Bernabò Brea & Cavalier 1980, 847-68.
47. Bernabò Brea & Cavalier 1980, 490.
48. Mentesana 1967; Spigo 1984-85, 866 (Gisira); Guerri 1991 (Fontanazza); Guzzardi 1993-94 (Vulpiglia); Scibona 1984-85 (Boccetta). For a review of Neolithic burials, see Robb 1994. A supposed Stentinello crevice burial near Petraro (Sluga Messina 1988) is no longer regarded as such by this author or others.
49. Cafici 1930-31.
50. Mannino 1991, 74.
51. Scibona 1984-85.
52. For Diana burials on Lipari and in Sicily: Bernabò Brea & Cavalier 1957, 115; 1960, 83-5; Tinè 1965, 141 (Biancavilla).
53. Maniscalco 1997a, 193.
54. Lewthwaite 1985.
55. Trump 1966.
56. De Miro 1961, 39-45.
57. Tinè et al. 1994.
58. Bernabò Brea & Cavalier 1968, 18; Maniscalco 1997a; Bernabò Brea 1965b.
59. Bacci Spigo 1993-94.
60. For example, Graziosi (1973, 162) for figures in the *domus de janas* at Branca (Sassari), a Sardinian Copper Age chamber tomb. This connection, therefore, can be added to the growing evidence for Sardinian links with western Sicily discussed in chapter 3.
61. Tusa 1993-94, 1521-26.

3. New Territories and Tombs

1. Alternative terms, 'Eneolithic' or 'Chalcolithic', emphasize the persistence of stone tools, but 'Copper Age' is more readily understood by non-specialists. For general surveys, see Cazzella 1972; Bernabò Brea 1976-77; 1988; Albanese Procelli 1988-89; Tusa 1992; McConnell 1997.
2. A subject discussed in several works by authors such as C. Renfrew, G. Barker, P. Halstead, A. Gilman and J. Lewthwaite (1981).
3. From a large bibliography on caves (cf. chapter 1) see: Tinè 1960-61 (Conzo, Chiusazza, Palombara, Novalucello, Fogliuta, Biancavilla, Lauro, Zubbia, Ticchiara, Monte Kronio); 1965 (Chiusazza); Tinè et al. 1994 (Monte Kronio); A. La Rosa 1986-87 (Caprara); Procelli 1989 (Monaci); Orsi 1907a (Calafarina); Orsi 1907b; 1930-31; Procelli 1992; Albanese Procelli 1988-89, 205; Privitera 1991-92 (Barriera, Biancavilla, Contrada Marca and other Etnean caves); De Miro 1961 (Infame Diavolo); Bovio Marconi 1944 (Villafrati, Fico, Chiusilla and others); 1979 (Vecchiuzzo); Maniscalco 1994 (Fontanazza).
4. Trump 1995-96. The Ggantija dates in the later 4th millennium cal. BC fit better with

Italian chronology than the early Zebbug dates in the late 5th millennium cal.BC, which also overlap with a date (4221-3797 cal.BC) for Red Skorba.

5. Trump 1995-96, 176; Skeates 1994, with references.

6. For central-western cemeteries: McConnell 1988 (Ribera); Tinè 1960-61 (Tranchina); Bovio Marconi 1944 (Conca d'Oro area); Cassano et al. 1975 (Uditore and others); Tusa & Di Salvo 1988-89 (Roccazzo); Spatafora & Mannino 1994 (San Cusumano, Roccazzello); Castellana 1995 (Piano Vento); Bianchini 1968 (Cozzo Busoné); Fiorentini 1980-81 (Marianopoli); La Rosa 1994, 289-90 (Serra del Palco).

7. The distinction is not always clear; the skeletal study suggests that the multiple burials were all in chamber tombs (Mallegni, in Castellana 1995, 185). The necropolis probably dates to an early phase of the Copper Age, as suggested by Piano Notaro ware, although the ^{14}C dates from tombs 9 and 15 (3990-3701 & 2399-2046 cal.BC) are widely divergent.

8. Fornaciari & Bartoli, and Di Rosa, in Castellana 1995. The mortality rate is lower at Roccazzo and Roccazzello: Tusa & Di Salvo 1988-89, 118; Di Salvo 1994, 224-5.

9. Bacci Spigo 1993-94; 1997.

10. Cafici 1879; 1899 (San Cono); Orsi 1908 (Piano Notaro); Bianchini 1968 (Cozzo Busoné); Procelli 1992,72 (Catania).

11. Spatafora & Mannino 1994; Di Salvo 1994, 225.

12. La Rosa 1994, 291-5; Mallegni et al. 1994. For partial burning from EBA sites see n. 65.

13. Albanese Procelli 1988-89 (Malpasso); Guzzardi 1980 (Calaforno).

14. Mannino 1971 (Salaparuta tomb); 1994 (Torre Donzelle); Tusa 1994 (Marcita and others), with further references.

15. For a review, see Whitehouse 1981.

16. Atzeni 1981, xlvii-iii.

17. Bernabò Brea & Cavalier 1980, 495-508, 681-7 (Piano Conte, Piano Quartara, with references); Cavalier 1979, 126-32 (Serra Fareddu); Cavalier & Bernabò Brea 1993-94, 989 (Serro Brigadiere); Genovese 1977 (Barcellona region).

18. Cavalier 1990; Villari 1995, 263.

19. Tusa 1992; Albanese Procelli 1988-89, 204; Cultraro 1988 (Etna region); Johns 1992 (Monreale survey).

20. Castellana 1988 (Rinollo, Zubbia); Castellana 1997 (Monte Grande, Pizzo Italiano).

21. Villari 1981, 113 (Fiumedinisi); Tusa 1992, 257, 288 (Poggio dell'Aquila).

22. Gullì 1993.

23. See n. 3.

24. Becker 1995.

25. Orsi 1928, 64-71; Arias 1938.

26. Giardino 1996. There are only vague hints of exploitation in classical sources, but better evidence for the Middle Ages to the 18th century, when small-scale workings produced copper and other metals. There are also references to iron production in the Messina region in the early Middle Ages. Villari 1981 (for Fiumedinisi).

27. Bovio Marconi 1944, 93, fig. 34; and other possible LCA-EBA examples: Orsi 1907b, 59; Tinè 1965, cat. nos.167-9, 397. For parallels in Corsica, Sardinia and elsewhere, see Camps 1988, 128-31.

28. Albanese Procelli 1988-89, 199-202; 1989.

29. In general, see Leighton 1989a; 1992 (ground stone); Nicoletti 1990; 1996; Nicoletti & Battagila 1991 (chipped stone).

30. The spectra of genuine Sicilian amber have an absorption band from 1230-1260cm-1 (mainly 1245cm-1): Beck & Hartnett 1993; Orsi 1892, 18-20 (Castelluccio).

31. From a dolmen at San Sebastien, west of Nice: Williams-Thorpe et al. 1984.

32. Cavalier 1960; Ceccanti 1980. I am not persuaded of a real connection between the Sicilian and Near Eastern vases illustrated by Cassano et al. (1975, figs. 30-33), with the possible exception of a spouted jar from Serraferlicchio (fig. 31,3), nor that postulated between Palestinian chamber tombs and those of Uditore (figs. 34-35). It is paradoxical that while vague East Mediterranean parallels are stressed, closer affinities between Piano Conte or Piano Notaro wares and Balkan Copper Age styles (for example, in the Albanian Malik II horizon), or Sardinian late Ozieri and Monte Claro wares, or Fontbouisse wares of eastern Languedoc, are ignored.

33. Renfrew & Whitehouse 1974, for a review and sceptical position on the whole question.

34. Barfield 1987; 1994; Tusa 1996b; Veneroso 1994.

35. Germanà & Di Salvo 1994 (using skulls from Chiusilla, Villafrati and Stretto). For a broad survey, see also Borgognini Tarli in Guidi & Piperno 1993; Becker 1995-96.

36. Germanà 1994.

37. 'BA' signifying *Bronzo Antico* or Bronze Age. For general surveys, see Bernabò Brea 1991-92; Tusa 1992; Malone et al. 1994; Procelli 1996; 1997.

38. Tinè 1965 (Chiusazza); Frasca et al. 1975 (Ramacca); La Rosa & D'Agata 1988 (Serra del Palco); Castellana 1994 (Ciavolaro).

39. Castellana 1997.

40. Bernabò Brea & Cavalier 1991, 210-15. Italian associations also imply an early start, perhaps from 2500 BC: Cazzella 1994. Vagnetti (1991) notes that the matt-painted sherds in the Aeolian islands do not necessarily antedate the LH I period.

41. Evans 1971, 224; Trump 1995-96; Tozzi 1978 (for Pantelleria).

42. Thompson (Morgantina, pers.comm.); Cultraro 1997 (Etna); Tusa 1991 (Pietraperzia); Johns 1992 (Monreale).

43. For example near Camarina: Pelagatti 1973a; 1973b; Procelli 1981, 85; Di Stefano 1993-94, 1385.

44. Holloway et al. 1990; McConnell 1995 (Muculufa); Orlandini 1962a (Manfria). Major EBA sites known from Orsi's work include: Orsi 1892; 1893a (Castelluccio); 1891a; 1893c (Melilli, Bernardina and Cava della Secchiera); 1895c (Priolo, Cava di Mostrinciano); 1898a (Monte Tabuto & Monte Racello); 1902a (Valsavoia); 1902b (Cava Cana Barbara); 1910 (Branco Grande and Settefarine); 1923 (Monte Sallia); 1926 (Sante Croci); 1928 (Monte Casale and San Basile).

45. Cruz-Uribe, in Holloway et al. 1990. The same species were also identified in old excavations by Orsi; doubts persist concerning the presence of horse (cf. chapter 2, n. 10).

46. Procelli, in press (Morgantina); Cultraro 1997, with references (villaggio Garofalo, Fogliuta); Pelagatti & Del Campo 1971; Pelagatti 1973a (Castiglione); Maniscalco 1997 (Le Salinelle); Di Stefano 1976-77; Nicoletti 1990 (Biddini); Guzzone 1993-94 (Garrasia).

47. Orsi 1901; Orlandini 1962a.

48. Bernabò Brea 1966 (Ognina); Voza 1972, 192-3 (Thapsos); 1968 (Timpa Dieri, Petraro). The wall at Naxos is more likely BA2 or Middle Bronze Age (Procelli 1983; 1991-92); and n. 43.

49. Frasca et al. 1975 (Torricella); Spigo 1984-85, 869-75 (Valsavoia); Di Stefano 1984, 114-24 (Baravitalla); Maniscalco 1997b (Santa Febronia).

50. Cazzella 1991.

51. For example, Camps 1988, 193-204 for the Corsican *castelli*.

52. Castellana 1990 (with references).

53. Orlandini 1968; Panvini 1990.

54. Holloway et al. 1990; McConnell 1995 (with contributions by several authors and further references).

55. Holloway et al. 1990; perhaps conditioned by analogies with sanctuaries in classical archaeology. The fact that the painted pottery here was of slightly different style might not necessarily mean that it was brought by visitors.

56. A vessel resembling a MBA form (Orsi 1892, 71) could suggest a MBA date for tomb 31. Contrary to a well-known reconstruction (Bernabò Brea 1957, 109; Tusa 1992, 378), the carved side of at least one slab (t.34) faced inwards (Orsi 1892, 75) (fig. 59:A).

57. Bernabò Brea 1966, 57.

58. Examples at Castelluccio, Melilli and Valsavoja. Maniscalco 1996 (S. Febronia, with further references); Bernabò Brea 1957, pl. 35-37 (Cava Lazzaro, Castelluccio); Di Stefano 1979 (Cava Lazzaro, or Cava Grande); De Miro 1961, 53 (Contrada Ragusetta); Procelli 1981 (Paolina).

59. For Sardinian tombs with spirals and pillars with chevrons, see Graziosi 1973, pl.184 (Enas de Cannuia); Atzeni 1981, xxxvii (Corongiu, etc.). These provide better analogies than the more elaborate spirals of Maltese temples, although it is possible that the Castelluccio culture was partially contemporary with the latter (Procelli 1981, 105; 1991)

60. Orsi 1898a, 202 (Monte Racello).

61. Orsi 1930-31 (Biancavilla); Cultraro 1997, with references (Grotta Maccarone).

62. Tusa 1997b; Recami et al. 1983, 71, 75 (Petraro); Di Stefano 1979 (Cava dei Servi); Palermo 1981, 105-7 (Polizzello). Local sources suggest that dolmens once existed in the Cava Lazzaro (Di Stefano 1984, 128). However, some doubts must remain about dating, particularly in the case of the Cava dei Servi and Polizzello monuments. At Monte Bubbonia, a small number of rather variable but not entirely dissimilar tombs built of masonry were recorded, which date to the later Iron Age: Pancucci & Naro 1992.

63. Despite many variations in form, the term 'dolmen' is used most frequently, albeit loosely: Whitehouse 1981 for a survey; Cipolloni Sampò 1994, 270.

64. The presence of dolmens in Sicily also raises the possibility of a Sicilian derivation for the Maltese examples (probably of the Tarxien Cemetery period), rather than an Apulian one (Evans 1971, 224). See Camps (1961) for the Tunisian monuments.

65. Castellana 1990; a more prosaic interpretation may be that this material represents debris removed from inside the tombs. For Muculufa: McConnell & Morico 1990; Riedel, in McConnell 1995. The use of old flint mines for burial, fire-setting and the partial burning of bodies in natural crevices, caves and tombs, is also attested widely in Italy and Sardinia (Cipolloni Sampò 1994, 274).

66. Evans 1971; Cipolloni Sampò 1994, 275.

67. Bernabò Brea (1985a, 47-52) links them with EH and MH jar burials in western Greece; Procelli 1983, 53, has noted Anatolian parallels, though not very close. For later developments, Albanese Procelli 1992, 44-6.

68. Maniscalco 1996. Elsewhere, however, some ambiguity persists: some of the finds from these forecourts may be due to the action of tomb-robbers who rifled the chambers for metal goods. At Castiglione and Baravitalla, the excavators believed that the material found in front of the tombs was left there by looters.

69. Facchini 1975; McConnell et al. 1990.

70. Bernabò Brea & Cavalier 1960 (Diana); 1968 (Calcara, Punta Peppa Maria, Serro dei Cianfi); 1980 (Lipari acropolis); 1991 (Piano del Porto, Capo Graziano Montagnola); Cavalier 1979 (Castellaro Vecchio, Contrada Monte and Fucile); 1981 (San Vincenzo); Cavalier & Bernabò Brea 1993-94 (Megna, Serro Brigadiere). Broader surveys: Bietti Sestieri 1982; Bernabò Brea 1985a.

71. Bernabò Brea & Cavalier 1991, 57-68; Cavalier 1985-86, 229-35.

72. Bernabò Brea & Cavalier 1980, 723-31. Analogies between Capo Graziano and Maltese vessels have often been noted (Evans 1971, 149-66).

73. Ciabatti 1978; Bernabò Brea 1985b (with further references).

74. I Faraglioni is discussed in chapter 4, although the earliest ^{14}C date (1949-1778 cal.BC) may suggest an initial BA2 phase of occupation (Holloway & Lukesh 1995). For Pantelleria: Orsi 1899b; Tozzi 1968; 1978.

75. See Evans 1959; 1971. Bernabò Brea (1966) suggested that Ognina might be a Maltese 'colony' in Sicily. However, the similarities in material culture between Malta, Ognina and probably other southern Sicilian sites, as yet little known, could reflect looser cultural or commercial links.

76. Bernabò Brea 1985a, for the idea of an initial colonisation, followed by local divergence. However, the parallels seem closer in the later phase, represented, for example, by the crossed lines underneath bowls, the widespread use of bowls with internal handles and terracotta 'anchors'. For a different perspective, more like that envisaged here, see Bietti Sestieri 1982.

77. For RTV 'sites', although many are only partially published: Cavalier 1970 (Tindari); Bovio Marconi 1964-65 (Boccadifalco); Bernabò Brea 1953-54 (Vallelunga); Bernabò Brea 1967 (Rodì); Procelli 1983 (Naxos); Bernabò Brea 1985a, 126-36 (Milazzo, Messina, & further references).

78. Bernabò Brea 1991-92; Procelli 1996, 90; Cultraro 1997 (for Etna sites).

79. Maniscalco (in McConnell 1995) uses the terms Naro and San Ippolito to describe early styles of Castelluccio ware. See also Pacci 1982; Pacci & Tusa 1991.

80. This has led to the designation of a 'Muculufa master' (Lukesh, in McConnell 1995, 187-98, with references); an inappropriate label in my opinion, although the attempt to define stylistic groupings is commendable.

81. Sluga Messina 1983.

82. Castellana 1997.
83. Giannitrapani 1997 for a survey of EBA links with Malta.
84. Orlandini 1968.
85. Albanese Procelli 1989; 1993-94; 1996a; Maniscalco 1997b (daggers); Cultraro 1997 (Grotta Maccarone cup).
86. The main study remains that by Evans 1956, to whom I am grateful for the illustrations; for different views, see Biancofiore & Ponzetti 1957; Holloway 1981, 17-19; Procelli 1991.
87. For example, Marazzi 1997a (with further references) on the genesis of long-distance contacts.

4. Interaction and Trade

1. In Italian terminology, the Late Bronze Age is subdivided into the Recent Bronze Age (13th century BC) and the Final Bronze Age (12th-10th century BC).
2. For recent discussions of Mycenaean contacts with Sicily and South Italy, see Peroni 1983; Voza 1985; Bietti Sestieri 1988; Tusa 1992; Leighton 1996b, with more references. For the wider context, see for example, recent contributions in Gale (ed) 1991.
3. See also Vagnetti 1991; Leighton 1993b.
4. Orsi 1895a; Voza 1972; 1973a; 1973b; 1984-85, 666-8, with further references. For other MBA sites in the region: Orsi 1891b; 1899c (Plemmyrion); 1893c (Molinello); 1893b (Cozzo Pantano); 1903a (Milocca, Matrensa); 1909 (Floridia); Bernabò Brea 1966 (Ognina); Procelli 1983 (Naxos).
5. Voza 1984-85, 671-2; Guzzardi 1993-94.
6. For central-western sites: Fiorentini 1993-94, 718-20 (Cannatello); Castellana 1987b; 1993-94, 741-7 (Madre Chiesa); 1992 (Scirinda); Falsone et al. 1980-81 (Monte Castellazzo); Mannino & Spatafora 1995 (Mokarta); Tusa 1993-94, 1536-7 (Erbe Bianche); Johns 1992 (Monreale survey). For MBA-LBA finds from Monte Saraceno and Monte Adranone, see Wilson 1996, 92, 99 with bibliography.
7. Orlandini 1965; De Miro 1980-81; Mollo Mezzena 1993, with further references.
8. Orsi 1899a; 1912a; Bernabò Brea 1990.
9. Messina 1993.
10. For Aeolian Milazzese sites, see Bernabò Brea & Cavalier 1968 (Panarea, Salina); 1980 (Lipari); 1991 (Capo Graziano).
11. Mannino 1982; Holloway & Lukesh 1995; 1997 (with further references). Unusual evidence of figurative stone sculpture has been published in the form of a carved tufa slab, resembling a cult figure, similar in style to some decorated handles of large pedestal vases from Thapsos. It has recently been suggested that, unbeknown to the excavators, this item was mischievously manufactured in recent times, and therefore I have omitted it pending further enquiries. The first excavator of the site (G. Mannino, pers. comm.) also maintains that the rock formations interpreted as tombs (Holloway & Lukesh 1995, 77) are natural features.
12. As suggested by Camps (1988, 99-109) for similar Corsican forms.
13. The estimate of just 25 adults (Holloway & Lukesh 1995, 10, 35) seems too low, given the size of the settlement and fortifications. Nor is there much to suggest restricted use by an élite.
14. Tozzi 1968; 1978.
15. Occasional cremations are documented in later Mycenaean chamber tombs by jar-urns, some of which resemble forms at Caltagirone and Pantalica (below).
16. Taylour 1958, 68; Voza 1985, 550; La Rosa 1979; 1986; Tomasello 1979; in Marazzi et al. (eds) 1986. The suggestion that the thermal building on Lipari known as the tholos of San Calogero was once a Bronze Age tomb seems less convincing: Bernabò Brea et al. 1990.
17. Orsi 1904. For other LBA cemeteries of the Pantalica I-II periods: Orsi 1912a; Panvini 1993-94, 810-23; 1997 (Dessueri); Orsi 1903b (Rivetazzo).
18. Orsi 1932; Fatta 1983; Anagnostou 1979; Palermo 1996, with further references.
19. Bernabò Brea & Cavalier 1959; Scibona 1971; Albanese Procelli 1992, for a survey.
20. Maniscalco 1997a.

21. A pioneering study by Taylour (1958) should be updated. Further articles in Vagnetti (ed) 1982; Marazzi et al. (eds) 1986.

22. Vagnetti 1991 (with further references).

23. D'Agata 1997, 456.

24. Jones & Vagnetti 1991.

25. Karageorghis 1995, 94; Leighton 1996b, 115. Suggestions as yet untested by scientific analysis.

26. Bernabò Brea & Cavalier 1968; Marazzi 1997b.

27. For 'Maltese' wares at Thapsos, see Voza 1973a; 1973b, 146-57 (with references); Evans 1971, 226.

28. Albanese Procelli 1993; 1996a; Giardino 1997.

29. D'Agata in Marazzi et al. (eds) 1986; Vagnetti & Lo Schiavo 1989.

30. In general, see Bietti Sestieri 1973. Oxhide ingot fragments are known from Thapsos, Cannatello and Lipari: Albanese Procelli 1993, 227; Giardino 1996, 129; for iron rods from Thapsos: Orsi 1895a, 127; Albanese Procelli 1993-94, 60.

31. Vagnetti 1968b; Lo Schiavo et al. 1985.

32. Cornaggia Castiglioni & Calegari 1978. See also n. 41 and chapter 3.

33. Giardino 1996.

34. Information from Giardino (1995) with bibliography.

35. Marazzi 1997a, 371 (with further references).

36. These sites undoubtedly share certain general features with the trading centres (e.g. gateway sites, community colonies and ports of trade) discussed by Smith (1987), although the historical contexts, character and complexity of the latter vary greatly, and therefore such analogies are of limited value.

37. This view was first outlined in Leighton 1996b.

38. Villari 1991a.

39. For example: Bérard 1957; Dunbabin 1948b; Manni 1962; Pareti 1956; Pugliese Carratelli 1956. Marazzi 1976, with more references, and various authors in *Kokalos* 34-35 (1988-89).

40. For example, Giangiulio 1983, from whom I have borrowed the phrase 'miti di precedenza'.

41. A tholos tomb, which contained MH to LH II-III material: Beck & Hartnett 1993.

42. Vagnetti 1993 (with references).

5. Realignments in Protohistory

1. For a definition of *protostoria* and surveys of peninsular Italy, see for example, R. Peroni 1994; Bietti Sestieri 1996. Some of the ideas in this chapter were first outlined in Leighton 1996b. For general surveys, see also Bietti Sestieri 1979; 1997; Bernabò Brea 1990. Sherratt & Sherratt 1993, for a sketch of the wider international context.

2. Leighton 1993b.

3. Frasca (1983) dates them earlier (10th-9th century BC), following the chronology of Bernabò Brea (1957). Likewise Pelagatti (1982a, 138). In my opinion, this is all probably 8th-century BC material.

4. Orsi 1912a (Pantalica); Steures 1980; Frasca 1981 (Finocchito, with references). Much of the Pantalica South pottery is more likely to be early colonial than EIA. Moreover, the serpentine fibula can no longer be regarded as a pre-colonial indicator: it occurs in native burials of the colonial period at Pantalica (eg. tomb SC6), Butera (Adamesteanu 1958), Finocchito (with 'navicella' fibulae and local geometric or Protocorinthian pottery in several tombs: E17; E27; S51; NW40; N44; Gium 11; Steures 1980) and in the 7th-century BC hoard of Mendolito (e.g. figs. 126, 133). Many of the tombs in the Calabrian Iron Age necropolis of Torre Galli (Pacciarelli 1986, with references) may well be later than the 9th-century BC date generally assigned to them.

5. Bernabò Brea 1971; Tinè 1965.

6. Voza 1973b, 146-57; 1980-81, 677-9; though initially dated to the Middle Bronze Age, the buildings uncovered by Bernabò Brea (1970) probably belong to the last phase (Bernabò Brea 1990, 56).

7. Orsi 1918, 429-32; Voza 1973c (Via Orsi tomb); Pelagatti 1982a, 138; 1982b; Frasca 1983 (with further references); Wilson 1996, 67.

8. Leighton 1993a (Morgantina, Cittadella); Rizza 1962; Wilson 1987-88, 114 (Lentini, Metapiccola). Similar structures of the mid-8th to 7th century BC have recently come to light at Monte San Mauro (chapter 6): Wilson 1996, 75.

9. Castellana 1992 (Scirinda); Panvini 1993-94; 1997 (Dessueri); Mollo Mezzena 1993 (Sabucina); Castellana 1993-94, 737 (predio Bellanti, Piano Vento).

10. Hut 1 is assigned to phase IIB2 (ca. 1350-900 BC) and hut 2 to phase IIB3 (ca. 900-750 BC): Trump 1961.

11. For later cremation urns in chamber tombs at Pozzo di Gotto and Finocchito, see chapter 6.

12. Orsi 1905 (Mulino della Badia); Bernabò Brea et al. 1969; Albanese Procelli 1992; 1994, with further references (Madonna del Piano).

13. Although these artefacts are not limited to cremations and cannot therefore have served only to gather ashes. See, for example, Peroni 1994, 74.

14. The bias in favour of females contrasts with that in favour of males noted in indigenous chamber-tomb cemeteries of the later Iron Age (chapter 6).

15. For Torre Galli, see Pacciarelli 1986.

16. Camerata-Scovazzo 1978 (and chapter 6).

17. Albanese Procelli 1982; 1988-89 (Carcarella and other Calascibetta cemeteries); Orsi 1899a (Cassibile); and chapter 4 for Pantalica, Dessueri, Sant'Angelo Muxaro and Mokarta.

18. Frasca 1982; Palermo 1982.

19. Leighton 1993a; Albanese Procelli 1996a.

20. Orsi 1918, 519-22.

21. Giardino 1996, 133.

22. Giardino 1995.

23. Bernabò Brea 1957, 157; Giardino 1995; 1996; 1997.

24. Evans 1953; 1971; also n. 10 and chapter 4.

25. Contu, in Bernabò Brea & Cavalier 1980, 829-36; Ferrarese Ceruti 1987 (Lipari); Leighton 1993a, 71 with bibliography (Pontecagnano); Bietti Sestieri 1992, 518-19 (Osteria dell'Osa).

26. Bernabò Brea & Cavalier 1960, 149-50.

27. Albanese Procelli 1993-94.

28. Bernabò Brea 1957, 183-200; Albanese Procelli 1993 (Syracuse Museum hoards); Giardino 1995 (for a general discussion).

29. Bernabò Brea & Cavalier 1980; Giardino 1995, 17 (for an Ausonian I or 12th-century BC date); Moscetta 1988 (for a slightly later dating: Ausonian II, or later 11th century BC).

30. Di Stefano & Giardino 1994.

31. Giardino 1987; 1996 (with further references).

32. Albanese Procelli 1993.

33. General surveys with further references by Ambrosini and Braccesi in Gabba & Vallet (eds) 1980; and by Peroni and La Rosa in Pugliese Carratelli (ed) 1989.

34. Bernabò Brea 1957, 136-9; Leighton 1993a, 152-4 with further references.

35. Bietti Sestieri 1979.

36. Bietti Sestieri 1996, 261.

37. A large bibliography exists on this question: see the recent conference proceedings in *Archivio Storico Siciliano* 14-15 (1988-89), and Spatafora 1996 with further references.

6. Indigenous Peoples in the 8th and 7th Centuries BC

1. From a vast bibliography on Greek colonisation in Sicily, see for example Morel 1984; various authors in Gabba & Vallet (eds) 1980; Pugliese Carratelli (ed) 1989; 1996. Surveys with more emphasis on indigenous peoples: Domínguez 1989; Albanese Procelli 1996b; Lyons 1996b; and several authors in *Forme di contatto e processi di trasformazione nelle società antiche. Atti del convegno di Cortona* (Scuola Normale Superiore and École Française de Rome, 1983); *Kokalos* 34-35 (1988-89).

2. Linguistic evidence has been examined in many works by Agostiniani and Lejeune; e.g. *Gli elimi e l'area elima, Archivio Storico Siciliano* 14-15 (1988-89), with references.

3. Recent reviews with further references: Gras 1986; Morris 1996.

4. A question discussed in several papers by G. Vallet and the excavators of Megara.

5. See, for example, Asheri in Gabba & Vallet (eds) 1980 (with further references).

6. Voza 1978.

7. Kearsley 1989, 101-4 (type 6); some doubts remain regarding the absolute dates.

8. Gras 1986, 7-8; Albanese Procelli 1996b, 168.

9. Orsi 1895b, 189; Coldstream 1996, 183-4.

10. Albanese Procelli 1993; 1996b; 1997a (with further references).

11. Pelagatti 1982b, for a general survey.

12. Gras 1986, 11.

13. Again the literature is vast. See, for example, Tusa and Bondì in Gabba & Vallet (eds) 1980; Moscati 1984-85; 1988.

14. Quotes, except for bracketed insertions, are from the Loeb edition: *Thucydides, History of the Peloponnesian War, with an English Translation by Charles Forster Smith* (London, Heinemann 1921).

15. Leighton 1981; Albanese Procelli 1993-94.

16. Falsone 1993.

17. Sherratt & Sherratt 1993, for a broad survey.

18. Ridgway 1992 (Ischia); Bartoloni et al. 1997, date the first Phoenician contacts with Sardinia in the 9th-8th centuries BC (but do not distinguish 9th- from 8th-century BC finds).

19. Falsone 1988, with further references.

20. See below n. 65.

21. Guzzardi 1991 (with references) mentions EIA 'ivory' combs in Sicily, none of which have been positively identified; they could be bone.

22. Various contributions and bibliography in the volumes: *Di terra in terra. Nuove scoperte archeologiche nella provincia di Palermo*, Museo Archeologico Regionale (Palermo 1993); *Archeologia e territorio* (Palumbo editore, Palermo 1997); Fiorentini 1995 (Monte Adranone).

23. For a general review, see Bérard 1957; Asheri (n. 5).

24. The word 'betrayed' is preferred by Graham (1988, 311). Orsi (1895a) suggested that a chamber tomb at Thapsos containing Protocorinthian cups (whence 'Thapsos' cups) was the grave of Lamis. Who expelled the Megarians from Thapsos is not clear: either locals or rival Syracusans?

25. Bernabò Brea 1968, following a suggestion by F. Villard (for Pantalica); Albanese Procelli 1996b, 168 (and others, for Villasmundo). Another proposal has been that of Melilli, about which little is known for this period.

26. Although see below and n. 43.

27. Shepherd 1995.

28. Dunbabin 1948a; van Compernolle 1984-85, 43. See also Coldstream 1993.

29. Orsi 1895b; see Shepherd 1995 for full references to the excavation reports.

30. Hencken 1958; and for contrasting theories about their origin, see Albanese Procelli 1982, 600-2; and Domínguez 1989, 179-89 on various local traits.

31. Orsi 1895b, 140. This shows the long duration of some typical LBA-EIA forms into the late 8th or 7th centuries BC.

32. Cébeillac-Gervasoni 1976-77, 597; Albanese Procelli 1997a (with references).

33. Orsi 1906b; Panvini 1996 (for a broad survey with references).

34. Bernabò Brea & Cavalier 1959.

35. Vallet et al. 1976 (Megara); Pelagatti 1982a (Syracuse); Vallet 1984-85; Di Vita 1996, with further references.

36. Voza 1980-81, 675-80.

37. Albanese 1978.

38. Vallet 1984-85, 141.

39. Frasca 1981, 93-4.

40. For example, tomb SC.6 (Orsi 1912a, 309): with vases betraying Greek colonial influence associated with a bronze serpentine fibula. This is a good example of the fact that many of these tombs do not belong to the Early Iron Age but to the later Iron Age; Leighton 1993b. The beaker (fig. 126:3) is unlikely to be pre-colonial, as suggested in *Prima Sicilia* vol. 2, 205.

41. Orsi 1900a (S. Aloe); Rizza 1962 (Metapiccola, San Mauro); Frasca 1982 (Carrube); Palermo 1982 (Pozzanghera); Rizza 1978, with further references.

42. Rizza 1978, 28, assigns these sherds to the Cassibile period, but they could be 8th century BC.

43. Lagona 1971 (Ossini); Voza 1978 (Villasmundo); Procelli 1989 (with references).

44. Procelli & Albanese 1992, 143-6.

45. Fortifications at native sites are not often closely dated, although this one is most easily regarded as an indigenous construction (Bonacasa Carra 1974, with references). On the cemeteries, see Steures 1980; Frasca 1981; 1996.

46. Orsi records about 150 skeletons for 81 tombs in a fairly well-preserved state (Steures 1980, 12), which would give a proportionate figure of about 1,100 individuals for a total of 600 tombs (covering about a century): but the real figure is likely to be higher.

47. Albanese Procelli 1996b, 172; 1997b.

48. Orsi 1898b; Wilson 1996, 75.

49. Pelagatti 1973b; Pelagatti & Del Campo 1971; Facchini & Brasili Gualandi 1977-79 (Castiglione; see also chapter 3); Facchini & Brasili Gualandi 1980; Fouilland et al. 1994-95, with references (Monte Casasia).

50. Pelagatti 1981; Procelli 1983; Albanese Procelli 1997a, 519.

51. Orsi 1919; Pelagatti 1978a, 140; 1982b.

52. Villari 1981 (Fiumedinisi); Orsi 1915 (Pozzo di Gotto). A later date than that proposed by Bernabò Brea (1967) better accounts for the proliferation of *oinochoai* and geometric decoration at Rodì.

53. Orlandini 1962b with references; Orsi 1912a; Panvini 1993-94; 1997 (Dessueri).

54. Adamesteanu 1958.

55. Rizza 1984-85.

56. Spigo 1980-81 with references; Costantini 1979 (botanical remains); Wilson 1996, 75.

57. Judson 1963.

58. Pancucci & Naro 1992, with references.

59. Albanese Procelli 1982; 1988-89. I would suggest lower dates for the Pantalica South tombs in this area, extending into the late 8th and early 7th century BC.

60. Lyons 1996a; 1996b; Leighton 1993a; Antonaccio 1997.

61. Fiorentini 1980-81, 599; Wilson 1987-88, 134.

62. Calderone et al. 1996 (Monte Saraceno); Mollo Mezzena 1993 (Sabucina).

63. Palermo 1981; De Miro 1988; 1988-89; Panvini 1992-93, 785-6.

64. Orsi 1932; Anagnostou 1979; Fatta 1983; Palermo 1996 with further references.

65. Only one of the four bowls has survived. The origin of the goldwork has been explained in various ways, and is even thought by some to represent indigenous manufacture (which seems unlikely): Rizza 1979. By contrast, Vagnetti 1972 suggested a Greek colonial product (perhaps from Gela). See also Falsone 1988. Greek interest in this region is also implied by a short-lived settlement (early 6th century BC) at Borgo Bonsignore on the western side of the Platani river mouth, which was succeeded around 550 BC by Heraclea Minoa: see Wilson 1981-82, 97 (with references).

66. See nn. 19 & 22; Wilson 1996, 92 with references. Panvini 1988-89 (Caltabellotta).

67. Castellana 1992; 1988-89.

68. Albanese Procelli 1996b.

69. De Miro 1980-81; 1983; 1988-89; including the idea (rather unlikely in my opinion) that these cults and the lively style of local painted ware in this area derive from the survival of Mycenaean traditions. See also n. 75.

70. Direct links between the Demeter shrines at San Biagio (Akragas), Bitalemi (Gela) and earlier indigenous cults now seem tenuous.

71. For example: Orsi 1899a, pl. VII:13,15-18; pl. XIII:12; see also chapter 4.

72. Peroni 1994, 296-314, for a general discussion.

73. Albanese Procelli 1993 (Mendolito); Vassallo in *Di Terra in Terra*, Palermo 1993 (Terravecchia di Cuti); Orlandini 1963, pl. XXXI:4 (Sabucina); Egg 1983; Wilson 1996, 110.

74. Tigano 1985-86 (Sabucina); Palermo 1981 (Polizzello, with further references).

75. La Rosa 1968. Kilian 1966, on South Italian symbolism. Neither a Mycenaean

derivation for the Polizzello trident, nor the suggested connection between an incised figure from Capodarso and a Mycenaean stirrup-jar seem convincing; Rizza 1979 with bibliography. See also n. 69.

76. Frasca 1992 (with full bibliography).

77. From a vast bibliography, see, for example, Manni 1980; Domínguez 1989, 563-9; Wilson 1990, 277-82.

Bibliography

Abbreviations

AJA = *American Journal of Archaeology*
ASSO = *Archeologia nella Sicilia Sud-Orientale.* Centre Jean Bérard Napoli, Siracusa 1973
AttiRS = *Atti, Riunione Scientifica dell'Istituto Italiano di Preistoria e Protostoria (Firenze)*
BAR-IS = *British Archaeological Reports, International Series.* Oxford
Basso Belice = Tusa, S. (ed) *La preistoria del Basso Belice e della Sicilia meridionale nel quadro della preistoria siciliana e mediterranea.* Palermo 1994
BPI = *Bullettino di Paletnologia Italiana*
Cronache = *Cronache di Archeologia*
Early Societies = Leighton, R. (ed) *Early Societies in Sicily. New Developments in Archaeological Research. Accordia Specialist Studies on Italy 5.* London 1996
MAL = *Monumenti Antichi dei Lincei*
MEFRA = *Mélanges de l'École Française de Rome, Antiquité*
NSc = *Atti dell'Accademia dei Lincei, Notizie degli Scavi*
PPS = *Proceedings of the Prehistoric Society*
Prima Sicilia = Tusa, S. (ed) *Prima Sicilia. Alle origini della società siciliana. (Albergo dei Poveri, Palermo 18 ottobre-22 dicembre 1997).* Ediprint, Palermo 1997
QuadMessina = *Quaderni dell'Istituto di Archeologia della Facoltà di Lettere e Filosofia dell'Università di Messina*
RA = *Rassegna di Archeologia*
RSP = *Rivista di Scienze Preistoriche*
SA = *Sicilia Archeologica*

Adamesteanu, D. 1958. Butera. Le necropoli di Piano della Fiera, Consi e Fontana Calda. *MAL*, 44: 205-672.

Agnesi, V., Macaluso, T. & Masini, F. 1997. L'ambiente e il clima della Sicilia nell'ultimo milione di anni. *Prima Sicilia*: 31-53.

Albanese, R.M. 1978. Avola (Siracusa). *Studi Etruschi*, 46: 569-71.

Albanese Procelli, R.M. 1982. Calascibetta (Enna). La necropoli di Cozzo S. Giuseppe in Contrada Realmese. *NSc*, 36: 425-632.

——— 1988-89. Calascibetta (Enna). Le necropoli di Malpasso, Carcarella e Valle Coniglio. *NSc*, 42-43: 161-398.

——— 1989. Una cuspide di lancia preistorica del museo archeologico di Siracusa. *QuadMessina*, 4: 1-8.

——— 1990. Appunti sui rapporti tra la metallurgia calabra e siciliana in età protostorica. In *A Sud di Velia. Ricognizioni e ricerche 1982-1988*: 117-32. Istituto per la storia e l'archeologia della Magna Grecia, Taranto.

——— 1992. La necropoli di Madonna del Piano presso Grammichele: osservazioni sul rituale funerario. *Kokalos*, 38: 33-68.

——— 1993. *Ripostigli di bronzi della Sicilia nel Museo Archeologico di Siracusa.* Accademia Nazionale di Scienze, Lettere e Arti, Palermo.

——— 1993-94. Intervento. *Kokalos*, 39-40: 58-65.

——— 1994. Considerazioni sulla necropoli di Madonna del Piano di Grammichele (Catania). In *La presenza estrusca nella Campania meridionale*: 153-69. Firenze.

——— 1996a. Produzione metallurgica e innovazioni tecnologiche nella Sicilia protostorica. *Early Societies*: 117-28.

——— 1996b. Greeks and indigenous people in eastern Sicily: forms of interaction and acculturation. *Early Societies*: 167-76.

Bibliography

—————— 1997a. Le etnie dell'età del ferro e le prime fondazioni coloniali. *Prima Sicilia*: 511-22.

—————— 1997b. Échanges dans la Sicile archaïque: amphores commerciales, intermédiares et redistribution en milieu indigène. *Revue Archéologique*: 3-25

Alimen, M.H. 1975. Les isthmes hispano-marocain et siculo-tunisien aux temps acheuléens. *L'Anthropologie*, 79: 399-436.

Ammerman, A.J. 1985. *The Acconia Survey: Neolithic Settlement and the Obsidian Trade*. University of London, Institute of Archaeology, Occasional Publication No.10, London.

—————— 1987. Recenti contributi sul neolitico della Calabria. *AttiRS XXVI*: 333-49.

Ammerman, A.J. & Bonardi, S. 1985-86. Ceramica stentinelliana di una struttura a Piana di Curinga (Catanzaro). *RSP*, 40: 201-24.

Ammerman, A.J. & Cavalli-Sforza, L.L. 1984. *The Neolithic Transition and the Genetics of Populations in Europe*. Princeton, Princeton University Press.

Ammerman, A.J. & Polglase, C. 1993. New evidence on the exchange of obsidian in Italy. In Scarre, C. & Healy, F. (eds) *Trade and Exchange in Prehistoric Europe*: 101-7. Oxbow Monographs 33, Oxford.

Anagnostou, H. 1979. S. Angelo Muxaro. Scavo nella necropoli meridionale del Colle di S. Angelo. *Cronache*, 18: 31-49.

Antonaccio, C. 1997. Urbanism at Archaic Morgantina. In Andersen, H.D., Horsnaes, H.W., Houby-Nielsen, S. & Rathje, A. (eds) *Urbanization in the Mediterranean in the 9th to 6th centuries BC*, *Acta Hyperborea*, 7: 167-93. Museum Tusculanum Press, Copenhagen.

Aranguren, B. & Revedin, A. 1992. Primi dati sugli scavi a Perriere Sottano (Ramacca, Catania). *RSP*, 42 (1989-90): 305-10.

—————— 1996. Problemi relativi all'insorgenza del mesolitico. *Early Societies*: 31-9.

Arias, P.E. 1938. La stazione preistorica a Serraferlicchio presso Agrigento. *MAL*, 36: 693-838.

Atzeni, E. 1981. Aspetti e sviluppi culturali del neolitico e della prima età dei metalli in Sardegna. *Ichnussa. La Sardegna dalle origini all'età classica*: xxi-li. Libri Scheiwiller, Milano.

Avellino, E., Bietti, A., Giacopini, L., Lo Pinto, A. & Vicari, M. 1990. Riparo Salvini: a new Dryas II site in southern Lazio. Thoughts on the Late Epi-Gravettian of middle and southern Tyrrhenian Italy. In Bonsall, C. (ed) *The Mesolithic in Europe*: 516-32. John Donald, Edinburgh.

Bacci Spigo, G.M. 1993-94. Un idoletto a violino di tipo egeo da Camaro presso Messina. *Kokalos*, 39-40: 171-80.

Bacci, G.M. 1997. Due idoletti di tipo egeo-cicladico da Camaro Sant'Anna presso Messina. *Prima Sicilia*: 295-7.

Barfield, L.H. 1987. The Italian dimension of the Beaker problem. In Waldren, W.H. & Kennard, R.C. (eds) *Bell Beakers of the Western Mediterranean*: 499-522. *BAR-IS* 331.

—————— 1994. Vasi campaniformi nel Mediterraneo centrale: problemi attuali. *Basso Belice*: 439-60.

Bartoloni, P., Bondì, S.F. and Moscati, S. 1997. La penetrazione fenicia e punica in Sardegna. Trent'anni dopo. *Atti della Accademia Nazionale dei Lincei, Memorie* 9 (1): 1-140.

Beck, C.W. & Hartnett, H.E. 1993. Sicilian amber. In Beck, C.W. & Bouzek, J. (eds) *Amber in Archaeology. Proceedings of the Second International Conference on Amber in Archaeology, Liblice 1990*: 36-47. Institute of Archaeology, Czech Academy of Sciences, Prague.

Becker, M.J. 1995. A revised interpretation of the function of La Grotta del Vecchiuzzo near Petralia Sottana and the Grotta dei Cocci at Capaci (Palermo, Sicily). *SA*, 28, 87-9: 7-17.

—————— 1995-96. Skeletal studies of Sicilian populations. A survey. *Accordia Research Papers*, 6: 83-117.

Bérard, J. 1957. *La colonisation grecque de l'Italie méridionale et de la Sicile dans l'antiquité. L'histoire et la légende*. Presses Universitaires de France, Paris.

Bernabò Brea, L. 1949. La Cueva Corruggi en el territorio de Pachino. *Ampurias*, 11: 1-23.

—————— 1953-54. La Sicilia prehistorica y sus relaciones con Oriente y con la Peninsula Iberica. *Ampurias*, 15-16: 137-235.

—————— 1957. *Sicily before the Greeks*. Thames & Hudson, London.

—————— 1965a. Segnalazioni di rinvenimenti paleolitici in Sicilia. *BPI*, 74: 7-22.

—————— 1965b. Palikè. Giacimento paleolitico e abitato neolitici e eneo. *BPI*, 74: 23-46.

—————— 1966. Abitato neolitico e indsediamento maltese del bronzo nell'isola di Ognina (Siracusa) e rapporti tra la Sicilia e Malta dal XVI al XIII sec. a.C. *Kokalos*, 12: 40-69.

—————— 1967. La necropoli di Longane. *BPI*, 76: 181-254.

—————— 1968. Il crepuscolo del re Hyblon. *La Parola del Passato*, 23: 161-86.

287

———— 1970. Thapsos. Primi indizi dell'abitato dell'età del bronzo. *Adriatica Praehistorica et Antiqua. Miscellanea Gregorio Novak Dicata*: 139-51. Zagreb.

———— 1971. Xuthia e Hybla e la formazione della facies culturale di Cassibile. *AttiRS XIII*: 13-28.

———— 1973. Giacimenti paleolitici del Siracusano. *ASSO*: 15-18.

———— 1976-77. Eolie, Sicilia e Malta nell'età del bronzo. *Kokalos*, 22-23: 33-110.

———— 1985a. *Gli Eoli e l'inizio dell'età del Bronzo nelle isole Eolie e nell'Italia meridionale.* Quaderni dell'Istituto Universitario Orientale, 2. Napoli.

———— 1985b. Relitto della prima età del bronzo di Pignataro di Fuori. *Bollettino d'Arte (supplement)*, 29: 48-52.

———— 1987. Il neolitico nelle isole Eolie. *AttiRS XXVI*: 351-60.

———— 1988. L'età del rame nell'Italia insulare: la Sicilia e le isole Eolie. *RA*, 7: 469-506.

———— 1990. *Pantalica. Ricerche intorno all'anaktoron.* Cahiers du Centre Jean Bérard XIV, Naples.

———— 1991-92. La Sicilia e le Isole Eolie. *RA*, 10: 105-21.

Bernabò Brea, L. & Cavalier, M. 1957. Stazioni preistoriche delle Isole Eolie. *BPI*, 46: 97-152.

———— 1959. *Mylai*. Istituto Geografico de Agostini, Novara.

———— 1960. *Meligunìs-Lipára I. La stazione preistorica della contrada Diana e la necropoli protostorica di Lipari.* Flaccovio, Palermo.

———— 1968. *Meligunìs-Lipára III. Stazioni preistoriche delle isole Panarea, Salina e Stromboli.* Flaccovio, Palermo.

———— 1980. *Meligunìs-Lipára IV. L'acropoli di Lipari nella preistoria.* Flaccovio, Palermo.

———— 1991. *Meligunìs-Lipára VI. Filicudi. Insediamenti dell'età del bronzo.* Accademia di Scienze, Lettere e Arti, Palermo.

Bernabò Brea, L., Cavalier, M. & Belli, P. 1990. La tholos termale di San Calogero nell'isola di Lipari. *Studi Micenei ed Egeo-Anatolici*, 28: 7-84.

Bernabò Brea, L., Militello, E. & La Piana, S. 1969. La necropoli detta del Molino della Badia: nuove tombe in contrada Madonna del Piano. *NSc*, 8, 23: 210-76.

Bertolani Marchetti, D. et al. 1984. Recherches géobotaniques sur les Monts Madonie (Sicile du Nord). *Webbia*, 38: 329-48.

Bianchini, G. 1968. Le due 'Veneri' di Busoné. *AttiRS XI-XII*: 129-43.

———— 1971. Risultati delle ricerche sul paleolitico inferiore in Sicilia e la scoperta di industrie del gruppo della 'pebble culture' nei terrazzi quaternari di Capo Rossello in territorio di Realmonte. *AttiRS XII*: 89-109. Firenze.

Bianchini, G. & Gambassini, P. 1973. La grotta dell'Acqua Fitusa (Agrigento). I. Gli scavi e l'industria litica. *RSP*, 28: 3-55.

Biancofiore, F. & Ponzetti, F.M. 1957. Tomba di tipo siculo con nuovo osso a globuli nel territorio di Altamura (Bari). *BPI*, 66: 153-88.

Biddittu, I. 1971. Considerazioni sull'industria litica e la fauna del Riparo della Sperlinga di S. Basilio. *BPI*, 80: 64-76.

Bietti Sestieri, A.M. 1973. The metal industry of continental Italy, 13th-11th century, and its Aegean connections. *PPS*, 39: 383-424.

————1979. I processi storici nella Sicilia orientale fra la tarda età del bronzo e gli inizi dell'età del ferro sulla base dei dati archeologici. *AttiRS XXI*: 599-629.

————1981. Economy and society in Italy between the Late Bronze Age and Early Iron Age. In Barker, G. & Hodges, R. (eds) *Archaeology and Italian Society: Prehistoric, Roman and Medieval Studies*: 133-55. *BAR-IS* 102.

———— 1982. Implicazioni del concetto di territorio in situazioni culturali complesse: le isole Eolie nell'età del Bronzo. *Dialoghi di Archeologia*, 4.2: 39-60.

———— 1988. The 'Mycenaean connection' and its impact on the central Mediterranean societies. *Dialoghi di Archeologia*, 6.1: 23-51.

———— 1992. *La necropoli laziale di Osteria dell'Osa.* Quasar, Roma.

———— 1996. *Protostoria. Teoria e pratica.* NIS, Roma.

———— 1997. Sviluppi culturali e socio-politici differenziati nella tarda età del bronzo della Sicilia. *Prima Sicilia*: 473-91.

Blanc, A. 1955. Il sacrificio umano dell'Addaura e la messa a morte rituale mediante strangolamento nell'etnologia e nella paletnologia. *Quaternaria*, 2: 213-25.

Bonacasa Carra, R.M. 1974. Le fortificazioni ad aggere della Sicilia. *Kokalos*, 20: 92-118.

Bonfiglio, L. & Piperno, M. 1996. Early faunal and human populations. *Early Societies*: 21-9.

Borgognini Tarli, S.M., Canci, A., Piperno, M. & Repetto, E. 1993. Dati archeologici e antropologici sulle sepolture mesolitiche della Grotta dell'Uzzo (Trapani). *BPI*, 84: 85-179.

Bibliography

Bovio Marconi, J. 1944. La Coltura tipo Conca d'Oro nella Sicilia Nord-Occidentale. *MAL*, 40: 1-170.

—— 1953. Incisioni rupestri all'Addaura (Palermo). *BPI*, 8,5: 5-22.

—— 1954-55. Nuovi graffiti preistorici nelle grotte del Monte Pellegrino (Palermo). *BPI*, 64: 57-72.

—— 1964-65. Il villaggio di Boccadifalco e la diffusione del medio bronzo nella Sicilia nord-occidentale. *Kokalos*, 10-11: 52-70.

—— 1979. *La Grotta del Vecchiuzzo presso Petralia Sottana. ΣΙΚΕΛΙΚΑ 1.* Bretschneider, Roma.

Braudel, F. 1972. *The Mediterranean and the Mediterranean World in the Age of Philip II*, Vol.1. Collins, London.

Broglio, A., Di Geronimo, I., Di Mauro, E. & Kozlowski, J.K. 1992. Nouvelles contributions à la connaissance du Paléolithique inférieur de la région de Catania dans le cadre du Paléolithique de la Sicile. In Peretto, C. (ed) *Il più antico popolamento della Valle Padana nel quadro delle conoscenze europee. Montepoggiolo*: 189-226. Jaca Book, Milano.

Brown, K. 1991. A passion for excavation. Labour requirements and possible functions for the ditches of the 'villaggi trincerati' of the Tavoliere, Apulia. *Accordia Research Papers*, 2: 7-30.

Burgio, E. 1997. Le attuali conoscenze sui mammiferi terrestri quaternari della Sicilia. *Prima Sicilia*: 55-72.

Cafici, I. 1879. Stazione dell'età della pietra a San Cono, in provincia di Catania. *BPI*, 5: 33-43.

—— 1899. Di un sepolcro scoperto a San Cono presso Licodia Eubea (Catania). *BPI*, 25: 53-66.

—— 1930-31. Sopra la recente scoperta di una fossa sepolcrale neolitica a Calaforno nell'agro di Monterosso Almo (prov. Di Ragusa). *BPI*, 50-51: 24-42.

Calderone, A. 1996. *Monte Saraceno di Ravanusa*. Messina.

Camerata Scovazzo, R. 1978. Ricerche nel territorio di Santa Margherita Belice: materiali e documenti inediti. *Kokalos*, 24: 128-55.

Camps, G. 1961. *Monuments et rites funéraires protohistoriques. Aux origines de la Berbérie.* Paris.

—— 1988. *Préhistoire d'une île. Les origines de la Corse.* Editions Errance, Paris.

Canci, A., Minozzi, S., Repetto, E. & Borgognini Tarli, S.M. 1995. Mesolithic skeletal remains from Grotta della Molara (Palermo, Sicily). *Rivista di Antropologia*, 73: 237-54.

Cardini, L. 1971. Rinvenimenti paleolitici nella Grotta Giovanna (Siracusa). *AttiRS XIII*: 29-35.

—— 1972. Dipinti schematici antropomorfi della Grotta Romanelli e su ciottoli dei livelli mesolitici della caverna delle Arene Candide e della Grotta della Madonna a Praia a Mare. *AttiRS XIV*: 225-35.

Cassano, S.M., Manfredini, A. & Quojani, F. 1975. Recenti ricerche nelle necropoli eneolitiche della Conca d'Oro. *Origini*, 9: 153-271.

Cassoli, P.F., Piperno, M., Tagliacozzo, A. 1987. Dati paleoeconomici relativi al processo di neolitizzazione alla Grotta dell'Uzzo (Trapani). *AttiRS XXVI*: 809-17.

Cassoli, P.F. & Tagliacozzo, A. 1982. La fauna della Grotta di Cala Genovesi a Levanzo. *RSP*, 37: 124-34.

Castellana, G. 1985-86. Il villaggio neolitico di Piano Vento presso Palma di Montechiaro. *QuadMessina*, 1: 19-26.

—— 1987a. Il villaggio neolitico di Piano Vento nel territorio di Palma di Montechiaro. *AttiRS XXVI*: 793-800.

—— 1987b. Ricerche nella Piana di Gaffe nel territorio di Licata. *La preistoria in Sicilia. I Quaderni di Sicilia Archeologica* 1: 123-52.

—— 1988. Capanne della cultura di San Cono-Piano Notaro-Grotta Zubbia alla Zubbia di Palma di Montechiaro (Agrigento). *RA*, 7: 546-7.

—— 1988-89. L'insediamento di Montagnoli nei pressi di Selinunte. Un contributo per la conoscenza delle popolazioni anelleniche lungo il corso finale del Belice. In *Gli Elimi e l'area elima. Atti del Seminario di Studi. Archivio Storico Siciliano*, 14-15: 325-33. Palermo.

—— 1990. Il santuario di Monte Grande presso Palma di Montechiaro e la stipe votiva del Ciavolaro presso Ribera: aspetti religiosi delle popolazioni del bronzo antico in Sicilia. *QuadMessina*, 5: 5-17.

—— 1992. Nuovi dati su scavi condotti nel versante orientale del Basso Belice e nel bacino

Bibliography

finale del Platani. In *Giornate Internazionali di Studi sull'Area Elima (Gibellina 1991). Atti, I*: 191-202. Pisa-Gibellina.

—— 1993-94. Ricerche nel territorio di Palma di Montechiaro, Ribera, Menfi e Favara. *Kokalos*, 39-40: 735-53.

—— 1994. Recenti acquisizioni preistoriche nel versante orientale del Basso Belice con riferimento ai nuovi dati delle ricerche nel territorio agrigentino. *Basso Belice*: 17-46.

—— 1995. *La necropoli protoeneolitica di Piano Vento nel territorio di Palma di Montechiaro*. Regione Sicilia, Agrigento.

—— 1997. Presenze egeo-levantine nell'agrigentino nella prima metà del II millennio a.C. *Prima Sicilia*: 375-87.

Cavalier, M. 1960. Les cultures préhistoriques des îles eoliennes et leur rapport avec le monde égéen. *Bulletin de Correspondence Hellénique*, 84: 319-46.

—— 1970. La stazione preistorica di Tindari. *BPI*, 79: 61-94.

—— 1971. Il riparo della Sperlinga di San Basilio (Novara di Sicilia). *BPI*, 80: 7-64.

—— 1979. Ricerche preistoriche nell'Arcipelago eoliano. *RSP*, 34: 45-136.

—— 1981. Stromboli. Villaggio preistorico di San Vincenzo. *SA*, 46-47: 27-54.

—— 1985-86. Nuovi rinvenimenti sul Castello di Lipari. *RSP*, 40: 225-54.

—— 1990. Archeologia e vulcanologia nelle isole Eolie. In Albore Livadie, C. & Widemann, F. (eds) *Volcanology and Archaeology. Proceedings of the European Workshops, Ravello November 1987 & March 1989*: 25-48. PACT 25, Strasbourg.

Cavalier, M. & Bernabò Brea, L. 1993-94. Attività della Soprintendenza: isole Eolie. *Kokalos*, 39-40: 987-1000.

Cazzella, A. 1972. Considerazioni su alcuni aspetti eneolitici dell'Italia meridionale e della Sicilia. *Origini*, 6: 171-298.

—— 1991. Insediamenti fortificati e controllo del territorio durante l'età del bronzo nell'Italia sud-orientale. In Herring, E., Whitehouse, R. & Wilkins, J. (eds) *Papers of the Fourth Conference of Italian Archaeology, 1. The Archaeology of Power*: 49-60. Accordia Research Centre, London.

—— 1992. Usi funerari nell'Italia meridionale e in Sicilia nel corso dell'età del bronzo: una riconsiderazione. *La Sardegna nel Mediterraneo tra il Bronzo Medio e il Bronzo Recente, XVI-XIII sec. a.C. Atti del III Convegno di Studi 'Un millennio di relazioni fra la Sardegna e i Paesi del Mediterraneo'. Selargius-Cagliari 1987*: 331-41. Cagliari.

—— 1994. Cronologia radiocarbonica calibrata e cronologia 'storica' nell'Italia centro-meridionale durante l'età del bronzo. In Skeates, R. & Whitehouse, R. (eds) *Radiocarbon Dating and Italian Prehistory*: 73-83. Archaeological Monograph of the British School at Rome 8, Accordia Specialist Studies on Italy 3, London.

Cébeillac-Gervasoni, M. 1976-77. Une étude systematique sur les nécropoles de Megara Hyblaea: l'exemple d'une partie de la nécropole méridionale. *Kokalos*, 22-23: 587-97.

Ceccanti, M. 1980. Contatti culturali tra Puglia, Sicilia ed il Mediterraneo orientale in epoca pre-Micenea (Età del Rame). In Best, J.G.P. & De Vries, M.W. (eds) *Interaction and Acculturation in the Mediterranean. Proceedings of the 2nd International Congress of Mediterranean Pre- and Protohistory. Amsterdam 1980*. Vol.1: 37-47.

Chilardi, S. 1993-94. Lo scavo paleontologico di contrada Fusco. *Kokalos*, 39-40: 1343-51.

—— 1997. Le faune pleistoceniche di contrada Fusco (Siracusa). *Prima Sicilia*: 77-81.

Chilardi, S., Frayer, D.W., Gioia, P., Macchiarelli, R. & Mussi, M. 1996. Fontana Nuova di Ragusa (Sicily, Italy): southernmost Aurignacian site in Europe. *Antiquity* 70: 553-63.

Ciabatti, E. 1978. Relitto dell'età del bronzo rinvenuto nell'isola di Lipari. *SA*, 36: 7-35.

Cipolloni Sampò, M. 1994. Paleobiologia delle popolazioni umane: l'eneolitico e l'età del bronzo in Italia centro-meridionale. *BPI*, 85: 261-86.

Coldstream, J.N. 1993. Mixed marriages at the frontiers of the early Greek world. *Oxford Journal of Archaeology*, 12.1: 89-107.

—— 1996. A question of Cycladic geometric amphorae. In Lanzillotta, E. & Schilardi, D. (eds) *Le Cicladi ed il mondo Egeo. Atti del seminario di studi, Roma 19-21 novembre 1992*: 171-86.

Compagnoni, B. 1991. La malacofauna del sito meso-neolitico della Grotta dell'Uzzo (Trapani). *RSP*, 43: 49-72.

Cornaggia Castiglioni, O. & Calegari, G. 1978. Due 'amber space-beads' siciliane. *RSP*, 33: 265-9.

Costantini, L. 1979. Monte San Mauro di Caltagirone. Analisi paleoetnobotaniche dei semi contenuti nei pithoi 4 e 6. *Bollettino d'Arte*, 4: 43-4.

—— 1989. Plant exploitation at Grotta dell'Uzzo, Sicily: new evidence for the transition from Mesolithic to Neolithic subsistence in southern Europe. In Harris, D.R. & Hillman,

290

Bibliography

G.C. (eds) *Foraging and Farming. The Evolution of Plant Exploitation*: 197-206. Unwin Hyman, London.

Costantini, L. & Stancanelli, M. 1994. La preistoria agricola dell'Italia centro-meridionale: il contributo delle indagini archeobotaniche. *Origini*, 18: 149-244.

Cottignoli, A. 1995. Geomorfologia dell'area dei fossati di c.da Stretto (Partanna – Trapani). Formazione e funzione. *SA*, 28: 135-41.

Cultraro, M. 1988. Distribuzione dell'eneolitico nella fascia etnea meridionale e sui margini della Piana di Catania. *RA*, 7: 550-2.

—— 1997. La civiltà di Castelluccio nella zona etnea. *Prima Sicilia*: 353-7.

D'Agata, A.L. 1995. L'unità culturale e i fenomeni di acculturazione: la media età del bronzo. *Prima Sicilia*: 447-57.

De Miro, E. 1961. Ricerche preistoriche a nord dell'abitato di Palma di Montechiaro. *RSP*, 16: 15-56.

—— 1962. La fondazione di Agrigento e l'ellenizzazione del territorio fra il Salso e il Platani. *Kokalos*, 8: 122-52.

—— 1980-81. Ricerche archeologiche nella Sicilia centro-meridionale. *Kokalos*, 26-27: 561-80.

—— 1983. Forme di contatto e processi di trasformazione nelle società antiche: esempio da Sabucina. In *Forme di contatto e processi di trasformazione nelle società antiche. Atti del Convegno di Cortona*: 335-44. Roma, Collection de l'École Française de Rome 67.

—— 1988. Polizzello. Centro della Sicania. *QuadMessina*, 3: 25-44.

—— 1988-89. Gli 'indigeni' della Sicilia centro-meridionale. *Kokalos*, 34-35: 19-46.

Di Geronimo, I., Di Mauro, E., Di Stefano, G. & Mangano, G. 1981-92. Riparo sottoroccia a Pedagaggi (Siracusa) con industria dell'Epigravettiano finale. *BPI*, 83: 9-26.

Di Salvo, R. 1994. Analisi preliminare dei resti cranici eneolitici della tomba di Roccazzello (Trapani). *RSP*, 46: 203-12.

Di Stefano, G. 1976-77. Saggi a Poggio Biddini sul Dirillo. *Kokalos*, 22-23: 647-50.

—— 1979. La collezione preistorica della 'Grotta Lazzaro' nel Museo Civico di Modica. *SA*, 12: 91-110.

—— 1983. Il villaggio neolitico di Pirrone sul Dirillo (Ragusa). *SA*, 52-53: 99-118.

—— 1984. *Piccola guida delle stazioni preistoriche degli iblei*. Ragusa.

—— 1993-94. Scavi e ricerche a Camarina e nel Ragusano (1988-92). *Kokalos*, 39-40: 1367-1421.

Di Stefano, G. & Giardino, C. 1994. Scicli (Ragusa). Il ripostiglio di bronzi in contrada Castelluccio sull'Irminio. *NSc*, 9: 489-546.

Di Vita, A. 1996. Urban planning in ancient Sicily. In Pugliese Carratelli, G. (ed) *The Western Greeks: Classical Civilization in the Western Mediterranean*: 263-308. Thames & Hudson, London.

Domínguez, A.J. 1989. *La Colonización Griega en Sicilia. Griegos, Indígenas y Púnicos en la Sicilia Arcaica. Interracción y Aculturación*. BAR-IS 549.

Dunbabin, T.J. 1948a. *The Western Greeks. The History of Sicily and South Italy from the Foundation of the Greek Colonies to 480 BC*. Oxford University Press, Oxford.

—— 1948b. Minos and Daidalos in Sicily. *Papers of the British School at Rome*, 16: 1-18.

Egg, M. 1983. Ein eisenzeitlicher Weihefund aus Sizilien. *Jahrbuch des Römisch-Germanischen Zentralmuseums Mainz*, 30: 195-205.

Evans, J.D. 1953. The prehistoric culture-sequence in the Maltese archipelago. *PPS*, 19: 41-94.

—— 1956. Bossed bone plaques of the second millennium. *Antiquity*, 30: 80-93.

—— 1959. *Malta*. Thames & Hudson, London.

—— 1971. *The Prehistoric Antiquities of the Maltese Islands*. The Athlone Press, London.

—— 1977. Island archaeology in the Mediterranean: problems and opportunities. *World Archaeology*, 9: 12-26.

Fabbri, P.F. 1993. Nuove determinazioni del sesso e della statura degli individui 1 e 4 del Paleolitico Superiore della Grotta di San Teodoro. *RSP*, 45: 219-32.

Facchini, F. I reperti scheletrici della necropoli di Castiglione (Ragusa) (età del bronzo). *Archivio per l'Antropologia e la Etnologia*, 105: 79-153.

Facchini, F. & Brasili Gualandi, P. 1977-79. I reperti scheletrici di età arcaica della necropoli di Castiglione (Ragusa) (VII-VI secolo a.C.). *Rivista di Antropologia*, 60: 113-58.

—— 1980. Reperti scheletrici della necropoli arcaica di Monte Casasia (Ragusa) (VII-VI secolo a.C.). *Studi Etruschi*, 48: 253-75.

Falsone, G. 1988. The Bronze Age occupation and Phoenician foundation at Motya. *Institute of Archaeology Bulletin, University College London*, 25: 31-53.

Bibliography

—— 1993. Sulla cronologia del bronzo fenicio di Sciacca alla luce delle nuove scoperte di Huelva e Cadice. In *Studi sulla Sicilia Occidentale in onore di Vincenzo Tusa*: 45-56. Aldo Ausilio Editore, Padova.

Falsone, G., Di Noto, C.A. & Becker, M.J. 1993. Due tombe arcaiche da Entella. In Nenci, G. (ed) *Alla ricerca di Entella*: 157-94. Scuola Normale Superiore, Pisa.

Falsone, G., Leonard, A. Fresina, A., Johnson, C. & Fatta, V. 1980-81. Quattro campagne di scavo al Castellazzo di Poggioreale. *Kokalos*, 26-27: 931-72.

Fatta, V. 1983. *La ceramica geometrica di Sant'Angelo Muxaro*. Fondazione G. Whitaker, Studi Monografici 2, Palermo.

Fedele, F. 1988. Malta: origini e sviluppo del popolamento preistorico. In Anati, A.F. & Anati, E. (eds) *Missione a Malta. Ricerche e studi sulla preistoria dell'arcipelago maltese nel contesto Mediterraneo*: 51-90. Jaca Book, Milano.

Ferrarese Ceruti, M.L. 1987. Considerazioni sulla ceramica nuragica di Lipari. In *La Sardegna nel Mediterraneo tra il secondo e il primo millennio a.C. Atti del II Convegno di Studi 'Un millennio di relazioni fra la Sardegna e i paesi del Mediterraneo'. Selargius-Cagliari 1986*: 431-42. Cagliari.

Fiorentini, G. 1980-81. Ricerche archeologiche nella Sicilia centro-meridionale. *Kokalos*, 26-27: 581-600.

—— 1993-94. Attività di indagini archeologiche della soprintendenza beni culturali e ambientali di Agrigento. *Kokalos*, 39-40: 717-33.

—— 1995. *Monte Adranone*. Roma.

Fouilland, F., Frasca, M. & Pelagatti, P. 1994-95. Monte Casasia (Ragusa). Campagne di scavo 1966, 1972-73 nella necropoli indigena. *NSc*, IX, 5-6: 323-583.

Francaviglia, V. 1988. Ancient obsidian sources on Pantelleria (Italy). *Journal of Archaeological Science*, 15: 109-22.

Frasca, M. 1981. La necropoli di Monte Finocchito. In *Contributi alla conoscenza dell'età del ferro in Sicilia. Cronache*, 20: 13-102.

—— 1982. La necropoli di Cugno Carrube in territorio di Carlentini. In *Scavi nelle necropoli di Leontini (1977-1982). Cronache*, 21: 11-35.

—— 1983. Una nuova capanna 'sicula' a Siracusa, in Ortigia: tipologia dei materiali. *MEFRA*, 95: 565-98.

—— 1992. Tra Magna Grecia e Sicilia: origine e sopravvivenza delle coppie-amuleto a figura umana. *Bollettino d'Arte*, 76: 19-24.

—— 1996. Iron Age settlements and cemeteries in southeastern Sicily: a short review. *Early Societies*: 139-45.

Frasca, M., Messina, F., Palermo, D. & Procelli, E. 1975. Ramacca (Catania). Saggi di scavo nel villaggio preistorico di contrada Torricella. *NSc*, VIII, 29: 557-85.

Gabba, E. & Vallet, G. (eds) 1980. *Storia della Sicilia. La Sicilia antica*. Storia di Napoli e della Sicilia Società Editrice, Napoli.

Gabrici, E. 1925. Polizzello, abitato preistorico presso Mussomeli. *Reale Accademia di Scienze, Lettere e Belle Arti, Palermo*: 3-11.

Gale, N.H. (ed) 1991. *Bronze Age Trade in the Mediterranean. Papers presented at the Conference held at Rewley House, Oxford, in December 1989*. Studies in Mediterranean Archaeology 90, Jonsered.

Genovese, P. 1977. Testimonianze archeologiche e paletnologiche nel bacino del Longano. *SA*, 33: 9-37.

—— 1978. Tracce di un insediamento neolitico stentinelliano a Barcellona. *SA*, 38: 85-91.

Germanà, F. 1994. Antropologia del campaniforme mediterraneo insulare occidentale. *Basso Belice*: 481-96.

Germanà, F. & Di Salvo, R. 1994. Il cranio trapanato di Stretto-Partanna nel quadro delle pratiche chirurgiche dell'Italia preistorica. *Basso Belice*: 411-22.

Giangiulio, M. 1983. Greci e non-Greci in Sicilia alla luce dei culti e delle leggende di Eracle. In *Forme di contatto e processi di trasformazione nelle società antiche. Atti del Convegno di Cortona (1981)*: 785-846. Scuola Normale Superiore and École Française de Rome, Pisa-Roma.

Giannitrapani, E. 1997. Rapporti tra la Sicilia e Malta durante l'età del bronzo. *Prima Sicilia*: 429-43.

Giardino, C. 1987. Il ripostiglio di Polizzello. *SA*, 65: 39-55.

—— 1995. *Il Mediterraneo Occidentale fra XIV e VIII secolo a.C. Cerchie minerarie e metallurgiche. The West Mediterranean between the 14th and 8th Centuries BC. Mining and Metallurgical Spheres*. BAR-IS 612.

292

Bibliography

———— 1996. Miniere e tecniche metallurgiche nella Sicilia protostorica: nuove linee di ricerca. *Early Societies*: 129-38.

———— 1997. La metallotecnica nella Sicilia pre-protostorica. *Prima Sicilia*: 405-14.

Gioia, P. 1984-87. L'industria litica di Fontana Nuova (Ragusa) nel quadro dell'Aurignaziano italiano. *Origini*, 13: 27-58.

Gliozzi, E. & Kotsakis, T. 1986. I vertebrati fossili del giacimento Epigravettiano finale di Pedagaggi (Siracusa). *Il naturalista siciliano*, 10: 35-42.

Graham, A.J. 1988. Megara Hyblaea and the Sicels. In Lordkipanidze, O. (ed), *Local Ethno-Political Entities of the Black Sea Area in the 7th-4th Centuries BC*. Materials of the 4th All-Union Symposium on the Ancient History of the Black Sea Littoral, Tsqaltubo-Vani 1985: 304-21. Tbilisi.

Gras, M. 1986. Aspects de la recherche sur la colonisation grecque. A propos du Congrès d'Athènes: notes de lecture. *Revue Belge de Philologie et d'Histoire*, 64: 5-21.

Graziosi, P. 1947. Gli uomini paleolitici della Grotta S. Teodoro (Messina). *RSP*, 2: 123-224.

———— 1950. Le pitture e i graffiti preistorici dell'isola di Levanzo nell'Arcipelago delle Egadi (Sicilia). *RSP*, 5: 1-43.

———— 1953. Nuovi graffiti parietali della Grotta di Levanzo (Egadi). *RSP*, 8: 123-37.

———— 1954. Pietra graffita paleolitica e ciottoli dipinti della Grotta di Levanzo (Egadi) (Scavi 1953). *RSP*, 9: 79-88.

———— 1956. Qualche osservazione sui graffiti rupestri della Grotta dell'Addaura presso Palermo. *BPI*, 65: 285-95.

———— 1962. *Levanzo. Pitture e incisioni*. Sansoni, Firenze.

———— 1968. Découverte d'outils du Paléolithique inférieur en Sicile. *L'Anthropologie*, 72: 399-488.

———— 1973. *L'arte preistorica in Italia*. Sansoni, Firenze.

Graziosi, P. & Maviglia, C. 1946. La grotta di S. Teodoro (Messina). *RSP*, 1: 277-83.

Grimaldi, G. & Scaletta, C. 1997. L'insediamento neolitico di contrada Stretto. *Prima Sicilia*: 213-22.

Guerri, M. 1991. Nuovi metodi di indagine: sepoltura stentinelliana in località Fontanazza (Catania). *Annali dei Musei Civici di Rovereto, Atti del Convegno 'Paolo Orsi e l'Archeologia del '900'*, 6: 223-8.

Guidi, A. & Piperno, M. 1993. *Italia preistorica* (2nd ed). Editori Laterza, Roma-Bari.

Gullì, D. 1993. Primi dati sull'insediamento preistorico di Eraclea Minoa. *QuadMessina*, 8: 11-20.

Guzzardi, L. 1980. Un ipogeo preistorico a Calaforno e il suo contesto topografico. *SA*, 42: 67-94.

———— 1991. Importazioni dal Vicino Oriente in Sicilia fino all'età orientalizzante. *Atti del II Congresso Internazionale di Studi Fenici e Punici (Roma 1987)*: 941-54.

———— 1993-94. Ricerche archeologiche nel siracusano. *Kokalos*, 39-40: 1299-1314.

Guzzone, C. 1993-94. Abitato Antico Bronzo in c.da Garrasia. *Kokalos*, 39-40: 845-50.

———— 1994. La ceramica del villaggio di Serra del Palco ed il territorio di Milena in età neolitica. *Basso Belice*: 305-22.

Hencken, H. 1958. Syracuse, Etruria and the North. Some comparisons. *AJA*, 62: 259-72.

Holloway, R.R. 1981. *Italy and the Aegean 3000-700 BC*. Louvain la Neuve & Providence.

Holloway, R.R., Joukowsky, M. & Lukesh, S.S. 1990. La Muculufa, the Early Bronze Age Sanctuary: the Early Bronze Age Village (Excavations of 1982 and 1983). *Revue des archéologues et historiens d'art de Louvain*, 23: 11-67.

Holloway, R.R. & Lukesh, S.S. 1995. *Ustica I. Excavations of 1990 and 1991. Archaeologia Transatlantica XIV*. Louvain-la-Neuve.

———— 1997. Ustica, località Faraglioni: perché castello? In *Archeologia e territorio*: 455-60. Palumbo editore, Palermo.

Johns, J. 1992. Monreale Survey. L'insediamento umano nell'alto Belice dall'età paleolitica al 1250 d.C. In *Giornate internazionali di studi sull'area elima (Gibellina 19-22 settembre 1991). Atti I*: 407-20. Pisa-Gibellina.

Jones, R.E. & Vagnetti, L. 1991. Traders and craftsmen in the central Mediterranean: archaeological evidence and archaeometric research. In Gale, N.H. (ed) *Bronze Age Trade in the Mediterranean. Papers presented at the Conference held at Rewley House, Oxford, in December 1989*: 127-47. Studies in Mediterranean Archaeology 90, Jonsered.

Judson, S. 1963. Stream changes during historic time in east-central Sicily. *AJA*, 67: 287-9.

Karageorghis, V. 1995. Cyprus and the Western Mediterranean: some new evidence for interrelations. In Carter, J.B. & Morris, S. (eds) *The Ages of Homer. A Tribute to Emily Townsend Vermeule*: 93-7. University of Texas, Austin.

293

Bibliography

Kearsley, R. 1989. *The Pendent Semi-Circle Skyphos. Institute of Classical Studies, Bulletin Supplement 44.* London.

Kilian, K. 1966. Testimonianze di vita religiosa della prima età del ferro in Italia meridionale. *Rendiconti della Accademia di Archeologia, Lettere e Belle Arti, Napoli,* 41: 91-106.

Kotsakis, T. 1979. Sulle mammalofaune quaternarie siciliane. *Bollettino del Servizio Geologico Italiano,* 99: 263-76.

Lagona, S. 1971. La necropoli di Ossini-S. Lio. *Cronache,* 10: 16-40.

Laplace, G. 1966. *Recherches sur l'origine et l'évolution des complexes leptolithiques.* École Française de Rome (supplement 4), Bonard, Paris.

La Rosa, A. 1986-87. Grotta Caprara, tomba dell'età del rame. *Atti e Memorie, Istituto per lo studio e la valorizzazione di Noto Antica,* 17-18: 113-25.

La Rosa, V. 1968. Bronzetti indigeni della Sicilia. *Cronache,* 7: 7-136.

―――― 1979. Sopralluoghi e ricerche attorno a Milena nella media valle del Platani. *Cronache,* 18: 76-102.

―――― 1985. Paolo Orsi e la preistoria della Sicilia. *Annali dei Musei Civici di Rovereto,* 1: 5-21.

―――― 1986. Nuovi ritrovamenti e sopravvivenze egee nella Sicilia meridionale. In Marazzi, M., Tusa, S. & Vagnetti, L. (eds) *Traffici micenei nel Mediterraneo. Problemi storici e documentazione archeologica. Atti del convegno di Palermo*: 79-88. Naples: Istituto per la storia e l'archeologia della Magna Grecia, Taranto.

―――― 1987. Un nuovo insediamento neolitico a Serra del Palco di Milena (CL). *AttiRS XXVI*: 801-8.

―――― 1989. Le popolazioni della Sicilia: Sicani, Siculi, Elimi. In Pugliese Carratelli, G. (ed) *Italia omnium terrarum parens*: 1-110. Milano.

―――― 1994. Le nuove indagini nella media valle del Platani. *Basso Belice*: 287-304.

La Rosa, V. & D'Agata, A.L. 1988. Uno scarico dell'età del bronzo sulla Serra del Palco di Milena. *QuadMessina,* 3: 5-24.

Leighton, R. 1981. Strainer-spouted jugs and the problem of the earliest Phoenician influence in Sicily. *Journal of Mediterranean Anthropology and Archaeology,* 1: 280-91.

―――― 1986. Paolo Orsi (1859-1935) and the prehistory of Sicily. *Antiquity,* 60: 15-20.

―――― 1989a. Ground stone tools from Serra Orlando (Morgantina) and stone axe studies in Sicily and Southern Italy. *PPS,* 55: 135-59.

―――― 1989b. Antiquarianism and prehistory in West Mediterranean islands. *Antiquaries Journal,* 69(ii): 183-204.

―――― 1992. Stone axes and exchange in south Italian prehistory: new evidence from old collections. *Accordia Research Papers,* 3: 11-40.

―――― 1993a. *The Protohistoric Settlement on the Cittadella. Morgantina Studies Volume 4.* Princeton University Press, Princeton.

―――― 1993b. Sicily during the centuries of darkness. *Cambridge Archaeological Journal,* 3(ii): 271-6.

―――― 1996a. Research traditions, chronology and current issues: an introduction. *Early Societies*: 1-19.

―――― 1996b. From chiefdom to tribe? Social organisation and change in later prehistory. *Early Societies*: 101-16.

Leighton, R. & Dixon, J.E. 1992. Jade and greenstone in the prehistory of Sicily and southern Italy. *Oxford Journal of Archaeology,* 11.2: 179-200.

Lewthwaite, J. 1981. Why did civilisation not emerge more often? A comparative approach to the development of Minoan Crete. In Krzyszkowska, O. & Nixon, L. (eds) *Minoan Society: Proceedings of the Cambridge Colloquium, 1981*: 171-84. Bristol.

―――― 1985. Social factors and economic change in Balearic prehistory, 3000-1000 b.c. In Barker, G. & Gamble, C. (eds) *Beyond Domestication in Prehistoric Europe*: 205-31. London.

―――― 1986. The transition to food production: a Mediterranean perspective. In Zvelebil, M. (ed) *Hunters in Transition. Mesolithic Societies of Temperate Eurasia and their Transition to Farming*: 53-66. Cambridge University Press, Cambridge.

―――― 1990. Isolating the residuals: the Mesolithic basis of man-animal relationships on the Mediterranean islands. In Bonsall, C. (ed) *The Mesolithic in Europe*: 541-55. John Donald, Edinburgh.

Lona, F. 1949. I carboni dei focolari paleolitici della Grotta di San Teodoro (Messina). *RSP,* 4: 187-97.

Lo Schiavo, F., Macnamara, E. & Vagnetti, L. 1985. Late Cypriot imports to Italy and their influence on local bronzework. *Papers of the British School at Rome,* 53: 1-71.

Bibliography

Lyons, C.L. 1996a. *The Archaic Cemeteries. Morgantina Studies Volume 5.* Princeton University Press, Princeton.

───── 1996b. Sikel burials at Morgantina: defining social and ethnic identities. *Early Societies:* 177-88.

Mallegni, F., Bartoli, F. & Ronco, D. 1994. I reperti umani del deposito funerario di contrada Menta (Milena, Caltanissetta). *Basso Belice:* 373-85.

Malone, C. 1985. Pots, prestige and ritual in Neolithic Southern Italy. In Malone, C. & Stoddart, S. (eds) *Papers in Italian Archaeology IV(ii):* 115-51. *BAR-IS* 244.

Malone, C., Stoddart, S. & Whitehouse, R. 1994. The Bronze Age of Southern Italy, Sicily and Malta, c. 2000-800 BC. In Mathers, C. & Stoddart, S. (eds) *Development and Decline in the Mediterranean Bronze Age:* 167-94. Sheffield Archaeological Monographs 8, Sheffield.

Maniscalco, L. 1994. Le ceramiche dell'età del rame nel territorio di Milena. *Basso Belice:* 323-38.

───── 1996. Early Bronze Age funerary ritual and architecture: monumental tombs at Santa Febronia. *Early Societies:* 81-7.

───── 1997a. L'insediamento preistorico presso Le Salinelle di San Marco (Paternò). *Prima Sicilia:* 193-8.

───── 1997b. L'insediamento castellucciano delle Coste di Santa Febronia (Palagonia). *Prima Sicilia:* 359-63.

Manni, E. 1962. Minosse ed Eracle nella Sicilia dell'età del bronzo. *Kokalos,* 8: 6-29.

───── 1980. Culti greci e culti indigeni in Sicilia. Problemi di metodo e spunti di ricerca. *Archivio Storico Siciliano,* 81: 5-17.

Mannino, G. 1962. Nuove incisioni rupestri scoperte in Sicilia. *RSP,* 17: 147-59.

───── 1971. La tomba di Contrada Pergola. *SA,* 15: 52-6.

───── 1978. Le Grotte di Armetta (Carini-Palermo). *SA,* 11: 73-83.

───── 1982. Il villaggio dei Faraglioni di Ustica. Notizie preliminari. In *Studi in onore di Ferrante Rittatore Vonwiller,* 1: 279-97. Como.

───── 1991. Ustica: nuove e più antiche testimonianze archeologiche. *SA,* 24: 65-85.

───── 1994. Ricerche preistoriche nel territorio di Partanna. *Basso Belice:* 125-76.

Mannino, G. & Spatafora, F. 1995. *Mokarta. La Necropoli di Cresta di Gallo. Quaderni del Museo Archeologico Regionale Antonio Salinas,* 1. Palermo.

Marazzi, M. 1976. *Egeo e occidente alla fine del II millennio avanti Cristo.* Dell'Ateneo, Roma.

───── 1997a. I contatti transmarini nella preistoria siciliana. *Prima Sicilia:* 365-74.

───── 1997b. Le 'scritture eoliane': i segni grafici sulle ceramiche. *Prima Sicilia:* 459-71.

Marazzi, M., Tusa, S. & Vagnetti, L. (eds) 1986. *Traffici micenei nel Mediterraneo. Problemi storici e documentazione archeologica. Atti del Convegno di Palermo 1984.* Istituto per la storia e l'archeologia della Magna Grecia, Taranto.

Martini, F. 1997. Il Paleolitico superiore in Sicilia. *Prima Sicilia:* 111-24.

Martini, F. & Sarti, L. 1973. La Grotta dell'Acqua Fitusa (Agrigento). II. Tipometrie dell'industria litica. *RSP,* 28.1: 57-105.

Massetti, M. & Vianello, F. 1991. Importazioni preistoriche di mammiferi alloctoni nelle isole del Mar Tirreno centro-settentrionale. *RSP,* 43: 275-92.

McConnell, B.E. 1988. Indagini preistoriche nel territorio di Ribera (AG): le tombe dell'età del rame in contrada Castello e a Cozzo Mastrogiovanni. *SA,* 66-68: 101-12.

───── 1995. *La Muculufa II. Archaeologia Transatlantica XII.* Louvain-la-Neuve.

───── 1997. Lo sviluppo delle prime società agro-pastorali: l'eneolitico. *Prima Sicilia:* 281-94.

McConnell, B.E., Morico, G., Corrain, C. & Capitanio, M. 1990. La Muculufa (Butera, Caltanissetta), stazione siciliana dell'età del bronzo antico. *Archivio per l'Antropologia e la Etnologia,* 120: 115-50.

Mentesana, M. 1967. La Gisira. *Notiziario Storico di Augusta 1:* 7-69.

Messina, A. 1993. Tre edifici del medioevo siciliano. *SA,* 82: 61-5.

Mezzena, F. 1976. Nuova interpretazione delle incisioni parietali paleolitiche della Grotta Addaura a Palermo. *RSP,* 31: 61-85.

Mollo Mezzena, R. 1993. Sabucina. Recenti scavi nell'area fuori le mura. Risultati e problematiche. In *Storia e archeologia della media e bassa Valle dell'Himera. Atti del Convegno Licata-Caltanissetta 1987:* 137-81. Palermo.

Momigliano, A. 1979. The rediscovery of Greek history in the eighteenth century: the case of Sicily. In Runte, R. (ed), *Studies in Eighteenth Century Culture,* 9: 167-87. Madison.

Morel, J-P. 1984. Greek colonization in Italy and the West. Problems of evidence and interpretation. In Hackens, T., Holloway, N.D. & Holloway, R.R. (eds) *Crossroads of the Mediterranean:* 123-61. Louvain La Neuve-Providence.

Bibliography

Morris, I. 1996. The absolute chronology of the Greek colonies in Sicily. *Acta Archaeologica*, 67: 51-59.

Morter, J. 1994. Four pieces of clay: 'tokens' from Capo Alfiere. *Journal of Mediterranean Archaeology*, 7.1: 115-23.

Moscati, S. 1984-85. Fenici e Greci in Sicilia: alle origini di un confronto. *Kokalos*, 30-31: 1-19.

—— (ed) 1988. *The Phoenicians*. Bompiani, Milan.

Moscetta, M.P. 1988. Il ripostiglio di Lipari. Nuove considerazioni per un inquadramento cronologico e culturale. *Dialoghi di Archeologia*, 1: 53-78.

Müller-Karpe, H. 1959. *Beiträge zur Chronologie der Urnenfelderzeit Nördlich und Südlich der Alpen*. De Gruyter, Berlin.

Muzzolini, A. 1989. La 'néolithisation' du nord de l'Afrique et ses causes. In Aurenche, O. & Cauvin, J. (eds) *Néolithisations. Proche et Moyen Orient, Méditerranée orientale, Nord de l'Afrique, Europe méridionale, Chine, Amérique du Sud*: 145-84. *BAR-IS* 516.

Nicoletti, F. 1990. Il campignano di Biddini (Ragusa). Approccio alle industrie bifacciali oloceniche e alla attività mineraria della Sicilia preistorica. *Archivio Storico per la Sicilia Orientale*, 86: 7-59.

—— 1996. Le industrie litiche oloceniche: forme, materie prime e aspetti economici. *Early Societies*: 57-69.

—— 1997. Il commercio neolitico dell'ossidiana nel mediterraneo ed il ruolo di Lipari e Pantelleria nel più antico sistema di scambio. *Prima Sicilia*: 259-69.

Nicoletti, F. & Battaglia, G. 1991. Ricerche tipometriche sui tranchets campignani di Poggio Biddini (Ragusa). *SA*, 76-77: 53-66.

Orlandini, P. 1962a. *Il villaggio preistorico di Manfria, presso Gela*. Banco di Sicilia, Palermo.

—— 1962b. L'espansione di Gela nella Sicilia centro-meridionale. *Kokalos*, 8: 69-121.

—— 1963. Sabucina, a) scoperte varie, b) prima campagna di scavo (1962). Rapporto preliminare. *Archeologia Classica*, 15:86-96.

—— 1965. Sabucina. La 2a campagna di scavo (1964). Rapporto preliminare. *Archeologia Classica*, 17: 133-40.

—— 1968. Statuette preistoriche della prima età del bronzo da Caltanissetta. *Bollettino d'Arte*, 53: 55-9.

Orsi, P. 1889-92. Megara Hyblaea, storia, topografia, necropoli e anathemata. *MAL*, 1.

—— 1890. Stazione neolitica di Stentinello (Siracusa). *BPI*, 16: 177-200.

—— 1891a. La necropoli sicula di Melilli (Siracusa). *BPI*, 17: 53-76.

—— 1891b. La necropoli sicula del Plemmirio (Siracusa). *BPI*, 17: 115-39.

—— 1892. La necropoli sicula di Castelluccio (Siracusa). *BPI*, 18: 1-34, 67-84.

—— 1893a. Scarichi del villaggio siculo di Castelluccio. *BPI*, 19: 30-51.

—— 1893b. Necropoli sicula presso Siracusa con vasi e bronzi micenei. *MAL*, 2: 5-36.

—— 1893c. Di due sepolcreti siculi nel territorio di Siracusa. *Archivio Storico Siciliano*, 18: 308-25.

—— 1895a. Thapsos. *MAL*, 6: 89-150.

—— 1895b. Siracusa. Gli scavi nella necropoli del Fusco a Siracusa nel giugno, novembre e dicembre del 1893. *NSc*: 109-92.

—— 1895c. Necropoli sicula del primo periodo presso Siracusa. *BPI*, 21: 150-2.

—— 1895d. Vasi siculi della provincia di Girgenti. *BPI*, 21: 80-5.

—— 1897. Sepolcro di Caldare. *BPI*, 23: 8-15.

—— 1898a. Miniere di selce e sepolcri eneolitici a Monte Tabuto e Monte Racello presso Comiso (Siracusa). *BPI*, 24: 165-206.

—— 1898b. La necropoli di Licodia Eubea ed i vasi geometrici del quarto periodo siculo. *Mittheilungen des Kaiserlich Deutschen Archaeologischen Instituts. Roemische Abtheilungen*, 13: 305-66.

—— 1899a. Pantalica e Cassibile. *MAL*, 9: 33-146.

—— 1899b. Pantelleria. Risultati di una missione archeologica. *MAL*, 9: 9-49.

—— 1899c. Siracusa. Nuove esplorazioni nel Plemmyrium. *NSc*: 26-42.

—— 1900a. Siculi e Greci in Leontinoi. *Römische Mittheilungen*, 15: 52-98.

—— 1900b. Villaggio preistorico di Matrensa. *NSc*: 208.

—— 1901. I siculi della regione gelese. *BPI*, 27: 153-63.

—— 1902a. La necropoli di Valsavoia. *BPI*, 28: 103-19.

—— 1902b. Sepolcreto di Cava Cana Barbara (Siracusa). *BPI*, 28: 184-90.

—— 1903a. Necropoli e stazioni siculi di transizione. Milocca e Matrensa. *BPI*, 29: 136-49.

—— 1903b. Necropoli e Stazioni Sicule di Transizione, III. La necropoli di Rivetazzo (Sir). *BPI*, 29: 23-8.

Bibliography

—— 1904. Caltagirone. *NSc*, 5,1: 65-98, 132-41, 373.

—— 1905. Necropoli e stazioni sicule di transizione, V. Necropoli al Molino della Badia presso Grammichele. *BPI*, 4,31: 96-133.

—— 1906a. Nuovi documenti della civiltà micenea e premicenea. *Ausonia*, 1: 5-12.

—— 1906b. Gela. Scavi del 1900-1905. *MAL*, 17.

—— 1907a. La grotta di Calafarina presso Pachino, abitazione e sepolcro. *BPI*, 33: 7-22.

—— 1907b. Caverne di abitazione a Barriera presso Catania. *BPI*, 33: 53-99.

—— 1908. Sepolcri Protosiculi di Gela. *BPI*, 34: 119-39, 155-68.

—— 1909. Floridia. Sepolcreto siculo con vaso miceneo. *NSc*, 6: 374-8.

—— 1910. Due villaggi del primo periodo siculo. *BPI*, 36: 158-93.

—— 1912a. Pantalica e M. Dessueri. *MAL*, 21: 301-408.

—— 1912b. Stentinello. *NSc*, 9: 356-7.

—— 1915. Necropoli sicula a Pozzo di Gotto in quel di Castroreale (Messina). *BPI*, 41: 71-84.

—— 1918. Gli scavi intorno all'Athenaion di Siracusa negli anni 1912-1917. *MAL*, 21: 353-754.

—— 1919. Taormina. Necropoli sicula al Cocolonazzo di Mola. *NSc*, 16: 360-9.

—— 1921. Megara Hyblaea (1917-1921). Villaggio neolitico e tempio greco e di taluni singolarissimi vasi di Paternò. *MAL*, 27: 109-50.

—— 1923. Villaggio, officina litica, necropoli sicula del primo periodo siculo a Monte Sallia presso Canicarao (Comiso). *BPI*, 42: 3-26.

—— 1926. Villaggio e sepolcreto siculo alle Sante Croci presso Comiso (Siracusa). *BPI*, 46: 5-17.

—— 1928. Miscellanea Sicula. *BPI*, 48: 44-98.

—— 1930-31. Abitazioni e sepolcri siculi di Biancavilla (Catania) entro caverne di lava. *BPI*, 50-51: 134-47.

—— 1932. La necropoli di Sant'Angelo Muxaro (Agrigento) e cosa essa ci dice di nuovo sulla questione sicula. *Atti della Reale Accademia di Scienze, Lettere e Belle Arti di Palermo*, 17: 271-84.

Pacci, M. 1982. Lo stile 'protocastellucciano' di Naro. *RSP*, 37: 187-216.

Pacci, M. & Tusa, S. 1991. *La collezione dei vasi preistorici di Partanna e Naro*. Palermo.

Pacciarelli, M. 1986. L'organizzazione sociale nella Calabria meridionale agli inizi dell'età del ferro: considerazioni preliminari sulla necropoli di Torre Galli. *Dialoghi di Archeologia*, 2: 283-93.

Palermo, D. 1981. Polizzello. In *Contributi alla conoscenza dell'età del ferro in Sicilia*. *Cronache*, 20 (1983): 103-47.

—— 1982. Leontini. Scavi nella necropoli di Pozzanghera. In *Scavi nelle Necropoli di Leontini (1977-1982)*. *Cronache*, 21: 67-86.

—— 1996. Tradizione indigena e apporti greci nelle culture della Sicilia centro-meridionale: il caso di Sant'Angelo Muxaro. *Early Societies*: 147-54.

Palma di Cesnola, A. 1994. Il paleolitico in Sicilia. *Basso Belice*: 99-119.

Pancucci, D. & Naro, M.C. 1992. *Monte Bubbonia. Campagne di scavo 1905, 1906, 1955*. Bretschneider, Roma.

Panvini, R. 1988-89. Scavi e ricerche a Caltabellotta tra il 1983 e il 1985. *Kokalos*, 34-35: 559-72.

—— 1990. Monte San Giuliano. In *Da Nissa a Maktorion. Nuovi Contributi per l'Archeologia della Provincia di Caltanissetta*: 11-19. Museo Civico, Caltanissetta.

—— 1993-94. L'attività della Soprintendenza di Caltanissetta tra gli anni 1992-93. *Kokalos*, 39-40: 783-823.

—— 1996. ΓΕΛΑΣ. *Storia e archeologia dell'antica Gela*. Società Editrice Internazionale, Torino.

—— 1997. Osservazioni sulle dinamiche formative socio-culturali a Dessueri. *Prima Sicilia*: 493-501.

Pareti, L. 1956. Basi e sviluppo della 'tradizione' antica sui primi popoli della Sicilia. *Kokalos*, 2: 5-19.

Pelagatti, P. 1973a. Villaggi castellucciani tra il Dirillo e l'Irminio. *ASSO*: 26-9.

—— 1973b. L'entroterra di Camarina. *ASSO*: 151-8.

—— 1976-77. L'attività della Soprintendenza alle Antichità della Sicilia orientale. *Kokalos*, 22-23, II,1: 519-50.

—— 1978a. Naxos nell'VIII e nel VII secolo a.C. *Cronache*, 17: 136-41.

—— 1978b. Materiali tardo geometrici dal retroterra di Siracusa. *Cronache*, 17: 111-12.

Bibliography

―― 1978c. Siracusa. Elementi dell'abitato di Ortigia nell'VIII e nel VII secolo a.C. *Cronache*, 17: 119-33.

―― 1981. Bilancio degli scavi di Naxos per l'VIII e il VII sec.a.C. *Atti del Convegno Internazionale Grecia, Italia e Sicilia nell'VIII e VII secolo a.C. Annuario della Scuola Archeologica di Atene e delle Missioni Italiane in Oriente*, 59: 291-311.

―― 1982a. Siracusa; le ultime ricerche in Ortigia. *Atti del Convegno Internazionale Grecia, Italia e Sicilia nell'VIII e VII secolo a.C. Annuario della Scuola Archeologica di Atene e delle Missioni Italiane in Oriente*, 60: 117-63.

―― 1982b. I più antichi materiali di importazione a Siracusa, a Naxos e in altri siti della Sicilia orientale. *La céramique grecque ou de tradition grecque au VIIIe siècle en Italie centrale et méridionale*: 113-80. Cahiers du Centre Jean Bérard III, Naples.

Pelagatti, P. & Del Campo, M. 1971. Abitati siculi: Castiglione. *SA*, 16: 31-40.

Peroni, R. 1983. Presenze micenee e forme socio-economiche nell'Italia protostorica. In *Magna Grecia e mondo miceneo. Atti del ventiduesimo convegno di studi sulla Magna Grecia*: 211-84. Istituto per la storia e l'archeologia della Magna Grecia, Taranto.

―― 1994. *Introduzione alla protostoria italiana*. Editori Laterza, Roma-Bari.

Pianese, S.P. 1968. Rassegna storica degli studi e delle ricerche sul Paleolitico in Sicilia. *Quaternaria*, 10: 213-50.

Piperno, M. 1997a. Il popolamento della Sicilia. Il Paleolitico inferiore. *Prima Sicilia*: 83-91.

―― 1997b. La Sicilia all'inizio dell'olocene. Aspetti del popolamento mesolitico. *Prima Sicilia*: 135-45.

Piperno, M., Scali, S., Tagliacozzo, A. 1981. Mesolitico e Neolitico alla Grotta dell'Uzzo (Trapani), Primi dati per una interpretazione paleoeconomica. *Quaternaria*, 22: 275-300.

Pluciennik, M. 1994. Space, time and caves: art in the Palaeolithic, Mesolithic and Neolithic of southern Italy. *Accordia Research Papers*, 5: 39-71.

Privitera, F. 1991-92. Castiglione di Sicilia. Contrada Marca – Grotta Sepolcrale della tarda età del rame e del bronzo antico. *Beni Culturali e Ambientali, Sicilia*, NS I-II: 21-5.

Procelli, E. 1981. Il complesso tombale di contrada Paolina ed il problema dei rapporti tra Sicilia e Malta nella prima età del bronzo. *Bollettino d'Arte*, 9: 83-110.

―― 1983. Naxos Preellenica. Le culture e i materiali dal neolitico all'età del ferro nella penisola di Schisò. *Cronache*, 22: 9-82.

―― 1989. Aspetti e problemi dell'ellenizzazione calcidese nella Sicilia orientale. *MEFRA*, 101,2: 679-89.

―― 1989. La grotta dei monaci. Stazione dell'età del rame presso Castelmola (Taormina) (1). *SA*, 71: 41-50.

―― 1991. Aspetti religiosi ed apporti transmarini nella cultura di Castelluccio. *Journal of Mediterranean Studies*, 1: 252-66.

―― 1991-92. Considerazioni sul passaggio dall'antica alla media età del bronzo nella Sicilia orientale: Catania e Naxos. *RA*, 10: 561-8.

―― 1992. Appunti per una topografia di Catania pregreca. *Kokalos*, 38: 69-78.

―― 1996. Sicily between the third and second millennium BC: a brief survey. *Early Societies*: 89-100.

―― 1997. La civiltà agro-pastorale siciliana matura: l'antica età del bronzo. *Prima Sicilia*: 343-51.

Procelli, E. & Albanese, R.M. 1992. Ramacca (Catania). Saggi di scavo nelle contrade Castellito e Montagna negli anni 1978, 1981 e 1982. *NSc*, 42-43 (1988-89): 7-159.

Pugliese Carratelli, G. 1956. Minos e Cocalos. *Kokalos*, 2: 89-103.

―― (ed) 1985. *Sikanie. Storia e civiltà della Sicilia graeca*. Milano.

―― (ed), 1989. *Italia omnium terrarum parens*. Milano.

―― (ed) 1996. *The Western Greeks. Classical Civilization in the Western Mediterranean*. Thames & Hudson, London.

Radi, G. 1972. Tracce di un insediamento neolitico nell'isola di Lampedusa. *Atti della Società Toscana di Scienze Naturali*, 79: 197-205.

Recami, E., Mignosa, C. & Baldini, L.R. 1983. Nuovo contributo sulla preistoria della Sicilia. *SA*, 52-53: 45-82.

Renfrew, C. & Whitehouse, R. 1974. The Copper Age of peninsular Italy and the Aegean. *Annual of the British School at Athens*, 69: 343-90.

Ridgway, D. 1992. *The First Western Greeks*. Cambridge University Press, Cambridge.

Rizza, G. 1962. Siculi e Greci sui colli di Leontini. *Cronache*, 1: 3-27.

―― 1978. Leontini nell'VIII e nel VII secolo a.C. *Cronache*, 17: 26-37.

―― 1979. S. Angelo Muxaro e il problema delle influenze micenee in Sicilia. *Cronache*, 18: 19-30.

Bibliography

—— 1984-85. La necropoli di Butera e i rapporti fra Sicilia e Creta in età protoarcaica. *Kokalos*, 30-31: 65-70.

Robb, J. 1994. Burial and social reproduction in the peninsular Italian Neolithic. *Journal of Mediterranean Archaeology*, 7.1: 27-71.

Scibona, G. 1971. Due tombe ad enchytrismos della media età del bronzo in contrada Paradiso a Messina. *BPI*, 80: 213-27.

—— 1984-85. Messina: notizie preliminari sulla necropoli romana e sul giacimento preistorico del Torrente Boccetta. *Kokalos*, 30-31: 855-61.

Segre Naldini, E. 1992. Arte mobiliare della Grotta Giovanna (Siracusa). *AttiRS XXVIII*: 347-54.

Segre, E. & Vigliardi, A. 1985. L'Epigravettien évolué et final en Sicile. *RSP*, 38: 351-69.

Shackleton, J.C., van Andel, T.H. & Runnels, C.H. 1984. Coastal paleogeography of the central and western Mediterranean during the last 125,000 years and its archaeological implications. *Journal of Field Archaeology* 11: 307-14.

Shepherd, G. 1995. The pride of most colonials: burial and religion in the Sicilian colonies. In Fischer-Hansen, T. (ed), *Ancient Sicily, Acta Hyperborea 6*: 51-82. Museum Tusculanum Press, Copenhagen.

Sherratt, S. & Sherratt, A. 1993. The growth of the Mediterranean economy in the early first millennium BC. *World Archaeology*, 24: 361-78.

Skeates, R. 1994. A radiocarbon date-list for prehistoric Italy (c. 46,400 BP – 2450 BP/400 cal.BC). In Skeates, R. & Whitehouse, R. (eds) *Radiocarbon Dating and Italian Prehistory*: 147-288. Archaeological Monograph of the British School at Rome 8, Accordia Specialist Studies on Italy 3, London.

Sluga Messina, G. 1983. *Analisi dei motivi decorativi della ceramica da Castelluccio di Noto (Siracusa)*. Roma.

—— 1988. Villasmundo. (Siracusa): tomba neolitica presso il villaggio preistorico del Petraro. *SA*, 66-68: 81-6.

Smith, T.R. 1987. *Mycenaean Trade and Interaction in the West Central Mediterranean 1600-1000 BC*. *BAR-IS* 371.

Spatafora, F. 1990. Monte Maranfusa (scavi 1986-87). In *Gli elimi e l'area elima. Atti del Seminario di Studi. Archivio Storico Siciliano, 14-15 (1988-89)*: 293-9. Palermo.

—— 1996. Gli elimi e l'età del ferro nella Sicilia occidentale. *Early Societies*: 155-65.

Spatafora, F. & Mannino, G. 1994. Tombe eneolitiche nella Sicilia occidentale. *RSP*, 46: 191-201.

Spigo, U. 1980-81. Ricerche a Monte San Mauro, Francavilla di Sicilia, Acireale, Adrano, Lentini, Solarino. *Kokalos*, 26-27: 771-95.

—— 1984-85. Ricerche e rinvenimenti a Brucoli (c.da Gisira), Valsavoia (Lentini), nel territorio di Caltagirone, ad Adrano e Francavilla Marittima. *Kokalos*, 30-31: 863-904.

Steures, D.C. 1980. *Monte Finocchito Revisited: Part 1: The Evidence*. Allard Pierson, Amsterdam.

Tagliacozzo, A. 1993. Archeozoologia della Grotta dell'Uzzo, Sicilia. *BPI* (supplemento) 84, II.

—— 1994. Economic changes between the Mesolithic and the Neolithic in the Grotta dell'Uzzo (Sicily, Italy). *Accordia Research Papers*, 5: 7-37.

Tagliacozzo, A. & Piperno, M. 1993. Una struttura di combustione associata ad una porzione di suolo d'abitato mesolitico nella Grotta dell'Uzzo (TP). *AttiRS XXX*: 261-76.

Taylour, W. 1958. *Mycenaean Pottery in Italy and Adjacent Areas*. Cambridge University Press, Cambridge.

Tigano, G. 1985-86. Ceramica indigena da Sabucina (Caltanissetta). Oinochoai trilobate a decorazione geometrica. *QuadMessina*, 1: 55-78.

Tinè, S. 1960-61. Giacimenti dell'età del rame in Sicilia e la 'Cultura tipo Conca d'Oro' (Relazione preliminare degli scavi eseguiti nel quinquennio 1954-1959). *BPI*, 69-70: 113-51.

—— 1961. Notizie preliminari su recenti scavi nel villaggio neolitico di Stentinello. *Archivio Storico Siracusano*, 7: 113-17.

—— 1965. Gli scavi nella Grotta della Chiusazza. *BPI*, 74: 123-286.

—— 1971. Lo stile del Kronio in Sicilia, lo stile di Ghar Dalam a Malta e la successione del neolitico nelle due isole. *AttiRS XIII*: 320-31.

Tinè, S., Tinè, V. & Traverso, A. 1994. La campagna di scavo del 1986 nell'Antro Fazello del complesso 'Stufe di San Calogero' del Monte Kronio di Sciacca (AG). *Basso Belice*: 245-61.

Tomasello, F. 1979. S. Angelo Muxaro. Nuove indagini sulla architettura funeraria del territorio. *Cronache*, 18: 59-75.

Bibliography

Tozzi, C. 1968. Relazione preliminare sulla prima e seconda campagna di scavi effettuata a Pantelleria. *RSP*, 23: 315-88.
—— 1978. Nuovi dati sul villaggio dell'età del bronzo di Mursia a Pantelleria. In *Un decennio di ricerche archeologiche. Quaderni de La Ricerca Scientifica*: 149-57. CNR, Roma.
Troja, S.O., Cro, A., Gueli, A.M. & La Rosa, V. 1996. Characterization and thermoluminescence dating of prehistoric pottery sherds from Milena. *Archaeometry*, 38: 113-28.
Trump, D.H. 1961. The later prehistory of Malta. *PPS*, 27: 253-62.
—— 1966. *Skorba. Excavations carried out on behalf of the National Museum of Malta 1961-1963*. Reports of the Research Committee of the Society of Antiquaries of London, No.XXIII. Oxford.
—— 1995-96. Radiocarbon dates from Malta. *Accordia Research Papers*, 6: 173-7.
Tusa, S. 1991. Functions, resources and spatial organisation in the Pietraperzia territory (Enna, Sicily) between the Copper and Bronze Ages. In Herring, E., Whitehouse, R. & Wilkins, J. (eds) *Papers of the Fourth Conference of Italian Archaeology. The Archaeology of Power*, Pt.1: 27-41. Accordia Research Centre, London.
—— 1992. *La Sicilia nella Preistoria*. Sellerio, Palermo (2nd edition).
—— 1993-94. Attività di ricognizione e scavo nel campo della ricerca archeologica preistorica, protostorica e subacquea nella provincia di Trapani. *Kokalos*, 39-40: 1493-1554.
—— 1994. Società e culture nel Belice fra la fine del III ed il II millennio a.C. *Basso Belice*: 387-410.
—— 1996a. From hunter-gatherers to farmers in western Sicily. *Early Societies*: 41-55.
—— 1996b. Complessi campaniformi e l'età del rame – prima età del bronzo nella Sicilia occidentale. *Early Societies*: 71-80.
—— 1997a. Origine della società agro-pastorale. *Prima Sicilia*: 173-9.
—— 1997b. Il megalitismo e la Sicila. *Prima Sicilia*: 333-42.
Tusa, S, & Di Salvo, R. 1988-89. Dinamiche funzionali ed organizzazione territoriale dell'insediamento eneolitico in Sicilia: l'evidenza di Rocazzo (Mazara del Vallo, Trapani). *Origini*, 14: 101-29.
Vagnetti, L. 1968a. Un vaso miceneo da Pantalica. *Studi Micenei ed Egeo-Anatolici*, 5: 132-5.
—— 1968b. I bacili di bronzo di Caldare sono ciprioti? *Studi Micenei ed Egeo-Anatolici*, 7: 129-40.
—— 1972. Un anello nel Museo archeologico di Firenze e le oreficerie di Sant'Angelo Muxaro. *Studi Micenei ed Egeo-Anatolici*, 15: 189-201.
—— (ed) 1982. *Magna Grecia e mondo miceneo. Nuovi documenti*. Taranto.
—— 1991. Le ceramiche egeo-micenee. In Bernabò Brea, L. & Cavalier, M., *Melìgunìs-Lìpára VI. Filicudi. Insediamenti dell'età del bronzo*: 263-305. Accademia di Scienze, Lettere e Arti di Palermo, Palermo.
—— 1993. Mycenaean pottery in Italy: fifty years of study. In Zerner, C. & Winder, J. (eds) *Wace and Blegen. Pottery as evidence for trade in the Aegean Bronze Age 1939-1989. Proceedings of the International Conference, American School of Classical Studies, Athens 1989*: 143-57.
Vagnetti, L. & Lo Schiavo, F. 1989. Late Bronze Age long distance trade in the Mediterranean: the role of the Cypriots. In Peltenburg, E. (ed) *Early Society in Cyprus*: 217-43. Edinburgh University Press, Edinburgh.
Vallet, G. 1962. La colonisation Chalcidienne et l'Hellénisation de la Sicile Orientale. *Kokalos*, 8: 30-51.
—— 1984-85. L'apporto del urbanistica. Le fait urbain en Grèce et en Sicile à l'époque archaïque. *Kokalos*, 30-31: 133-55.
Vallet, G. & Villard, F. 1960. Les fouilles de Mégara Hyblaea (1949-1959). *Bollettino d'Arte*, 45: 263-73.
Vallet, G., Villard, F. & Auberson, P. 1976. *Megara Hyblaea 1. Le quartier de l'agora archaïque*. Rome, École Française de Rome.
van Compernolle, R. 1984-85. La Sicilia e la Grecia arcaica fino alla fine del VI secolo: l'apporto delle fonti letterarie. *Kokalos*, 30-31: 23-35.
Veneroso, P. 1994. Osservazioni tecniche sulle ceramiche campaniformi siciliane. *Basso Belice*: 461-80.
Venezia, M. & Lentini, L. 1994. Il Paleolitico nel Basso Belice. *Basso Belice*: 71-92.
Vigliardi, A. 1968. L'industria litica della grotta di S. Teodoro in provincia di Messina (Scavi Graziosi-Maviglia). *RSP*, 23: 33-144.
—— 1982. Gli strati paleo-mesolitici della Grotta di Levanzo. *RSP*, 37: 79-134.
Villari, P. 1981. I giacimenti preistorici del Monte Belvedere e della Pianura Chiusa di

Bibliography

Fiumedinisi (Messina). Successione delle culture nella Sicilia nord-orientale. *SA*, 46-47: 111-21.

—— 1991a. Faunal remains from Thapsos. *Bulletin du Musée d'Anthropologie Prehistorique de Monaco*, 34: 109-24.

—— 1991b. Le faune del villaggio di Capo Graziano nel contesto archeozoologico eoliano e siciliano dell'età del bronzo. In Bernabò Brea, L. & Cavalier, M., *Melianunìs-Lipára VI. Filicudi. Insediamenti dell'età del bronzo*: 317-30. Accademia di Scienze, Lettere e Arti di Palermo, Palermo.

—— 1995. *Le Faune della Tarda Preistoria nella Sicilia Orientale*. Ente Fauna Siciliana, Siracusa.

Voza, G. 1968. Villaggio dell'età del bronzo in contrada Petraro di Melilli. *AttiRS XI-XII*: 173-92.

—— 1972. Thapsos. Primi risultati delle più recenti ricerche. *AttiRS XIV*: 175-205.

—— 1973a. Thapsos. *ASSO*: 30-52.

—— 1973b. Thapsos. Resoconto sulle campagne di scavo del 1970-71. *AttiRS XV*: 133-57.

—— 1973c. Siracusa. Esplorazioni nell'area delle necropoli e dell'abitato. *ASSO*: 81-107.

—— 1978. La necropoli della valle del Marcellino presso Villasmundo. *Cronache*, 17: 104-10.

—— 1980-81. L'attività della Soprintendenza alle Antichità della Sicilia Orientale. *Kokalos*, 26-27: 674-93.

—— 1984-85. Attività nel territorio della Soprintendenza alle Antichità di Siracusa nel quadriennio 1980-1984. *Kokalos*, 30-31: 657-77.

—— 1985. I contatti precoloniali col mondo greco. In G. Pugliese Carratelli (ed) *Sikanie. Storia e civiltà della Sicilia greca*: 543-62. Milano.

Whitehouse, R. 1981. Megaliths of the Central Mediterranean. In Evans, J.D., Cunliffe, B. & Renfrew, C. (eds) *Antiquity and Man. Essays in Honour of Glyn Daniel*: 106-27. Thames & Hudson, London.

—— 1992. *Underground Religion. Cult and Culture in Prehistoric Italy*. Accordia Specialist Studies on Italy 1, London.

—— 1994a. The British Museum ^{14}C programme for Italian prehistory. In Skeates, R. & Whitehouse, R. (eds) *Radiocarbon Dating and Italian Prehistory*: 85-98. Archaeological Monograph of the British School at Rome 8, Accordia Specialist Studies on Italy 3, London.

—— 1994b. Società ed economia nel neolitico italiano; la problematica dei fossati. *Basso Belice*: 275-85.

Williams-Thorpe, O. 1995. Obsidian in the Mediterranean and the Near East: a provenancing success story. *Archaeometry*, 37: 217-48.

Williams-Thorpe, O., Warren, S.E. & Courtin, J. 1984. The distribution and sources of archaeological obsidian from Southern France. *Journal of Archaeological Science*, 11: 135-46.

Wilson, R.J.A. 1981-82. Archaeology in Sicily, 1977-81. *Archaeological Reports*, 28: 84-105.

—— 1987-88. Archaeology in Sicily, 1982-87. *Archaeological Reports*, 34: 105-50.

—— 1990. *Sicily under the Roman Empire. The Archaeology of a Roman Province, 36 BC – AD 535*. Aris & Phillips, Warminster.

—— 1996. Archaeology in Sicily 1988-1995. *Archaeological Reports for 1995-1996*, 42: 59-123.

Zampetti, D. 1989. La question des rapports entre la Sicile et l'Afrique du Nord pendant le Paleolithique superieur final: la contribution de l'archeologie. In Hershkovitz, I. (ed) *People and Culture in Change. Proceedings of the Second Symposium on Upper Palaeolithic, Mesolithic and Neolithic Populations in Europe and the Mediterranean Basin*: 459-76. BAR-IS 508.

—— 1990. Il paleolitico superiore del Riparo del Castello a Termini Imerese (Palermo): analisi di una collezione. *Origini*, 13: 59-97.

Zampetti, D. & Mussi, M. 1991. Segni del potere, simboli del potere: la problematica del Paleolitico Superiore Italiano. In Herring, E., Whitehouse, R. & Wilkins, J. (eds) *Papers of the Fourth Conference of Italian Archaeology. The Archaeology of Power, 2*: 149-60. Accordia Research Centre, London.

List of illustrations and sources

302

Tables

Index

311